Who Speaks for Margaret Garner?

WHO SPEAKS FOR MARGARET GARNER?

Mark Reinhardt

UNIVERSITY OF MINNESOTA PRESS

Minneapolis

London

Royalties from the sale of this book will be donated to Free the Slaves, a nonprofit organization dedicated to ending slavery and human trafficking around the world and to helping former slaves rebuild their lives. http://www. freetheslaves.net.

Portions of the Introduction were previously published in "Who Speaks for Margaret Garner? Slavery, Silence, and the Politics of Ventriloquism," *Critical Inquiry* 29, no. 1 (Fall 2002): 81–119.

Published by the University of Minnesota Press
111 Third Avenue South, Suite 290
Minneapolis, MN 55401-2520
http://www.upress.umn.edu

Library of Congress Cataloging-in-Publication Data
Reinhardt, Mark.
    Who speaks for Margaret Garner? / Mark Reinhardt.
        p.   cm.
    Includes bibliographical references and index.
    ISBN 978-0-8166-4258-8 (hc : alk. paper)
    ISBN 978-0-8166-4259-5 (pb : alk. paper)
1. Garner, Margaret—Trials, litigation, etc. 2. Garner, Margaret—Public opinion. 3. Trials (Infanticide)—Ohio—Cincinnati. 4. Infanticide—Ohio—Cincinnati—History—19th century. 5. Fugitive slaves—Legal status, laws, etc.—Ohio—Cincinnati. 6. Fugitive slaves—Legal status, laws, etc.—United States. I. Title.
    E450.G225R44 2010
    306.3'62092—dc22
    [B]   2010030721

Printed in the United States of America on acid-free paper

The University of Minnesota is an equal-opportunity educator and employer.

17   16   15   14   13   12   11   10   10   9   8   7   6   5   4   3   2   1

For Simon, Max, and Dulce

CONTENTS

PREFACE

In February 1856 the *Pittsburgh Visitor* made the following prediction: "The name of Margaret Garner shall be a memento of which posterity shall be proud, and will certainly be cherished by good men and women for ages yet to come." Garner, the paper wrote, was "destined to imperishable fame." Other voices offered the American public similar assessments.[1] Margaret Garner was then very much in the news, a protagonist in one of the most widely publicized and symbolically charged fugitive slave cases the nation had ever seen. Her liberty was at stake in the courtroom drama, but she was not alone in that. Eight Garners spanning three generations had escaped servitude in Kentucky, only to be captured in Cincinnati the following morning. Seven had survived, and the fates of all of them now hung on how the case was decided by a federal fugitive slave commissioner. Margaret, however, stood at the center of the national discussion. Her fame was due to an act she committed at the moment her family's bid for freedom was thwarted: when an armed party of federal marshals stormed the house in which the Garners were hiding, Margaret killed her two-and-a-half-year-old daughter, Mary. Reports suggested that she had tried to kill her three other children, too.

The press immediately seized on, and sensationalized, the deed. Detailed accounts of the dramatic flight and capture circulated widely, and with them came a host of questions. What did it mean that a mother would rather have her children die than see them returned to the life they had just fled? What did it suggest about slavery and about the slave who took such a drastic step? What should become of her now? How should this case be resolved—by what principles and which authorities? In the end, all of the surviving family members were forcibly returned to

Kentucky, but from the day the Garners were captured until well after the machinery of the Fugitive Slave Act landed them back in slavery, their contemporaries took up such issues again and again, making the case a matter of intense political and cultural contention. The struggle was waged not only in the courtroom and front-page news reports but in the halls of governors' mansions and on the floors of state legislatures, in citizens' assemblies and city streets, in sermons, pamphlets, editorials— even fiction and poetry.

It is hardly surprising that many antislavery commentators believed that the woman who had triggered so substantial a dispute was assured a permanent and prominent place in American political memory. As it turned out, these observers were wrong: Margaret Garner did not become an enduring household name or even one of the nation's minor political icons. At least as a matter of public discourse, the case faded into obscurity soon after the Civil War. Although the Garners appeared a few times in the margins of later scholarly writing on antebellum conflicts over slavery, their story remained largely forgotten until 1987, when Toni Morrison's novel *Beloved* was published. Morrison let it be known that she had found inspiration for her book, one of the most celebrated American novels of the past half-century, in an antebellum interview with Margaret Garner. As she also stressed, *Beloved* is not a fictional recounting of Garner's life or the family's legal struggle: the novelist did not research the events in detail, and her alchemical imagination transmuted her source into a story that follows a very different trajectory.[2] The novel's success nevertheless returned Garner to public attention and helped launch a series of scholarly studies of the case. Now there are a handful of secondary accounts devoted to the events in Cincinnati, including one full-length narrative history, Steven Weisenburger's *Modern Medea.* Morrison recently completed the circle, incorporating many of the historical characters and incidents into her opera *Margaret Garner.*[3]

While following in the footsteps of other scholarly works, *Who Speaks for Margaret Garner?* differs fundamentally in its approach and aspirations. Its central purpose is to put many of the most important primary sources into the hands of today's readers. The documents gathered here include the first news reports on the Garners' escape and capture, detailed accounts of the court proceedings, the last recorded interview with Margaret Garner's husband, Robert, and, finally, the (perhaps dubious) recollections of a descendant of Archibald K. Gaines, the man who claimed Margaret and her children as his property. There are also letters from several key participants in the legal struggle; editorial commentaries;

excerpts from debates in the Ohio legislature; selections from notable speeches, sermons, and interviews; representative examples of the literary renderings of the events that began appearing even while the fugitive slave hearing was still under way; and a few key cultural sources on which such renderings drew. Although a few documents give us glimpses of the Garners' situation after their return to slavery, the primary focus of this collection is not the life histories of the participants (which, with the Garners as with so many enslaved persons, can be traced only sketchily) but the public struggle waged over both the meaning of what Margaret did and the question of whether she and her family should attain the freedom they had so fiercely pursued. Whenever possible, the selection of texts aims to represent the ideological and geographic diversity of views, for the struggle exposed, and exacerbated, the fault lines running through a nation that was already drifting toward civil war. The sources in this volume tell us much about contending understandings of slavery and freedom, race and gender, party and region, law and politics at a critical moment in American history.

What they have to say is largely for the reader to determine. The task is not always easy. While the written record of the Garner case is in many respects rich and illuminating, it is also marked by notable omissions, flagrant contradictions, and all of the intense biases of the men and women who fashioned it. From beginning to end, matters of motive and meaning are bitterly disputed. For all that was written about Margaret Garner, we learn remarkably little about her own thoughts and sentiments: of the many words gathered here, only a small minority are attributed directly to her or to other members of the Garner family, and few of those that are give us reason to have confidence in the attribution. Even some questions of basic fact remain fundamentally ambiguous or obscure. The documentary record does not cohere into one seamless, coherent narrative.

Nor do I seek to provide one in my own analyses in the subsequent chapters of this book. This does not mean, of course, that the reader is left without any guidance. The Introduction briefly retells the history of the case, places it in context, and discusses some of the political and interpretive battles that made it so significant. Each group of documents and a number of the individual sources are prefaced by brief commentaries. The chronology at the end of the book is intended to be a reference for those who are reading selectively or are confused by the documents' bewildering parade of names and events. Anyone seeking a fuller retelling of the story will have to turn to other scholarly studies, for the conviction behind this volume is that there is something uniquely instructive in reconstructing the events through one's own encounter with the antebellum sources.

To pursue such an encounter, today's reader must undertake the difficult work of historical analysis, facing the methodological and moral quandaries that such labors involve. More than a century and a half after the fact, the Garner archive, like the events at its center, retains its power to disturb. The challenge of making sense of the materials republished here is thus more than a matter of keeping track of who did what, when, or of deciding which sources to trust and for what reasons—though it does involve such decisions, and they can be perplexing. It involves more, too, than determining the interests and causes that drove the various parties and attending to the institutions through which they pursued their objectives—important as those tasks are. To grasp how Americans of the nineteenth century responded to this complex and emotionally fraught case, it is crucial to identify the means by which they sought to make the events fit the forms of explanation and expression that their culture provided. One must, that is, explore all of the problematical ways in which such coherence as the primary documents offer us was imposed. Examining these impositions, or what one might call the scripts through which the case was made into a story for public circulation, calls our attention to what could be said in such a conflict, and by whom, while also allowing us to identify what the documents do not tell us, the important questions left unanswered or unasked. At times, the scripts even confront us with the peculiar ways in which a case of death, captivity, and legally enforced subjugation was made to provide certain narrative thrills and satisfactions. Engaging these dimensions of the sources will surely give readers a better understanding of the politics of this crucial episode and of the society in which it unfolded. My hope is it will also preserve something that was not always evident in the responses of Margaret Garner's contemporaries: a sense of humility in encountering the heart and mind of a mother driven to kill her child.

AN EXTRAORDINARY CASE?

Flight, capture, a murdered daughter, protracted legal struggles, and then—despite considerable public sympathy and some reason to hope for emancipation—forcible return to slavery: the story of Margaret Garner and her family is so dramatic in its twists and turns, so disturbing in its details, so heartbreaking, that it is easy to overlook what it shared with other fugitive slave cases of the day. Of course, the Garners' circumstances after their arrest in Cincinnati were hardly ordinary. When the captives were led by federal marshals out of the county jail, through the city's streets, past agitated crowds, into the packed courthouse, and before a federal commissioner, they became publicly visible in a way that few enslaved persons would ever experience. They were not, however, the only ones who underwent such a change in condition during the decade before the Civil War. Between the passage of the Fugitive Slave Act in September 1850 and the Garners' arrival in Cincinnati on the morning of January 28, 1856, plenty of fugitives had been caught, and a few cases had made headlines, finding their way into the midst of an intensifying national debate.

Boston, especially, had been the site of highly publicized clashes between abolitionist forces and the act's enforcers. In February 1851 Shadrach Minkins avoided a return to slavery when a group of black men active in the city's antislavery movement rescued him in court, wresting him from his captors and ultimately arranging his escape to Canada. When another fugitive, Thomas Sims, was brought before the same federal commissioner two months later, city and federal officials prevented a rescue by surrounding the courthouse with chains; after the commissioner found for his owner, Sims was marched to Boston Harbor by U.S. Marines and taken south on a government warship. Anthony Burns was returned to slavery in a similar fashion in 1854 only after an assault on the courthouse by hundreds of sympathizers failed to liberate him.[1] The struggle over the outcome and meaning of these episodes was far too broad to be confined to the courtroom and the streets of Boston. Nor was Massachusetts the only stage for such conflicts. Although the Boston cases were among the most widely reported, similar incidents took place across the free states. Cincinnati saw more than its share of controversies, and while the Burns affair was the last of the great Boston struggles, Cincinnati's were still growing more intense. Less than a year before the Garners were captured, for instance, opponents of slavery used a writ of habeas corpus to pry sixteen-year-old Rosetta Armstead from her Kentucky master's agent as he was transporting her through Ohio. The resulting legal contest, which pitted not only master against slave but federal against state courts while involving many of the parties who would play leading roles in the Garner case, ended with Armstead's winning her freedom. During that conflict, too, crowds surged into Cincinnati's streets, and the national press took notice of the tumultuous events in the "Queen City of the West."[2]

By the time the Garner hearings began, such spectacular cases had come to inform popular understandings of the workings of the Fugitive Slave Act. That the spectacles were not at all typical of the experiences of fugitive slaves did not seem to matter: these legal controversies were significant episodes in the political life of antebellum America.[3] Much of this significance derived from preexisting sectional and partisan animosities, but the great fugitive slave trials of the 1850s also shaped and sharpened those hostilities, providing one of the important channels through which the underlying conflicts unfolded. They did so at a distinctive moment in American political development. Struggles over slavery took on a new ferocity just as the system of political parties was undergoing the most dramatic transformation in a generation—as seen, most obviously, in the formation and rapid rise of the Republican Party—and as the processes of electoral competition were becoming thoroughly entangled with an incipient mass culture. As slavery and sectional tensions provided the material for such wildly popular entertainments as blackface minstrel shows, so partisan struggles were highly theatrical, scripted, staged.[4] Reflecting this convergence, the rhetoric through which fugitive slave cases were contested tended to be highly stylized and to draw on narrative forms shaped by commercial and literary, as well as more narrowly political and legal, imperatives.

So it was with the Garners. Their story was narrated through familiar genres and stock characters, taking much of its texture, and even its political meaning, from the language and techniques of melodrama and sentimental fiction. Turned into national symbols, they were spoken about and spoken for in ways over which they exercised limited control. Like other fugitives whose trials became sites of significant controversy, they were drawn into battles that they did not initiate and that would continue long after they left the public stage. In these respects, the Garners' situation was hardly singular, and the title of this chapter is misleading. Yet in crucial ways their case *was* unique: even when compared with other famous and bitterly contested fugitive slave incidents, it stands out. For one thing, their legal ordeal was longer. The Fugitive Slave Act was designed to ensure the swift return of captured slaves. Many federal hearings were completed in a matter of hours, even minutes, and it is doubtful that any other case lasted nearly the four weeks that Commissioner John L. Pendery took to rule on the family's status.[5] By providing more occasions for dramatic front-page reporting in the daily press, the drawn-out dispute in his court added to the exceptional public prominence of the Garners' attempts to avoid a return to slavery. The dispute was also singular in this respect: Margaret Garner is the only fugitive known to have testified in a federal hearing brought under the Fugitive Slave Act, which explicitly barred such testimony.

Surely, though, it was neither the length of the hearing nor even a fugitive's legal testimony that led the American Anti-Slavery Society, voicing a common sentiment, to call this "the most remarkable . . . the most touching, and the most terrible" of fugitive slave cases.[6] To many commentators it was of course Margaret's killing of her daughter that made the controversy swirling around the family so extraordinary and gave her story an unmatched symbolic power. In general, claims about how Margaret's deeds illuminated her character and the institution of slavery were, at least for opponents of the institution, at the core of assertions about the case's political importance. Many made her a rebuke to slavery's apologists; many of those sympathizers celebrated her for her heroism. Yet even for sympathizers, her actions were often unsettling as well—difficult to assess, disruptive of familiar classifications. Her conduct also, if for different reasons, proved difficult for proslavery polemicists to engage. Despite all that was familiar or ritualized in the speeches, writings, and arguments about Margaret Garner, then, her case also strained against the available ways of telling the story of slavery. That certainly did not keep her story from being told. It was narrated again and again, as the documents gathered in this volume show. But those documents also reveal the difficulties a mother's killing of her daughter posed to partisans on all sides of the slavery issue. The Garner archive illuminates the controversy over slavery both for what this case shares with other prominent cases and for the ways in which it is unique. It is hard to address either aspect, however, without first—as so many commentators did—making a narrative of the events. Here, then, is one brief telling.

The Story

Late on January 27, 1856, at Richwood, in rural Boone County, Kentucky, a group of eight slaves slipped into the cold night and made a bid for freedom. One member of the group, twenty-one-year-old Robert Garner, had stolen two horses and a sled, and was joined by his parents, Mary and Simon Garner, his twenty-two-year-old wife, Margaret, and her four young children, Thomas (usually Tom), Samuel (usually Sam), Mary, and Cilla. They headed for the Ohio River, about sixteen miles away. Well before dawn, having eluded the night patrols that swept the highways, they reached the town of Covington, on the river's Kentucky bank. Turning the horses loose and abandoning the sled, they crossed the frozen river on foot. At Western Row, they entered Cincinnati, in the free state of Ohio.[7]

The family headed two miles into town to the home of their relatives, the Kites, freed blacks who had formerly lived in Kentucky. The fugitives entered the house before daybreak. For the first time in over twelve hours, they were hidden from view. After an early breakfast, Margaret's cousin, Elijah Kite, set off to get help from Levi Coffin, a prominent white "conductor" on the Underground Railroad. Coffin urged Kite to act immediately: the family must be moved to safer quarters in another part of the city, from which they could be sent north after nightfall.[8] The peril, however, was even greater than Coffin knew. Not long after the Garners left, their flight had been detected. Around the time Coffin was speaking with Kite, the family's pursuers completed their own race from Richmond to Cincinnati. On arrival, Archibald K. Gaines, who claimed Margaret and her children, and Thomas Marshall, whose father, James, owned the other adults, moved swiftly to make use of the provisions of the Fugitive Slave Act. Soon enough, federal Commissioner John L. Pendery issued a warrant for the Garners and assigned several federal marshals to the case. Even before these proceedings were complete, a group of deputies made their way to the Kite house. How they knew to go there is not clear. Robert Garner would later suspect Elijah Kite, whose errand to Coffin dragged on longer than Robert thought necessary. Whether these suspicions were justified, by the time Kite returned, his house was being watched. As the morning dragged on, the posse outside continued to grow. At about 10:00 a.m., the men approached the house. Flanked by Gaines and Marshall, a deputy marshal demanded entry. When they were refused, the whites tried to force their way in. The Garners resisted. In the ensuing commotion, Robert shot one deputy marshal with a pistol, forcing him to retreat. But soon enough, the fugitives, outnumbered and overwhelmed, yielded.[9]

It was as the whites were about to enter that Margaret Garner began her attempt to kill her children. Before the men found her, she had succeeded in killing two-and-a-half-year-old Mary by slitting her throat. One local paper described the aftermath from the marshals' point of view:

> In one corner of the room was a negro child bleeding to death. His throat was cut *from ear to ear,* and the blood was spouting out profusely, showing that the deed was but recently committed. Scarcely was this fact noticed, when a scream issuing from an adjoining room drew their attention thither. A glance into the apartment revealed a negro woman holding in her hand a knife literally dripping with gore over the heads of two little negro children, who were crouched to the floor. . . . They were discovered to be cut across the head and shoulders, but not seriously injured, although the blood trickled down their backs. . . . The negress avowed herself the mother of the children, and said that she had killed one, and would like to kill the three others rather than see them again reduced to slavery.[10]

The surviving Garners were taken into custody, but this did not put an end to the day's battles. News of the murder and capture raced through the city. The marshals took the fugitives to the U.S. Court House, where Gaines and Marshall might have expected a quick, perfunctory proceeding ending in victory and an immediate return to Kentucky. Instead, Pendery, citing the lack of proper documentation from Marshall, refused to turn over the fugitives or to rule immediately on their status. The Garners would have to be held in the city for at least a night. When seeking to move them to the cells at the Hammond Street station, however, the marshals were forced to contend with a large and threatening multiracial crowd. More challenges soon followed. Cincinnati's organized antislavery forces had also sprung into action, and they began by questioning the federal government's right to detain the fugitives. At around 3:00 p.m., the locally prominent abolitionist lawyer, John Jolliffe, appeared before antislavery Probate Court judge John Burgoyne seeking a writ of habeas corpus for the Garners. Burgoyne complied, asking Deputy Sheriff Jeffrey Buckingham to take custody of the fugitives. When Buckingham and a group of sheriffs arrived at Hammond Street, however, the marshals refused to cooperate. The dispute was heated, and over the next few hours it only grew more so. As the turbulent and unpredictable crowd swirled around the two forces, first one party, then the other seemed to have the upper hand; some—contested—reports in the daily press even claimed that a deputy marshal threatened the sheriffs with his pistol drawn. By around 8:00 p.m., the sheriffs finally succeeded in placing the fugitives in the county jail, though the question of who held rightful custody was not resolved.[11]

It would only grow more complex. Burgoyne's writ had been issued in anticipation of criminal charges against the Garners, and two days later, even as the case before Commissioner Pendery commenced in earnest, Ohio officials issued a warrant for the arrest of all four of the adult Garners on the charge of murder. Jolliffe had done all he could to encourage them: seeking any means that would put the fugitives in the hands of Ohio courts and forestall a return to Kentucky, antislavery forces argued from the beginning that the criminal case took priority over Gaines and Marshall's federal fugitive slave claims. Thus began a conflict over jurisdiction between the state and federal judicial systems, which—played out in four different courts and marked by contending writs, rulings, and contempt citations—persisted throughout the Garner affair. Although Pendery repeatedly refused to allow the criminal charges to interrupt or otherwise inform the fugitive slave proceedings before him, the state's courts would challenge the claims and conduct of federal officials up through and even weeks beyond the moment that the commissioner ruled in the owners' favor. Widely understood as an important test of the North's willingness to enforce the Fugitive Slave Act, this multifaceted struggle over the Garners' status drew in the Republican governor of Ohio, Salmon Chase, who (at least initially) encouraged intervention by Judge Burgoyne, while the administration of President Franklin Pierce clearly wanted the fugitives returned to slavery. Despite the fundamental differences of interest and perception among them, participants and observers concurred on one point: much hung on the outcome of the case.

The conflict of the courts was among the elements that drew sustained and impassioned commentary from across the political spectrum, both locally and nationally, but it was the drama in Pendery's courtroom that loomed largest. Outside, special deputies hired by Cincinnati's U.S. marshal, Hiram H. Robinson, patrolled the streets and regulated access to the building, at times preventing people of color from joining the audience. Inside, the hearing turned on disputed questions of both fact and law. Witnesses for the Garners testified that the adults had all in previous years been on free soil in Cincinnati in the company or with the knowledge of their owners. The Garner lawyers argued that this had been sufficient to emancipate them and, by extension, the children free as well. Jolliffe, their chief counsel, also produced an extended constitutional argument against the Fugitive Slave Act and put slavery itself on trial. The lawyers for Gaines and Marshall ridiculed Jolliffe's arguments, and the owners and their witnesses denied that any of the slaves had been to Ohio before their escape. Even after nearly two weeks of hearings, Pendery, citing the complexity and significance of the issues that had been raised, announced that he would require four more weeks to reach a decision.[12]

Only two weeks later, on February 26, he read that decision to a courtroom packed with white and black spectators. Summarily dismissing all antislavery constitutional claims, but accepting as plausible the evidence that at least some of the Garners had previously been in Ohio with the consent of the masters, he announced that the case boiled down to one question: "'does the fact of the temporary visit [to Ohio] . . . affect the rights of the claimant?'" His answer was an elaborately argued no. Invoking a number of precedents, Pendery concluded that the issue was a settled one in American law. He did concede that had the fugitives refused to return to Kentucky after being brought to Ohio, instead seeking protection from the free state, they would in all likelihood have succeeded. Since they would not be fugitives under the terms of the Fugitive Slave Act, they would be beyond the act's reach and would thus "become, practically, free." But the case at hand, Pendery reasoned, was fundamentally different. If "the slave having been brought to Ohio by the master, returns with him voluntarily to the State of Kentucky," the practical freedom is dissolved, for "the claim upon the State of Ohio for protection against violent abduction was not made. *The right to be free was waived.* In coming to Ohio the master voluntarily abandoned his legal power over his slave, and in returning voluntarily the slave has equally abandoned his claim to freedom."[13]

Despite Pendery's decision, the Garners remained in the county jail in Cincinnati. Asserting custody and the priority of the pending murder case, the Hamilton County sheriff refused to release them to the marshals. Two days later, however, Federal District Court Judge Humphrey Leavitt ruled that the federal claim under the Fugitive Slave Act took precedence, thereby denying the state courts or local law enforcement any jurisdiction over the fugitives. Less than an hour after Leavitt finished reading his decision to another large crowd, the Garners were returned to Kentucky, escorted by Robinson and several hundred of his special deputy marshals.[14]

Even this was not the end of the legal struggle on the Garners' behalf. Governor Chase sought to extradite Margaret and the other adults from Kentucky so Ohio could pursue the murder charge, and Kentucky's governor, Charles Morehead, attempted to comply, but the effort came too late: despite earlier disavowals of any intention to do so, Gaines sent Margaret and her family down the river to be sold just before Ohio officials arrived to collect them. The passage south was marked by more turmoil. On March 8 the boat carrying the family collided with another boat. Twenty-five lives were lost, among them that of the Garners' infant daughter, Cilla. Some stories in the press reported that Margaret expressed joy at seeing one more of her loved ones rescued from slavery. After that, her movements become more difficult to trace. Gaines recalled her to Kentucky. Once more, Ohio attempted extradition; once more, before officials arrived to retrieve her, Garner was gone—this time to Arkansas and, soon after, New Orleans.[15] There, it has often been said, Margaret's trail disappears.[16]

Beyond the Story

What can be said about this story? That it was at times told inaccurately is already evident in the quoted description of the murder scene, which refers to Margaret's daughter as a boy. This reflects a broader pattern: the news coverage and court testimony are full of contradictory claims about even elementary factual matters. Depending on which version one chooses to believe, Margaret either was or was not found with knife in hand. She did or did not use the knife on her boys. She did or did not ask her mother-in-law, Mary, to help her kill the children, and Mary did or did not respond by refusing and hiding under a bed. Margaret's husband,

Robert, either was or was not "screaming as if bereft of reason" and did or did not urge Margaret to do the killing. For that matter, Robert either was or was not Robert: witnesses for James Marshall, his owner, claimed his name was and always had been young Simon or Simon Jr., that he had never been known as Robert by anyone, while Jolliffe insisted that the warrant for the arrest of one young Simon could not apply to his client without being amended, as Simon certainly was not Robert's name, and each side in the court battle tended to use the different names throughout the case. Even the basic fact that aroused so much popular interest, that is, a mother's killing of her child, is contested in the record, for one—unsubstantiated and wildly implausible—article from a Kentucky paper claimed that a free member of the Kite family killed young Mary, and Margaret then agreed to take the blame (presumably to stave off her return to slavery and to help make abolitionist propaganda).[17]

The contradictions and inaccuracies extend to the belief that the Garners disappeared in New Orleans. The outlines of their subsequent journeys and circumstances remain visible, however sketchily, in the documents. Yet even though it is belied by the facts, the claim of disappearance nevertheless expresses a significant cultural truth: as an important force in antebellum American politics, the Garner story essentially reached its final chapter when the second requisition attempt failed. It is not that the family vanished from public discourse immediately after their two months of celebrity or notoriety. From the spring of 1856 through the Civil War, Margaret continued to be invoked, if less frequently, as a symbol in the struggle over slavery. But what happened to the biographical Margaret Garner in the next stages of her life did not shape the public symbol. The figure who mattered to the struggle was the slave who had escaped, been captured, chosen death over bondage for her daughter, and, despite the entreaties of antislavery forces and the criminal claims of the state of Ohio, been returned to Kentucky slavery, only to disappear into the Deep South.

To say that is the story we need to bear in mind in order to understand the political and cultural struggle is not to take this version at face value. To make sense of the meanings of the Garner controversy, it is crucial not only to bring a skeptical eye to the handling of evidence but to go beyond the story, both in the sense of placing the events that went into the narratives in a larger social and institutional context and in the sense of critically exploring how the most common tellings were constructed. The remainder of this introduction pursues those two tasks, in that order, by examining the following topics: the Cincinnati to which the

Garners fled, particularly what we can know of the role played in their case by individuals and organizations from the community of free blacks; the legal context of the courtroom disputes that followed the Garners' capture; the workings of the antebellum press; how, in the press and elsewhere, different actors formulated and fought over narratives of the case, what resources they drew on, what purposes they pursued, and what elements they excluded; the place of the Garners' own voices in those narrative struggles; and the political consequences of these assorted versions of their story. It might be best to begin, however, by saying a bit more about the broader pattern of slave escapes, how the Garners did and did not fit that pattern, and, most important, the lives of subordination they tried to leave behind.

Glimpses of the Fugitives' World

Most of the evidence about how each of the adults viewed his or her particular situation in Kentucky—apart from what can already be inferred from their resistance at the moment of capture and their decision to seek freedom in the first place—comes from what was said or written during the legal struggle in Ohio. The record of their lives before their escape is meager, evidence of their views and sentiments still more so. The archives, of course, offer us no letters or diaries in which the enslaved Garners discuss their experiences. Almost all of the firsthand "slave testimony" in the nation's written records is by ex-slaves, looking backward. That is no accident. Denying slaves the right and the means of speaking for themselves—on the principle that "the slave could only be known through his master"—was a central pillar of slave-holding society in the United States.[18] White Southern families thus tended to be far better documented than slaves, and as the Gaines family was more prominent than most, the record they left behind is correspondingly fuller. Those surviving papers, however, have relatively little to say about the troubles and aspirations of the slaves.

Still, while it is difficult to conclude much about the Garners' inner lives in slavery, some of the family's basic circumstances in the small farming community of Richmond are clear enough.[19] About half of the people living in Richmond were slaves, more than double the percentage for Kentucky as a whole. Margaret and her children lived with Archibald Gaines on his farm, Maplewood, along with his second wife Elizabeth (sister of his deceased first wife), and two children from each of the marriages. The farm of James Marshall, which at the time of the escape was home to Robert, Mary, and Simon, was less than a mile away. Each farm had roughly a dozen slaves and, although the owners grew assorted crops, the central economic activity was raising livestock, particularly hogs.[20]

Margaret Garner was born on June 4, 1833, roughly one year before Robert. Both were born in Richmond. For the first sixteen years of her life, Margaret was the slave of John P. Gaines, Archibald's oldest brother, who owned Maplewood at the time and was raising his family there. As Margaret grew up, John Gaines became a notable public figure. Considered a hero by his neighbors for his role in the Mexican–American War, he served a term in Congress from 1847 to 1849. In the fall of 1849, only months after he lost the seat to a primary challenger, a new political opportunity arose when President Zachary Taylor offered him the governorship of Oregon. Gaines accepted and promptly sold Maplewood and his slaves, including Margaret, to Archibald, who returned from raising cotton in Arkansas to take up residence in Richmond. Robert and Margaret had evidently already begun their relationship: Margaret, then sixteen, was pregnant with her oldest son, Thomas. Thomas was born in March 1850, and the remaining children followed quickly thereafter: Sam in 1852, Mary in 1853, Cilla in April 1855.[21] Only months after Cilla's birth, Margaret seems to have conceived again, for she was apparently pregnant at the time of her capture.[22]

Press coverage during the trial before Commissioner Pendery gives us glimpses of life in slavery as the Garners knew it. Long before his son Robert was born, Simon was sold away from his wife to another northern Kentucky farmer, rejoining her on the farm only weeks before their escape, when Marshall repurchased him. He had been gone nearly twenty-five years. Since both Simon and Mary appear to have been in their fifties at the time of the court proceedings, they had spent roughly half of their lifetimes separated from each other, far more than they had been together as a couple. Mary was hired out at various points and said that she had borne eight children, most of them sold away, too. Several news articles report her invoking harsh and abusive treatment by Mrs. Marshall as a reason for the decision to escape. Like his parents, Robert was also periodically hired out. Both when he labored for Marshall and for others, his duties included helping raise the hogs and—if the testimony of the Garners' witnesses was reliable—drive them to market in Cincinnati. Margaret, who one brief article also characterizes as complaining of cruel treatment and who bore a scar on her face that she said came from being struck by a "white man," worked in the Gaines household, caring for the Gaines children and devoting at least some of her time to Archibald's elderly mother, Eliza—so much so that in court she suggested that old Mrs. Gaines was in fact her owner.[23]

These details underscore the degree of control exercised by the Gaines and Marshall families, but at certain moments the courtroom reporting also allows us to see that the Garners, like many other slaves, found avenues for autonomous action beyond their masters' knowledge or understanding. One such moment is the dispute over naming. It seems likely that when Jolliffe called his client "Robert," and Marshall's witnesses countered that the fugitive in court had "never" been known by any name other than "young Simon," both sides were telling the truth as they knew it—that "Robert" was how the man in court identified himself and was known among family and friends even while he was always "Simon" to Kentucky whites. Such a gap between social worlds would not have been unusual. Masters sometimes tried to control slaves' first names, but often without complete success. For both parties, naming was an important avenue for self-assertion, a way to influence the balance of power. We can see this not only in Robert's insistence on refusing to be known in court by the master's name but in the prolonged if undeclared struggle over what to call Margaret. For Archibald Gaines, she was "my negro woman Peggy," which is how his witnesses in court referred to her as well, while, rejecting the diminutive, she gave her own name as "Margaret," and Jolliffe and her assorted public supporters tended to follow suit (though they did not do so with perfect consistency). Many, perhaps most, slaves also had surnames, even though most masters did not know it or at least did not know what those names were. Mary Garner fit this pattern: "The old lady, speaking to me of the witnesses, said, 'She won't know me as MARY GARNER; I was called when she knew me MARY MARSHALL. My old man, whose name I took when I married him, was gone from me 24 years and while he was gone I went under my master's name, but when he came back, I took his name again.'"[24]

The very thing, however, that enabled the Garners to define some of the terms of their world—the ability to keep certain choices and actions invisible to white people—also placed these efforts largely outside the documentary record, making them difficult to reconstruct in detail. According to one report, for instance, Mary Garner had been "a professor of religion" for roughly twenty years before the family's escape, but there is no evidence that she belonged to an official church recognized by whites, and, hence, there is no other archival trace of her spiritual activities. Unsanctioned or even covert religious gatherings were among the most vital aspects of American slave culture, sources of profound meaning and of resistance to the masters' accounts of social reality, but what Mary's professing involved, to whom it was directed, and where it took place are now unknowable. Yet official membership in a white-sanctioned church might not have told us much more, either. Records of the Richmond Presbyterian Church reveal that, less than a year before the escape, "Margaret a woman of colour" was examined on her faith, baptized, and admitted as a member. While the evidence suggests that this was in all likelihood Margaret Garner, one can assess what her entry into the church meant to her and how it informed her thinking about her escape and killing of her daughter only by indulging in the most baseless forms of speculation. This, unfortunately, is all too typical of what the records can and cannot show today's readers about most of the important aspects of the Garners' lives in slavery.[25]

Gaines family letters offer brief indications that, beyond the insecurity and fears of separation that were generalized parts of slave life, Maplewood slaves may, at times, have had specific reasons to worry that sale might be imminent—but the evidence is murky. Much the same can be said of the other traces of slave resistance at Maplewood. Members of the Richmond Presbyterian Church admonished one Hannah, probably the same Hannah who belonged to Archibald, for defying her masters, but it is difficult to discern how this fit in the broader patterns of relations between Gaines and those in bondage to him. Similar ambiguities and uncertainty mark the brief glimpses of Margaret's parents afforded by the archives. Her reputed father, Duke, was enslaved on Maplewood when she was born and during her childhood, but is not clearly among the farm's slaves listed on the 1850 census. Virtually nothing is known about him. Margaret's mother, Cilla, was still enslaved on the farm at the time the Garners fled and may have been among the four slaves who successfully escaped three days later, but that is not clear, either. Even Cilla's full name is a matter on which the evidence is ambiguous.[26]

Indeterminacy of this kind hampers efforts to get to the bottom of a significant question that clearly preoccupied the Garners' contemporaries during the trial before Commissioner Pendery, suffusing many antebellum responses to the case, even as it has fascinated some later scholars: who fathered Margaret's children and was this matter of paternity a clue or key to the meaning of her actions? Were her flight and her decision to kill her daughter responses to sexual violation by a white man, and, if so, was that man Archibald Gaines? As discussed below, public discourse about the children was marked by coded insinuations, and occasionally more direct claims, of white parentage. There is no question that these remarks were important to the political contest over the case. Gaines's lawyer, Francis Chambers, anxiously sought to suppress the issue when it arose in testimony before Pendery. There is also every reason to think that even indirect public references to the issue infuriated Gaines himself, that he perceived them as part of a broader assault on his honor.[27] What they can tell us about the actual paternity of the children is a far more contestable matter.

Steven Weisenburger has made an extended circumstantial case that "Archibald Gaines probably fathered one or more of Margaret's children." In addition to invoking as evidence the conduct of both Archibald and Margaret following her escape, Weisenburger makes three main points. First, Sam, Mary, and Cilla, all notably lighter than their brother Tom, were the three children born after Archibald bought Margaret from his brother, during a period in which he would have been the only white male at Maplewood. Second, because Robert was sold away, he was far from Margaret at the time when the younger children were conceived. Third, with each of those children as well with the child she was carrying at the time of her capture, Margaret became pregnant a few months after Gaines's wife, Elizabeth—which is to say during the period when, according to the conventions of the milieu and the era, white women were likely to make themselves sexually unavailable to their husbands.[28] On this account, Gaines had, in the parlance of crime fiction, the means, the motive, and the opportunity.

That verdict, however, is best taken as a cautionary tale about what can and cannot be concluded from evidence of this kind. Certainly the color of the children offers ambiguous testimony, especially given the intimate intermingling of black and white in the American South: Robert and Margaret, who was classified in both the 1850 census and court documents as being of mixed race, could have themselves produced children of various hues. Furthermore, Weisenburger misconstrues the court reporting, imputing to Robert the labor history of his father, for it was the older man, *not* the younger, who was sold by James Marshall. Once this error—a consequence, presumably, of the struggle over naming, the presence in so many documents of two different Simons—is corrected, it is no longer obvious that Robert and Margaret were out of reach of each other at the relevant times.[29] Nor are the sources unambiguous even in their support for the claim that Margaret conceived during the late stages of Elizabeth Gaines's pregnancies.[30] If Archibald Gaines *did* become sexually involved with Margaret Garner, then, it may not have been because her husband was absent and his own wife was unwilling.

None of this means that he was not the father of her children: noting these problems of evidence and inference no more suffices to establish Robert's paternity than it refutes the antebellum insinuations that so angered Gaines. The literature of slavery overflows with cases of sexual relations between master and slaves, relations always structured by vast disparities in power and sometimes taking the most brutal and violent forms.[31] In light both of the broad historical tendencies and of the more specific circumstances of the Garner case, there are reasons to raise the question of paternity. But given the available evidence, there is no answer that warrants confidence: we simply cannot know. All we can say with certainty is that, for whatever reasons—and American, race-based chattel slavery provided the men and women who endured it with plenty of reasons, even when a master's sexual attention was not among them— the Garners resolved to run.

By setting out that night in Richwood seeking a new life in freedom, the Garners were already departing from the general pattern of slave behavior. It is easy for contemporary readers to miss the magnitude of the departure. As they did in the 1850s, fugitives have continued to loom large in the American imagination of slavery, partly because the relatively few slaves who left a notable imprint on public records tended to be those who, like Frederick Douglass, managed to escape their condition. But most enslaved persons did not flee, and most of those who ran away did not end up reaching, or even seeking, a free state. The historians John Hope Franklin and Loren Schweninger estimate that roughly two thousand succeeded each year, "a mere trickle from among . . . millions."[32] Slaves were most likely to head north—and had the best chances of success—when they lived near free territory, in places such as northern Kentucky, but even those living as close as the Garners did faced daunting challenges; many escapees never connected with agents of the Underground Railroad or even made it across the heavily watched Ohio River.[33] Margaret and her family, then, got farther than most.

They also stood out for escaping as a family. About 80 percent of runaways were young men seeking freedom alone. Often these men had no wives, or at least no children. Most male runaways who were married or had children left their families behind. Women, more strongly tied to children, were less likely to run (and typically slave girls had begun having children by their late teens). Few fugitives were as old as Simon and

Mary. Few were as young as the Garner children. Very few parties were families, and even when families did escape together, they tended to do so in smaller clusters, not groups of eight, spanning three generations.[34] Such were the general trends for the slave South. In the Garners' immediate northern Kentucky environs, family escapes were somewhat more common.[35] And when slaves did escape, it was also common for them to seek the aid of kin, as the Garners did; free blacks in an urban setting, like the Kites, could be especially helpful. But there were obvious practical reasons for the general predominance of young adults and small parties among fugitives: larger, more heterogeneous groups had a much poorer chance of success. As Franklin and Schweninger observe, "Perhaps the most difficult task was for an entire family—husband, wife, children, grandparents, grandchildren—to try to escape together"; those who tried "rarely made it to freedom."[36] Whether the Garners felt their own odds were better than these national tendencies suggest or whether they saw their bid for freedom as a desperate long shot is, it should be clear by now, impossible to say.

However they imagined their chances, and whatever the statistics indicated, it is easy to see how everything could have turned out differently. Had Gaines and Marshall discovered the escape a few hours later, or had Kite returned home earlier, enabling the Garners to follow Coffin's advice and hide with another household in another part of the city—or had Kite simply bypassed the consultation with Coffin and acted on his own to place his relatives with another black family—perhaps the masters and the assorted officers who assisted them in the work of slave catching would have failed to find the fugitives. Then, as Coffin had hoped that morning, it might have been possible to send the family north out of the city under the cover of darkness. Like the four Maplewood slaves who followed them on January 31, they could have disappeared without a trace.

Black Cincinnati Responds

Such things did happen in Cincinnati. A beacon for slaves thinking of crossing the river, it was a city that had much to offer the fugitives who made it there, even those who, unlike the Garners, lacked relatives among the free black population. There were people in town—Kite among them—from whom escapees had reason to expect not only sympathy but also knowledge of what to do and a willingness to risk defying the Fugitive Slave Act and the powerful institutions that enforced it. Despite this allure, though, the Queen City was hardly a *safe* destination for fugitives. The alacrity and tenacity of the federal marshals' response reflected something important about the city, too. Organized, dedicated antislavery activists, both black and white, were important presences, but they were in no position to set the political tone. Cincinnati straddled the border not only geographically but culturally, occupying free soil yet conducting much of its business with slave owners and slave states while serving, too, as a major gateway to the West. Dense and crowded, it was growing rapidly, in part through waves of German and Irish immigration. In 1850 the population stood at just over 115,000. By 1860 it would top 160,000 (making Cincinnati the seventh largest city in the country and, after New Orleans, the largest outside the Eastern seaboard). During this period of expansion, residents both rich and poor, black and white, were scattered through virtually all quarters in a heterogeneous mixture. When the Garners arrived, there were roughly 3,500 black residents. That was enough to constitute one of the largest and most significant black communities in the free states, but still a community dwarfed by a white population that was far more accepting of slavery, and hostile to abolition, than were other parts of Ohio.[37] Anything that threatened the interests or sensitivities of the business partners so vital to the city's economy—and nothing did that like public attacks on the Fugitive Slave Act—would draw censure and resistance from significant forces, both popular and elite. With many white Cincinnatians, those who aided fugitives were deeply unpopular.

Electoral politics reflected this tendency. When the Garners arrived, Salmon Chase had just taken office as governor. A man who had been so central to antislavery legal advocacy in the state over the past twenty years that he was sometimes called the "attorney-general for runaway negroes," Chase was the chief architect of Ohio's newly formed Republican Party. Although he had triumphed in the race for the state's highest office, he had finished only third on election day in Cincinnati and surrounding Hamilton County, getting under 20 percent of the vote there. Similarly, Ohio would back Republican nominee John C. Frémont in the presidential election that coming fall, but in June, just months after the Garners were shipped south, the Democratic Party held its national nominating convention in Cincinnati; the delegates there embraced James Buchanan, as Hamilton County voters would in the fall as well when, largely on the basis of a near-sweep of the slave states, the Democrat went on to a decisive victory.[38] The clashes between the parties in Ohio were sharp even by the standards of the era, and though the Republican Party was still a fragile mix, internally divided over the politics of both race and immigration, Democrats were relentless in painting their opponents as "Black Republicans"; stoking antiblack sentiment was central to Democratic tactics and strategies. But although the broadest of sketches would portray a Democratic city at odds with other parts of a Republican state, Cincinnati, too, was of course intensely divided—the era's political and cultural frontiers ran right through it. The most vituperative charges and countercharges found expression, week in and week out, in the city's highly partisan newspapers, only fitting in a community that encompassed everyone from antislavery officials such as Judge Burgoyne to pro-Southern "doughfaces" like Marshal Robinson and his underlings. It was an explosive mix.

The city, then, was no paradise for its black residents. In this, it shared much with the state as a whole, for hostility to slavery did not by any means necessarily entail opposition to white supremacy. Ohio's discriminatory constitution and a series of "Black Laws" had imposed severe burdens for most of the century, using race-specific financial and bureaucratic regulations to make immigration to the state difficult, barring blacks from voting, denying them poor relief available to whites, and, until very recently, excluding residents of color from public education even while taxing them as fully as white citizens.[39] In Cincinnati the animus expressed in such laws had repeatedly turned violent, even deadly. In 1829, 1836, and 1841 the city had seen major riots in which mobs of marauding whites assaulted blacks (and in some instances attacked the property of white abolitionists). The first episode was so severe that roughly half of Cincinnati's black population emigrated to Canada (founding the community of Wilberforce), and the most recent riot was the largest such attack in any American city up to that moment. The 1841 assaults, however, had been met with considerable black resistance, a sign not only of the resilience and assertiveness of the community but also of its capacity for self-organization, something that would continue to bear fruit in the coming years.[40]

By 1856 black people in Cincinnati had created a rich institutional life. Theirs was one of the nation's most active communities in doing the work of the Underground Railroad, not surprising given the city's location and the fugitives who took advantage of it. Many of those who had fled to the city had been sheltered and sent onward entirely without the assistance of whites (just as, for the nation as a whole, the job of protecting fugitives from federal marshals most typically fell to black men and women). Largely Southern-born, predominantly literate, and highly focused on education, Cincinnati's black community had a well-developed leadership structure. Just days before the Garners' escape, some of the city's most important black men had been the moving forces at the state's Convention of Colored Men, which had addressed both the antislavery struggle and Ohio's discriminatory laws.[41] Later in the year, black Cincinnati would finally win its long struggle to secure tax-funded, community-controlled, public education.[42]

Given this history, there is every reason to imagine that Cincinnatians of color and their organizations played a major role in the struggle over the Garners' attempt to avoid a return to slavery. Like much of the Garners' lives in Kentucky, however, the details of this participation prove elusive. Once again, the reasons have to do with who shaped the documentary record and how. Cincinnati's black leaders and institutions drew nothing like the kinds of newspaper coverage that white elites received. While the Garners were the subjects of voluminous reports, speculations, and commentaries during their legal struggles, very few of the free blacks working to help them gain freedom appear in the press in any guise other than as members of an anonymous mass. Nor is there much in the way of written documentation of the internal life of black organizations, especially those concerned with the dangerous and illegal activities involved in defying the Fugitive Slave Act. When such scraps of information about black institutions as do survive provide the names of associations—the Sons of Enterprise, the Sons of Liberty, the Daughters of Samaria, the Life Guards, the Anti-Slavery Sewing Society—they often, unfortunately, do not tell us much more than that.

Historians have established that the Life Guards sheltered and aided fugitives, while the Anti-Slavery Sewing Society provided clothing, but the written record offers only a few fleeting glimpses of how these groups or their members responded to the Garners' escape, capture, and trial. Some of the names that emerge in scholarly studies of the city's black leadership also appear in the margins of antebellum reporting on the case. Ann Smith, a witness who testified in support of Margaret's claim to having been taken north as a child to nurse the Gaines children, is listed on the membership rolls of the protemperance Daughters of Samaria. Jesse Beckley, who at Jolliffe's request filed a habeas corpus motion before Judge Burgoyne alleging that the Garner children were being detained illegally, was among the wealthiest of Cincinnati's black citizens, reportedly a member of the Life Guards, and would soon (aided by Jolliffe) pursue a legal case for his right to vote in city elections. His brother William, the man Jolliffe sought to have appointed by Commissioner Pendery to serve subpoenas to the witnesses for the Garners, played a key leadership role in the community, serving, for instance, on the Colored Schools Board of Trustees. Behind these actors' brief appearances in press accounts there must have been a rich web of associations and activities, but the details simply do not appear in the printed record: when we are limited to what the political scientist James Scott calls "the public transcript," much about the organization of black resistance remains invisible.[43]

Consider, for instance, this editorial warning shot, fired by the *Daily Enquirer*: "The negroes, in this fugitive slave matter, are acting very injudiciously, and if a riot is not gotten up it will not be their fault." The "injudicious" conduct was the "negro meeting" held two nights previously, which had passed a resolution indicating, "That we view with indignation the attempt made to exclude colored persons from the trial now progressing before Commissioner Pendery." Given the city's broader political climate and demographic character, such a gathering was a bold and risky act of community assertion. The *Daily Enquirer*'s outrage is one measure of the risks. But who was behind the decision that the risks were worthwhile? Who attended? What deliberations and arguments—surely of a different character from those made in court and reported in the daily press—shaped the resolution's language? Press accounts do not take us inside the meeting: they do not detail the debates in the way that marked coverage of some white forums that addressed the case.[44] Not even the narrative of the Garners' story produced by Levi Coffin discusses such events or the men and women who made them happen, for Coffin, too, focuses on the doings of whites in the city.[45]

Yet those sketchy reports and commentaries on the action of black crowds and anonymous individuals remain of great value. For all they do not say, they help us gauge the response of Cincinnatians of color. Even when they are as hostile as the *Daily Enquirer*'s editorial, such sources at least convey the intensity of black public feeling. Newspaper accounts, furthermore, demonstrate that acts of black public assertion were not limited to organized meetings: while black Cincinnatians were being kept outside the courtroom, they were busy mobilizing for the Garners in the streets. Here is the *Cincinnati Daily Times,* describing the scene as the family was led from Commissioner Pendery's court at the close of the first day's proceedings:

[A] large crowd of colored men and women, intermixed with prominent whites of a certain political stamp, blocked up the passing way and stubbornly refused to give room that the prisoners might be taken out.

When a passage was at length cleared . . . the officers . . . were greeted by this mob with indecent curses and imprecations, and the slaves urged to "stand by their freedom" and "not to give up," and the poor woman, whose hands are stained with the blood of her own child, cheered for the murderous act. Several attempts were made to rescue the prisoners, but they were all successfully repulsed by a strong police force in attendance.

During the skirmish, two black men, Minstin Hays and Jerry Fassett, were arrested.[46] The next day, events outside the court took a similar course, with "two or three hundred persons, mostly colored people" again challenging the officers' ability to control the Garners' movements. After the prisoners had been confined in the omnibus that would take them to jail, "they opened the windows and shook hands with the colored people within reach. As the vehicle started, some cheered and some hooted, the colored people following it. . . . When near Fifth, a rescue was proposed, but the officers immediately making an arrest, it divided the crowd, and no further molestation was experienced." The arrest was of a black man, unnamed in any reporting, accused of throwing a stone at officers sitting atop the omnibus.[47]

Struggle in the streets was not limited to men. Women of color's militance can be detected even when viewed through the belittling lens of the *Daily Enquirer*: "'D———n you!' shouted one of these saddle-colored ladies, who, by the way, was dressed in the extreme of fashion, in answer to a request of one of the officers to stand back, 'D———n you, I'm free born, half white, and as good as any white-livered b———h in Ohio!' The officer took no notice of her or her companions."[48] A more sober, if less detailed, assessment can be found in the *New York Daily Times*: "Four or five decently dressed colored women in the crowd seemed the most bent upon resistance and opposition."[49] Despite the daily press's Olympian distance from the social networks through which opposition was solicited and organized, black resistance registers clearly enough.

Such reports, however, waned as the case continued: it is clear that the degree of turbulence in the streets subsided over time. There were no major violent clashes, and no systematic effort to effect a forcible rescue was ever launched. The procession escorting the Garners to the river when they were returned to Kentucky was far more subdued than the crowds that greeted their first day in court. Among the recriminations that flowed in the aftermath of the trial were complaints that there had been no more ambitious attempt to use physical force to extricate the family from the clutches of the legal system. It was not as though Cincinnatians simply lacked the will or ingenuity shown by those Bostonians who had rescued Shadrach Minkins. Just three years before the Garners drew so much public attention, a notable escape had thwarted another fugitive slave hearing in Cincinnati. During the proceedings in court, the fugitive, Louis, had moved away from the bar. With the silent and surreptitious assistance of black and white spectators, he worked his way back through the crowd until, unnoticed by his master, the federal marshals, or officers of the court, he slipped out the door and into the streets. He hid in the city with a black family until agents of the Underground Railroad were able to help him flee to Canada, disguised as a woman. Jolliffe had been the attorney in this case, too, and he clearly had not minded being relieved of his duties in this way.[50] Why, some then wondered, did the Garner case fail to produce a similar act of triumphant defiance? Some focused in particular on the black community: what did it suggest that Cincinnatians of color had not done more to take matters into their own hands?[51]

In retrospect, there is nothing surprising about the lack of a more ambitious rescue attempt. Marshal Robinson did a lot to ensure that none would take place. A man who embraced his role with zeal, Robinson expanded his force of special deputies rapidly in the first few days, until it reached about four hundred men. This, as Weisenburger observes, effectively placed the city "under martial law."[52] Robinson appears to have had a strong ideological identification with the claimants. He must also have known that a successful rescue or escape would damage not only his reputation but also his pocketbook: under the Fugitive Slave Act, he would be subject to a fine of up to $1,000.[53] Such a fine had been imposed in the Louis case. Evidently, Robinson was determined to ensure that nothing like that happened this time, and he was able to command considerable government funds in pursuit of that goal. Those who in the aftermath called out for an insurrectionary confrontation led by the city's most marginal population were proposing what would in all likelihood have been a bloodbath.[54] Rather than see the lack of escape as a testimony to the passivity of Cincinnati's black and abolitionist communities, it may be more appropriate to take the massive scale of the marshal's militarization of the city's streets as a backhanded acknowledgment of the determination and potential strength of Garners' allies, of the real threat that they would succeed—despite the Southern and Democratic sympathies of so many white Cincinnatians—in preventing the family from being taken South. Since there was no rescue, however, the legal process ran—if much more slowly, and amid an unusually complex array of challenges from assorted state officials and courts—until it reached the end so clearly intended by the authors of the Fugitive Slave Act, when federal courts sided with the men who claimed the Garners as their property.

The Law and the Courts

The Fugitive Slave Act was a crucial and controversial piece of the Compromise of 1850, the massive legislative package aimed at preserving the Union by dampening sectional antagonism. Like the Fugitive Slave Clause of the U.S. Constitution and the Fugitive Slave Act of 1793, the new law mandated the return of slaves who escaped to free territory, but it departed from its predecessors in requiring the federal government to assist in the return, and it detailed procedures, incentives, and obligations designed to ensure that this requirement would be met. The law authorized federal judges to appoint commissioners who would rule on the claims of masters and issue warrants for the arrest of fugitives; it required federal marshals to execute these warrants and, if a commissioner deemed this necessary, oversee the captives' return to slavery. Even while stipulating that alleged fugitives could not testify in their hearings, it essentially established the claimant's sworn word as sufficient proof to establish rightful ownership. In an attempt to shut down abolitionist disruptions, the law also prescribed punishments for ordinary citizens who assisted fugitives, and barred any interference from state courts once the federal proceedings were under way. And as if to clear up any lingering uncertainty about the optimal resolution to a case, the Fugitive Slave Act, notoriously, tied commissioners' pay to their verdicts: they received a fee for each ruling, $10 for finding for the claimant and $5 for finding for the alleged fugitive, with payment made not by the federal government but by the claimant. This summary should make it obvious why, although the broader Compromise of 1850 had something to offer a range of different actors, interests, and locales, in the Fugitive Slave Act itself, "the South got the law it wanted."[55]

For all of its blunt specificity about duties, fines, and punishments, the language of the law was delicate on one fundamental point: the word "slave" appears nowhere in the text. In terms that closely follow the equally evasive language of the U.S. Constitution, escaped slaves are referred to as "fugitives from service or labor." One might see the euphemisms of the later texts as nothing more than a trace or echo of the well-known reluctance of some of the Founders to see slavery projected indefinitely into the future by being written into the nation's permanent charter, but the choice of words had other effects, too. As Stephen M. Best has observed, such language casts the slave as a debtor, and the fugitive as one who has reneged on a debt.[56] Those whose every product could be appropriated by men or women with whom they had signed no contract and made no agreement are here portrayed as thieves. A thief is still, of course, a human being, and in this the language of debt reinforced a dynamic that marked the law of American slavery more generally: slaves were construed as at once persons and property. Even a partial acknowledgment of the slave's humanity might appear to open the door to those who argued that slavery was unjust, but it could also, in a particularly painful irony, serve to deepen the subordination of slaves; certainly the instability between personhood and property could work to the advantage of owners inside the courtroom. It did just that at a key moment in the Garner case, as the sheriffs and marshals were battling for custody before Judge Leavitt. James Headington, the counsel for Marshal Robinson, argued that it was precisely because slaves were "not property, but persons," that they fell within the terms of federal and state laws that authorized the marshal to hold custody over "prisoners" in the county jail; with this point established, Headington later pivoted, reminding Judge Leavitt that there was no way in which a state criminal claim could supersede or interrupt an in-process "*property*" claim under the Fugitive Slave Act. The next morning's *Cincinnati Daily Enquirer* published an editorial praising him for this "masterly effort," and Leavitt, despite personal antislavery sympathies, ruled for Marshal Robinson.[57]

In some respects, as this example shows, the law worked as intended: it tilted the legal struggle in the free states toward masters. More than 80 percent of cases brought under the Fugitive Slave Act resulted in rulings for the claimants followed by the successful return of slaves, often, as with Garners, under escort by federal marshals. The midfifties were the peak period for returns, and rescues grew less frequent as the decade wore on. The law was particularly effective in the border states, as proximity made it relatively inexpensive for slave owners to pursue their claims and as the white populations were less broadly hostile than in New England. Ultimately, though, the Fugitive Slave Act produced frustration and resentment on both sides. Every victory won by a fugitive slave in court was a source of outrage to the South; high-profile cases in which fugitives were returned became important occasions for building the antislavery movement. By bringing the apparatus of slavery more visibly into the free states, the law only heightened their anxieties about what many in the North perceived as both a Southern campaign to nationalize slavery and a broader pattern of national domination by the forces of what critics had come to call "the Slave Power." Yet the South, offended by any show of free state resistance to the law, substantially exaggerated its extent. Many Southerners also misconstrued or were unwilling to recognize the practical consequences of the law, underestimating the high rate at which commissioners returned slaves and the frequency with which these returns were paid for by the federal government. When a Kentucky editorialist commenting in the aftermath of the Garner case remarked that "the Fugitive Slave Law is very near a nullity," he was at variance with the facts but not with prevailing sentiment in his region.[58] By 1856, then, the Fugitive Slave Act was facilitating both the return of slaves and the polarization of the polity.

Antislavery lawyers had by then also brought the conflict inside the judicial system by repeatedly challenging the law's constitutionality in court. One attack was on the law's use of commissioners, glorified petty bureaucrats—judicial underlings neither appointed by the president nor confirmed by the Senate as the Constitution required judges to be—whose rulings were not subject to appeal by fugitives. Another common challenge, not surprisingly, was to the way commissioners were paid. Neither challenge ultimately succeeded, however, and the Fugitive Slave Act would continue to stand, as written, until its repeal near the end of the Civil War.[59] In keeping with the common practice of those in the antislavery bar, Jolliffe did raise some questions about the legitimacy of Commissioner Pendery's position, but they were peripheral to the constitutional case he presented in the commissioner's court. His main challenge, one he had invented himself a few years earlier, was that the Fugitive Slave Act violated the First Amendment guarantee of freedom of religion by compelling ordinary citizens, regardless of the tenets of their faiths, to cooperate with the return of fugitives. It is hard to imagine, however, that Jolliffe really believed that this argument would succeed with Pendery or in any other federal court. Clearly, on this point he was aiming, through the press, at the court of public opinion, at advancing the broader, longer-term struggle over the future of slavery in the United States. As for advancing the immediate interests of his clients, Jolliffe was—insofar as the federal courts were in a position to decide whether the Garners were slaves—for all practical purposes condemned to accept as a given the framework established by the Fugitive Slave Act.[60]

That framework appeared to offer little room for maneuver: if the Garners were indeed owned by Gaines and Marshall, then the law gave the fugitives no recourse. Yet Jolliffe and his team managed to turn what might have been a swift administrative formality into a sustained legal dispute, one that left at least some journalists uncertain about how the case would be decided. While it seems clear that the immense publicity accompanying Margaret's murder of young Mary, and the skirmishes that this set off among the different officials and courts, slowed the case before Pendery, Jolliffe's most important legal theory played a part in extending the case in the commissioner's court to an unprecedented length, too. Many of the developments in that court arose from the argument that because of the Garners' prior visits to free soil, they were not, in fact, slaves under the law. It was because of this argument that Pendery allowed Jolliffe first to search the city for and then examine on the stand witnesses who testified that they had seen Robert and his parents in Cincinnati. There was no such witness, however, who could vouch for having seen Margaret or her children, as even on her own account she had not been across the river since she was a young girl, and her children had never been at all. That was why it seemed so momentous when the commissioner, for reasons that remain unclear, allowed Jolliffe—over the objection of opposing counsel and in violation of both the letter and the spirit of the Fugitive Slave Act—to call Margaret to testify as a witness. Although, nominally, she was permitted to testify only on behalf of her children, the testimony concerned her own journey to free soil as a girl; since under Jolliffe's legal theory, this was sufficient to emancipate her, it would make all her offspring free as well. Gaines and Marshall would then have no legitimate claim.

A court had first proclaimed the doctrine that bringing or allowing slaves onto free soil was sufficient to set them free in England's famous *Somerset's Case* of 1772. By 1856 the history of that doctrine in American courts was tangled, and its status not altogether clear. State courts in Ohio had in recent years proved sympathetic, thanks in no small part to Chase's pressing of this argument when he served as counsel to various fugitives. In the 1840 case of *State v. Farr,* the Ohio Supreme Court chief justice declared that even a momentary visit to Ohio soil was sufficient to set a slave free; even though this remark was dictum, made in passing, rather than the reasoned finding of the whole court, the state's lower courts had on a number of occasions cited it as sufficient reason to rule on behalf of fugitives. A county judge had done so in setting Rosetta Armstead free in Cincinnati in 1855, and when Marshal Robinson promptly rearrested her and brought her into federal court, the commissioner in the case—John Pendery—had freed Armstead, since she could no longer be considered a fugitive.[61] But when they came before Commissioner Pendery one year later, the Garners had not—despite the best efforts of antislavery forces—previously been before any kind of state court, and federal precedent was not nearly so favorable. Chase himself had failed to sway the U.S. Supreme Court with free soil arguments in the 1847 case of *Jones v. Van Zant,* and in the much-discussed *Strader v. Graham* (1851), which concerned slaves who had worked in the free states and then returned to Kentucky, the Court unanimously ruled in a way that favored the aggrieved Kentucky master. There was some uncertainty about what precise rules and principles that case had established, but in Pendery's court the lawyers for Gaines and Marshall made much of *Strader v. Graham,* arguing that under this precedent it was the laws of Kentucky, not Ohio, that determined the Garners' status—and under the laws of the slave state there was no doubt by this time that they were slaves. Whether or not he was swayed by that argument, at the core of Pendery's eventual ruling was the idea that in returning to Kentucky, the Garners had placed themselves back under its laws. In the end, after prolonging the case, and shaping much of the testimony on both sides, Jolliffe's argument failed.[62]

In this context, the repeated efforts by Jolliffe and assorted state officials to get the Garners brought before a state court were both predictable and rational. Because of the main tendencies in federal jurisprudence, antislavery activists regularly appealed to state courts to intervene in Fugitive Slave Act cases, and, despite the language of the law, those courts regularly obliged. Ohio was a particularly fierce battleground of such intercourt struggles.[63] The interventions of Judge Burgoyne, who as an officer of a probate court had by rights little to do with fugitive slave cases, was in fact fairly typical. But none of his efforts, including an order forbidding Marshal Robinson to remove the Garners from Ohio without Burgoyne's express permission, was able to prevent the fugitives' return to Kentucky. Nor did the murder case ever amount to more than procedural wrangling. That case was hardly typical—indeed no previous fugitive slave case had involved a competing effort by a state to pursue a murder case—but because Commissioner Pendery would not allow the murder trial to interrupt or supersede the fugitive slave case, the Garners never appeared before Judge Samuel Carter on the murder indictment he had issued. These legal proceedings certainly contributed to the range and intensity of commentary on the case, and had Gaines not deliberately thwarted the Kentucky governor's effort to return the adult Garners for trial, the murder case might well have drastically altered the outcome. The Garners' sympathizers clearly hoped, as many supporters of the Fugitive Slave Act clearly feared—both perhaps with reason—that once the family appeared before a state court, means might be found for all of them, one way or another, to escape slavery permanently. When Gaines defied Morehead, however, the Garners' legal battle was over. What remained were the final stages of the rhetorical battle in the press.

Newspaper Politics

Just as they were for the American party system, the 1850s were a transformative moment for journalism. Indeed, the two changes were intimately connected elements of what the media scholar, Michael Schudson, calls "the politics of narrative form": how Americans read about politics in the press changed as the political world itself shifted significantly. Senators and congressmen, especially the most militant among them, began for the first time to use debates in their chambers as occasions to read aloud long, polished, and increasingly divisive speeches that addressed not their colleagues in the room but partisan publics outside the capital. Newspapers were the conduits. In changing how they presented the words and deeds of politicians, they helped speed the collapse of the partisan order that had existed through the passage of the Fugitive Slave Act, facilitating both the reconfiguration of the Democratic Party through the push and pull of sectional conflict, and the emergence of the Republican Party as the dominant force in the free states and the Democrats' main challenger for national power.[64] Viewed from the perspective of the present, however, the new features of the antebellum press are less striking than what the papers shared with their immediate predecessors: a striking degree of overt partisanship.

The partisanship of the press at the time of the Garner case was expressed both in newspapers' organizational affiliations and in the conventions of their writing. Although the coverage of the case certainly shows differences between pieces that are pure editorial commentary and stories concentrating on recounting the events of the previous day, the distinction between reporting facts and expressing opinions was much fuzzier for antebellum journalists and readers than it would be for their successors. The editorial page had not yet emerged as a wholly separate, clearly demarcated section of the paper, and the idea or ideology of journalistic "objectivity" was still well in the future. The press had long been tied to American political parties, indeed had been integrated into their mobilization and recruitment efforts. This was beginning to change by midcentury, as some began to embrace the ideal of a newspaper sufficiently insulated from external forces that it could criticize the choices and positions of any party.[65] Even so, the practical state of things when the capture of the Garners thrust them into the press was that the overwhelming preponderance of American papers was aligned with political parties, and tied to their affairs.

Judged by today's standards, at least, it is hard to imagine an illustration more striking than Cincinnati's main Democratic organ, the *Daily Enquirer.* Until just after the Garners were shipped South, the paper's editor and publisher was none other than Hiram H. Robinson, the U.S. marshal who had done so much to ensure their return to Kentucky. Robinson was a significant figure among the Democratic politicians of the city. In the journalistic world of his time and place, there was nothing scandalous in his involvement with the party or, still less, in an editor's fiercely Democratic sentiments. Still, it is extraordinary that he was a key player in this case in so many different ways: legal custodian over the Garners during their captivity (at least according to the rulings of the federal courts); chief organizer and paymaster of a vast cadre of special deputies hired to control the streets throughout the trial and prevent a rescue; the person financially liable if such a rescue were to happen; the ultimate authority evaluating his paper's daily reporting on the case; and presumably, a main writer of the *Daily Enquirer*'s editorials not only on the fate of the Garners but on the legal contest that centered on his own, highly disputed, conduct as a government official ("presumably," because in the *Enquirer* as in other dailies, most articles of any kind were unsigned).

Given such multifaceted institutional entanglements, it is understandable that the clashes that marked party life in a bitterly divided city appear in the press not only in reports and commentary on the events of the day but in sniping among the city's major papers. The *Daily Enquirer* feuded throughout the case with both the (Republican) *Daily Gazette* and the *Daily Commercial* (which had, like the *Gazette,* been an organ of the now-defunct Whigs and which was now cautiously inching its way toward alignment with the Republicans). The sniping ran both ways, with the sides not only rebutting each other's specific reports on and analyses of all aspects of the Garner case but also attacking rival papers in far more sweeping terms. The *Enquirer* was particularly full of invective, referring to the *Commercial* and the *Gazette* as organs of disloyalty and disunion; both papers pushed back angrily and ultimately devoted significant critical coverage to questions about whether Robinson had mismanaged federal funds during the hiring of deputies for the Garner case.[66]

Though the Garners dominated the front pages of the Cincinnati papers for weeks, looming large in the rest of Ohio and in Kentucky as well, the journalistic struggle over the case was no mere local affair. Through reprints from the Cincinnati press and through their own special reports from correspondents in the city, newspapers in many other parts of the country picked up the story, and the editors of a number of these papers added their own commentaries on the meaning of Margaret's conduct and the proper resolution of the complex struggle among the different courts. It was through the daily press, more than any other channel, that the Garners came to play, if briefly, an important role in the national conflict over slavery. This is not quite the same, however, as saying that theirs was a truly national news story. While papers in cities as diverse as Boston, Chicago, New York, and Washington, D.C., all devoted significant resources to the case, the degree of importance placed on it varied considerably, for it was based on the politics of the publication in question. This can be seen, for example, by comparing coverage in New York City's three most important papers, the *Daily Herald,* the *Daily Tribune,* and the *Daily Times.* The latter two, already aligned with the new Republican Party and hostile to the expansion of slavery, featured the case prominently for weeks, while the Democratic *Herald,* the South's favorite Northern paper, dropped its coverage after a few days and, during the turmoil in the streets of Cincinnati, published a report from a correspondent who, making no mention of the case, claimed that the city was "dull enough at present."[67]

The greatest difference, however, was regional. If the Garners made important news, they did so largely in the free states. There were exceptions, certainly. There was significant coverage in slaveholding Washington, D.C., but the capital city was a unique locale, and the bulk of the stories ran in its abolitionist weekly, the *National Era* (the paper that had first published *Uncle Tom's Cabin,* as a serial). The coverage was more prominent in the border state of Kentucky, where the Garners' escape, resistance, and legal struggles were economically important local news, directly involving not only Richmond masters and slaves but also the hundreds of Kentuckians who served as deputy marshals throughout the hearings. A charged moment in the state's fraught relationship with its neighbor across the river, the case was unavoidable. Kentucky also stood out among slave states for the degree to which slavery was a contested issue and press reporting on political matters was unrestrained.[68] The Deep South was quite another matter. Some major Southern papers simply did not mention the events; none covered them in any depth. Those that referred to the legal case went to extraordinary lengths to avoid mentioning the details of the murder or the circumstances that occasioned it.[69] The omissions and evasions did not arise because Southerners saw the case as too trivial or uninteresting to discuss, for the press in this region generally reported in detail on notable fugitive slave cases. It is thus clear that, whether it arose from inarticulate discomfort or explicit policy, the response of Southern papers is best understood as an act of political censorship.

Outside the South, though, the volume of reporting was considerable, and, if the frequency of coverage was proportionate to a paper's hostility to slavery, the case was nevertheless reported on from a wide range of political perspectives. From radical abolitionists, black and white, through the more politically mainstream supporters of the Republican Party, through the Know Nothings, the ever-dwindling remnants of the defunct Whigs, and on to the most pro-Southern and even proslavery supporters of the Democratic Party, diverse journalists thought the case was exciting news. Newspapers clashed over the course Judge Pendery should take, with assessments of the appropriate ruling following, predictably, from the papers' positions on the Fugitive Slave Act. The disagreements about the relative claims of the Ohio and federal courts were similar, though on this point the antislavery press was more divided among itself, and many papers sympathetic to the Garners were more cautious on this matter. Perhaps most revealing, though, are the responses to what so many writers took to be the center of the story, Margaret Garner's killing of Mary.

Some, especially pro–Fugitive Slave Act and pro-Southern editorialists, used the act to diminish, or even demonize the mother, and, by extension, to question the capacities of slaves and free blacks and the wisdom or virtue of abolitionists. For Robinson's *Daily Enquirer*, the "brutal and unnatural murder" was indisputably the work of a "crazed and frenzied negress," one unusually blind to the relative blessings for black people of life under the care of a master. The paper railed for months against all who would defend the deed or the doer. The *New York Express* was more moderate in its criticism but still concluded that the mother could have attacked her children only after being made "wretched" by "abolition excitement and passion." That only the intervention of fanatical whites could account for the murder was, understandably enough, a popular line in the Kentucky press. The *Covington Journal,* claiming local knowledge, told readers, "The truth is, Peggy is a very common, cross tempered, flat nosed, thick lipped negro woman, whose father was a very bad character. She was cruel to her children at home. . . . The murder of the child was the result of vexation and disappointment, arousing to a pitch of phrenzy a revengeful and devilish temper, inherited from her father, and her new formed friends taught her the beautiful morality found in the *higher law,* that it was noble to cut the throat of her offspring."[70]

But representations of Garner as villain or dupe were in the minority. In contrast to the wide range of opinions represented in discussions of the proper legal outcome, most writing that focused on the murder took it to be an indictment of slavery in general and powerful testimony on the unjustified sufferings that had been endured by this particular family of slaves. Margaret, especially, was treated sympathetically. Repeatedly, her attack on her children was portrayed as a blow for freedom, and she herself was rendered a political heroine. She was heroic precisely because, in killing her daughter to save her from slavery, she showed she valued freedom above life itself. This choice of death before slavery revealed not only the horrors of "the peculiar institution" but also the true character of those who were unjustly subjected. Garner's heroism and love of freedom were staples of sympathetic commentary. In referring to the "excitement" and "thrills" provided by the case, the commentators commonly invoked the intensity of her resistance to slavery. Abolitionists, of course, pushed the point especially far. As the culmination to a long argument that "power concedes nothing without a demand," that freedom would come only through "struggle" and "agitation," Frederick Douglass declared, "every mother who, like Margaret Garner, plunges a knife into the bosom of her infant to save it from the hell of our Christian slavery, should be held and honored as a benefactress." The *Anti Slavery Bugle* underscored the nature of the benefit: "Let the spirit of this despairing mother seize upon her oppressed race over the South and the whole Union cannot enslave them."[71]

In abolitionist commentaries, there were regular comparisons to Bunker Hill, and Patrick Henry. These were, transparently, attempts to construe Garner's action as the very same kind of sacrifice celebrated in foundational American political myths, to align the spirit of the American Revolution with the critique of slavery. Abolitionists had long sought to invoke the revolutionary tradition for their cause and had often appropriated Daniel Webster's celebrated unionist speech, which used the symbolism of the Bunker Hill monument to invoke the founders' heroism.[72] That the Garner case could be deployed in this familiar way was one reason for its political import.

If certain familiar scripts were important to the telling of story, however, key facts of the case were altogether out of the ordinary, and much about Margaret Garner herself fundamentally confounded prevailing expectations. To come to terms with her contemporaries' fascination with the case, it is important to understand this interplay, to grasp how she both fit and defied established narrative conventions. Much of the strangeness of the Garner archive lies in how, in the struggle over the import of her actions, various political actors used the imperfect resources available to them in imposing a narrative form on her confusing, disturbing, yet also compelling conduct. The documents reprinted in the book offer a variety of illustrations, but as an introduction to them it may be helpful to analyze at some length one exemplary case: what did it mean to see Margaret Garner as an American heroine?

A Slave Tragedy?

Patrick Henry and the soldiers at Bunker Hill—masculine cases, it should be noted—remind us that among the central qualities attributed to heroes are courage and a willingness to sacrifice themselves for greater causes. Margaret Garner, however, did not only risk herself in the struggle for freedom: she killed a child. At the center of her story is an act of horrifying violence. The act is difficult to come to terms with now; all the evidence suggests it was difficult then. Whatever rhetorical purposes it served and genuine solidarity, or even admiration, it solicited, the killing also unsettled those who would use her experiences for political ends. Reformers of the period repeatedly invoked the mother–child pair in their efforts. In a culture preoccupied with redemption, political discourse, especially that of sentimentalism, presented mothers and children as singularly capable of redeeming others. Deliverance through a child's death, and "salvation through motherly love" were, as Jane Tompkins observes, among the nation's "favorite stor[ies] about itself."[73] The Garner story gained some of its symbolic power by bringing these two plots together, offering antislavery commentators two potentially transformative narrative moments: a child's death and a loving mother saving that child from slavery. Yet of course the mother's love was not supposed to drive her to bring about the child's death: *this* was hardly the version of the salvation story that the culture already loved to tell itself over and over again.[74] What did it mean to bend the story to include the likes of Margaret Garner?

Historians believe that infanticide was very rare among slaves, and there is no known case in which a slave mother killed her child in so public, so overtly defiant, a way—but child-murder of a kind had become a part of literary and political culture.[75] Antislavery commentators had long exploited rumors of infanticide by slave mothers, as Harriet Beecher Stowe did with Cassy in *Uncle Tom's Cabin*: resolving to spare her two-week-old son the pain of growing up under slavery, Cassy kills him by giving him an overdose of laudanum. Yet such stories provided no precedent for the type of iconic figure that Garner became. Cassy's killing is unconfrontational, covert, unknown by her master or nearly anyone else. Nor does the novel present her action as in any way heroic: she is less a redeemer than a woman in need of the redemption that Stowe tries to give her at the end.[76] What kind of political salvation and what kind of heroism could a mother like Garner offer?

The *New York Daily Times* ran its first full report on the Garner case under the headline "The Slave Tragedy in Cincinnati," and references to the case as a tragedy came up repeatedly in reporting and other writings. Obviously, this was a way of stressing that something terrible had happened, but it is clear that the repeated turn to tragedy offered more than that vague sense of the term. Tragedy offered a familiar framework for contemplating heroism and horror in a political way. Yet although the Garner case recalls the depth and power of the great dramas, a "slave tragedy" was, by prevailing standards, something of an oxymoron. For all of their delight in putting comic, blackface slave characters on stage, antebellum whites were reluctant to treat black figures as having the dignity of a tragic hero. The existence of slavery on American soil was often viewed as tragic but, as Elizabeth Spelman argues, this view tended to render *white* Americans the protagonists in a story about the betrayal of noble ideals (just as to refer, now, to slavery as "the American tragedy" is to invoke a national sin that was redeemed, belatedly, through the shedding of blood).[77] The political attempt to present not just slavery but *slaves* as tragic—to put their suffering at the center of a momentous drama with a claim on everyone's attention—required substantial rhetorical labor and cultural invention. In the decades leading up to the Garner case, the most important such work had been done by sentimental novelists of an antislavery bent. Shaped by the very political culture they would resist, they had found tragedy in the lives of slave women with "white blood." As the case of Cassy illustrates, however, they had not created a tragic character to whom Margaret Garner could easily be assimilated. Garner was understood to be a woman of mixed ancestry, but her course of action escaped the destinies rigidly prescribed for the "tragic mulatta," a stock character who, invariably, "either dies of grief when her white lover abandons her for a wife of his own race, or . . . becomes a 'raving maniac' when sold to a profligate upon the death of her master."[78]

Despite this lack of fit, invocations of tragedy arose again and again even amid discussions of Garner's heroism. From the beginning of the case, those discussions repeatedly invoked the ancient Roman character Virginius. As presented by the Roman historian Livy, Virginius is a brave centurion who kills his freeborn daughter, Virginia, to save her from sexual violation by the tyrant Appius Claudius, who had used a blatantly corrupt legal process to declare her a slave. In response to the killing, the hitherto intimidated Roman people rally around Virginius, overthrow Appius, and restore the Roman republic.[79] The advantages of identifying Margaret's virtues with those of this classical hero are obvious. In understanding that there are things worse than death, things worth the deliberate sacrifice of human life, Virginius is the quintessential man of honor; that is why he deserves the freedom that is restored to him when the people join him in defeating tyranny. The comparison with Virginius was used, repeatedly, to argue for the Garners' legal emancipation and to condemn any court that would enforce the continuation of their servitude. One of the Garners' lawyers, Samuel S. Fisher, sounded this theme when appearing before Commissioner Pendery: because Margaret had proven herself the equal of Virginius in her love of liberty, her actions were "an unanswerable reply" to those who justified slavery by saying that slaves lacked that love. In a typical editorial commentary, the *New York Tribune* agreed, arguing that, by matching Virginius's heroism, Margaret revealed American slave law to be as corrupt as Appius's notorious pursuit of Virginia.[80]

Yet as the Roman father became the black American mother, the characteristics of the heroic deed changed in an important way. Virginius's act was one of supreme control and deliberation. He was able to kill his daughter only because he hid his feelings well enough that he was allowed to draw near to her and carry out a surprise attack. In the story, his control functions, like his sense of honor, as a sign of his political virtue, his fitness for freedom and the rigors of self-government. Such control, however, was only rarely attributed to Margaret Garner. Her killing of her daughter was instead presented as born of delirium. The adjectives used to characterize her state of mind—used repeatedly, with remarkable lack of variation—were "frantic" and "frenzied," as in "the instinct of the frantic mother was truer than reason" and "perhaps . . . a jury of freemen would have found a mitigation of the crime in the sudden frenzy of the mother."[81] The choice of terms is revealing. The synonyms *frantic* and *frenzy* share an origin in the Latin *phreneticus* and, before that, in a variety of ancient Greek words for derangement. That origin marks English usage and meaning: the first definition for frantic in the *Oxford English Dictionary* is "afflicted with mental disease, lunatic, insane. . . . violently or ragingly mad," and, before this century, the term had a technical status in both law and medicine.[82]

To murder in the grip of temporary insanity seems a far cry from the stoic resoluteness of the Roman republican hero, yet the invocation of Margaret Garner's delirium was not an alternative *to* the figure of Virginius but an alteration *of* it; the authors who equated her with her composed Roman predecessor also, and even more frequently than others, described the murder as a "frenzied" or "frantic" act. The implications of that description flatly contradict those of the classical comparison, a contradiction all the more striking because some evidence suggests that, like the Roman hero, Garner actually was, or at least claimed she had been, steady, deliberate, "cool."[83] Yet if this common way of representing her act was factually questionable and logically inconsistent, it made powerful cultural sense. Neither half of the incoherent picture, alone, was enough to give most sympathetic commentators a fully satisfying way to articulate the meaning of the murder. Fused into a whole, the portrait of Garner as a frantic Virginius enabled her partisans to navigate the difficult terrain surrounding this disturbing case.

No small part of that difficulty came from antebellum American culture's overwhelmingly Christian commitments. The Christianity woven into the sentimentalist story about the redemptive power of a mother's love and a child's death could not easily accommodate the killing of a child for secular political ends. Nor could that story comfortably assimilate murder as an act of maternal care—even though the chief rhetorical opportunity the case provided lay in denouncing the institution that made such an act thinkable. The emphasis on Garner's delirium provided a way around these obstacles: underscoring mind-destroying maternal grief made it possible to use the murder as a politically compelling indictment of slavery while setting limits to the challenge to fundamental Christian beliefs. By itself, emphasizing the frenzied quality of the act would have provided antislavery propaganda but it could not have enabled the—also crucial—uses of Margaret Garner as heroic icon. A merely deranged murderess can be the object of sympathy but cannot be celebrated as an inspiration in the struggle for freedom. To make Garner a fully potent antislavery symbol, it was necessary to draw on the heroic connotations of Virginius's precedent while also domesticating it.[84]

The use of Virginius is a reminder, too, of the ultimate hope of those who sought to use the Garner case to inspire antislavery action; the result of his violence is a political rebellion that reestablishes freedom. If Margaret's motherhood made it hard to render the killing purely heroic, it also accentuated the profoundly subversive character of what she had done. At the core of slave status is, in Orlando Patterson's classic formulation, the "social death" of "natal alienation," the denial that a person has any legitimate ties to ancestors or descendants. As Patterson reports, slaveholding societies have often recognized marital unions but have *never* given slave parents custodial power over children.[85]

Slave mothers in antebellum America lived a painfully ironic form of this alienation. By determining slave status matrilineally, slave law granted a deadly form of recognition to motherhood even while denying mothers themselves any affirmative agency or maternal rights. By dealing death to her daughter, Margaret Garner refused the social death imposed on her family.[86] Whatever her motivations or self-understanding, in asserting a mother's right to control the destiny of her children, she struck a blow against the material and cultural foundations of American chattel slavery. The Virginius story helped provide a framework for articulating and affirming that assault, at once underscoring the radicalism of Garner's disturbing challenge and assimilating it to a familiar precedent.

This was not the only significant cultural work performed by that precedent, for it also provided an elliptical way to talk about sex. Virginius kills his daughter to save her honor; he knows that Appius seeks a slave to use for his sexual pleasure. What about Margaret Garner? Equating her with Virginius allowed observers to suggest that she might have been motivated by a similar concern about her daughter's sexual future and that such concerns might have been rooted in her own experiences. This point was at once present and absent in the coverage of the case. The question of violation, or at least interracial sex, was alluded to in various ways but only rarely raised with any directness: sexual fascination courses through the press reports, but it is disguised or sublimated. It appears most frequently in the elaborate taxonomies of color applied to members of the Garner family.

Press reports describe Robert Garner as a "negro" and Margaret as a "mulatto." Margaret's five-year-old Tom is described as "a negro," and four-year-old Sam is a "mulatto," while the murdered Mary is described as "almost" or "nearly white" and infant Cilla is "much lighter in color" than her mother, even "light enough to show a red tinge in the cheeks."[87] Reports from the courtroom return to such details compulsively, but without any acknowledgment of where the compulsion comes from or what the details mean. None is really needed: reading them, it is clear that for many spectators the case's "tinge of fearful, although romantic interest," as the *Daily Enquirer* put it, had everything to do with all that was conjured by the skin's near whiteness, the cheek's red tinge.[88] In this context, the Virginius story provided an acceptable language of indirection, a way to point to Garner's concern about her daughter's sexual future without transgressing antebellum norms of delicacy and propriety. Not that it is likely that such propriety would have satisfied Archibald Gaines: if comparing Margaret Garner to Virginius underscored her concern for honor, it by the same measure challenged that of her master.

Fugitive Voices, Popular Scripts

The recurrent comparisons also underscore one of the most striking aspects of the telling of the Garner story—the way it was shaped by, and perhaps became a part of, antebellum mass culture. The majority of commentators who referred to Virginius most likely knew the story not from reading Livy but from attending a play by the popular English writer James Sheridan Knowles, whose *Virginius: A Tragedy in Five Acts* was one of the most widely performed dramas of midcentury America.[89] That a popular dramatic spectacle provided the most common referent for Margaret Garner's heroism is one small part of a much larger pattern. Mass culture did more than provide the occasional reference for thinking about the meaning of the Garner case. It helped structure how the case was perceived, understood, and narrated. Popular genres provided the forms into which the Garners' deeds and words were compressed, so much so that the fugitives' own voices are hard to detect.

The absence of slave voices from a fugitive case is by no means unusual. The Fugitive Slave Act was, after all, designed to ensure that absence: in barring fugitives from testifying, it treated them presumptively as property, bringing into free state courtrooms the Southern principle that slaves should be spoken for by those who owned them. The Garner case, however, would appear to have violated that principle, at least for a moment, since Margaret did testify. But while the fact of her testimony is remarkable, indeed unique, the substance is not very revealing. Many other witnesses before Commissioner Pendery are quoted vividly and at length; Margaret's words (at least as reported in the press) take up merely a long paragraph. Flat, affectless, they offer little about how she understood her experiences or her situation.[90] There were, however—and also to an unusual degree for a fugitive slave case—other venues and other occasions to pursue that understanding. Amid the broad fascination with the case in general and with the details and the meaning of the murder in particular, several sympathetic white writers and activists spoke with the Garners in court or in jail and then presented accounts of the captives' opinions of their past, their case, and their prospects. Yet even here it is difficult to locate the Garners' voices in the record the visitors produced. It is as if the white men and women who spoke with the Garners, and the sympathetic members of the broader white reading and listening public, were at once eager for those voices and unable to hear them. They were by no means indifferent to the fugitives' words, but, even so, the reports more often than not reveal less about the Garners than about the longings and aspirations of their white contemporaries. The documents gathered in this volume—which include the most important accounts of interviews—make that clear.[91]

It is not that the accounts can tell us nothing about the Garners. Even when approached with appropriate skepticism, the reports shed some light on the Garners' actions and motives. For instance, all accounts of those who spoke with Margaret have her saying that she killed her daughter and that her intent was indeed to kill all of the rest of her children to save them from the experiences that would come with a return to slavery. There is enough consistency on this point that it seems safe to conclude that she did indeed say something to that effect. But if we consult the relevant texts to learn about the experiences that led her to view the problem that way, to know what specific travails and indignities she wished to spare her children or the precise content of her hopes and concerns, we will find little detail, and perhaps not much to inspire confidence. Instead, the Garners are largely confined within the familiar set pieces of the era's sentimental literature.

All communication obeys conventions, of course. No matter what their white interlocutors had done, the Garners could not possibly have addressed the public in a way that simply stood outside all of the era's scripts. For instance, the slave narrative, the genre in which fugitives and emancipated slaves most frequently and successfully spoke to white American audiences, certainly *was* a genre, which is to say a highly stylized form of communication. Slave narratives enmeshed the men and women who wrote them within linguistic, moral, and economic constraints set by white patrons and readers. Yet what made this genre one of the monumental achievements of nineteenth-century black culture was how, writing amid that very entanglement, artful slave narrators such as Frederick Douglass and Harriet Jacobs found ways to contest and transform the expectations and assumptions of their readers even while maintaining moral sympathy and soliciting political solidarity.[92] Now, that some black men and women were able to exploit or create openings in antebellum culture does not ensure that the Garners would have made effective use of a greater opportunity to speak. Whether Margaret, for instance, would have wished to address the nation in similar ways is impossible to say, and even if she had, there is no way to know whether her own reflections would in fact have significantly affected either the course of events or the antebellum discourse of race. The burying of the Garners' voices beneath the clichés of sentimentalism, however, meant that the opportunity did not even arise.

For all of the failures in the courts and in the streets, and for all of the ways in which the era's hierarchies shaped the telling of the Garner story, it is important not to lose sight of that story's subversive elements. Margaret Garner's actions enabled a variety of militant responses by those who took up her cause and spoke in her name. Nascent feminists were able to identify, directly, the problem of sexual violation that the other commentators addressed only in code, thereby intensifying the—always volatile—"sectional contents of sexual politics."[93] Standing up to address the audience in Commissioner Pendery's court, Lucy Stone made this problem the key to the murder: "The faded faces of the negro children tell too plainly to what degradation female slaves submit. Rather than give her little daughter to that life, she killed it."[94] The black abolitionist press offered the most consistently unrestrained and unambivalent portraits of Garner's heroism, as when the *Provincial Freeman* editorialized that she was a "more than model of modern woman" who would long "live in the minds, and be cherished in the hearts, of every true man and woman."[95] And Garner's return to slavery summoned forth calls for black militancy that pushed abolitionist discourse to its outer limit:

> I would have this Fugitive Slave Bill, (not Law), set at defiance in practice, as well as theory, throughout the land, and more especially by the Colored People. . . . Let us make battle ground of every foot of free soil where an attempt is made to get a fugitive back. If Liberty is dear to white men, let us feel that it is equally dear to black men; and if Sharp's rifles are to be used to defend the rights of free white men in Kansas, let us use them to defend free black men upon free soil.[96]

That a subversive edge inhered in public discussions of Garner is demonstrated by the most obviously tactical of the silences in this case, by the newspaper coverage she did *not* get—by the degree of Southern censorship. It is clear that the reason for the refusal of the Southern press to engage the Garner case, and particularly Margaret's actions, is that the events in Cincinnati were simply too threatening to cover. Why? Obviously, like other fugitives, all of the Garners disrupted the story of slave contentment, but the challenge Margaret posed to Southern tellings ran far deeper than that. It ran deeper, too, than the white South's taboo on publicly acknowledging the pervasiveness of sex between master and slave. While Margaret Garner's killing of her child could be presented by the Kentucky press as evidence of both her own savage temper and the destructive consequences of abolitionist interference, her evident preference for death over slavery also threatened to subvert any attempt to attach a proslavery moral to the tale. Her conduct undercut the very core of the ideology of slavery, the conception of slaves as persons without honor, which is to say persons unwilling to risk or sacrifice life in the struggle for freedom and dignity. Among the definitions of "slave" in the 1847 edition of Webster's *American Dictionary of the English Language,* for instance, is the following: "One who has lost the power of resistance; or one who surrenders himself to any power whatever." It would be difficult to find either submission or fear of death in Margaret Garner, and it was thus difficult to obscure her honorable preference for liberty. Yet to recognize her as a woman of honor would be to acknowledge her as a person deserving of a dignified life; indeed, such recognition would be tantamount to setting her free.[97] No proslavery organ, of course, wished to perform this act of literary emancipation. Given that danger, silence or evasion was the only safe response to the case.

Although Margaret Garner could be spoken about and for in various ways, then, her story was still bounded: it did not admit of an infinite range of telling, and it was not equally available to all sectors of the American polity. It could be bent far, put in the service of contending interests and arguments, but there was a limit beyond which Garner's contemporaries were unable to stretch it. The white South's need for silence reveals that in some ways Garner was among the authors of her story, a person who helped determine how her actions were understood. She did not control the means of cultural reproduction, and could not affect the ways her words were used or invented by her supporters, but, despite that, she did commit an act that could not safely be recorded in some of the culture's key venues, locales, and forms. If her deed was horrifying from many vantage points, and co-optable by some, it was also, at its core, radical. Perhaps it is because this was recognized—if dimly, uneasily, and not in these precise terms—that Margaret Garner was made a heroine by slavery's opponents.

Furthermore, the Garners helped *produce* the political cleavages that responses to their situation reveal. Entering the court system in a legally problematical and symbolically potent case, they forced whites (at least in Kentucky and the free states) to respond. One striking instance is how their struggles burst into both chambers of the Ohio legislature. The debates on the floor touched on the deepest principles and most visceral political and cultural anxieties, exacerbating regional and partisan polarization over racial order and the states' appropriate relationship to slavery and slave catching. Although these debates were in themselves probably far more important than their legislative outcomes, a Republican majority passed both a resolution against the Fugitive Slave Act and a law that responded to the specific facts of the Garner case by seeking to give state judges more efficacy in aiding fugitives and thwarting the efforts of federal courts and marshals—the very kind of law that infuriated the South.[98] The fugitives' actions, and the reactions that followed, fueled sectional animosity. This was a common consequence of highly publicized fugitive slave cases, but because of Margaret Garner's killing of her daughter, her case probably aroused more emotion and generated more responses than any other. Even at the very moment it was forcibly denied by a law that declared these men and women to belong to others, the Garners' political agency affected the contours of power: they were returned to slavery by a federal government that they had helped push closer to civil war.[99]

Coda: The Garners in Later Days

How would the War's arrival and the emancipation that followed benefit the Garners? Like the details of their lives before escape, much about the circumstances of their later years remains obscure. In the few documents that survive, Simon simply drops out of the discussion. Mary's whereabouts and condition are unclear. Margaret's pregnancy remains a mystery: it is impossible to tell if she carried her child to term or, if she did, what became of him or her, for none of this is mentioned anywhere. Thomas and Samuel appear, though fleetingly. The documents do make clear that Robert found freedom and lived into Reconstruction, though one source may indicate that he died while still young, in 1871.[100] Margaret did not even make it out of slavery: she did not escape again and died before emancipation came. Even the year of her death, however, is the subject of competing accounts and problematic sources.

In September 1862 the *New York Daily Tribune,* by then the North's most important newspaper, published a report on the Garner family on its front page.[101] This time, it is Robert who stands at the center of the narrative: in keeping with the iconography of a nation spilling the blood of so many men at war over slavery, it is *his* heroism in fighting against his family's capture that the article renders so commendable. The *Tribune*'s story is putatively based on a letter from Robert, received "in a 'red, white, and blue' envelope," though, in his (intentionally?) elusive wording, the reporter leaves unclear whether he has read Robert's letter himself or simply had it described to him. Regardless, the story is full of details, however accurate, bringing readers up to date on the fortunes of the family since the legal system sent them South. Newly emancipated, Robert is aboard the Union gunboat Benton. He reports that "Sammy and Tommy are still living." He seeks news of his mother, who, the article suggests, is still in Kentucky. And he informs his correspondent that Margaret had died over a year earlier, on May 14, 1861.

Despite the prominence of the venue, this story seems to have had little effect. An 1863 recounting of the Garner case, showing no awareness of the *Tribune*'s account, dismissed any fears that so heroic a woman could die in slavery: "Let us rather think of Margaret as having safely reached New Orleans, and when, in the course of time the 'Linkum gunboats' drove the chivalry from those shores, Margaret was among the first to welcome the unfolding of the Stars and Stripes over the rebellious land; and, as events hastened on, the enrollment of her race begins, and we behold her, rejoicing in the day of freedom, and zealous in every good work to aid the contraband soldier in his warlike toils." A year later Salmon Chase, who one would have expected to follow the *Tribune*'s version of the news, claimed that "nothing has been heard from the Garner family" since the failure of the requisition. I have come across no Civil War–era texts that incorporate the *Tribune*'s news. Perhaps it should not be surprising, then, that assorted scholarly accounts of the case written over the years claimed that Margaret Garner had simply disappeared from view in New Orleans, or that as late as the 1990s, a literary scholar who had researched the case could consider whether Garner did, as rumored, end up in postbellum Cincinnati claiming anachronistically to be the inspiration for Harriet Beecher Stowe's Eliza.[102] Perhaps Garner's contemporaries deemed the manner of her death unfit for a political heroine. Perhaps it intensified the elements of discomfort that always marked the case. Whatever the reason, Margaret Garner's end in obscurity and amid oppression is the element of the case that was most swiftly and thoroughly forgotten.

What, though, do we really know about that end? Not much, and not with clarity or cause for confidence. Besides the *Tribune*'s account, there is one other plausible narrative source on the later history of the Garner family, but it tells a somewhat different story. In 1870 a journalist for the *Cincinnati Chronicle* interviewed Robert in the offices of a lawyer who was representing him in a civil suit over a workplace injury. Robert told him that Margaret Garner died of typhoid in 1858, while enslaved on the plantation of Judge Bonham, in Tennessee Landing, Mississippi. There are reasons to consider this account more reliable. While it is hard to determine how far removed the *Tribune* journalist is from his putative documentary source, clearly the *Chronicle*'s reporter spoke directly with Robert. It is hard to imagine that Robert misremembered the date of his wife's death by three years, even though his recollections here come much later. Presumably one can accept his account of the cause of death, too, and Mississippi did see a typhoid epidemic in 1858. Census records also appear to lend support to the *Chronicle*'s dating, for by 1860 there does not seem to be anyone matching Margaret's description on Bonham's Tennessee Landing—though the census evidence is not in this instance wholly reliable.[103] The disparity between the sources remains instructive. That the two news reports on Margaret's death are both attributed to Robert and yet cannot be reconciled on the basic facts suggests something about the gaps between text and event and between black speech and white recounting, that marks so much of the Garner archive.[104] Given that gap, and the paucity of sources, prudence suggests a certain caution even in settling on something as ostensibly clear-cut as a date of death. The Garner case has much to tell us about the terms and dynamics of political and cultural struggle in the antebellum era, but, to the end, Margaret Garner eludes those who, combing through the scraps surviving in the archive of America slavery, seek to know her.

DOCUMENTS

CHAPTER 1

ESCAPE AND CAPTURE

Beginning on the day the fugitives were captured, accounts of the Garners' story spread far and fast, dominating the local press and gaining prominence across the free states, especially in the papers of such major cities as New York, Boston, and Chicago. Most of the early news published elsewhere was reprinted from the Cincinnati papers, whose reporters had the most direct access to witnesses and participants and provided the most detailed coverage; the Kentucky press also presented the case in detail. Although this chapter contains only a few of the many articles printed at this time, it reveals the main contours of the reporting on initial events. We can see in several of these documents, for instance, the sensationalism characteristic of most responses to the killing of the Garners' young child. We can see, too, the factual inaccuracy and uncertainties, the contradictions among versions, that mark much of the Garner archive. Whose horses did the fugitives steal to make their getaway? What was the sex of the murdered child? Who was the killer? How old were the surviving children? Like the broader pool of stories, the reports reprinted in this chapter offer conflicting answers even to these basic factual questions. They also remind us of how journalistic accounts of the events expressed partisan allegiances. Closely tied to political parties, antebellum papers typically functioned as explicitly political organs. Cincinnati was no exception, and so, for example, how each reporter characterized the immediate response to the case in the city reflects his paper's party affiliation and its position on the local and national struggle over slavery.

Cincinnati Daily Enquirer, January 29, 1856

Although one paper printed a story on the evening of the Garners' capture, and the Associated Press sent out a brief account over the wire as well, the most substantial initial reports ran the next day, in assorted morning papers. This document was among the most thorough of them. More than any other publication, the Enquirer, *one of the city's two most significant papers, was intimately tied to the Garner case. Since editor and primary owner Hiram H. Robinson was also the city's U.S. marshal, he was in charge of capturing and returning fugitive slaves. He had previously played a prominent part in some of Cincinnati's most highly publicized and contested cases. Though out of town at the time the Garners were caught, Robinson soon took charge, organizing a vast security force during the trial and triumphantly taking the family back across the river at the end of the case. While he was doing everything in his power to see the fugitives returned to slavery, his paper was editorializing relentlessly on behalf of the men who claimed the right to own the Garner family and against all who sought to keep the family on free soil. In general, the Democratic* Enquirer *was the Cincinnati paper most inclined to defend the Fugitive Slave Act and to take the side of the slave states in the struggles of the day. Of course, the paper was not merely a political but a commercial enterprise, concerned, above all, with selling newspapers. It is clear that the* Enquirer *saw this story as a significant opportunity to grab readers' attention. The Garner case would reappear on the paper's front page many times in the coming weeks.*

A TALE OF HORROR!
An Arrest by the U.S. Marshal
A DEPUTY U.S. MARSHAL SHOT.
A Negro Child's Throat Cut from Ear to Ear
by the Father or Mother, and
Others Wounded!
CORONER'S INQUEST.
Writ of Habeas Corpus Taken Out.
GREAT EXCITEMENT!

The city was thrown into much excitement yesterday morning by the information that a party of slaves, sixteen in all, had made a stampede from Kentucky to this side of the river. Other circumstances, however, which afterward transpired, have imparted a degree of horrible interest to the affair different to that which usually attends a stampede of negroes. The particulars are as follows: Three of the slaves, who bore the relationship of father, mother and son, the two former apparently about fifty years of age, the son twenty-five, were the property of Mr. James Marshall, of Richwood Station, Boone County, about sixteen miles back of Covington, and five others, consisting of a woman named Peggy and her four children, the oldest about five years of age, the youngest an infant at the breast, belonging to Mr. Archibald K. Gaines, who resided in the immediate vicinity of Mr. Marshall. Peggy was married to young Simon, the slave of Mr. Marshall, and the son of the old couple with whom he ran away. It seems that about ten o'clock on Sunday night the party took a pair of horses and a sleigh, belonging to Mr. Marshall, with which they drove to Covington, where they left the team standing outside of the Washington House, where it was found by the landlord, the horses very much blown from the severe manner in which they had been driven. In the meantime the party of eight crossed the river on the ice and took refuge in a house, the fourth below Millcreek bridge, tenanted by a negro named Kite, a son of old Joe Kite, well known for years in this city. Young Kite was well acquainted with the parties, for he has himself lived in their neighborhood, having been formerly owned there, but his freedom was purchased some time since by his father.

Early yesterday morning, Mr. Gaines, accompanied by a son of Mr. Marshall, arrived in this city in pursuit of the fugitives.

Application was made to United States Commissioner Pendery, who, thereupon, issued his warrant, which was placed in the hands of the United States Marshal, who, having received information of the hiding place of the fugitives, collected a *posse* of officers, some from Kentucky and others belonging to this city, and with Mr. Gaines, Mr. Marshall, jr., and Major Murphy, who accompanied them from Richwood, they proceeded to the residence of Kite. Arrived there they found the doors and windows fastened, but, upon thundering at the door, Kite looked out of a window, and at first agreed to admit them, but afterward refused to do so, and at this juncture, as they were about to force an entrance, young Simon fired from the window with a revolver, the ball from which struck the finger of one of the deputized marshals, named John Patterson, and then lodged in his upper lip, leaving the finger hanging by a mere thread. Upon this the door was burst in, when Simon fired three more shots at the party, fortunately, however, without either taking effect. Mr. Gaines seized him by the wrist and wrenched the pistol from his hand before he could shoot the other two barrels off, it being a six-shooter. But a deed of horror had been consummated, for weltering in its blood, the throat being cut from ear to ear and the head almost severed from the body, upon the floor lay one of the children of the younger couple, a girl three years old, while in a back room, crouched beneath the bed, two more of the children, boys, of two and five years, were moaning, the one having received two gashes in its throat, the other a cut upon the head. As the party entered the room the mother was seen wielding a heavy shovel, and before she could be secured she inflicted a heavy blow with it upon the face of the infant, which was lying upon the floor. The whole party having been arrested, medical aid was procured for the little sufferers, whose wounds were not of a fatal character, and then all were carried to the office of the United States Marshal, when United States Commissioner Pendery fixed the hearing of the case for this morning at nine o'clock.

Coroner Menzies immediately hastened to the spot where the dead body of the child was found, and summoned a jury, when, after examining five of the parties who first burst into the house, not one of whom, however, could throw any light as to whether the father or mother of the child had committed the bloody deed, the further hearing of testimony was postponed until this morning.

The only information derived from the eldest boy, in reply to who had injured him and the other children, is that the folks in the house did it. When taken to the office of the United States Marshal, the woman declared that they had received their wounds in the *melee* which followed the entrance of the *posse* into the house, but this is known to be untrue. The fearful act lies between one or the other of the miserable parents, perhaps both, but, doubtless, the truth will be brought out by the Coroner to-day.

The old couple are mild and rather intelligent in their appearance, the mother of the children is a good-looking, hearty negress, while her husband bears the appearance of having been well cared for, in fact, young Mr. Marshall states that he has always treated him more as a companion than a slave; they have been playmates in childhood and have grown up together, "And now," said he, "if money can save him from the effect of any rash act he has committed I am willing to give it to any amount." After the United States Commissioner had adjourned the hearing of the case until this morning, a couple of hackney coaches were procured for conveying the fugitives to the Hammond street Station house, but a crowd was assembled in the street, whose threats alarmed the hackmen for the safety of their carriages, and the prisoners were accordingly walked under the conduct of a strong escort. Some threats were made by a portion of the mob, but no violence or attempt at rescue was made, subsequently, they were lodged for safer keeping in the County Jail.

In the meantime the leading Abolitionists busied themselves, and a writ of *habeas corpus* was procured, commanding the United States Marshal to produce the fugitives before Judge Burgoyne of the Probate Court; they, however, were allowed to remain in Jail, and will be brought before the United States Commissioner, as previously arranged.

At the time of the flight of Messrs. Gaines and Marshall's negroes, a gang of eight left Covington, six belonging to Mr. Levi P. Dougherty, five men and one woman, and two men owned by John W. Stevenson, Esq., both residents of Covington. The Marshal of Covington, with several officers of this city, supposed they were upon their track, but, after a fruitless search . . . at a late hour last night no clue had been obtained of their lurking place. In the meantime there is much excitement existing, the bloody episode having invested the affair with a tinge of fearful, although romantic interest. The Abolitionists regard the parents of the murdered child as a hero and heroine, teeming with lofty and holy emotions, who, Virginius like, would rather imbue their hands in the blood of their offspring than allow them to wear the shackles of slavery, while others look upon them as brutal and unnatural murderers. At any rate the affair will furnish some employment to lawyers as well as officers, an extra force of the latter being necessary to prevent a rescue while the case is pending.

Louisville Daily Courier, January 30, 1856

=======

The Daily Courier *here reprints a story in which the* Columbian *reports on the killing of the Garners' daughter, Mary, in minute detail. Though not all of these details are accurate (note what becomes of Mary's gender), the paper's account does correctly indicate that it was Margaret who killed her own child, and it gives readers more information than other papers did on this date about the struggle for jurisdiction between (Republican) city sheriffs and (Democratic) U.S. marshals, and between state and federal courts—a struggle that would run through, and even beyond, the moment of the family's forced return to Kentucky. Few editions of the* Columbian *survive, and it is hard to assess its perspective on the case.*

[From the Cincinnati Columbian, 29th.]
HORRIBLE AFFAIR!
Arrest of 8 Fugitive Slaves.
DESPERATE RESISTANCE.
A CHILD SLAIN BY ITS MOTHER.

The Negroes Demanded from the U.S. Marshal by virtue of a Writ of Habeas Corpus—He at first Refuses, then Coquettes, and Finally Consents—The People Growing Deeply Interested—Prospect of still Greater Excitement—Danger of Conflict between the United States and State Authorities.

Scarcely ever did we witness, in this city, greater excitement than that occasioned yesterday afternoon by the arrest of a number of fugitive slaves, their desperate resistance and a tragic event in connection therewith. The circumstances, as elicited by diligent inquiry, are about as follows:

Night before last, eight fugitive slaves, two men, two women and four children, the property of Mr. James Marshall and of Mr. Archibald Gaines, both of whom reside near Richwood Station, in Boone county, Kentucky, ran away from their masters. To expedite their flight a team of horses and a sleigh, belonging to Mr. Gaines, were brought into requisition. They struck the road for Cincinnati, thinking undoubtedly to take the underground railway at this point for Canada. The distance, 18 miles, was soon made, and, arriving at Covington, they crossed the ice to this city.

Unfortunately for them their pursuers were close on their track, as they became aware before their Abolition friends could provide for their departure or concealment. They sought refuge and obtained it for a short while in the house of a negro, on the road, about one mile below the Mill Creek bridge. Their pursuers, it seems, were too swift for them, and came upon them in time to ascertain their retreat. The house was closely watched while a messenger, in the person of Mr. Gaines, went to procure a warrant from United States Commissioner Pendery, for their arrest as fugitive slaves.

The application was successful, and at noon (Marshal Robinson being absent from the city) the warrant was placed in the hands of Deputy Marshal John Ellis, who in connection with a strong posse, including officers Francis and Butts, of Covington, proceeded to the spot to effect the capture of the negroes.

Arriving at the premises, word was sent the fugitives to surrender.

A firm and decided negative was the response. The officers, backed by a large crowd, then made a descent. Breaking open the doors, they were assailed by the negroes with cudgels and pistols. Several shots were fired, but only one took effect, so far as we could ascertain. A bullet struck a man named John Patterson, one of the Marshal's deputies, tearing off a finger of his right hand and dislocating several of his teeth. No other of the officers was injured, the negroes being rendered powerless before they could reload their weapons.

On looking around, horrible was the sight which met the eyes of the officers. In one corner of the room was a negro child bleeding to death. *His throat was cut from ear to ear,* and the blood was spouting out profusely, showing that the deed was but recently committed. Scarcely was this fact noticed, when a scream issuing from an adjoining room drew their attention thither. A glance into the apartment revealed a negro woman holding in her hand a knife literally dripping with gore over the heads of two little negro children, who were crouched to the floor and uttering the cries whose agonized peals had first startled them. Quickly the knife was wrenched from the hand of the infuriated negress, and a more close investigation instituted as to the condition of the infants. They were discovered to be cut across the head and shoulders, but not very seriously injured, although the blood trickled down their backs and upon their sleeves.

The negress avowed herself the mother of the children, and said that she had killed one, and would like to kill the three others rather than see them again reduced to slavery. By this time the crowd about the premises had become prodigious and it was with no inconsiderable difficulty that the negroes were secured in carriages and brought to the United States District Court Rooms. . . . The populace followed the vehicles closely, but evinced no active desire to effect a rescue. Rumors of the story soon circulated all over the city. Nor were they exaggerated, as is usually the case. The incidents were too horrible in themselves to need exaggeration. For once, reality surpassed the wildest thought of fiction.

The door was besieged with applicants for admission, but all, officers alone excepted, were refused admittance. U. S. Commissioner Pendery held a momentary session of Court, and fixed this morning at 9 o'clock as the time of investigation, ordering the prisoners to be kept in the close custody of the Marshal until that hour.

After the crowd had mostly dispersed, the negroes were removed to the Hammond-street Station House, and there confined during the afternoon. Here, as in the former case, access was denied all excepting officers and friends of the masters. The application of this rule seemed somewhat to displease an amiable looking gentleman, whose meek and modest mien were generally voted to be those of an Abolitionist.

Toward evening Deputy Sheriff Jeff. Buckingham arrived with a writ of *habeas corpus* from Judge Burgoyne, of the Probate Court, requiring the production of the negroes forthwith before him, and summoning Deputy Marshals Bennett and Ellis to show cause why they made the arrest. To this proposal, so far as the production of the negroes was concerned, Bennett at first refused to accede, claiming that, under Judge McLean's ruling, no State Court had a right to demand and enforce the presence of prisoners held under the United States law. A disposition being evinced by the State officers to see the mandate of Judge Burgoyne complied with, a compromise was finally agreed to, by which the negroes were to be committed to the county jail until morning, and then placed at the disposal of the Marshal, he agreeing to bring them before the Probate Court by 11 o'clock, A. M., on condition that he should not be interfered with in taking them to the U.S. Commissioner's room, at 9 o'clock.

An omnibus was then sent for in which to remove the negroes. Arriving in front of the door, they were taken from their cells, and then it was that we caught a glimpse of their ebony proportions. One of the men and one of the women are very largely built and seem almost of Herculean strength. The other male and female are not above the medium height. The smaller one of the women it was who murdered the child.

Making enquiry of Mr. Gaines, he informed us that the women and children were his property, and the two men belong to Mr. Marshall. There was something of intelligence in the countenance of the younger female, and nothing of that ferocity that might have been expected. She held a babe in her arms and seemed to regard it with the usual tenderness of a mother.

Finally, the party of slaves were placed in the omnibus, and Deputy Marshal Bennett and Deputy Sheriff Buckingham got inside the vehicle with the negroes. Deputy Marshal Ellis took the seat with the driver. Reaching Fourth street, the omnibus turned to the left instead of the right toward Sycamore street. Soon the driver paused in front of the United States Court-room. The door of the omnibus was thrown open, and the negroes, assisted by the Marshals and Deputies, were hurried upstairs before the Sheriffs were fairly aware of the game being played upon them.

They did appreciate it, however, before it was entirely consummated, and strongly expressed their disapprobation. They even faintly attempted to resist the Marshals, but their force was too small to enable them to do so effectually. Besides, Deputy Marshal Ellis called on all the people, in the name of the United States, to assist, and flourished a huge revolver, threatening to use it, if the emergency required, sooner than to relinquish his prisoners.

By this time the slaves were up stairs, but with them was Jeff Buckingham, who soon appeared at the balcony, and, in a loud voice requested the friends of justice and "State rights" to inform Sheriff Brashears of his position, and request him to send a sufficient force to secure possession of the negroes, in accordance with the requirement of the Probate Court.

The commotion caused by this announcement brought another crowd to the spot, which augmented for a half an hour, and then dwindled away as the prospect of a collision grew less and less apparent.

Cincinnati Daily Commercial, January 29, 1856

This and the following document offer brief excerpts from the Commercial's *first two (long and detailed) reports on the capture and immediate aftermath. The* Commercial *was considered an antislavery voice, and it consistently supported the Garners' case. Despite this, the paper presented itself as transcending sectional and partisan interest, rejecting the abolitionist label that the* Enquirer *and the Kentucky press tried to pin on it.*

After the conflict was over a bloody and melancholy spectacle presented itself. One of the slave children was discovered lying on the floor with its head nearly severed from its body, two others, boys, aged about four and five years were bleeding from the wounds in the neck and head, and an infant in the arms of Margaret had its head much swollen and was bleeding quite freely at the nose. The officers state that Simon and Mary, the eldest of the party made no resistance, but that Robert and Margaret fought with the ferocity of tigers, and that during the affray she struck her infant on the head with a fire shovel, in the opinion of many with the intention of taking its life.

During a conversation with Margaret, she stated to us that she was eating breakfast in company with the other fugitives, when she heard some one cry out, "They are coming, they are coming." They sprang up in alarm, but before they had time to fly, their captors burst in upon them. She fought with all the strength with which she was capable and cannot tell how her child was killed and the others wounded, but only knows that the death and the wounding occurred during the affray. This is her story, but it is evident that the bloody tragedy was perpetrated while the officers were seeking admittance, and she is said to have acknowledged the fact of killing her child and wounding the others during the excitement incident to the arrest.

Cincinnati Daily Commercial, January 30, 1856

The appearance of the fugitives is favourable in regard to their physical well being, looking as though they had been well fed; their clothing is good and comfortable. We do not hear of them making any complaint of unkind usage on the part of their masters, and we learn from one of the witnesses that when the officers were breaking down the door, Mr. Gaines expressed his anxiety that nothing should be done inconsistent with the law; and especially desired that no harm whatever should be done to the little children.

The mother is of an interesting appearance, a mulatto of considerable intelligence of manner, and with a good address. In reply to a gentleman who yesterday complimented her upon the looks of her little boy, she said "You should have seen my little girl that—that (she did not like to say—was killed)—that died, that was the bird."

The little boy has a severe wound on his head from which the blood was trickling when the officers made the arrest. He says his mother hit him there with a shovel.

The face of the infant, 9 months old, is much swelled and battered, and one eye swelled, doubtless, from being struck with the same instrument. A shovel was found on the premises, by which, it is supposed, the wounds were given.

Cincinnati Daily Gazette, January 30, 1856

On January 29 Coroner John Menzies conducted an inquest into the death of Mary Garner. Press reports of the findings largely put to rest the conflicting stories over, and public doubt about, who killed her. The most pointedly antislavery of the city's main papers, the Gazette had

*originally been a Whig organ but was by the time of the Garner case
allied with the recently formed Republican Party. In the Cincinnati
press at the time, only the Enquirer was as prominent and influential.
The two papers feuded regularly, though for all of their differences over
the Garner story both kept it on the front page for weeks.*

THE FUGITIVE SLAVES. —Yesterday morning the Sheriff made a return on the writ of Habeas Corpus, that the slaves were in the custody of
the U.S. Marshal, and therefore, without his jurisdiction. This returned
the slaves to the custody of the Marshal. By an agreement with all, the
parties permitted the slaves to remain in the county jail all day yesterday, with the understanding their examination should commence this
morning.

We learn that the mother of the dead child acknowledges she killed
it, and that her determination was to have killed all the children, and
then destroyed herself, rather than return to slavery. She, and the others,
complain of cruel treatment on the part of their master, and allege that as
the cause of their attempt to escape.

The Coroner's Jury, after examining the citizens present at the time
of the arrest, went to the Jail last evening and examined the grandmother
of the child—one of the slaves. She testified that the mother, when she
saw they would be captured, caught a butcher knife and ran to the children, saying she would kill them rather than to have them return to slavery, and cut the throat of the child, calling on the grandmother to help
her kill them. The grandmother said she would not do it, and hid under
a bed.

The Jury gave a verdict as follows: —That said child was killed by
its mother, Margaret Garner, with a butcher knife with which she cut its
throat.

Two of the jurors also find that the two men arrested as fugitives
were accessories to the murder.

It is expected the examination of the fugitives will commence this
morning before Commissioner Pendery.

CHAPTER 2

IN THE COMMISSIONER'S COURT

Archibald Gaines first sought Commissioner John Pendery's help in recovering the Garners on the morning of January 28, shortly before the fugitives were captured. Pendery did not announce his ruling on the case until February 26. The Garners, their lawyers, or both appeared in Pendery's court fourteen times in that interval, often for a full-day session. The written record of the proceedings in this, the central site of struggle over the family's fortunes, is thus both substantial and very rich: for all of the uncertainties that characterize the broader story of Margaret Garner and her family, we can arrive at a pretty clear picture of what went on in the commissioner's court. The official transcripts of the proceeding were lost in a courthouse fire long ago, but the era's newspapers provide a reasonable substitute. Reporters were in court every day, and the Cincinnati dailies were especially detailed in their presentation of the arguments and proceedings. Although sometimes the stories briefly summarize or even skip over what transpired—in general the reports abridge the technical legal arguments about precedent as well as the most humdrum or routine aspects of testimony, concentrating on the more exciting or theatrical moments of the proceedings—they often follow the give-and-take point by point, on occasion even offering what are presented as the speaker's precise words.

The following selection covers most of the proceedings and all of the key moments of legal maneuvering and argument, drawn primarily from the Enquirer *and the* Gazette. *Each paper tended to give more coverage to the side it favored, so I reproduce the former where the main point of the selection is to feature the speeches of the lawyers for the claimants, and the latter where the emphasis is on the arguments of the*

Garners' lawyers. The Gazette's *reporting, however, tended to be more streamlined and easier to follow, and the paper lacked* Enquirer *editor Robinson's direct entanglement in the legal contest; I have employed the* Gazette *as the default paper of record when the focus is on the proceedings more generally, using other papers only when there was a compelling reason to do so.*

Cincinnati Daily Enquirer, January 31, 1856

January 30 saw the beginning of the substantive hearing on James Marshall's and Archibald Gaines's claims that the Garners were subject to return under the Fugitive Slave Act. At the outset, Commissioner Pendery announced one decision that would affect all that followed in his court: he would split the case in two, first hearing Marshall's claim to the return of Simon, Robert, and Mary Garner, and only then turning to Gaines's claim to Margaret Garner and her children. Because Margaret's case came second, the most substantial arguments and many of the most dramatic moments would appear in the case of her husband and in-laws.

Reporting on the day's events, the Enquirer *not only gives a detailed account of the legal maneuverings inside the courtroom but also notes the skirmishes on the outside. At great expense, Marshal Robinson had hired several hundred deputies to control the crowds in the streets and prevent any attempt to wrest the fugitives from captivity. As his paper makes clear, though, this did not prevent verbal confrontations. Furthermore, in its brief references to habeas corpus writs, the article also registers the continuing struggle between the parties, waged elsewhere, over which agency of law enforcement should have custody of the fugitives and which court had the right to answer that question.*

THE FUGITIVE SLAVE CASE.
Before U.S. Commissioner Pendery,
Courts of the Defense,
AFFIDAVITS OF THE FUGITIVES.
INTENSE EXCITEMENT.

Yesterday morning the escaped slaves were taken from jail, where they had been placed for safe keeping by the United States Marshal, and conducted in an omnibus, attended by a strong *posse* of officers, into the

United States Court, the Hon. John L. Pendery presiding. A crowd accompanied the omnibus, and the Court-room, a few minutes after it was opened, was jammed with eager spectators, many of whom evidently would have expressed their sympathy for the fugitives in an audible manner but for the rigid order enforced by the Deputy Marshals.

The cases were submitted to His Honor as follows:

James Marshall, claimant, *against* Simon Garner, sr.; Simon Garner, jr.; Mary Garner, fugitives from labor and service; and Archibald K. Gaines, claimant, *against* Margaret Garner, Tom, a negro boy; Sam, a negro boy; Miller, a negro boy; fugitives from labor and service. Case arising under the Fugitive Slave Law.

Hon. John W. Finnell and S.T. Moore, of Kentucky, and Colonel Francis T. Chambers, of Cincinnati, attorneys for the claimant; John Jolliffe attorney for the fugitives.

Mr. Jolliffe, attorney for defendents, submitted a motion for continuance, which was resisted by Colonel Chambers.

Mr. Jolliffe stated that by reason of the issuing of the rite of *habeas corpus* by Judge Burgoyne, and the action of the Sheriff of Hamilton County in returning to the Marshal of the Southern District of Ohio the fugitives on an alleged informality in the said writ of *habeas corpus,* he (Mr. Jolliffe) had not caused any subpoena to issue for witnesses on the part of the defense.

Colonel Chambers, in reply, said that the warrant upon which the fugitives are held had been issued on the 28th of January, thus allowing the attorney, Mr. Jolliffe, ample time to have his subpoenas issued, served and returned.

Colonel Chambers would require a showing in writing, giving the names of the witnesses and what he expected to prove by them.

Mr. Jolliffe said he would prepare the affidavits of the defendants themselves to show that they had at various times been brought by their owners, or the agents of the owners, into this state; and having done so, Mr. Jolliffe then read to the court the affidavit of Mary Garner, which was as follows. Previous to the reading of the affidavit, the court, on motion of Colonel Chambers appointed Mr. J. Bell Pollock the official reporter, it having been agreed that the testimony, as taken down by the reporter, should be read to and signed by the witnesses, and should be considered the correct testimony in the case. The following is the affidavit of Mary Garner:

Mary Garner having been duly sworn, states that about five years ago Cas Warrington, of Covington, Ky., hired this deponent of James

Marshall, who claimed her as his slave and brought her to Covington, Ky., and about the time of the said hiring the said Cas Warrington asked said Marshall if he was afraid the said Mary would run away, to which said Marshall replied, in the hearing of this deponent that deponent might pass and repass to Cincinnati whenever she pleased; that he was not afraid she would run away; that she lived in Covington with said Warrington better than twelve months, and while she so lived with him she frequently came over to the city of Cincinnati to attend worship in the Methodist Episcopal Church, of which she was and now is a member; that sometimes the said Warrington knew of her crossing here to church, and at other times he did not know of it; that she never made any effort to conceal her coming from the said Warrington or any other person, and never heard him object to her so coming to the city of Cincinnati. And further, she says that while she so lived with said Warrington she came over to the city of Cincinnati, state of Ohio, to market; sometimes she came to Cincinnati with said Warrington and at other times with Polly Warrington, his wife, and at other times with Sally Stuart, sister of Mrs. Warrington; Benjamin Conolly, Mrs. Warrington's brother, knows that she came over on said errands; Mr. Kennedy, who kept the ferry-boat between Cincinnati and Covington, knows, as she believes, that she came over frequently from Covington to Cincinnati. She has been in jail in Cincinnati ever since Monday last, and has no means to employ lawyers in her behalf, and prays the court to protect her in her rights in this matter. She hopes to obtain the testimony of said witnesses, but has no means to pay the fees of said witnesses.

her

MARY X GARNER

Mark.

Col. Chambers submitted a motion to the court to determine whether it would grant a continuance as to Mary Garner, alleged slave of Marshall. Commissioner Pendery stated that this morning, when a motion was made for continuance, he understood that the motion applied to all the alleged slaves, both of Messrs. Gaines and Marshall. However, he would first hear all the affidavits read and then he would pass upon cases separately.

Mr. Joliffe then read the affidavits. Robert (*alias* Simon, jr.) Garner, as follows:

Robert Garner, of lawful age, being duly sworn, on his oath states that about five weeks before Christmas of the year 1855, Thomas

Marshall, a son of James Marshall, an agent of James Marshall the claimant, brought this deponent from Ky. to the city of Cincinnati in the state of Ohio, and kept him in Cincinnati about four hours and then returned him to Kentucky; and that about four years ago William Timberlake, who is a storekeeper and lives in Covington, had this deponent hired, and while he was so hired said Timberlake bought some wheat in Ohio and brought this deponent over to Ohio to measure said wheat, and this deponent did measure said wheat at the house of a man named Scott, near Dayton, Ohio, and this deponent came over on Monday morning and returned on the Saturday night following to Covington, Kentucky.

This deponent, on his oath, further says that the same James Marshall who now claims him as a slave or fugitive, about six years ago brought this deponent over from the State of Kentucky into the State of Ohio with a drove of hogs, that the hogs were sold to a man by the name of Mr. Rice, a Dutch butcher, and that deponent was on that occasion brought into the State of Ohio by the consent of his alleged master five days and five nights.

That about six years ago James Poor hired him from said Marshall for eight months, and that he did live with said Poor for eight months in Covington, Ky., and while he was in the service of said Poor, the brother-in-law and sister of said Poor were about to go to Texas, where he lived, and this deponent was sent over to Cincinnati by said Poor to carry the boxes and trunks of his said sister-in-law, and he did come into the State of Ohio in said conduct and did carry the trunks and a satchel for the sister-in-law of Poor.

This deponent hopes to be able to prove these facts if he is allowed time to obtain the testimony. He has been in prison since Monday night.

His

Robert ✗ Garner

Mark.

Mr. Jolliffe then stated upon his professional honor that he had not had time to prepare his part of the case thoroughly. He had fully prepared the case with reference to a trial before Judge Burgoyne, but *had not* with a view of a trial here.

Colonel Chambers said, the gentleman and myself have had the same length of time to prepare. The parties are here who claim the alleged fugitives, and by the laws of the United States the course of proceeding in these cases was intended to be summary, and not to be delayed on every pretense urged. Mr. Jolliffe has had ample time to examine the Fugitive

Slave Law, which has been in force some years, and has been adjudicated upon in nearly every State in the Union. There was not a word in the affidavit which had been read by Mr. Jolliffe giving a sufficient reason why a continuance should be granted.

Mr. Jolliffe replied that the rights of the defendants ought to be observed as well as the rights of those who claimed them as slaves. Why should these persons not be entitled to have their witnesses present, that every word they may have to say should be heard? The Court should grant a continuance of a day, a week, a month, aye, a year, if necessary, to give these people a chance to bring their witnesses and establish their right to freedom.

Mr. Jolliffe then read the affidavit of Margaret Garner, *alias* Peggy, as follows:

Margaret Garner, being duly sworn, saith [t]hat when she, the said Margaret Garner, was a girl, she was brought from Kentucky into the city of Cincinnati, in the State of Ohio, by John Gaines and Eliza Gaines, his wife, the said John Gaines being then the person who claimed to be her owner; that she was brought to Cincinnati to nurse Mary Gaines, daughter of the said John Gaines, who now lives with her uncle, Archibald Gaines, in Kentucky; that she came here in the morning and went back on the evening of the said day.

Eliza Gaines, wife of the said John Gaines, is dead; the said John Gaines now lives, as deponent believes, in Oregon Territory, to which place he went about six years ago; she prays that her case may be continued until she can obtain the testimony of said John Gaines in her behalf, and that commission may issue, and a stay of proceedings be had to obtain his testimony. William Garner, about six years old, Samuel Garner, about five years old, and Miller [*sic*] Garner, about nine months old, are co-defendants with this deponent and her children, and each of said children has been born since the time when deponent was brought into the State of Ohio.

Her

MARGARET ✗ GARNER

mark.

Colonel Chambers said he found the same objections to the sufficiency of this affidavit as he had to the others. The case has its painful aspects. It has its reasons for an appeal to the sympathies of every one, with which the Commissioner has nothing to do. It has been ably argued by the members of the Congress which enacted the law, and the responsibility which, though a great and painful one, rests upon your Honor. Into the moral view of the question it is not your province to inquire; it is for you to decide the case upon the facts.

Mr. Jolliffe replied that the freedom of these persons might rest upon the motion which he had made for a continuance. Besides which, these infants are under the special care of your Honor, and you should guard their rights zealously. We wish at least to have time to attempt to get these witnesses.

Commissioner Pendery—This motion is one addressed entirely to the discretion of the Court. The case is not one of an ordinary character, and, therefore, should be carefully examined. As to whether the testimony which the defendants allege they can procure would be of any service to them in this case, I do not think it necessary at this time to determine. It is a new point and a difficult one to decide, and the Court will not hear and determine without being fully advised as to all the facts and the law. If the alleged slaves have any rights they should be inquired into as well as those of the claimants. I shall grant a continuance as to Mary Garner, one of the alleged fugitives of Mr. Marshall, until to-morrow morning, at nine o'clock A.M., and will not determine as to the others until after the disposition of that case.

The court then remanded the fugitives to the custody of the Marshal, and adjourned until this morning at nine o'clock.

Before the Court was adjourned it was understood that a warrant had been issued by Justice Clark for the four adult slaves upon the verdict of the Coroner's inquest, finding Margaret Garner guilty of killing her child, and the slaves with having been accessories. It was understood, however, that the warrant would not be served until after the disposition of the case by the United States Commissioner. In the meantime another writ of *habeas corpus* had been issued by Judge Burgoyne, directed to George S. Bennett, United States Deputy Marshal, the Sheriff having made a return in answer to the first writ that the negroes were in the custody of Mr. Bennett, and not under his, the Sheriff's control. The fugitives, however, still remain in the custody of the United States Marshal.

Previous to the removal of the prisoners from Court-room to the omnibus, to be conveyed back to Jail, a large crowd had collected in the streets, and there was considerable excitement. The principal promoters of the fuss where some mulatto women, who were extremely lavish of opprobrious epithets to the officers that guarded the way leading to the vehicle.

"D——n you!" shouted one of these saddle-colored ladies, who, by the way, was dressed in the extreme of fashion, in answer to a request of one of the officers to stand back, "D——n you, I'm free born, half white, and as good as any white-livered b——h in Ohio!" The officer took no notice of her or her companions, but not so with a pair of masculine dark-ies who undertook to express their disapprobation of the proceedings in a rather noisy manner, and who were in consequence pounced upon and, in spite of their own strugglings and some little demonstration of a rescue, hurried to the Hammond-street Station-house and locked up.

Nothing more occurred during the progress of the fugitives to the Jail, to which they were accompanied by the same strong constabulary force that escorted them from thence.

Cincinnati Daily Gazette, February 1, 1856

The Fugitive Slave Case.
BEFORE U.S. COMMISSIONER PENDERY.
THIRD DAY.

On the opening of the Court at 9 1/2 o'clock yesterday morning, Mr. Jol-liffe stated that he had been informed that warrants had been issued against those of the fugitives who were adults, on a criminal charge, and that an arrangement had been made between the U.S. and the State offi-cers, by which they were not to be served until this investigation had ter-minated. He would therefore move if any officer had such warrants, he should be permitted to serve them at once.

The law of 1850, provides that no warrant in any event shall be served upon the fugitives in case they are remanded to the custody of their owner. Not even a warrant for murder could prevent their being returned to bondage.

Col. CHAMBERS said, he was not surprised at this motion, or to see the gentleman the champion of the sovereignty of the State of Ohio, and using all his endeavors to bring their people under her laws, but the sov-ereignty of the Union he had entirely set aside.

Mr. JOLLIFFE—"No sir, not me."

Col. CHAMBERS said he knew not what might be the sentiment of the multitude, whether they loved the Union better than any thing else, but he must say the motion of the gentleman quite surprised him.

Commissioner PENDERY said that since the opening of the Court this morning he had been called upon by the City Marshal with two war-rants, claiming four or more of the fugitives, and that he had told him that in order to prevent a collision between the authorities he would not grant them until the investigation was through. Between the termination of the investigation and the time he would take for giving his decision the warrants could be served.

Mr. JOLIFFE still pressed his motion. It might seem strange that as the attorney for these people he should demand that they be given upon a charge of murder, but each and all of them had assured him *that they would go singing to the gallows rather than be returned to slavery.*

JACOB FLINN, who appeared for the Marshal, said he would look into the matter so as to give the proper advice to the Court.

Commissioner PENDERY declined to make the order then.

Col. CHAMBERS, attorney for the claimant, said he did not wonder so much at these people preferring the gallows to slavery. He should do so too were there no alternative, but he should prefer to be remanded and take a chance for an underground slide at some other time, and he hoped these parties might have that chance.

Mr. JOLLIFFE said he understood that the Marshal was excluding a certain class of (the colored) people from the Court Rooms. He would ask if any such order had been issued. With the same propriety might the foreign born population have been excluded in the trial of the Irish filibuster cases.

Commissioner PENDERY stated that the Court had made no such order. If such a thing had been done, it must have been by the Marshal without authority.

Mr. JOLLIFFE rose and said he must go and hunt up his witnesses, for as many of them were colored people, they had not been permitted in the Court Room.

Col. CHAMBERS—"I won't wait for any such thing."

Commissioner PENDERY stated that there was no law providing for the subpoenaing of witnesses for the defendants or fugitives in such cases. The law provides for the serving of subpoenas issued by the masters, but for none on the behalf of the slave. The U.S. Marshal was under no obligation to serve them, and therefore refused.

Col. CHAMBERS denied this.

Commissioner PENDERY replied that experience had taught him differently. He had sent accounts for such service to head quarters, and the Comptroller at Washington had refused to allow them.

The Court was then informed that the Marshal disregarded its order, and was still refusing to admit colored people to the Court Room. Commissioner PENDERY stated that he had spoken with the Marshal about it, and he had said that he wanted to preserve order in the Court Room, and did not wish to disobey the order of the Court, but still did not like to admit the colored people. So they were still excluded.

Mr. JOLLIFFE stated that the subpoenas they had issued on behalf of the fugitives had been returned to them by the U.S. Marshal. He declined to serve them. Mr. Jolliffe, therefore, asked the appointment of a special deputy Marshal by this Court to serve these subpoenas. He asked the appointment of a special deputy in order that the Court might have the power to issue attachments for witnesses who refused to come. If served by volunteers the Court would have no such power. He would, therefore, ask that Wm. Beckley be appointed. (Wm. Beckley is a light colored mulatto.)

Col. CHAMBERS objected to the appointment.

Mr. Jolliffe stated that Beckley was a citizen of Ohio, and a voter.

Commissioner PENDERY said, after talking aside to the Marshal, that to prevent trouble the Marshal would serve these subpoenas, and he (the Commissioner) would pay the fees out of his own pocket.

Mr. JOLLIFFE—"Oh no, you shan't do that."

The Marshal then took the subpoenas to serve.

Mr. JOLLIFFE then desired the warrant to be amended as to the fugitive named in it as young Simon. His name was not Simon, but Robert Garner.

Mr. JOLLIFFE then moved that this prosecution be quashed, on the ground that the warrant had no seal upon it. It had in its place simply a scroll, made with a pen, and the word seal written there. That such would be sufficient on a deed or bond, in the State of Ohio, he did not deny, but on process issued from a United States Court it was not sufficient. This was not the Commissioner's fault. The Congress that passed the Fugitive Slave Law had failed to provide a seal for the Commissioner, and if there was a hiatus in the proceeding, it was thank God, so much the better for the cause of human freedom. In processes between different States, the seal was the only evidence to authenticate them.

Commissioner PENDERY said he thought when he undertook the business of issuing the warrant he knew what he was about. When he undertook the office he had consulted with a Justice of the Supreme Court, about his duties, and was told that a seal was not necessary. He did wish [*sic*] to delay this trial, but the question might be argued at any time. Besides, the warrant, whether defective or not, did not now hold the prisoners. They were now in the custody of this Court.

Mr. JOLLIFFE then moved a continuance, to allow them to get the witnesses in behalf of Robert Garner, from Dayton, Covington, and other places, to prove that he had been brought into the State of Ohio; also to hunt up Rice, a Dutch butcher, to whom his master had sold hogs in this city and brought Robert over to assist in killing them.

Commissioner PENDERY decided that if Rice was dead, and could not be had, there was no cause for continuance on that account; and that the case must be preceded with.

The case of James Marshall, who claims the two men and the old woman was then commenced.

TESTIMONY FOR THE CLAIMANT.

JAMES CORBIN—Am acquainted with James Marshall; he lives in Boone County, Kentucky; know Simon Garner (the colored man here, the oldest of the two); he belongs to Mr. Marshall; have known him for thirty years; he sold him to Anderson about twenty-four years ago, and promised Simon that when he was able he'd buy him back; Anderson kept him till last spring, when Mr. Marshall bought Simon back from the widow, Mr. Anderson having died; he had lived with a nephew most of the time.

Young Simon belongs to Mr. Marshall; have known him ever since he was born, and have never heard him called by any other name. I know Mary Garner, she belongs to James Marshall; I last saw them at Mr. Marshall's farm two weeks ago.

Cross examined—Do not know how long it is since Geo. Anderson died; I think he left no brothers or sisters, or children; do not know who were his heirs at law.

THOMAS MARSHALL being sworn said: I know James Marshall. Have known Simon Garner (the fugitive there,) since my father bought him in April last. Have known young Simon, ever since I can recollect. I was raised with him. I shall be 19 next March. Know Mary Garner. I know all these persons owed service to Mr. Marshall, under the law of Kentucky. I saw old Mary and old Simon, in Kentucky on Sunday evening. Young Simon I saw there on Friday night; the old folks were at my brothers, and young Simon at my fathers, they escaped last Sunday night. I next saw them by the Hamilton and Dayton depot after they were caught last Monday. About 5 weeks before last Christmas I started from my father's to go to Arkansas for a gentleman, young Simon went with me to Covington, we got there on Wednesday evening; I had a little difficulty with the gentleman and returned home; I crossed from Covington to Cincinnati on that occasion; young Simon did not cross with me; did not see him in Cincinnati then; if he was there I do not know it; I crossed about the middle of the day; did not pay ferriage for myself and Simon. I left Simon hired to Mr. Ellison in Covington.

I have not said in the hearing of Mr. George Guilford that Simon had often been in Cincinnati; did not tell him so in the U.S. Marshal's office on the day they were arrested; did not hear *these people* say to Mr. James Elliott that they had often been in Ohio. (Mr. Elliott was pointed out to witness.) He said he had never seen him. The language the witness used was: "I know not the man." Mr. Guilford was pointed out to him, and he denied having spoken to him in the Marshal's office; was not an agent for his father in general, was only sent after these negroes.

G.W. Marshall—Am a nephew of Mr. Marshall, who claims these negroes. I'll be twenty-three years old in February. All *these people* owed service to Wm. Marshall. Lived in Covington five years. Young Simon did not live there with a man named James Poor—he did live with Poor's mother some years ago.

He lived with Mr. Timberlake, in Covington, some seven years ago. That was before I moved to Covington.

James Marshall never told him that young Simon had killed hogs for him in Cincinnati. James Marshall was not in the habit of bringing his boys over to this side when he brought hogs over. Re-examined—Never knew of any of *these people* ever being in the State of Ohio by their master's permission. Never knew them to be here at all until this time.

W.B. MURPHY, (the Major Murphy who assisted to make the arrest,) was called and sworn. Said: I know *these people* as the slaves of Mr. Marshall. They were Mr. Marshall's property by the laws of Kentucky. Cross-examined.—Was present at the arrest; went down to the house where they were taken about three-quarters of an hour before Mr. Gaines and the Marshal got there. Saw Elijah Kite, whom I knew, and wanted through him to get to talk with the old man. Knew if I could talk with him, there would be no difficulty about getting them to go back. (This testimony was objected to by Col. Chambers as being irrevelant.) Didn't go into Kite's house.

Question by Mr. JOLLIFFE—Was any one murdered during the arrest? Objected to by Col. Chambers—he did not wish to go into all these fancy matters.

Mr. JOLLIFFE, replied that the fact he intended to bring out, was that the mother of these children, frantic, at the time of the arrest, had murdered one of her children, (a little girl) rather than have it taken back into slavery. He did not regard this as a "fancy matter" as Col. Chambers termed it.

The Court rejected the question, when Mr. Jolliffe put it in another form.

Col. Chambers thought this was trifling with the dignity of the Court. Commissioner Pendery said the Court, understood how to maintain its own dignity, and would ask Mr. Jolliffe what object he had in proving the fact of the death of the child.

Mr. Jolliffe's Remarks.

Mr. JOLLIFFE replied that he intended on the final argument of this case, not only to allege, but to demonstrate conclusively to the Court; that the Fugitive Slave Law was unconstitutional and as part and parcel of that argument, he wished to show the effect of carrying it out. That it had driven a frantic mother to murder her own child, rather than see it carried back to the seething hell of American slavery. [Here loud bursts of applause from the multitude effectually drowned for a moment the marshal's cries of "order, order."] This law was of such a character that its execution required human hearts to be wrung and human blood to be spilt.

The Constitution expressly declared that Congress should pass no law prescribing any form of religion, or preventing the free exercise thereof. If Congress could not pass any law requiring you to worship God, still less could they pass one requiring you to carry fuel to Hell. (Applause, order, order, cried the Marshal.)

The Commissioner was there as the guardian of religious liberty in the United States, and if he acted wisely he would bring happiness to thousands and tens of thousands, but if he followed evil counsel the consequences could not easily be foretold. In a brief time, perhaps in less than six months, the Union might be severed. The stars and stripes might float over separate nations and blood flow between them. He desired to introduce this evidence simply to show the legitimate effects of this law.

For a few moments after Mr. Jolliffe sat down shouts of applause and cries of order filled the Court Rooms.

Mr. Finnell's Remarks.

Mr. Finnell replied to Mr. Jolliffe. He was here, he said, as a Kentuckian and as a slaveholder, and he knew some slaves that he loved better than he loved white folks, still he wished most sincerely that there was not a slave in the universe. But there were other systems of slavery beside ours. The Irish were enslaved by England and that man, (looking towards Mr. Elliott) fresh from the bog, had better stayed there and helped his enslaved brethren than come here to meddle with our institutions. He told the story of the flat boatman who entered a bayou of the Mississippi and thought himself at sea, so his friend Mr. Jolliffe had drifted clear out at sea in his remarks. He had gone off to the discussion of morals, which did not belong to the case.

It being then 4 o'clock, the Court adjourned to 1/2 past 9 this morning . . .

Cincinnati Daily Times, February 1, 1856

Here, the Times *(a paper at this moment aligned with the very short-lived American Party, the electoral arm of the nativist Know Nothing movement) gives us a particularly vivid view of the struggle in the streets and the dispute over who should be allowed to watch the proceedings in court. In the opening days of the case, the paper repeatedly warned that antislavery forces were seeking to stir up a riot and prevent the rule of law.*

THE FUGITIVE SLAVES
EFFORTS TO INCREASE THE
EXCITEMENT!

Unsuccessful efforts are still being made to get up additional excitement relative to the fugitive slave case. Special indignities now seem to be leveled against those persons who, by virtue of their office, are compelled to guard the fugitives, and prevent their escape. Last night handbills were posted all over the city headed, "Geo. S. Bennett, U.S. Deputy Marshal." They read as follows:

Let the public mark this man, and let the nation fear for his safety when LECHEROUS, DRUNKEN TYRANTS are in power.

Commissioner Pendery has declared that his court room is a FREE one, that all citizens who are willing to depart themselves quietly are at liberty to enter. Yet in the face of this, GEORGE S. BENNETT declares with profane and insulting emphasis that "no damned niggers" are to be admitted. And the ruffian crowd who have deserted their proper duty as city policemen to aid him in his degrading work of slave catching, stand ready to insult and maltreat NATIVE TAX PAYERS who desire to enter the court room, as is their right."

After accusing Bennett of having intruding himself into a colored ball . . . the poster thus closes:—

"Blood hounds should always be treated thus. But his brazen front knows no shame. The people of Ohio send Sharp's rifles to Kansas, yet permit their own soil to be invaded by bullying Kentuckians, sided by their dog BENNETT. We hope you will not fill the measure of your shame by permitting a woman who deserves Immortality, to be dragged to that slavery she dreads worse than death.

Great God!! what a blot on our nation that men and women should seek in the gallows, a refuge from that slavery to which our laws threaten to consign them.

JUSTICE"

Though generally read, the poster seems to create no excitement.

The colored man arrested last evening for an alleged attempt to create a disturbance as the prisoners were being conducted from the court room to the jail, had not been tried, when our reporter left the Police Court this morning. He is accused of throwing a stone at the officers who were sitting on top the omnibus.

We stated yesterday that one of the colored men, punished for attempting to raise a disturbance the evening previous, seized the Mayor by the throat—such was the testimony given in Court, but Mayor Faran informs us this morning that such is not the fact. He saw a crowd around the colored man, some hitting, and some kicking him, and he ran in to keep those who were attacking him from seriously hurting him. As he lay his hands on the colored man, a white man caught him by the collar, to pull him back, but the colored man did not touch him. —The witnesses were entirely mistaken.

Cincinnati Daily Gazette, February 2, 1856

The Fugitive Slave Case.
BEFORE U.S. COMMISSIONER PENDERY.
FOURTH DAY.

On the opening of the Court yesterday morning, Col. Chambers announced that the claimant had no more witnesses and rested here.

TESTIMONY FOR THE SLAVES.

Charlotte Armstrong, a colored woman, being sworn, was asked if she ever saw that woman, (pointing to Mary, the older of the women claimed as slaves.) She replied yes, she had seen her about four years ago at the

Bethel Chapel on Sixth street, in Cincinnati. The second time I saw her was in the same chapel, she sat then, in the next pew to me; the third time I saw her I was going down to the river and met her coming up with a market basket, going towards Fifth street market. This was some three years ago, and between eight and nine o'clock in the morning. I said to her you come over to market very often. She replied yes.

Col. Chambers objected to the conversation. Mr. Jolliffe contended that so much of the conversation as was connected with the act at the time, such as what was said about going to market when she had a market basket on her arm, was admissible. The Court overruled it, and the examination was resumed.

I saw her again on Fifth street market, she was buying marketing, had a basket pretty full. She said it was for her owners.

Col. Chambers—"Never mind what she said."

Question—Is that the same woman? Yes sir, that's the same woman, if I was to be qualified to death.

Questions were then asked about her history, and how long she had lived in Cincinnati; these were objected to by the claimants, and they admitted that the witness was a highly respectable woman.

Edward John Wilson, a black man, was called. Had seen that young gentleman, (pointing to young Simon,) before. Was passing down Broadway from my dwelling. It was near the corner of Fourth. That man (young Simon) asked me if I could tell him where Mr. Kite lived. I told him he lived on Sixth street, right near, if I'm not mistaken, to the Bethel church, which is called the old church. He said he wished to go there to stop all night. I then placed him right, and told him the place as near as I could. It is beneath my dignity to tell what time it was. The question was repeated and witness replied:

It is very hard for me to draw these old intellects of mine on that pint. Think its near two years ago, as near as I can come at it. Know him by his complexion, and by his feet, he turns them a little out. Have no doubt in my own mind that it is the same man, but can't explain myself any better, as I'm not much in court business, but his face is too plain to be mistaken. There was a white man with him. Think it was that man there, (pointing to Marshall, the claimant.)

Cross-examined—Ques. —What time in the year was this? Ah, that's where you got me—when a man asks me a question, I'm out and gone again.

Re-examined. —Lived in Cincinnati about eleven years, as near as I can recollect.

George J. Guilford called—(Mr. Guilford was called to contradict the statement made by young Marshall, the son of the claimant that he had never told Mr. G. that these people had been frequently in Ohio.— REP.) He said:

On the day these fugitives were brought to the office of the United States Marshal, I had a conversation with the young gentleman referred to, Thomas W. Marshall, the son of the claimant, in regard to the time and manner of the escape of these fugitives—names of the claimants and of the defendants—inquired about the manner in which they were treated at home; asked him if they had ever expressed any dissatisfaction with their condition, or had ever evinced any inclination to be free. His reply in substance was that they had always seemed contented. He never imagined that they desired to run off. (Col. Chambers rose to object to this testimony, but finally consented to its admission, as it was designed to contradict and impeach Mr. Marshall.) Witness continued: Marshall said these people had been on this side of the river frequently. By *these people* he meant the fugitives here. He did not distinguish between the slaves of Mr. Marshall and Mr. Gaines. I was inquiring into these facts, not with any thought of being used as a witness, but for the purpose of publication; I am reporter for the *Commercial* newspaper. Maj. Murphy was present at a part of this conversation; and I also explained to him my object in making the inquiries. I called Marshall from the stove to the window, and took out my note book and put down what he said at the time.

Cross-examined—Don't think I can be mistaken as to the identity of Marshall. He was pointed out to me as the son of the claimant, and I have seen him since in Court. Was present at this examination as a witness.

Maj. Murphy came up during the conversation with an expression of inquiry on his countenance, and I explained to him the purpose for which I was making the inquiries.

Re-examined—Took the substance of the conversation down at the time, and published such as I thought proper afterwards. Have not my notes now. Copy is not preserved in a newspaper office. Mr. Guilford pointed out young Marshall, and said, "that is the man." . . .

Joseph Kite sworn—I know that young man, (young Simon) he was in my house sometime this winter; took supper with me, and he remarked he was glad he took supper with his uncle once. His wife and my son are cousins. Her father was my wife's brother. I lived over in Boone county, Kentucky, for years. Saw him here more than once or twice—once driving hogs here, but not positive about it. It was on Broadway; don't know the time, but it was in the winter of this year.

James Elliott sworn—Heard on last Monday there were some fugitives in the U.S. Marshal's office, and went there. I made inquiries about the case. Saw Thomas W. Marshall, the son of the claimant, there. That's him. I asked the colored persons, in Mr. Marshall's presence, if they wanted a lawyer. (Objected to by Col. Chambers. Mr. Jolliffe explained that the object was to contradict Mr. Marshall's statement.) After some arguments witness went on.

I asked the negroes in young Marshall's hearing, if they had ever been in Ohio.

Ques. —What did they reply?

Objected to by claimant, and a long argument ensued. Witness said "Mr. Marshall asked me my name."

Ques. By Mr. Jolliffe. —How come he to do so?

Objected to by claimant.

When I remarked that they must have a lawyer and I would furnish them one, Mr. Marshall remarked that they were in the hands of the U.S. Officers now, and I said they could not be taken away without a trial. He said we are ready. He then asked me my name, and I told him it was Elliott.

Mr. Jolliffe moved that Rev. A.A. Livermore be appointed a guardian, *ad litem,* for Cilly, (Priscilla) the child nine months old, and one of the defendants in this case. Objected to by Col. Chambers.

(From 10 o'clock till half past two, the Court was waiting for the appearance of witnesses.)

A habeas corpus, *ad testificandum,* for one of the witnesses for the fugitives, who had been arrested by the Marshal, and sent to jail by the Police Court yesterday, was asked for and granted.

Wm. Alexander, a colored man, sworn. —Said: I have seen that young man, (pointing to Simon.) Saw him once before Christmas and once on the Christmas. Was coming up Sixth street, and met him just below Broadway, coming down. He asked me where Mr. Kite lived. The next time I saw him was at my own house. Had an hour and a half's conversation with him. Next time was him, he was in company with a white man.

That was three or four weeks before Christmas. They were driving hogs up Broadway, when he was at my house. I asked him if he was the same man. (Objected to and ruled out.) Was positive that this is the same man I saw on Broadway. . . .

At 3 1/2 o'clock, Court adjourned to 10 o'clock this morning.

Cincinnati Daily Gazette, February 4, 1856

The Fugitive Slave Case.
BEFORE U.S. COMMISSIONER PENDERY.

Messrs. Chambers, of Cincinnati, and Wall & Finnell, of Kentucky, for the Claimant—Messrs. Jolliffe & Gitchell for the Slaves.

The City Police who had preserved order in the U.S. Court Rooms, on Friday, were excluded on Saturday, and the Court was entirely in the charge of the U.S. Marshals and the Covington (Ky.) Police. One tall, bony, gaunt Kentuckian, (said to be a Negro catcher by profession,) with a small, red, sunken eye, hollow cheeks, and a sharp chin, stood erect within the bar watching over the Commissioner. Occasionally he would mount a settee near the railing and wave a huge club (which he carried in lieu of a cane) over the heads of the multitude of white, black, and yellow folks outside the bar. During the day he would occasionally look cudgels at the "free niggers," then suddenly putting his hand to his ear he would dodge his head down to catch a whisper that passed between Mr. JOLLIFFE and his clients, but he spoke never a word.

A number of Kentuckians remain about the Court, and when it adjourns form a double line of men from the Court Room door to the prisoners' van, and between the files of men the fugitives are passed out. They then follow the omnibus to prevent a rescue. It is said these men have stated that they were prepared to carry the fugitives back to Kentucky at all hazards, but we cannot believe that this is any thing more than bluster.

TESTIMONY FOR THE SLAVES.

ALFRED GILMORE, (a colored man) sworn—Saw that young man (young Simon) during all the Christmas at the People's Theater, in this city, at night, as many as four times; once I accompanied him there from corner Sixth and Broadway. Met with him there on the street. Mr. Ellis, the Deputy Marshal, also saw him there, for I heard him remark about his bushy hair. Mr. Ellis is usher at the People's Theater. I am certain that is the man.

Wm. MARSHALL was called for, but could not be found.

SARAH KITE, colored woman, sworn. —Young Simon was at our house during the Christmas. Was there part of a day off and on. Am sure that is the same man.

J. KNIGHT, a white man, sworn—Stated that he was a butcher, but had never slaughtered hogs for the farmers. Knew a butcher by the name of Rice that did, and gave his address, and a subpoena was issued for him.

W.M. MARSHALL, sworn—(Marshal is the policeman who was dismissed by the Mayor on a charge of arresting Mr. Hayes, of Vicksburg, for the sake of extorting money from him. Having been turned out of the police department, he has been selected as a proper person for the office of special U.S. Marshal, to guard these fugitives. He had stated in conversation that he had frequently seen young Simon in Cincinnati; that from his long experience as a policeman he never forgot a face.

He was called for to testify to this fact; he could not for some time be obtained, but finally came. When on the stand he did not reply to questions directly, but his answers were so evasive and equivocal as not to place the character of the witness for candor and fairness in a highly favorable light. Those who had any lingering doubts about the propriety of the Mayor's act in suspending him, and heard this testimony had them removed.) He said:

Have seen that man (young Simon) before this arrest. Mr. Guilford and I had a conversation about him last Monday, when I drew his attention to him. I first saw him on this side of the Ohio. Have studied the matter over since. Have been over in Kentucky, and might have seen him here. I asked him if he'd ever peddled apples or potatoes on Front street. If he told me the truth, I was disposed to think I'd seen him on Front street. Have seen him there more than once, if he told me the truth. No doubt I have seen him there if he told me the truth. If he did'nt tell me the truth, I have doubt. Knew a man from Kentucky who used to peddle watermelons seven or eight years ago, and this man came about, near the time he left. Am a policeman. . . .

ELIJAH KITE sworn—Saw these people (the fugitives) last Christmas. Young Simon came to my house on Christmas—was there in the evening—went away about 10 o'clock and came back the next day. Never saw him in Ohio before that. He was here two days, one after the other. Was'nt there afterwards till Monday. My house is in Ohio.

SPENCER CASH, copper colored, was sworn—Saw that man (young Simon) driving hogs in Cincinnati. It was a few days before the Strader's chimneys blew off, (near Christmas.) Saw him three times on that day. Am sure that was the same man.

Here a delay occurred. The Court waited for the appearance of witnesses who had been subpoenaed. Col. Chambers protested against the delay. Mr. Jolliffe explained that he had stated when he went into the case, that he was not ready, and had done so on condition that he should have time to get his witnesses.

Here JACOB FLINN, attorney for Mr. BENNETT, Deputy U.S. Marshal, rose and wished to have the reporters correct their report of his remarks on day before yesterday. The *Gazette,* however, fell into no error about it, for it did not report them.

He wished also to vindicate the Marshal from the charge of having made a rule to exclude colored people. He said, "the Marshal made no such law himself, but acted in strict conformity with the instructions laid down by the Commissioner."

JOHN FARRAR—a very light mulatto, sworn. —Saw that man (old Simon,) in Cincinnati, going down towards the river from Lower Market, a short time before last Christmas. Am certain that is the man.

A GERMAN BUTCHER, *to whom Marshall had sold hogs, appears and testifies that Marshall brought the two slaves to Ohio, and stayed with them all night at his house, but fails fully to identify Marshall.*

JACOB RICE, (a German butcher) sworn. —Have seen that man (old Simon,) before. Have seen him with Mr. Marshall. Mr. Marshall sold me some hogs. I cannot tell how many hogs he had along with him. He fetched two black boys (nagurs) along. The first day he fetched the hogs, and the next day he weighed the hogs. He left one of the boys in my house over night. I cannot tell how many nights he stayed in my house. In the night I tell Mr. Marshall, "Mr. Marshall, where we lay the boy?" and do he say, "very well, lay 'em on the ground—makes no difference where he lays." My old woman tell me, "now, old man, take the boy over to the childers, and put them over to the childers in the bed." In the morning Mr. Marshall tell me, "where is the boy?" He said to my old woman, "what's the reason you give him a bed?" Well, then my old woman tell Mr. Marshall, she said how, "these people like us." He said he no call them people; they same like anoder ting—he wouldn't say a dog; and then the next morning he take 'em, and he goes 'long home. That's all I knowed.

My house at that time was out on Hamer street, between Vine and Main, in Cincinnati. Ques. —How long ago? Well, my friends, that's too long—8 or 9 years ago. Think bought the hogs of him yonder side of Covington. Would not know him now.

He was told to look at the two Negro men, and said:

I know this man very well—that one was a little boy 10 years ago. Believe that man is the man, though he was a boy then.

Col. C. —You know the old man? "Oh, I knew him long ago"; had seen him before. I can't tell when—a good many times. My wife is dead. My children's names are Margaret and Emily. Margaret is married to Frederick Fisher, and they live in my house; Emily to John Reybold—he lives in Lick Run.

Cross-examined—About 10 years since I knew that old man. He (young Simon) looks like the boy that was along. One was a man grown and the other a little boy. (Showed how high, about 4 1/2 or 5 feet.)

Court—Point out Mr. Marshall. Ans. He is in the Court like a gentleman, and he comes to my house like another man. He comes to my house with hogs, looking like his nagur, and now he dressed like a gentleman. Mr. Marshall was a high (tall) man, large.

The Court then waited for some time for the appearance of Margaret Fisher, the daughter of Mr. Rice, who was immediately sent for. During this interval, Mr. Rice talked with Robert.

JACOB RICE re-called, and asked again as to young Simon said— "Yes, I recollect him now; that's the same boy I saw in my house."

MARSHALL FULLY IDENTIFIED BY THE BUTCHER'S DAUGHTER.

MARGARET FISHER, daughter of the last witness, having arrived, was seated for a moment, close by the fugitives, and spoke to young Simon. She was then sworn and told to look at the fugitives, and state if she had ever seen any of them before. She said:

I think I've seen that young man before. I think he is the very boy that staid at our house years ago, but he's grown very much. He stayed all night at Mr. Rice's—my father's. My father lived then at the corner of Hamer and Black streets. Been about ten years ago. I believe the boy slept with the journeyman. Ques. —Are you satisfied that is the same boy? Ans. —Yes, sir, I think it is. Ques. —Have you any doubt about it? Ans. —I think it's the boy. I have no doubt of it at all.

He was brought there by a gentleman whom father had hogs of. Can't recollect his name just now, but would know it if I heard it. Ques. —Was it Marshall? Ans. —Yes it was. Ques. —Can you pick him out? Col. Chambers objected, and the Court took the witness and asked her if Marshall was in the room. The witness stood up and looked around for some time. It was a moment of intense interest, for the identity of Marshall with the man who stayed with the Negroes at the butcher's was all that was wanting to make the evidence complete. A brother of Marshall, who resembles him strongly, rose, and witness looked at him eagerly as though about to recognize him as the man, but did not speak. Next to him was a man crouching down, with the head of his cane to his lips and looking stealthily out of the corner of his eyes. —At length witness said: "THAT MAN WITH THE STICK TO HIS MOUTH IS HIM." It was Marshall.

Cross Examined. —Ques. —"Why did you look so hard at the man that rose up?" Ans. —I was just a going to say it was him, and then I looked at him right, and saw it wasn't him.

Ques. —You changed your mind then? Ans. —I didn't change my mind at all. I just thought it was'nt him. It's so long ago a body has to take a good look before they know. Ques. —Did you know the young man there (young Simon) as soon as you came in the room. Ans. —"Yes sir, I did so." Ques. —How old and large was he then. Ans. — He was about 10 or 11 years old then. (Showed how large—4 ½ or 5 feet) Never saw him since till to-day. Can't say whether he stayed three or four nights.

Witness was directed to look at Marshall. She said his face was fuller then than now. Could'nt say if his body was fatter, but knew his face. Don't know how he was dressed. Had clothes like the farmers generally have on. Don't remember that old man, (old Simon). Don't remember he was along.

Ques. —Had Mr. Marshall whiskers on? Ans. —Well I guess he did have whiskers.

Ques. —Can you point out in the Court room any other man who sold hogs to your father? Witness. —"And stayed all night?" Col. Chambers. —"No."

Well I did'nt bother about them. My business was in the house, and I only noticed those that stayed all night. Witness pointed out another Kentucky hog drover that she had seen at her father's. No other boy stayed there. Might have been other boys just come with him, but they did'nt stay there all night. Mr. Marshall slept alone; when he started to bed father asked him if the boy would sleep with him; he said no, he could lay on the bare floor. Boy slept with the journeyman, and ate at our table. The little boy behaved first rate; everything his master told him to do he done. Don't know whether his hair was combed the way it is now; he had on a cap. I am going on 27 years old. Have not talked with any body about this case. Nobody has told me anything about this case to-day. Simon did not point out his master to me. Did not point his finger to him while I talked with him. Ques. —How did you come to say that the very boy staid at our house all night? Ans. —Because you asked me.

Ques. By Col. Chambers—"What's the name of that young man (pointing to Simon)? Ans. —If I didn't know you've told me often enough. I didn't converse with Simon about this trial. I sat down by him and he asked me if I knew him. That's all he asked me. Have talked with no one about this case.

Re-Examined. —Don't know anything about what my father stated in Court. That man (pointing to the Marshal) came for me, and I came right down.

It being half past four, Court adjourned to Monday morning at 10 o'clock.

Cincinnati Daily Enquirer, February 5, 1856

On the morning of February 4 each side introduced a few final witnesses to address the question of whether Robert Garner had previously been in Ohio and under what conditions. The afternoon was given over to John Finnell's lengthy argument on behalf of the claimants. The Enquirer's *sympathetic coverage of that argument is presented below.*

FUGITIVE SLAVE CASE,
Before U.S. Commissioner J. L. Pendery.
CLOSE OF TESTIMONY.
Argument of J. W. Finnell, Esq.

The unparalleled length of this case, and the continued interest manifested in the probable result draws an immense crowd of spectators to the Court-room. The opening argument of Colonel Finnell for the claimant was a master effort, and the deep attention manifested during the period of its delivery gave proof that it was appreciated by all who heard it. . . .

At the appointed time the Court re-assembled, when the argument was opened by . . . Finnell . . . as follows:

If your Honor please, I do not desire to weary the patience of the Court, already tired out by the protracted length of the case, but I propose to come as briefly as possible to the claim of James Marshall to the services of the slaves at the bar, to wit: Simon Garner, sr., Simon Garner, jr., and Mary Garner. It is no province of mine to discuss the moral aspect of slavery; as a citizen of Kentucky I have no right to defend the institutions of that State. I will not discuss here whether it were a crime in my forefathers to introduce in this fair country the institution of slavery. I do not come here to discuss the abstract question of slavery whether it be right or wrong; the people of the slave States have rights to this species of property. The Federal Constitution, under which we live, and I hope may continue to live while the suns shines upon this beautiful land, which now extends from the Atlantic to the Pacific, recognizes the institution of slavery, and it also requires laws to be passed to protect the slave property of the Southern States of this Union, as well as the so-considered and acknowledged property of the North. I know how common it is for men of ability and standing in the North to denounce us of the South as slave owners, slave catchers and tyrants over human flesh, but that cannot annul the Constitution and the law. I say we stand not here as citizens of Kentucky nor of Ohio, but of the Union, and in the investigation of this case we are only bound by the laws passed by Congress on this subject. What have we to do with the right or wrong of slavery. It is here in our midst, and we cannot rid ourselves of the evil, if evil there be. Whence did we derive our institution of slavery? From the cupidity of the Yankee slave-dealers who may say they have rid themselves of the crime of holding slaves.

I claim these people for my client not under the law of the State of Ohio but under the Constitution of the United States and the laws passed in pursuance thereof—the former almost universally acknowledged, and the latter the law of the land since 1850. What was the position of Kentucky forty years ago toward the State of Ohio? Less than half a century ago the North-western borders of Ohio were menaced by a cruel savage foe. Kentucky was secure from the danger, and to her the appeal was made, and upon every battle-field fought in defense of your homes, your firesides, your women and your children, the blood of Kentuckians flowed freely. The last time I ever made a speech in the presence of so large an assemblage of persons in Ohio as this was on the occasion of receiving the bones of those of the sons of Kentucky who fell in defense of Ohio women and Ohio children, to convey them to Kentucky; and I ask you, is it not time to pause in the consideration of these conflicting questions, if conflicting they be, and recur to scenes enacted when with Kentucky the language was, "I will stand by you, for you are my brethren?"

We have fallen upon evil times. I was educated in a school that knew nothing but the perpetuity of the Federal Government. I admit as fully as the gentleman can do the doctrine of State sovereignty, but I do not admit the ultra Southern doctrine of nullification. What are we without the doctrine of supremacy of the Federal Government, leaving to the States their peculiar province? It is only the care of a mother for her children, only superintending their general progress, and never insisting on more than their provisional and educational care. The Constitution of the United States covers this whole ground: Whatever ultra men may say at the South, or ultra men may contend at the North, there is but one interpretation, which is that *property* in slaves or otherwise shall be held sacred. The idea of *nullification* can as well be entertained in a slave case on the part of those who set at nought the laws of Congress on a weak plea as of those who for State's rights were willing to make an issue on the part of a State, in contradistinction to a law of Congress regulating the tariff. When this right of nullification was claimed by South Carolina, what was the course pursued by President Jackson? He promptly said to the nullifiers, "The Constitution and laws of the Union are the supreme law of the land, and to them you must yield obedience." This order he forced them to obey. I would to God that we had some other Andrew Jackson to administer the laws of the Government at present, who would say to the nullifiers of the Northern States as *he* did to those of South Carolina, "You shall not nullify the Constitution and the laws of the Union." My friend indicated the other day that he knew of a higher law than the Constitution! Sir, I am not a Christian; would to God I were! But I am the son of a Christian mother, and I know of no higher law in civil matters than the Constitution, and the laws made in pursuance thereof. I do not yield that his admiration of the Divine law is any greater than my own. I recognize no lawgiver in civil and constitutional matters but the Congress of the United States, and no lawgiver for all other purposes but the Author of Divine law.

I think there can be no doubt but that these persons escaped from the custody of James Marshall, the claimant, as is alleged by him. The Congress of the United States has, in pursuance of the Constitution of the United States, passed the Fugitive-slave Law, directing what shall be the mode of proceeding to enforce that law. The claimant has shown all that by the law referred to he is bound to, to-wit: that these persons owed labor and service to Mr. Marshall by the laws of the State of Kentucky, and that while so owing service and labor they escaped in Ohio. I shall not discuss the questions as to whether the Fugitive-slave Law is unconstitutional or infamous. It has been adjudicated upon by a majority of the judges of the Supreme Court on their circuits, and by the subordinate courts of every State of the Union, except three. It has, by the people of the Union, been held to be constitutional. The next point is that these persons have been in the State of Ohio, and having stepped upon free-soil became free men. I will read your Honor some of the decisions upon this point:

Mr. Finnell here read the case of Graham *vs.* Strader in *V B. Munroe,* 181.

In this case the fact was that two slaves had been in Ohio, and having been brought back into Kentucky, the question arose as to whether, by the laws of Kentucky, they were free. The Court held that they were not entitled to their freedom, because their masters or the agent of their masters having brought them into this State without the intention of remaining here, and they having returned into Kentucky without changing the relation of master and slave; the condition as to slavery had never changed. Now, sir, the Supreme Court of the United States say that the law of Kentucky must govern this case, and the law of Kentucky is plain that the persons are not free. Wherever a slave has made a case in the courts of Kentucky they have always received where they had a shadow of right; the most liberal construction they could give in favor of this freedom is always given and I know of no lawyer of any respectability in Kentucky who would refuse to take the case of any negro against the claims of any master who endeavored to retain him in slavery without having the most unqualified right to the labor and service of the negro. But in Ohio, if an owner claims under the laws of the United States, his property he must be set upon by those who are fanatics in morals, bigots in religion and demagogues in politics, who run after them to drive them from the State, bestowing upon them the most opprobrious epithets in the English language. What concern is it of yours what the domestic institutions of Kentucky are? You cannot stretch the arm of your legislation across me in Kentucky; still less can you judge the moral right or wrong of its institutions. I do not claim the right to these persons as a citizen of Kentucky, but as a citizen of this great and glorious Union, protected as I am by the flag of my country. I claim it as one who is protected by the national emblem of the Union—as one who is protected by the Federal Constitution. Shall it be said to the people of my State by the people of Ohio, You come here, if you do come at all, according to my understanding of the Federal Constitution and of your institutions. I have the supremest scorn for the Political Abolitionist; I consider him as the most loathsome thing upon the face of this earth. I cannot find in the whole vocabulary of the language a name to properly express my opinion of what he is. But I have a respect for the honest anti-slavery man. It is not to be believed that a man, reared in the North to hate the institution of slavery can be, in a moment, transformed into a pro-slavery man. There are some of the best men in Kentucky who detest and do not fear to cry out against the institution peculiar to the South. I am no alarmist on the subject of the safety of the Union; but we must make compromises if we would preserve it. The Constitution of the United States is, itself, a compromise. I love the Union better than I love any of its institutions, and I love the liberty of the white man better than that of the black man. I trust, sir, that, however we may be divided upon the subject which now agitates this Union, to-wit: that of slavery, as to its moral right or wrong, we all stand together upon the great question of the Union, that it must and shall be preserved.

The action of the Legislature of Ohio in the passage of certain resolutions, copies of which have been placed in my possession, is one of the most injudicious acts that has ever been enacted by a sovereign State of this Union. What has the Legislature of Ohio to do with this case. There is a plain and unmistakable section of the Constitution of the United States which contains all the law upon this question, and the members of the Legislature of Ohio should look well into this matter before passing resolutions which can possibly teach nothing better than to instruct the mob to resist the execution of the laws of the United States. I would have your Honor do no wrong to these alleged fugitives. If these people are free by the Constitution and laws of the United States, let them go hence from this Court free. If Mr. Marshall wants this man and he be free, then I am not his counsel. I trust, sir, you will carefully consider all the law on this matter and give your decision without fear or favor.

The Court, upon the conclusion of Mr. Finnell's argument, adjourned until two o'clock this afternoon. . . .

Cincinnati Daily Gazette, February 7, 1856

On February 5 James Gitchell, John Jolliffe's assistant, began his side's rebuttal of the arguments that had been made the previous day by John Finnell. Gitchell rehearsed the defense evidence that the Garners had crossed the Ohio River with consent of their masters, arguing that this emancipated them, and he challenged the constitutionality of the Fugitive Slave Act, claiming, among other things, that Congress lacked the authority to regulate slavery and that the law's creation of federal commissioners (such as Pendery) violated the Constitution's strictures on the appointment of judges. Although the courts had ruled on such arguments before, with recent federal arguments going against the fugitives' side, Gitchell argued that the key issues remained unresolved. None of the papers, however, seemed interested in the jurisprudential substance of these arguments, and the record left to us is thin. When Jolliffe added his own three-hour summation the next day, however, his remarks were amply reported. Whatever its constitutional merits, Jolliffe's central argument that the Fugitive Slave Act violated the First Amendment guarantee of religious liberty had not been previously adjudicated by higher courts, for it was original to him.

THE FUGITIVE SLAVE CASE.
BEFORE U.S. COMMISSIONER PENDERY.
Messrs. Chambers, of Cincinnati, Wall & Finnell of Kentucky, for the Claimant—Messes. Jolliffe & Gitchell for the Slaves.
SPEECH OF MR. JOLLIFFE.

On the opening of the Court yesterday morning, Mr. JOLLIFFE commenced his argument. He said: I have reason to rejoice to-day in behalf of my clients and of the country, that this case is to be tried before a gentleman who has tried similar cases, and had the moral courage to decide against the claimant. It was not the pride of opinion that controlled his judgment, but a sincere conviction of the truth and justice of such a course.

I will first notice the arguments of my courteous opponent, Mr. FINNELL. He said Kentucky and Virginia were not responsible for Slavery, but the Yankees, who sold them the negroes. Others have charged that England forced Slavery upon us. But when his ancestors and mine went down to Norfolk to buy slaves, were they not to be blamed? The merchants and traders—sold them for gold—for gold they would have sold the planters as well. But were not they who tempted the merchants to bring them slaves, equally guilty with those who brought them?

He said, also, that it was the Abolitionists who were creating all this agitation, and he denounced them as "pot house politicians." Now, who are the Abolitionists? I know those in Ohio, perhaps, as well as that gentleman, but I do not know among them a single man to whom the phrase, "pot-house politician," could be applied.

The gentleman was ill-advised in his attack. He was firing his grape and cannister into the ranks of his allies, and at every charge they fell. The Union savers, they are the pot house politicians—men who love everything but God and the poor— for the meaner and more degraded a white man is, the more he hates a negro. He further charged us with being ungrateful to Kentucky, who assisted to fight our battles in the Northwest. When Kentucky renders any service to the Union, she, as a State, claims credit for it; but when sacrifices are expected from Ohio, we are to make them entirely for the sake of the Union.

But we do return the kindness. When a poor and friendless Kentuckian comes here naked, we clothe him; hungry, we feed him; oppressed, we relieve him; bound on a journey, we put him on a certain railroad and have him through in lightning speed. If Kentucky feels aggrieved, let her ladies retaliate. Let them set up sewing societies for the poor Ohioans; and as hospitable Kentucky is better than picayune Ohio, let them send ten for one of our poor people to Texas, Kansas, or any such place as they desire to emigrate. (Applause and cries of order.)

No, poor Kentuckians even the most destitute, had friends and counsel here. For all these people, on both sides of this case, are Kentuckians. The only difference between them is that while they (looking towards the slaves) are basically struggling for freedom, that man (looking at Mr. Marshall) comes into Court, his hands all dripping with warm blood, and asks to take the father of that murdered infant back into interminable slavery and the grandfather back into everlasting bondage. (Applause, and cries of order.)

But the gentleman says the Constitution of the U.S. gives him a right to these fugitives.

Oh, star-eyed science, hast thou wandered there
To bring us back the message of despair?

That a straight line is the shortest distance between two points, is an axiom. The proposition on which I shall base my argument is no less plain. It is: THAT EVERY MAN ON EARTH HAS THE RIGHT TO DO EVERY THING THAT GOD HAS MADE IT HIS DUTY TO DO. Or, as I am not here as a theologian to discuss difficult points, but only as a civilian asserting rights, and as some duties are more clearly stated in the Bible, than others, I will vary the form, and say: That every man on earth has the right to do everything that GOD, IN THE BIBLE, HAS CLEARLY MADE IT HIS DUTY TO DO.

God made it the duty of Daniel to pray, though the Persian Empire forbid it—of the three holy children to refuse to bow down before an idol—of the Apostles to preach the doctrine of the resurrection—of Cranmer and Ridley to refuse to bow down to the sacrifice of the Mass—and in doing so they all asserted their right. Right and duty are correlative terms, as inseparably mingled as the light and heat of the sun. Sir, (to the

Commissioner,) it is your right, sitting there as a Commissioner of the U.S., to love God with all your heart, and your neighbor as yourself. It is your right to keep a conscience void of offense. This is a right for which the martyrs suffered, and for which our fathers poured out their blood like water—the right of every American citizen to take the Bible as the man of his council. You have a right to love that old man, (putting his hand on the head of old Simon) as you love yourself, and to do to him as you would have others do to you and it is your duty sitting here in his court of Justice to exercise that right.

Your oath to support the Constitution imposes an obligation to support it all, not only the 3d article of the IV section, but the WHOLE CONSTITUTION.

The Constitution says (1st Amendment) "Congress shall make no law respecting an establishment of religion or prohibiting the free exercise thereof." This may embrace the religion of China and of the Hindoos, but it certainly does embrace the Christian religion. What then is the Christian religion? Its vital principle is too love God with all your heart, and your neighbor as Yourself," and every law that interferes with this (as do the acts '93 and '50 [*sic*]) pierces the very vitals of the Christian religion as the spear of the Roman soldier pierced the heart of Christ on the cross.

Should Congress pass a law forbidding you to read the Bible, does any man doubt that it would be unconstitutional? When Congress passes a law forbidding you to obey the Bible, is not that unconstitutional? What binding force would a law have declaring that there is no God? How much better is an act which says there is a God, but you shall not obey him? The Bible commands to feed the hungry—clothe the naked—shelter the outcast—to break every yoke and let the oppressed go free. The Abolitionists—the hated, the despised—have for the last 25 years been asserting these rights, unconsciously bearing upon their own shoulders the rights of the whole American people.

A few years ago all Christendom were indignant because the Madiar family were imprisoned for reading the Bible. But what difference is there between imprisoning a man for reading the Bible in Italy, and for obeying it in the United States?

All men have a religion, no matter whether members of churches or not—deep down in the heart of every man, is a sense of responsibility to his maker. It may not show itself till called to do some gigantic wrong, but then it rises up to restrain his hand.

When called upon to decide upon a question like this, it is your duty to listen to its voice.

That man (putting his hand on young Simon) is here a prisoner, guilty of no crime, his wife in jail in a delicate situation, needing her husband's aid, and Mr. Marshall asks you to tear him from his wife's arms. His three children, one an infant at the breast demand his care, and you are asked to tear him from both wife and children that this man may take him into Kentucky, to sell his flesh, blood and bones, and soul, on the auction block. Do your duties as a christian, interfere with that? Can you do it and keep your conscience void of offense? Can you do it and maintain for the people of the U.S. the right of religious freedom? When we consider the great question of religious freedom involved in it, the rights of these people become insignificant. It is your right and mine.

Never in the history of jurisprudence has a question of such importance been submitted to the decision of a single man. If you sustain these rights, you sustain religious freedom for us all; if not, you betray humanity.

He then considered the rules of construction by which this Article of the Constitution was to be interpreted, and the purpose for which it was made. Now, said he, if Congress cannot pass a law compelling you to worship God, can they pass a law compelling you to sin against God?

The trouble is this. The Congress of the United States have endeavored to pass a law declaring that wrong was right. There is danger in thus disregarding rights, for every law that supports slavery strikes down some right of the slaveholder. The principle that gives you a right to your slave, may take away your right to your land.

He then read from the Bible the account of the creation of man, "In the image of God created he him," "to have dominion over every living thing that moveth upon the earth." Can man, the lord of creation, be made property? Wherever man is found—no matter how degraded his condition, even the naked negro basking in the sun or lying in the palm tree's shade—he is still the lord of creation. The distinction between man and those over whom he rules is this: that man everywhere, no matter how debased or ignorant, can be taught to love and obey God; brutes never can. Congress had no more right to pass a law that man should bow down before man than that he should bow before the consecrated wafer. Both are heresies—one of America and the other of Europe. What right had Congress to enforce one heresy and refuse the other. It is an article of religious belief in me that man cannot hold property in man. I take it from the Bible. Catholics and Mormons are protected in their creed—why not I in mine?

The law of '50 (The Fugitive Slave Law) commands you to treat those people as slaves; the Bible as men. As slaves they may not learn to read the Bible—nor attend divine service—nor preach the gospel to every creature—nor bring up their children in the nurture and admonition of the Lord—nor cherish their husbands and wives; but as men they enjoy all these rights. Don't you see that the Bible is on one side and the Fugitive Slave law on the other? By the hallowed memory of the Mothers who taught us to reverence that Bible—by the battle fields of our revolutionary sires we must not—dare not relinquish this great and glorious right of loving our neighbor as we love ourselves. The President may send steel clad men to compel us—all the woes of the human race may fall on us, but still on our bended knees and with outstretched hands will we cling to their rights.

Here is an old woman (putting his hand on old Mary's head) for 20 or 30 years an honored and respected member of the Church of Christ. If we could see all things as they are, we should see in this room a host of angels around her—we should see Jesus here. "Whatsoever ye do to the least of these ye do it unto me." If you send her to slavery you send the Saviour—if you send her to the auction block you send Christ there. "Whosoever shall offend one of the least of these, it is better that a millstone be hanged about his neck and that he be cast into the depths of the sea." If Congress enjoins you to pluck out an eye or a hand would you do it? But would it not be better to enter into Heaven without an eye than having two eyes to be cast into Hell fire?

My friends, (turning to the counsel for Mr. Marshall,) what would you have? Just so sure as you tear that sucking babe from the bosom of its mother, the very stones will rise against you, (not in mob violence,) but in six months the Union will be at an end; and better far that it should end, than to sanction such violence. The constitution does not require you to do an act which shall wrap this land in flame and drench it in blood. You have only to assert your own religious freedom. By doing so you refuse Mr. Marshall his fugitives, but you secure him a greater, a dearer right. What right have you to send a writ to the Marshal, requiring him to execute such monstrous wrong? Suppose he were as conscientious as John Wesley—could you ask him to do it? Suppose him, on the other hand, a degraded and wicked man. (I am not alluding to the present Marshal, for I scarcely know him,)—what right have you to add another drop to his cup of iniquity?

It is for you to decide whether this man shall be free to worship God without the haughty shadow of his master between him and his Creator—free to go where he pleases—free to embrace his wife and his children. Then, though all the calamities of earth come upon him, no slaveholder can enter his cabin to drag his loved ones away to helpless bondage. No! thank God, that is (rightly considered) now the law of the land—that is our glorious heritage.

I am aware that this argument has not been used by any of our great men in the Congress of the nation, but the path that the eye of the Vulture hath not seen, may be discovered by animals of more limited vision. Eureka! I have found it! I see it plainly. Do not Kentuckians love religious freedom as well as we do? Do you think because they are slaveholders they mean to go down to Hell? No. What is slavery? Atheism. Not that which denies the existence of a God, but that which denies the immortality of man.

Our friends are those who tell us our faults, and help us to correct them, and the abolitionists are your very best friends, (to Mr. Finnell). These men that are pimping to your vices, are doing so that they may get your money or your votes. They care not whether its you or your black man that's a slave, so they get money by it. But you know where to find us. We speak out and tell you of your vices. But we know that you are a generous open hearted race, and as brave men as ever trod the earth, save only those of Old Virginia.

Slavery is cannibalism, not that of eating, but of selling human flesh and blood, one cuts the man up for food, and the other sells him for money. Now sir, are you required to dip your hands in this bloody system of Cannibalism.

He then read from the Institutes of Justinean, an act commencing, *In nomine domini Jesu Christi.* The way in which civil enactments then commenced. The New Testament has it "do all in the name of the Lord Jesus Christ." Would you head your mandates? In the name of the Lord Jesus Christ, hurl back that old servant of the Lord who has served him thirty years into the seething hell of American slavery? The error in Daniel Webster was that he took but half the Constitution. You must enlarge the basis, and take it all. The theory in matters of civil government is, that there is no higher law. My theory is, that there is a God, and that human governments are valuable only so far as they enable men to obey God. Daniel Webster said in his speech at Cacapon Springs—near where I was born—"the North mountain is higher than the Blue Ridge, and the Allegheny higher than that, but this higher law soars an eagle's flight above them all." Sir, this higher law rises higher than ever eagle flew. If you take the wings of the morning and fly to the uttermost parts of the earth, it is there. Descend to the depths of Hell, and it is there—it follows man through life, through death—and that higher law is with Daniel

Webster to-day, wherever he may be in the universe of God. To send this man back, would be to separate him from his wife, for as she is to be tried separately, the Court will presume her free, until proven otherwise. Can you find a law to separate husband and wife?

Had such a provision been inserted in the act, it would never have been passed. Ask for a law to tear that babe from its mother's breast. When Shakespeare put in the mouth of lady Macbeth "I tear the nipple from its boneless gums and dash its brains out," the poet's imagination could go no farther. But this is not to dash its brains out, (oh its mother would kneel and implore you to do so,) but to send it back to the roaring, seething, hissing hot hell of American slavery.

Will you do it? (To counsel for claimant) Gentlemen, look to it if there is any such law. Take your pound of flesh, but not one drop of blood.

He then recapitulated the testimony, in relation to the fugitives having been in Ohio, and said that the maxim of law was "once free, always free." The Kentucky courts did not deny this, but decided that the freedom must be asserted at the time. But young Simon was then a minor, and Mary a femme covert, so this neglect could not prejudice their case.

Now here is the last one, (putting his hand on the old man's head,) although I most earnestly desire his freedom, yet I cannot misrepresent the testimony. I believe it was Robert's (young Simon) oldest brother, Simon's son, that was here, and the resemblance accounts for the mistake of the witnesses.

I now leave the religious liberty of the U.S. in your hands. Such a case has never before arisen, and if you separate these people it will be such a judgment as has never seen given since Pontius Pilate sat upon the judgment seat.

Mr. Jolliffe closed about half past 12 o'clock, and Col. Chambers said that in view of the new course of argument, he was not prepared to reply, and requested the Court to adjourn to 9 o'clock this morning. . . .

Cincinnati Daily Enquirer, February 8, 1856

On the final day of the first hearing, Chambers's concluding case for the owners was still longer than Jolliffe's argument for the fugitives. Chambers attacked the factual claims made by witnesses for the Garners but then argued that the factual claims were irrelevant, anyway. His legal argument

was largely familiar by this point in the case: much as his colleague Finnell
had a few days earlier, Chambers touched on the import of the Fugitive
Slave Law; the relevance of the Supreme Court's Strader v. Graham *deci-*
sion; the priority that decision gave to the laws of the slave state; and Ken-
tucky laws under which the Garners were still considered slaves. He also
responded to Jolliffe in personal and political terms that ranged well beyond
the legal points at issue before Commissioner Pendery. The following text is
a brief excerpt from that portion of his response.

COL. CHAMBERS

. . . My friend opens upon the claimant, and says he comes into this
Court with hands dripping with warm blood and seeks to tear the
mother from her child, and send it into the seething hell of American
slavery. This is unjust to my client. I know him; he can hold up his
hands with Mr. Jolliffe or any one; he is not answerable for the blood of
that child. If there is guilt resting upon any one besides its mother it is
upon those who invited the mother to do the deed—telling her to take
its life, that it might be laid upon the altar of, freedom and help the glorious cause. What matter though she might go to the gallows, it would
help, and promote the cause of freedom. My client is not guilty of the
blood of that child. . . .

Sir, the action of Abolitionists has deterred the freedom of the slaves
in many of the States; if it had not been for their conduct a law would
have been passed in Kentucky that after 1866 there should be no slaves
born in that State. The disturbances in Kansas would never have taken
place had it not been for the damnable excitement produced by Abolitionists; in endeavoring to save thousands they have bound the shackles
tighter on millions. Their acts tend to the dissolution of the Union, and
the parceling out of the States to Queen Victoria, Prince Joseph and Louis
Napoleon, just as Poland is parceled out now. My friend has graphically
portrayed the battle-field that would be seen when brother should be
arrayed against brother and State against State.

Sir, the man who could cry over the blood of one child and not feel
more affected in contemplating the carnage that would ensue along the
borders of the free and slave States in case of civil war comes under the
cognomen of a fanatic; but I will not pursue the theme further; you are to
decide the matter according to the law and the facts.

Cincinnati Daily Gazette, February 11, 1856

Arguments in the first case concluded on Thursday, February 7. The trial concerning Margaret and her children was expected to begin the following day, but neither the Garners nor Jolliffe appeared in court on Friday. Instead, Commissioner Pendery's courtroom was taken over by the ongoing dispute over who had rightful custody of the fugitives, as lawyers for Marshal Robinson and Hamilton County Sheriff Gazoway Brashears pressed their competing claims. The fugitives were housed in Brashears's county jail, but legal custody resided with the federal marshals; the sheriff sought to replace the marshals as legal custodian. The day's session ended without any resolution. On Saturday morning, Brashears refused to release the Garners into the marshals' hands until the commissioner ruled on his motion. Pendery swiftly ruled against Brashears, who then delivered the fugitives. The official legal case of Margaret Garner and her children began moments later. The following document reports on the first day's testimony and argument.

The Fugitive Slave Case.
First Day of the Trial of the Mother and her Children.

Archibald K. Gaines, Claimant, *vs.* Margaret Garner and her three children.

Court met at 9 o'clock, but the fugitive did not appear for some time.

A little after 10 o'clock, Margaret and her children were brought in. She is about five feet three inches in height, and rather stoutly than delicately made. She is a mulatto, showing from one-fourth to one-third white blood. Her forehead is high, and has a protuberance (not so large, of course,) but something like that which made Daniel Webster's so striking. Her eyebrows are delicate lines finely arched, and her eyes, though not remarkably large, are bright and intelligent. The African appears in the lower part of her face—in the broad nose and thick lips. Her ear is small; her wrist and hand large, and she wears a plain gold or brass ring on the little finger of the left hand. She is twenty-two or three years of age.

She was dressed in a dark calico, with a small handkerchief on her shoulders, pinned closely about her neck, and a yellow cotton handkerchief was wrapped turban-like or *a la ole Virginy* around her head.

The child in her arms is a little girl about nine months old, and is much lighter in color than herself—light enough to show a red tinge in its cheeks.

Her eyes during the trial were generally cast down. She would look up occasionally for an instant with a timid, apprehensive glance at the strange faces around her. The babe, with its little hands, was continually fondling her face, but she rarely noticed it, and her general expression was one of extreme sadness. Only once when it put its hand to her mouth we observed her smile upon it, and playfully bite its little fingers with her lips.

On the left side of her forehead, just above the outer extremity of her eye brow is an old scar, and on the cheek bone of the same side, another. We asked her how those scars came there. She said "White man struck me."

The boys are four and six years old, respectively and are bright-eyed, wooly-headed, cunning looking little fellows, as almost all little black boys are. Their fat cheeks dimple when they laugh, and they amused themselves most of the time during the trial, by sitting on the floor and playing with the turned table legs.

The murdered child was almost white—and was a little girl of rare beauty.

MR. ARCHIBALD K. GAINES, the master, is not a large man, being but little above medium height, and quite slender. His head is small—his hair bushy, standing up, and gray. He wears whiskers, meeting at the chin, also gray. His face is thin, the lower part quite narrow, and marked with numerous lines. He has a small foot and hand; the latter looks rough, but more from exposure than labor. His dress is careless, but his general manner and appearance rather gentlemanly. There is nothing coarse, disagreeable or repulsive about his appearance, but on the contrary, he seems to be, (and we have no doubt he is,) an agreeable and intelligent gentleman. He is a member of the old school Presbyterian church—is regarded as very orthodox, and is the chief supporter of the church clergyman of that denomination in his neighborhood.

THE COURT having announced that it was ready to proceed with the case,

MR. JOLLIFFE applied for a continuance, on the ground that the only witness by whom they expected to prove Margaret's having been in Ohio by the consent of her master, was now in Oregon, and they wished time to get his deposition.

MARGARET'S DEPOSITION was offered, which stated that when a small girl she had been brought by John P. Gaines (who then owned her) and Eliza Gaines, to Cincinnati to nurse their daughter, Mary Gaines, who is now living with her uncle in Kentucky, and that her children have all been born since she was thus brought into Ohio. She asks time to get the deposition of John P. Gaines, who now lives in Oregon Territory, of which he was not long since Governor.

THE COURT decided that the case should go on, but in the event that the Commissioner should decide this point material to the case, he would then make proper provision for obtaining this testimony.

MR. JOLLIFFE then rose and made a professional statement (the first he had made in the case). It was to the effect that he verily believed the deposition of Margaret to be true, and that if the cases of the mother and children could be severed, and she made a witness, that she would state the facts given in her deposition. He therefore asked that the mother and children be tried separately, in order that she might be a witness for them.

MR. WALL objected to this "most strenuously." They were all claimed together as slaves under one warrant, and what the mother might swear to after the frenzy she had exhibited, they did not know, and would not risk.

MR. JOLLIFFE replied, that if on sending for Mr. Gaines' deposition he should prove to be dead, this would be depriving them of their own chance to prove their freedom.

THE COURT decided against a severance.

MR. JOLLIFFE then asked that Rev. A. A. Livermore be appointed as guardian *ad litem* for "Cilley," the babe.

COL. CHAMBERS thought such a proposition too absurd for argument. It was bringing the case where the gentleman had all along tried to put it, viz: within the humanities.

THE COURT decided against the appointment of guardian, and the evidence for the claimant was then commenced.

TESTIMONY FOR THE CLAIMANT.

DR. ELIJAH SMITH CLARKSON sworn, said—I know that woman and two of the children—the two oldest. The woman is called Peggy, (for Margaret) largest boy called Tom—the next, Sam. These people are under the laws of Kentucky slaves to Archibald K. Gaines, the claimant here. Have known her 20 years—from a child two years old. Has all that time been a slave. She has belonged to claimant about 10 years I should think—before that time she was owned by Major John P. Gaines, late Governor of Oregon. The mother also belonged to Major Gaines. Peggy is twenty-three or four years old to the best of my knowledge. Has had a child within a year—did not attend her on that occasion—went over the next day and found her doing well enough.

Cross examined—Margaret or Peggy's mother's name was "Cilley." They both belonged to Jno. P. Gaines, and became the property of this claimant by purchase. I lived in the neighborhood at the time of the alleged purchase. Have lived within a mile and a half of Mr. Gaines for 20 years. It is customary to transfer slaves by bill of sale, but have known sales without this. J. P. Gaines had a daughter—Miss Mary Gaines—who is probably about 17 at this time. She is now in Kentucky. I presume John P. Gaines to be now in Oregon. Been there about 6 years. I was family physician for John P. Gaines. Mr. Gaines has other brothers,—Richard, Benjamin, William, and Le Grand. One of them lives near Natchez, and one I think in New Orleans. Their mother lives with Mr. Archibald Gaines; is a widow. Do not know whether Mrs. Elizabeth Gaines does not claim to be the owner of Peggy during her life. Mr. Gaines has several other slaves beside these. She is the wife of Simon. —Ques. —"Is he the father of these children?" Col. Chambers— "We admit that."

MAJOR WM. B. MURPHY sworn said: I know Peggy, there; have known her for some time. I declare I can't say how long; she is said to belong to Mr. Gaines; claimed by him as his slave, and served him as such. Known her as such from six to ten years. Live some three and a half miles from Mr. Gaines.

CROSS EXAMINED—When I first saw her it was said she was the property of Jno. P. Gaines. He was then living where Archibald K. Gaines now lives. Was not present when she was sold to the present claimant. Am not certain I ever saw her on the plantation of Mr. Archibald Gaines. Have seen her about the neighborhood and knew her as Mr. Gaines' woman. Miss Mary Gaines is now about 15 or 16 years old.

First saw Peggy in Ohio last Monday week. —Mary Garner and her husband and Simon were with her, and her three children that she has here, and another one. It was at a house below Millcreek bridge; I saw the other child; its throat was cut. Objected to by Col. Chambers. COURT stated that as the warrant embraced four children it was proper to show what had become of the other one. It was finally admitted that one child was killed, and that the mother attempted to kill the other three, at the time of the arrest; that one has a cut on its throat; one, on its head, and the infant a blow.

Ques. by MR. JOLLIFFE—Did Simon, this woman's husband, shoot one of the persons making the arrest at the time? Objected to by Col. Chambers, and objection sustained by the Court.

Adjourned to Monday morning at 10 o'clock.

After the crowd passed out, the little negro boys were carried down in the arms of the Marshal, and the woman Peggy, taking the proffered arm of the polite Deputy U. S. Marshal, Mr. Brown, was escorted to the omnibus.

Cincinnati Daily Gazette, February 12, 1856

The dispute before Commissioner Pendery over Margaret Garner and her children moved more quickly than had the proceedings on Robert, Simon, and Mary Garner. While it was Margaret's actions on the day of her capture that made this case so notorious and legally complex, by the time her hearing began the lawyers had already rehearsed their main theories and arguments. The most important break from the pattern established in the earlier proceedings came on the second day of Margaret's case, when she gave evidence in court. That she was able to do so was exceptional. Under Section 6 of the Fugitive Slave Act, alleged slaves whose cases were being decided by a federal commissioner were not permitted to testify (see appendix). When Jolliffe sought to call Margaret to the stand, it was thus entirely predictable that opposing counsel Chambers would object. The equally predictable response by Pendery would have been to sustain that objection. Surprisingly, Pendery accepted Jolliffe's device for smuggling in Margaret's testimony, allowing her to speak as a witness for her children, not herself. The following article thus documents what may well be the only instance in which a fugitive captured under this law was allowed to testify in court. But what kind of record of that testimony does the Gazette *provide? The account of Margaret's words is clearly something of a paraphrase. Although it is thus not entirely certain how much of the blandness and brevity of her remarks is due to the reporter's way of rendering her answers, none of the versions offered in the coverage by the other local dailies differs meaningfully from this one in either content or tone.*

The Fugitive Slave Case.
Second day of the Trial of the Mother and her Children.

Archibald K. Gaines, Claimant, *vs.* Margaret Garner and her three children.

Court met at 10 o'clock.

On entering we were surprised to see a large number of gentlemen wearing the badge of the Legion of Honor (a red ribbon in the button hole). The first thought was that they might be distinguished Frenchmen—invited guests to the 22d February celebration—but we afterwards learned that the special U.S. Marshals appointed to guard this Negro woman and her three children, had so high an appreciation of the duty that they had thought proper to compliment the Legion of Honor by assuming its badge.

TESTIMONY FOR THE CLAIMANT CONTINUED.

PETER NOLAN sworn, said:

Know the woman and her three children—knew them for four or five years in Boone Co., in Mr. Gaines' possession—as his slaves.

I lived a year on Mr. Gaines' place, and worked more or less with him for the last five years.

CROSS-EXAMINED—Lived not much over a quarter of a mile from Mr. Gaines' house. Know that this woman is Mr. Gaines' slave only from seeing her on the place, and understanding that she belonged to him. Mr. Gaines' family consists of four children and his wife. His mother lives with him, and has ever since I can recollect. Am not sure that this woman Peggy does not belong to old Mrs. Gaines. Never heard her claim her.

A bill of sale from John P. Gaines to the claimant was then offered, and on Mr. Finnell's stating that he knew it to be Jno. P. Gaines' handwriting—that he corresponded with him, etc., it was admitted without being legally proven. It read as follows:

"I have sold and delivered to A. K. Gaines five slaves. Sam, Harry, Peggy, Hannah and Charlotte, and all my right and interest thereto, for the sum of $2,500, which sum I acknowledge the receipt of. Given under my hand this 17th day of November, 1849.

JNO. P. GAINES."

Col. Chambers explained the recent date of this by stating that it was given to supply an old one that was lost.

JOHN ASHBROOK sworn said: Know Peggy; the two eldest children, the youngest I don't know; have known Peggy for fifteen or sixteen years; she was then the slave of John P. Gaines; about six years since he sold out to Archibald Gaines, the claimant here; I have been in the habit of purchasing Mr. Gaines stock.

JAMES MARSHALL (the owner of Simon, Peggy's husband, and the claimant in the former case) was called and said: I know Peggy and the two oldest boys; have known her for twenty years; she belonged to Major John P. Gaines during a part of that time and the residue to Archd. K. Gaines; she escaped from Kentucky last Sunday night two weeks; know Simon, Peggy's husband; he was born mine; Peggy has belonged to Mr. Archibald Gaines some 12 or 14 years.

CROSS EXAMINED. —Lastly saw Peggy in Kentucky a while before Christmas.

Statutes of Kentucky were then offered in evidence especially that part of them from page 627 to 648 relating to slaves, also page 364, where it states a slave after five years possession, becomes absolute property, so that no proof of title or bill of sale is necessary.

The claimant rested his case here.

TESTIMONY FOR THE SLAVES.

ANN SMITH, a colored woman, sworn. —Am a nurse. Commenced nursing between 5 and 6 years of age. They were white children—in the families where I lived. It is a common thing for children 5, 6 or 7 years old to nurse white children in the families they belong.

CROSS EXAMINED—Am 38 years old. Have lived in this State some 20 odd years.

MARY LIPSCOM, colored—It is a common thing for colored children of 5 or 7 years old to nurse white children. I had the whole charge of Mr. Piatt's child by his first wife, (he now has his third wife) when I was 7 1/2 years old.

CROSS EXAMINED—Don't know exactly how old I am. Think I am about 28 or 9.

ANN COX (colored) sworn—Made a statement similar to that of the last witness.

CROSS-EXAMINED—Knew a lady to take with her, on a journey, as a nurse, a little dark girl between six and seven years of age. The lady was Mrs. John Forsyth; she was sister of Mrs. Judge Riddle, in Pittsburgh. Knew another instance: Mrs. Eldred of Harrisburg, where I was born. I am 36 years old; lived in Cincinnati since the high water in 1847.

MRS. LEWIS, colored, sworn, said, she commenced nursing in Charlottesville, Va., when she was between five and six years old.

CROSS EXAMINED—Am 25 years old now.

MRS. DIANAH BAKER, black, sworn, said she began to nurse in Charleston, S.C., when she was between six and seven years old. Nursed two children one an infant and one just able to get around about.

CROSS EXAMINED—Was born on the very day that Lafayette celebrated South Carolina.

DR. WILLIAM. PRICE, having affirmed, said—I graduated as a physician in 1809, at the Pennsylvania Medical College; have practiced ever since; practiced in Philadelphia and in this city; children at the age of 5 and 6 are frequently employed in families to nurse children; not to have the entire charge, but to assist in nursing.

CROSS EXAMINED—Never lived in a slave State; have seen an infant placed in the charge of a child not more than 6 years old, for an hour or more; would not be any thing unreasonable to take a child of that age on a visit, 18 miles distant, to nurse the infant.

MR. JOLLIFFE then said:

I now offer in evidence a duly certified copy of an indictment found by the Grand Jury of Hamilton county against Margaret Garner, charging her with murder in the first degree.

COL. CHAMBERS objected.

MR. JOLLIFFE wished to introduce this to prove that he cannot have the certificate for the transfer of Margaret Garner that he is asking for. That the indictment was a bar to it. It was for the Court to decide whether the Fugitive Slave law over rides the law of Ohio to such an extent that it cannot arrest a fugitive slave, even for the crime of murder. He then read the 10th amendment to the Constitution, stating that all rights not delegated in the Constitution are reserved to the States, etc., etc. This execution of its own criminal laws every State has reserved to itself, and no act of Congress can interfere with it.

These slaves cannot, after being remanded, be re-claimed as fugitives from justice. A demand for a fugitive from justice must be based on affidavit that the person so demanded fled. She cannot flee when she goes by force—by order of Court and against her will. She cannot be arrested under any process after the Commissioner shall have granted his certificate. The writ of capias under an indictment for murder cannot stay the delivery. If the certificate is granted, it wrests from the State the right to punish murder.

If this was decided to be the law a fugitive could, on the trial, shoot down the Marshals, or even the Commissioner, and he could not be punished for so doing. Paramount is this right—the right of the State is superior to all private claims.

COL. CHAMBERS—This was a repetition of the old story that this woman preferred the gallows to delivery in Kentucky.

The practical effect of all these sort of motions was to abolish the Fugitive Slave Law at once. —All a fugitive would have to do would be to commit some trifling offence and he would become the prisoner of the State of Ohio.

The Court observed that it could not be received because it had already a motion pending on this question.

MR. JOLLIFFE. —We have one other witness—we want Margaret Garner sworn as a witness, not for herself, but on behalf of her three children.

COL. CHAMBERS objected on the ground that being a fugitive the provisions of the Fugitive Slave Law directly forbid her being a witness for herself or any body else.

After a long discussion the Court stated that it had refused to sever the cases, simply on the ground of delay, but could see no objection to admitting the woman's testimony in behalf of her children and she was accordingly put on the stand and sworn.

MARGARET GARNER (the mother of the three living and of the murdered child) being sworn, was asked: Were you ever in Ohio before? Ans. Yes, sir. Ques., When? Ans. I came here when I was about seven years old. (To other questions from time to time, her answers were as follows:) I came here with John Gaines and his wife; her name was Eliza Gaines. They came on a visit to Mr. Bush's who lived in Covington, and staid there a week. During that time they spent one day over here, and they brought me over to nurse the baby; that was Mary Gaines. Mary wasn't quite as large then as my baby. (Her baby is about nine months old.) They brought me across the river to Cincinnati. We came over pretty soon in the morning, and staid tolerable late in the evening.

Don't know whether it was a tavern or private house they stopped at. Don't remember the name of the people where they stayed. Was never over any other time than that. I'll be 23 years old the 4th day of next June. Miss Mary Gaines is very near 17 years old. She's at her uncle Archibald's in Boone county. John P. Gaines was my master at that time. That was before he sold me to Archibald K. Gaines. Don't recollect anything particular on that day I was over here, except that my mistress was very particular in keeping me close by her. Kept me sitting by her side all the time. Don't know what they came over here for. Mrs. Jno. P. Gaines is dead. She died in Oregon. John P. Gaines is in Oregon. Pretty near 7 years since he went there. These three children here with me are mine. All been born since I was here in Ohio with John P. Gaines.

As far as I understand old Mrs. Gaines owned me; I lived with her; often heard her say, when Mr. Gaines was by, that I was her servant; never heard him deny it; never heard him say it was so.

MR. JOLLIFFE. Take the witness.

COL. CHAMBERS. I've nothing to say to her.

At 2 o'clock Court took a recess for 30 minutes.

MR. GEO. J. GUILFORD, of the *Commercial,* was called for, but not appearing, it was agreed to admit Mr. Guilford's testimony on the first trial, to wit: that Mr. Marshall had told him that these people had all been in Ohio before their escape.

Court met again, after the recess, at 3 o'clock.

REBUTTING TESTIMONY FOR THE CLAIMANT—JAMES MARSHALL re-called—Never knew a child 7 years old employed as a nurse in Kentucky; never heard of the like before to-day. Cross Examined—never knew one of that age employed to nurse a child even in the presence of her mistress; have no recollection of ever seeing a girl 7 years old take a child.

W. D. GRIFFING, JOHN C. HUGHES, and JOHN ARMSTRONG, were also called to the same point and made statements similar to Mr. Marshall's.

The testimony of both parties closed here. It being four o'clock, the commencement of the argument was postponed until this morning.

Adjourned to nine o'clock this morning.

Cincinnati Daily Times, February 12, 1856

On February 12 both sides made their concluding arguments. Three lawyers summed up the Garners' case, with Samuel S. Fisher joining Gitchell and Jolliffe, while Samuel T. Wall argued for the claimants. For reasons that are impossible to determine at this remove, the day's reporting in Cincinnati's press was unusually spotty. None of the papers, regardless of political orientation or views on the case, reported the arguments of Gitchell or Jolliffe in any detail. Only the Enquirer *offered a lengthy account of Wall's argument for Archibald Gaines, while the* Cincinnati Daily Times *was*

*alone in reporting extensively on Fisher's advocacy for the Garners. The
next two documents are drawn from the stories in the two papers. (Fisher's
remarks are reprinted first, even though he addressed the court hours after
Wall. Because the* Daily Times *was an evening paper, its report appeared on
the day the arguments were made, while the* Enquirer's *account of Wall's
remarks appeared the following morning.)*

    *Much of Fisher's argument followed the by now familiar pattern,
asserting the priority of state's rights over federal power and reiterating the
theory that an earlier visit to free soil had emancipated his client, placing
her beyond the reach of the Fugitive Slave Act. But Fisher also questioned
whether the Peggy on the bill of sale submitted to the court was in fact
Margaret Garner and, in his conclusion, offered a political analysis of the
meaning of Garner's decision to take her daughter's life. That latter commentary is included in the excerpt below.*

In alluding to the murder of the child, Mr. F. said he regreted that the
circumstance had occurred, and while he did not regard it in any other
light than a crime, he could not assent to the belief that it was committed
in mere ignorance and exasperation. No! he believed the love of liberty
had something to do with it—it was done for freedom. He would ask
what was the difference between the story of Virginius, who killed his
daughter in the Roman forum, and the story of this woman who killed
her child. In his case it was for liberty, in this case it was the same: they
are parallel. There is but little doubt that she intended also to have killed
herself. I thank God, sir, that such a result did not transpire. My southern
brethren love liberty, but they say that their slaves do not. This act of the
mother was an unanswerable reply to them, and must forever shut the
mouths of those who claim that the ignorant do not rank with the educated in their instinctive love of freedom. . . .

    Mr. Jolliffe followed Mr. Getchell [*sic*] in his usual pathetic and forc-
ible manner. During his remarks the Court room was honored by the
presence of Mrs. Lucy Stone Blackwell, who took a seat and listened
attentively to the speaker. After he had concluded, she was introduced
to Mr. Gaines, the claimant, with whom she had considerable conversation, the nature of which we did not ascertain. She afterwards spoke with
Margaret for some time. We have heard it said her object is, in case the
slave-mother should be sent back to slavery, to purchase her freedom, if
found out on what terms her emancipation can be secured.

Cincinnati Daily Enquirer, February 13, 1856

The following is the complete text of Wall's remarks, as the Enquirer *rendered them.*

FUGITIVE SLAVE CASE.
Before U.S. Commissioner J.T. Pendery

Arguments of S.T. Wall, Esq., of Covington, for the Claimant, and Messrs. Fisher, Gitchell and Jolliffe for the Defense.

S.T. Wall, Esq., addressed the Court as follows:

If the court please, I cannot but admire the patience with which your Honor has disposed of questions, sometimes for and sometimes against me, and which latter I have always borne without murmur.

This will always be a leading case in the slave cases of this country, and the endeavor of your Honor to discover the truth and to declare your honest opinion upon this law from the evidence before you and to give a decision worthy of the great case in which you have so long been engaged. I shall not pander to the passions of the people of the South; I shall not discuss the chivalry of the Southern people nor the magnanimity and benevolence of the people of the North. We have had, during the investigation of this case, a great number of strong men and delicate if not fair women, who always conducted themselves with propriety while in the court-room.

I must say that the attorneys for the defense have resorted to every device (legitimate of course) to protract the already long-protracted continuance of this case, and have entirely failed to prove anything worthy of the time consumed in the hearing of the case.

What was the condition of these people in Kentucky? They were well cared for, as is evidenced by their appearance in Court. They were enjoying the comforts of a family in which themselves and their ancestors have long been held as slaves and from whom they always received great kindness.

The slavery of Kentucky is in so mild a form that I infinitely prefer it to the poverty of the North. The condition of slaves in the South is much better, I assure your Honor, than the half-starved free colored people of the North.

The desire of these people to go into the seething cauldron of Northern fanaticism is not attended with any beneficial results, either to themselves or their brethren in the South. It only serves to fasten the chains of slavery more firmly around them. It only serves to bind the fetters closer.

There are mutual confidences in the South between the master and slaves, and they will be destroyed and each will distrust the other by the occurrence of such scenes as these; and further, sir, I am bound to say that had it not been for fanaticism in the North there would already have commenced a gradual emancipation of the slaves in Kentucky. It may be, sir, that slavery will be abolished in Kentucky, but the slaves will not receive any benefit from that abolition. They will be sold from their own homes to districts further South, from their old associations.

Abolitionism is a weed of recent growth. Even in my recollection (twenty five years), it was not invented. Such a word was not then in the language. At that time my father, a large slave owner, was discussing how gradually to emancipate his slaves and how to get rid of the evil. Why, sir, in Kentucky thief and Abolitionist are synonymous terms. I confess, sir, that I, living on the borders of my State, have known and do now know Abolitionists in whom I have every confidence, and I would lie down with them with money in my pocket fearless of being robbed.

Kentucky is not the aggressor. The debt which Ohio owes to Kentucky, and which she owes to the mother of States, Virginia, ought to be better repaid than by stealing slaves from these States.

Sir, there was a man who died fifty-eight or nine years ago, named Washington, who was what Kentucky would be, an emancipationist. He got rid of his slaves, who were there and his, not by any act of his own, but thrown upon him by his father. By his will he devised among other things that his slaves should be free, and made some provision for their comfort. His conduct, sir, is but a type of what Kentucky would have done had it not been for the hair brained fanatics of the North.

There was a man whom I have heard of who said, rather than be driven to do right he would do wrong. This, sir, is the condition of the State of Kentucky. I freely confess it. Instead of making laws for the gradual abolition of this evil, she has passed more strenuous laws for the perpetuation of the institution. And this, sir, is the consequence of the Abolition excitement of the North. Reference has been made to the present and past relations of the States of Ohio and Kentucky. I have no reason to complain about the present condition of my native State, which has produced as much of genius, patriotism and ability as any State or Territory of equal dimensions in the world.

I remember several years ago of having seen the Indians of Ohio on their way to the far West. They were removing from their old homes, from their hallowed associations in the land of their birth, and by whom, sir, were they removed? Not by the aid of British arms, or sympathy, but, sir, by the benevolent, magnanimous, tender hearted people of Ohio. By those who cry out whenever an occasion offers, and often when there is no such occasion, against the people of the South and their peculiar institution of slavery. By those who would subvert the Constitution of the United States and the laws made to pursuance thereof, and would make them subject to the so-called sovereignty of Ohio.

But now, sir, the State of Ohio has become, at least partially so, Abolitionized, and the reverend Abolition infidels have come from England, and other reverend gentlemen Abolitionists have united together, for what purpose? Why, sir, to steal Kentucky negroes. To steal that property which is sacred to us, and which is protected by our National Constitution. What effect will your decision have on the interests of the people of the South? I need not examine the testimony. We have proved the property to be A.K. Gaines', and that we are entitled to the possession of that property. We have been disposed to give no offense. Instead of taking these slaves back to Kentucky (as we might have done by the aid of the friendly bridge of ice) by force from the house of Elijah Kite, we have appealed to the courts of the country.

The defense in this case is, I understand, two-fold. The Grand Jury of Hamilton county have, on their oaths, presented an indictment for murder in the first degree against Margaret Garner, and she is liable, according to the gentleman's proposition, to be suspensus per cullum— hanged by the neck—when ever the public prosecutor shall see fit to so order. This, sir, is one of the defenses made by the gentleman—that this woman, having violated the criminal laws of the State of Ohio, ought to answer to that charge now. A very singular device, indeed, sir, to avoid the responsibilities of the Fugitive slave Law.

The other theory of the defense, is raised by the testimony of Margaret Garner, who was sworn on behalf of her children, and who testified to facts which your Honor perfectly remembers. Now, sir, what is that testimony? She says that some twelve or fifteen years ago she came to Ohio to nurse Miss Mary Gaines, a daughter of her owner at that time (Major John P. Gaines) and that these three children have been born since she so came to Ohio. This, sir, is the testimony of this woman who has barbarously murdered one of her children, whose hands have been imbued in the blood of her offspring. Of what benefit can her testimony be. Not being competent as to herself, how can it avail her children. She has not been proved by any other than her own testimony ever to have been in Ohio; and such being the fact, that no such testimony has been presented to the Court as will prove conclusively that the mother has been in Ohio, the testimony of the mother cannot be of any benefit to her children. And these remarks I make, sir, taking it for granted that the theory of the defense is correct, to wit.: That free soil makes free men.

It is not my province to argue the moral right or moral wrong of slavery; I have only given to the Court my humble views upon the facts in this case, and I leave the matter with the Court. . . .

Cincinnati Daily Gazette, February 14, 1856

Arguments before Commissioner Pendery concluded on February 13. Even as he left the scene, however, his courtroom provided a platform for the antislavery activist Lucy Stone to enter the battle for public opinion. Different versions of her remarks on this day circulated in papers across the free states. Now regarded as one of the century's most important suffragists, Stone was at the time she took up the Garner case already renowned both for her magnetism as a speaker and for her uncompromising advocacy of women's equality. (There is a reasonable chance, then, that when Archibald Gaines first spoke with her in the court, he knew something about who she was and what she stood for.) Stone had only recently married fellow suffragist and abolitionist Henry Blackwell in a ceremony during which the bride and groom's denunciation of existing marriage law was read aloud. The couple formally agreed that Stone would retain her name, an arrangement often credited as the oldest such instance on record in the United States. The agreement clearly did not impress all journalists and editors, though, for they often violated it when reporting on her activities.

The Fugitive Slave Case.
Fourth day of the Trial of the Mother
and her children.

ARCHIBALD K. GAINES, CLAIMANT, VS. MARGARET
GARNER AND HER THREE CHILDREN

CONCLUSION OF THE ARGUMENT—SPEECHES BY COL.
CHAMBERS AND LUCY STONE.

Colonel Chambers commenced his argument a little after 10 o'clock, yesterday morning, and closed at ten minutes before 3 P.M. In the course of it he alluded, several times, to Mrs. Lucy Stone Blackwell, who had been present the day previous, but was not then in the Court Room. He alluded, also, to an interview Mrs. Blackwell had had with the slave mother, in the course of which, said the Colonel, she asked of the Deputy U.S. Marshall Mr. Brown, the privilege of giving her a knife, that she might destroy herself in case she was remanded back to slavery.

On the close of Col. Chambers' remarks, Mr. Jolliffe, after correcting a misrepresentation of himself by the Colonel, expressed regret that Mrs. Blackwell was not present to answer the attack he had made upon her. Col. C. joined in the regret, and just at that moment Mrs. Blackwell entered, and on application by Mr. Jolliffe, opposed by counsel on the other side, the COURT gave her permission to reply to Col. Chambers. She however preferred not to speak at the bar, but as it was near the time of closing, requested the audience to remain a few moments after the adjournment to hear her explanation.

The COMMISSIONER then stated that as many new points had arisen in this case which had never been fairly adjudicated he should in justice to all parties and to himself take ample time for investigation. This he should do conscientiously, endeavoring to know nothing but the law and the facts in this case. He had fixed Wednesday the 12th of March (4 weeks from to day) to give his decision.

Col. CHAMBERS objected to fixing so distant a day, on account of the expense to his clients, and Jacob Flinn thought it would be better not to announce the day, so as to avoid collision between the Sheriff and the U.S. Marshal. In consideration of these objections, the Court stated that if they felt prepared to give the judgment sooner, notice would be given to the counsel.

The Court then adjourned to Wednesday, the 12th March, and the fugitives were immediately taken out in the custody of Mr. Brown, Special Marshal.

The Marshal, Mr. Bennet, then called the meeting to order, and Mr. Pullen was appointed Chairman.

LUCY STONE BLACKWELL'S SPEECH

Mrs. Blackwell then took the platform and said:

I am only sorry that I was not in when Col. Chambers said what he did say about me, and about my giving a knife to the poor woman who has just gone out. I returned to town only yesterday or I should have been here during every day of this trial. When I came here and saw that poor fugitive, took her toil-hardened hand, and read in her face deep suffering and an ardent longing for freedom, I could not help bid her be of good cheer. I told her that a thousand hearts were aching for her, and they were glad that one child of hers was safe with the angels. Her only reply was a look of deep despair—of anguish such as no word can speak.

I thought then that the spirit she manifested was the same with that of our ancestors to whom we had erected the monument at Bunker Hill—the spirit that would rather let us all go back to God than back to slavery.

The faded faces of the negro children tell too plainly to what degradation female slaves submit. Rather than give her little daughter to that life, she killed it. If in her deep maternal love she felt the impulse to send her child back to God, to save it from coming woe, who shall say she had no right to do so? That desire had its root in the deepest and holiest feelings of our nature—implanted alike in black and white by our common Father. With my own teeth would I tear open my veins, and let the earth drink my blood, rather than wear the chains of slavery. How then could I blame her for wishing her child to find freedom with God and the angels, where no chains are?

I know not whether this Commissioner has little children, else I would appeal to him to know how he would like to have them torn from him; but I feel that he will not disregard the Book which says, "Thou shalt not deliver unto his master the servant which is escaped from his master unto thee: he shall dwell with thee, even among you, in that place which he shall choose in one of thy gates, where it liketh him best."

After talking with this poor slave woman, I talked with her master, (no, I cannot say her master, for one [*sic*] is your master, even Christ.) I told him that these were heroic times, and that his heroic action of his slave might send his name to posterity as her oppressor—or if he choose—as the generous giver of her freedom. He said, "If I get her back to Kentucky, I mean to make her free."

After she concluded, Col. Chambers rose and said that he was authorized by his client to deny the statement made by Mrs. Blackwell that he would free Margaret. He said when he got her back to Kentucky, he would consider whether he would free her or not.

Mrs. Blackwell repeated that he had promised her to free Margaret, and said this was an evasion. He had told her just what she stated.

The meeting then dispersed.

Cincinnati Daily Gazette, February 27, 1856

---

*Although Commissioner Pendery had announced that he would issue his
ruling on the Garner case on March 12, he tried to conclude as early as the
morning of February 21. His attempt that morning was thwarted, however,
when the custody fight reignited: Sheriff Brashears and a crew of armed
deputies evicted the marshals from the city jail, refusing to let them bring
the Garners to court. When Pendery seemed indecisive in responding,
Marshal Robinson turned to a loftier federal authority, petitioning Judge
Humphrey Leavitt for a writ that would force the sheriff to back down. At
noon on February 26, arguments before Leavitt, held in the same courtroom
used by Pendery, concluded. Less than two hours later, Pendery entered
the court and read his ruling aloud from the bench. Though it could not
take effect until Judge Leavitt resolved the struggle between the sheriff and
the marshal, Pendery's decision was an unequivocal victory for Gaines and
Marshall, and a disaster for the Garners. The versions of that decision provided in Cincinnati's papers the following morning differ in minor details,
but are the same on all important points and even on most of the wording,
so we can be confident that the following document renders Pendery's text
accurately enough.*

THE FUGITIVE SLAVE CASES.
DECISION OF COMMISSIONER PENDERY.
The Fugitives remanded back to Slavery.

At half-past one o'clock yesterday afternoon, Commissioner Pendery
opened his Court in the U.S. Court Rooms, (Judge Leavitt giving way)
and gave his decision. He commenced by saying:

Previous to the disposition of the cases now before us, we shall pass
upon the motion: "That we discharge Margaret Garner, Simon Garner,
senior, Simon Garner, junior, and Mary Garner, from the custody of the
U.S. Marshal and deliver them into the possession of said Sheriff." This
motion is based upon an indictment found by the Grand Jury of Hamilton County, Ohio, charging them with the crime of Murder in the First
Degree, and a capias issued upon said indictment for their arrest.

We find no law to warrant us in making such order, and therefore
overrule the motion.

He then proceeded to consider the claim of Marshall to Simon Garner, Senior, Simon Garner, Junior, and Mary Garner.

On the 28th of January, 1856, Archibald K. Gaines, a citizen of Boone county, and State of Kentucky, made an affidavit, etc., that one negro man named Simon Garner, Senior, aged about 55 years; one negro man named Simon Garner, Junior, aged about 25 years; and one negro woman named Mary Garner, aged about 50 years; who owe labor and service to James Marshall, for life, under the laws of Kentucky, escaped from the State of Kentucky.

The testimony for the claimant shows that these persons are held by the said James Marshal as slaves for life under the laws of Kentucky, that the above named persons are the identical ones described in the claimant's affidavit, and that they escaped on the night of the 28th day of January last, from said county and State into the Southern District of Ohio, where the U.S. marshal made the arrest.

The testimony for the defense is, in substance, that Simon Garner, junior, and Mary Garner, have both been in Ohio previous to their escape, with the claimant's consent; but no proof of that kind is offered as to Simon Garner, senior.

These are the principal facts elicited in the investigation of this case.

The only question which we propose to discuss in this case, is, "does the fact of the temporary visit to Ohio of Simon Garner, junior, and Mary Garner, with the consent of their master, prior to their escape, affect the rights of the claimant?" Or, in other words, James Marshal having permitted these persons to come into Ohio, and they having voluntarily returned into his service, is their relation as master and slave changed?

Upon what principle, then, are we to find young Simon and Mary Garner to be free, when in Ohio by the consent of their master. Is it in the clause of our State Constitution, which declares there shall be no Slavery in this State, nor involuntary servitude, except for the punishment of crime? Article 1st, Section 5th.

The most recent case bearing upon this point is that of Strader et. al. vs. Graham, 5 B. Munroe, 173. The facts in this case were: Strader & Gorman were the owners of the steamboat Pike, and had permitted three slaves of Graham to come on their boat from Louisville to Cincinnati, whence they escaped into Canada. The defense made by Strader & Gorman was that these negroes were musicians, and allowed to travel about by the complainant as free negroes; that the complainant gave them written consent to come to Ohio, and that they remained here for a long time, then returned into the State of Kentucky, into the service of their master, and, therefore, that they were free. Judge Marshall, in delivering the opinion of the Court, held:

1st. That a master residing in Kentucky, and taking his slave with him to Ohio, for a temporary purpose, is not to be understood as renouncing his right to his slave, and on the return of the slave to Kentucky he cannot, on that ground, assert a right to freedom.

2d. The owner of a slave who resides in Kentucky, who permits his slave to go to Ohio in charge of an agent for a temporary purpose, does not forfeit his right of property in such slave."

This case was afterwards removed to the Supreme Court of the United States by a writ of error, and Chief Justice Taney delivered the opinion of the Court, as reported in 10 Howard's Supreme Court Reports, 92. He says: "Much of the argument on the part of the plaintiffs in error has been offered for the purpose of showing that the judgment of the State Court was erroneous in deciding that these negroes were slaves, and it is insisted that their previous employment in Ohio had made them free when they returned into Kentucky."

Although the Chief Justice decided that this was not the question before him, he states: "That the condition of the negroes as to freedom or slavery after their return depended altogether upon the laws of Kentucky, and could not be influenced by the laws of Ohio; that it was exclusively in the power of Kentucky to determine for itself whether their employment in another State should or should not make them free on their return, and that the Court of Appeals having decided that by the laws of that State, they continued to be slaves, that decision was, in his opinion, conclusive."

This same doctrine is also fully maintained by the Supreme Court of the United States, in the case of the United States vs. The Ship Garonne, 11 Peters, Reports, 73. The facts of the case were, that Mrs. Smith, a widow lady of Louisiana, had visited France, and had taken with her the slave Priscilla. Afterwards she was brought back by the son-in-law of Mrs. Smith, and lived in Louisiana as his slave.

Chief Justice Taney, in delivering the opinion of the Court held: That even assuming by the French Laws, that Priscilla was entitled to her freedom, upon her introduction into that country, the Court was of opinion that there was nothing in the act of Congress to prevent her mistress from bringing her back to her place of residence, and continuing to hold her as before in her service, and that, although the girl had been staying for a time in France, in the service of her mistress, yet in contemplation of law, she still continued an inhabitant of Louisiana.

To return to the question; When brought within the State of Ohio for a temporary purpose by the consent of the master, did they become free in consequence of that clause of the Constitution of Ohio which declares

"There shall be no slavery or involuntary servitude within her limits?"
We think not; the true effect of that clause being to prevent slavery as
an institution within her limits, rather than to execute the act of manu-
mission upon foreign slaves temporarily upon our soil with the master's
consent.

Supposing that Ohio has the right under her Constitution to pass
laws making the slave free the moment he stands upon Ohio soil, by the
consent of the master, it is sufficient for the purpose of this case that, at
the time Mary Garner and Simon Garner were in the State of Ohio as
alleged, there was no law declaring that the relations they held to their
master as slaves were dissolved and at an end.

Had they refused to return to Kentucky, it is quite possible that the
owner would have invoked the aid of legal process to compel their return
in vain. The Federal Courts could not have remanded them to the custody and control of their master, because they were present in Ohio by
act of the master, and not as fugitives who had escaped into Ohio. The
Constitution and laws of the United States; all powerful as they are, and
I trust always will be, in national and inner State affairs, were inopera-
tive when by the act of the parties, the whole case was brought within the
jurisdiction and disposal of the State of Ohio.

The aid of legal process from Ohio Courts could not have been
obtained, for Ohio has enacted no laws for the control and management
of foreign slaves while, for the purpose of sojourn or transit, temporarily
within her borders.

With this state of the law, slaves asserting their freedom become,
practically, free. The master has no longer the right of violent subjection
to his command, but the State of Ohio extends to both parties the protection of equal laws.

But this possible freedom, this freedom in *posse,* rather than in *esse,*
is something which the law of Ohio rather protects than creates. That the
slave brought by his master into Ohio, and refusing to return, becomes
free, is one of the inevitable results of the proposition that slavery is a
creature of law, and cannot maintain itself where the laws do not regulate
it, and provide for its continuance.

But the slave having been brought to Ohio by the master, returns
with him voluntarily to the State of Kentucky, what, then, is the relation
between them? While in Ohio, the Ohio courts could have determined
that, for the whole matter was properly within her control. The act of the
parties again changed the jurisdiction, and the whole matter rested again
within the control of the State of Kentucky.

The claim upon the State of Ohio for protection against violent abduction was not made. The right to be free was waived. In coming to Ohio the master voluntarily abandoned his legal power over his slave, and in returning voluntarily the slave has equally abandoned his claim to freedom.

Upon the return of slaves voluntarily to Kentucky with their master, their relations become confirmed by the laws and jurisdiction of that State, and with that settlement of the question the Supreme Court of the United States has declined to interfere. The law, as thus determined, we have already stated in the earlier part of our opinion.

With reference to the particular case before us, we therefore are under the necessity of holding that these defendants, Mary Garner, Simon Garner, jr., were legally held in slavery at the time of their escape on the 26th of January, 1856.

We have given those cases which in our opinion are the leading ones upon this subject, and which throw light upon the issues to be met in this case. They are the landmarks by which we have been guided in our decision.

The next and last question to be settled arises under the Constitutional provision for the rendition of fugitives from labor, under the Fugitive Slave Law, and the facts proved in the case render our duty a clear and unmistakeable one.

The question is not one of humanity that I am called upon to decide. The laws of Kentucky and of the United States make it a question of property. It is not a question of feeling, to be decided by the chance current of my sympathies. There are to be adjudicated the rights of an institution so agreed to in the formation of our Government as to make it both municipal and federal in its character. It is the essence of the institution that the slave does not possess equal rights with the freeman. The abstract rights to life, liberty and property are in his case replaced by statutes providing expressly for his condition. It has been our duty, as a Court, to listen with attention, and, we trust, with courtesy to all of those arguments which have urged the decision of this question upon moral rather than legal grounds. We conceive that our highest moral obligation in this case is to administer impartially the plain provisions of the law.

However painful the result may be to the defendants in this case, it is my duty to deliver them, Simon Garner, Sr., Simon Garner, Jr., and Mary Garner, fugitives from service, into the custody of the claimant, James Marshall.

He then proceeded to consider:

The claim of Gaines, to Margaret alias Peggy Garner, a mulatto woman; Tom, a negro boy; Sam, a mulatto boy, and Silla, an infant girl; claimed by Archibald K. Gaines, of Boone county, Kentucky, as fugitives from service and labor in the State of Kentucky.

In this case it is claimed by the defense, that Peggy, when about six years old, was permitted by her previous master to come to the State of Ohio; and upon that fact they claim that she is entitled to her freedom; and that being free at that time, and her children being born since, they are also entitled to freedom.

These facts present for our consideration the same question which was raised in the case of Marshall vs. Simon Garner et al, and the decision which we have just announced applies equally in this case.

We shall therefore make the order that the parties named, to wit: Peggy, Tom, Sam, and Silla, be delivered into the custody and possession of the claimant, Archibald K. Gaines.

CHAPTER 3

RETURN

*Two days after Commissioner Pendery handed Archibald Gaines
and James Marshall their victory, Judge Leavitt ruled on the custody
dispute between Marshal Robinson and Sheriff Brashears, finding for
the marshal. Even though Leavitt found that Ohio had no right to interrupt federal processes in a fugitive slave case, and that Pendery's ruling
should now be put into effect, some observers thought that the orders
of Ohio Probate Judge John Burgoyne (see chapter 5) would at least
temporarily prevent Robinson from proceeding. In the event, however,
as soon as Leavitt brought his session to a close, Robinson and his vast
cadre of deputies retrieved the Garners from the sheriff and brought
them over the river to Kentucky.*

Cincinnati Daily Gazette, February 29, 1856

THE FUGITIVE SLAVES.
JUDGE LEAVITT'S DECISION IN THE HABEAS CORPUS.
The Fugitives Returned to Kentucky.

At 3 o'clock yesterday afternoon Judge LEAVITT gave the following decision on the Habeas Corpus case:
EX-PARTE, H. H. ROBINSON, MARSHAL, ETC., HABEAS CORPUS.
    . . . The question presented on these facts is one of conflict between
the Marshal and the Sheriff, as to the legal custody of these persons. It
is insisted by the counsel of the Marshal; that they were in his custody

under lawful process from the Commissioner, and that it was not competent for the Sheriff to arrest them, under the process of the State, while they were so held under process issued by authority of the laws of the United States. On the other hand, it is claimed by the counsel for the Sheriff, that the proceeding against them under the Fugitive Slave Act, then pending, and their commitment to the jail of Hamilton county, did not shield them from arrest on a charge of a violation of the criminal law of the State of Ohio.

In disposing of this question, I am free to confess I have had some anxiety to find a legal basis on which I could satisfactorily reach the conclusion, that these fugitives could properly be held in custody under the process of the State, notwithstanding the fact of their being in the prior legal custody of the Marshal. And my first impressions were strongly in favor of the position, that as the claim of the owner in the proceeding under the fugitive slave act, was the mere assertion of a civil right, it must be subordinate, and yield to, the right of the State to assert and enforce its criminal laws. But upon a closer examination of the principal involved, and the cases referred to as bearing on the question, I am prepared to adopt a different conclusion.

If the question as to the rightful custody of these four persons could be controlled and governed, with exclusive reference to the rights asserted by their owner and claimant, I should have no hesitancy in holding that those rights could not be protected at the hazard of infringing upon the rights and dignity of the State of Ohio. But there is obviously another phaze on this subject, that presents it in a different and far more imposing aspect. In sustaining, as I am always inclined to do, the just powers and sovereign rights of the State, the claims of the national government, and the necessity of sustaining and vindicating its laws, must not be overlooked. In our compound system, the National and State Governments have their appropriate functions and duties; and it is vital to the healthful action of the system, that each should move within its constitutional orbit; thereby avoiding conflicts and collision.

But without extending my remarks in this direction, I may observe that if the four persons named in the writ of habeas corpus, came at the time of their arrest by the Sheriff, in the custody of the Marshal under process issued by authority of a law of the United States, I do not see how that custody can be superseded. And I may here remark, that speaking judiciously, this question is not affected by the fact that the law of the Untied States under which the process issues, and these persons are in custody, may be viewed, even by a majority of community as inexpedient, unjust, or oppressive. Until repealed, or adjudged void on the ground of unconstitutionality by the proper judicial tribunal of the Union, it must be respected and observed as law.

In holding as I must do in this case, that the right of the Marshal to the custody of the person in question must be respected, I am not to be understood as asserting that a fugitive slave is not responsible for the violation of the criminal laws of the State to which he may have fled. It is the undoubted right of every State to punish crime committed within its limits. A State destitute of this right in its freest and fullest exercise, could have no just claim to sovereignty. And if an escaped slave could violate law with impunity, many of the States of this Union would be in a most defenceless condition. It is not asserted, therefore, that they are not liable to punishment, but merely, that if they are in custody of an officer, under a law of the United States before their arrest for crime against the State law, the latter arrest can not be enforced till the disability existing by the prior arrest is removed. In other words, the slave being in the custody of an officer acting under the authority of another, and for the purposes of this question, a foreign jurisdiction, he cannot, by the mere force of a subsequent arrest, be delivered from such custody.

In Dorr's case, 3 Howard Rep. 105, Judge McLean, in giving the opinion of the Supreme Court, strongly sustains the position just stated. That was an application for habeas corpus to deliver Dorr from imprisonment in the State of Rhode Island, under a sentence for treason committed against that State. Judge McLean says: "Neither this or any other Court of the United States, or Judge thereof, can issue a *habeas corpus* to bring up a prisoner who is in custody, under a sentence or execution of a State Court, for any other purpose than to be used as a witness. And it is immaterial whether the imprisonment be under *civil or criminal process*. . . .

It is said in argument, that if these persons cannot be held by the arrest of the Sheriff under the State process, the rights and dignity of Ohio are invaded without the possibility of redress. I cannot concur in this view. The Constitution and Laws of the United States provide for a reclamation of these persons, by a demand on the Executive of Kentucky. It is true, if now remanded to the claimant and taken back to Kentucky as slaves, they can not be said to have fled from justice in Ohio; but it would clearly be a case within the spirit and intention of the Constitution and the act of Congress, and I trust that nothing would be hazarded by the prediction, that upon demand properly made upon the Governor of Kentucky, he would order them to be surrendered to the authorities of

Ohio, to answer to its violated law. I am sure it is not going too far to say, that if the strictness of the law did not require this, an appeal to comity would not be in vain. . . .

The Delivery of the Fugitives.

About 4 o'clock the U. S. Marshal, with a large number of assistants, went to the county jail to receive the fugitives. They were brought out into the reception room one by one by the jailors, and then delivered by the Sheriff in person to U. S. Marshal Robinson and his deputies. Mr. Russel carried in "Silly" the infant, while Mr. Brown offered his arm to Margaret, and J. Bill Pollock walked arm in arm with Simon to the omnibus. When about to start Mr. Robinson called to the driver to stop. Some of Margaret's clothes (given to her since in jail) had been left. They were brought out, and the omnibus then moved on. H. H. Robinson and Geo. S. Bennett, led the way in a buggy, and the omnibus surrounded by a number of deputy Marshals followed. They proceeded down Sycamore to Ninth, thence to Walnut, and down Walnut to the Covington ferry landing.

A large crowd which had gathered around the jail followed, but with the silence and order of a funeral procession. They were attending the funeral of the sovereignty of the State of Ohio.

The moment the omnibus drove on the ferry boat "Kentucky" she was cut loose. Marshall, one of the claimants, was on the bow deck surrounded by crowds of his friends, and warm congratulations were exchanged. "Oh," said one, "ain't this worth a thousand dollars?" "Yes," replied another, "we've got that d——d abolition State under foot now, and by G——d we'll keep it there;" "Oh, its too good," said a third, in great exultation.

The omnibus drove up to the jail and deposited the fugitives. Women with children in their arms came to the door steps and in the street, and beautiful, dark haired girls, gleaming with jewels, filled the open windows—all to see the procession pass. It reminded us of the recent jubilee in Cincinnati on the 22d of February.

After the Negroes were deposited, the white men went to the Magnolia House to hold a congratulatory meeting. The bar was opened, and for some time liquor flowed freely, without money and without price.

The Congratulatory Meeting in Covington.
Speeches by Robinson and Flinn, of Cincinnati,
and Finnell and Gaines, of Kentucky.

Mr. Robinson, the U.S. Marshal, being loudly called for, took a position on the balcony of the Magnolia House, while the crowd gathered in the street below. He commenced by saying, "We in Ohio may well be proud this day that our sovereignty as a state has been maintained, by vindicating the sovereignty of the state of Kentucky." (Applause.) He then denounced, in good round terms, the abolitionists of Ohio—spoke of his own personal courage, and his determination to do his duty. He did not claim that he had in this case done anything more than his duty.

MR. FINNELL'S SPEECH.

Mr. Finnell was next called out. He said, that though Mr. Robinson claimed no credit for doing anything but his duty, yet in doing that, he had well merited the commendation in the good book, of "Well done, good and faithful servant." (Applause.) He said he loved the Union, and that it was far dearer to him then than it was two hours ago. (Applause.) "You may talk as much as much [*sic*] as you please about the chivalry of Kentucky; I tell you the salvation of Kentucky and of the South, and the continuance of our domestic institution depends entirely upon the integrity and continuance of our Federal Union." (Tremendous applause.)

"Flinn" and "Gaines" were then loudly called for. Flinn came forward and was introduced by Mr. Finnell as the counsel of the Marshal. He made a "glorious Union" speech, but stopped short, and said he was dry, and must go down to get a drink. (Applause.)

Mr. Gaines was then called for.

Mr. Robinson came forward and apologized for Mr. Gaines' non-appearance by stating that he had been appointed a committee of one to go over the [*sic*] and invite Mr. Jolliffe to come over and get a drink.

This was received with shouts and laughter; but the multitude still persisted in calling, "Gaines," and he finally came forward.

MR. GAINES' SPEECH.

Mr. Gaines said, "I'm ten thousand times obliged to you gentlemen, for your diligence in preserving the laws and carrying them out; but I am no speech maker. Mr. Flinn will speak for me."

Jacob Flinn then said: He could assure them that no mercenary motive actuated Mr. Gaines in pursuing these slaves. It was a pure matter of principle with him, for they had cost him more money than would boulder that whole street with wooly-heads.

THE ASSAULT ON OUR REPORTER.

As it was getting dark and the crowd began to disperse, our reporter then left. While he had been standing in the crowd, with his pencil in his hand, he frequently heard such remarks as "See that d——d abolition reporter,"

"What business has he over here from Ohio?" but thought nothing of them. He had gone two or three blocks from the Magnolia House toward the river, when he was suddenly struck behind. He turned around, but was immediately surrounded by a crowd, struck by a number of persons, and knocked down. One respectable looking man remonstrated with the crowd, but with no effect. They cried "Tar and feather him," "Duck him." "He's a d——d abolitionist, give him h——ll." "Take him down to the river, and put him on a cake of ice, and let him go to the d——l." The last suggestion seemed to delight them, and they surrounded him and proceeded toward the river. He noticed a number of men in this crowd whom he had seen in the Court Rooms, during the trial of the case, serving as special deputy marshals from Kentucky.

Just as they reached the levee they were joined by a small party, some of them deputy Marshals from Ohio, who had come over to assist in bringing over the fugitives. Mr. Lee, late deputy city Marshal of Cincinnati, recognized our reporter: the Ohio party drew their shooters and ordered the Kentuckians to stand back. They obeyed. But the moment the ferry boat had left the landing, the Kentuckians crowded on the wharf boat and shouted their curses and threatenings, swearing that if they ever again caught the d——d abolition reporter on that side of the river they would kill him.

Cincinnati Daily Times, February 29, 1856

The Fugitive Slaves Safe in Kentucky—
Their Arrival and Reception.

As soon as Judge Leavitt had given his decision and signed the order remanding the Fugitive Slaves into the custody of the United States Marshal, Marshal Robinson and his posse proceeded to the jail when the Sheriff delivered the slaves into his possession. A looker-on informs us, that Mr. Marshall approached young Simon, and told him he was going to take him back to Kentucky, and asked him if he was not sorry he ran away, and if he didn't want to go back, and live as he had lived heretofore, to which Simon replied that he wouldn't care to go back if he was treated right, and not knocked about. His master asked him who had knocked him about to which he replied, "all about the farm" or some such answer.

An omnibus was provided to take them to the river, into which the slaves got, and as many deputies as could get in. Marshal Robinson and his chief deputy, Geo. S. Bennett, preceded the omnibus in a buggy, some two hundred or more deputies and others walking on each side of the streets they traversed. In this way they reached the river.

We noticed attorney Jolliffe standing on the corner of Walnut and Third streets, and saw one or two of the Kentuckians shake hands with him as they passed. We suppose they were so elated with obtaining the slaves that they were even willing to take by the hand the man who had done his utmost to free them.

The omnibus took them across to the Covington Jail, where the slaves are and all were delivered to the Jailor, Andy Herod, who will retain them in custody until their owners shall make what disposition of them they may see proper.

We heard Mr. Marshall remark to old Simon, at the Jail door, "How are you Simon—you are in Kentucky now. Do you know me? You didn't know me in Ohio?" to which the old man made no reply. We didn't hear a word of remonstrance from any of the negroes during the entire way from one jail to the other.

The Kentuckians appeared to be highly gratified with the finale of the trial, many remarking that it proved to them we had still a Union, whose laws would be respected and maintained, notwithstanding the efforts of bigoted fanatics and one-idea abolitionists.

CHAPTER 4

REQUISITION?

Archibald Gaines had professed a willingness to see Margaret Garner returned to Ohio to face a murder charge after the courts had upheld his claim and returned her to Kentucky. As soon as the Garners were sent back, antislavery forces immediately pressed for an extradition— a process that Ohio did initiate, but which failed to return any of the Garners to Ohio soil. The roots of that failure are complex and, at this historical distance, not easy to disentangle. Clearly, Gaines did all that he could to thwart the efforts of Ohio's antislavery governor, Salmon P. Chase, even while proclaiming his full cooperation. Gaines's efforts to move the Garners out of reach ended up keeping the case in the nation's newspapers when the boat taking the family down the river collided with another boat in a freak accident, and the family's youngest child, Cilla, drowned.

The resulting outpouring of commentary on Gaines's duplicitous conduct ultimately prompted him to defend himself in print on two occasions, most comprehensively in his second letter to the editor, reprinted in this chapter. But he was not the only figure to come under fire for the failed requisition. Critics also questioned Chase's motives and the seriousness of his legal efforts on the Garners' behalf, not least because when speed was essential, he took days to formulate his requisition order. Both this rather labored document and Kentucky Governor Charles Morehead's barbed, but ultimately acquiescent, reply offer a valuable behind-the-scenes view of these public questions. At stake in this controversy were not only the Garners' fortunes and Gaines's reputation but also, perhaps, the ambitious Ohio governor's political future.

Chase was already angling to be selected as the presidential nominee at the first Republican national convention, scheduled for that summer. Eight years later, while he tried to put himself in position to unseat Abraham Lincoln as the party's nominee, he was still defending his performance in the Garner case against pointed public criticism from the kinds of prominent antislavery militants whose support he desperately needed. Chase's letter to John T. Trowbridge, reproduced at the end of this section, was written in order to be published during the 1864 campaign; in this late reconstruction of the case, Chase tries to show that he did all that a governor could do on the Garners' behalf. He thus reveals how he understood Margaret's actions and the Garners' aspirations—or, at least, how he wanted to present them to the Civil War public.

Chase to Morehead

Columbus, March 4, 1856.
To his Excellency,
Charles S. Morehead,
Governor of the State of Kentucky

Sir:

Annexed to this letter you will find a requisition for Margaret Garner, alias Peggy Garner, Simon Garner, Robert Garner, alias Simon Garner Jr., & Mary Garner, as fugitives from the justices of this State, together with a copy of this indictment on which it is founded.

As the circumstances under which these persons have been removed from this State has given rise to some doubts whether they come within the description of the second clause of the second section of the fourth article of the Constitution of the United States, which provides for the demand and surrender of fugitives from justice, I have thought it due to you that a full release statement of all material facts should accompany the requisition. . . .

The Constitutional provision which determines our extraction duties is necessarily familiar to you, but for the purpose of making perfectly clear to the court actions which have determined me to make the present requisition, I will quote it. It is as follows:

"A person charged in any State with treason felony or other crime, who shall flee from justice and be found in another State, shall on demand of the Executive authority of the State from which he fled, be delivered up & be removed to the State having jurisdiction of the crime."

That the persons named in the indictment herewith transmitted are charged with felony committed in this State, that they have left this State and . . . are to be found in Kentucky are facts which do not admit of question.

That they must be delivered up on my requisition to be removed to this State for trial is equally clear. . . .

It was due however to the State which I represent as well as to the State of which you are the honored Chief Magistrate that I should carefully examine this question for myself, under the lights of reason and authority, with a sincere desire, not merely to ascertain my own duty in the premises but to avoid also all action in the premises, which, upon like consideration, would not probably commend itself to your approval.

With these impressions I have attentively considered the whole matter submitted to me by the Prosecuting Attorney of Hamilton County & my conclusion is that I am authorized by the Federal Compact and required by my duty as Chief Magistrate of this State to ask of you the surrender of these persons.

The most respected authorities upon international law have constantly insisted that it is the duty of each action, and independently of treaty stipulation, to deliver up to the justice of another nation, those who having been guilty of crime within the jurisdiction of the latter are found within the jurisdiction of the former. By other authorities this doctrine, though committed to be salutary, has been doubted or denied as an obligatory principle of the law of action.

To remove all doubts upon a question so important a positive stipulation for the mutual extradition of persons charged with crime was introduced in 1778, into the Articles of Confederation & Perpetual Union between the original thirteen American States. The same stipulation, in substance, was transferred in 1789, into the Federal Constitution, and constitutes the provision which now determines the reciprocal rights and obligations of the Existing States.

The mischief to be remedied was the allowance of asylum in one State to persons charged with the commission of crime in other States. The mode in which said persons might come into States where found was entirely unimportant. It was absolutely immaterial whether they might come in the ordinary course of travel or with a positive intent to elude responsibility for guilt.

It can hardly be maintained that the wise framers of the Constitution intended to make a circumstance of this nature a criterion of liability or nonliability for extradition. Why then, it may be asked were the words, "who shall flee from justice" introduced into the extradition claim of this instrument?

To this question the proper and sufficient answer seems to be this: not for the purpose of requiring evidence of actual flight as a prerequisite to complain with a demand for extradition, but for the purpose of limiting the obligation of extradition to persons charged with crimes committed within the State making the demand. . . .

But even if evidence of actual flight should then be necessary, such evidence, it seems to me, is not wanting in the present case.

The flight contemplated by the Constitution can, at most, be nothing more than departures from the State where the crime was committed. . . . It is immaterial whether this departure be the voluntary act of the alleged criminal or an act compelled by a superior person.

If a person should commit murder in Kentucky and should be immediately seized & brought into Ohio against his will as one, I however, would say that the murderer, caught for extradition, must remain as furnished. For if a fugitive then should commit murder in Ohio & should be immediately seized by the master, exercising the power of recaption recognized by the Federal Supreme Court, some, however, would deny the right of the Executive of Ohio to demand as the duty of the Executive of Kentucky to surrender him. In both cases there would be a flight, but it would be properly regarded as the flight of the criminal, since, for the time, his will must be considered as based on the will of the captors, and it could make no difference in respect to the contest supposed whether conveyance into another State might be in the exercise of the power of recaption by direct force or in the exercise of the same power through the agencies provided in the Fugitive Slave Act.

These considerations can direct one to the conclusion that the persons mentioned in the annexed indictment are properly subject to extradition and I therefore make the usual requisition.

I have thought it my duty under the peculiar circumstances of this case to make this explanation of the grounds upon which I proved that the whole matter may be fairly and completely before you, and that you may be assured that I ask nothing which I am not ready to concede I make as requisition with which I would not promptly comply, if addressed to myself.

I have the honor to be

With the greatest respect,
Your Svt.,

S.P. Chase

Morehead to Chase

Gov. C. S. Morehead
March 7/56
Frankfort, March 7, 1856

To his Excellency
S. P. Chase
Governor of Ohio

Sir,

I received on last evening a requisition from your Excellency for Peggy Garner, Simon Garner, Robert Garner and Mary Garner, as fugitives from the justice of the State of Ohio, accompanied by a duly authenticated copy of an indictment against them in this Court of Common pleas of Hamilton County, Ohio, for the crime of murder. The circumstances under which the indictment was found—the effort made by its intervention to obstruct the delivery of these persons as fugitive slaves from Kentucky to their owners, and the final action of the Judge in remanding them to this State, were of such public notoriety, that I should have been but an inattentive observer of passing events, not to have formed an opinion in advance as to my duty in the event of a requisition being made by you. I was therefore prepared to act immediately upon the presentation of your demand. But accompanying it, was a statement made by the prosecuting attorney of Hamilton County, a copy of the opinion pronounced by the District Judge of the United States, for the Southern District of Ohio, with a letter from yourself in which you state, "as the circumstances under which these persons have been removed from this State, have given rise to doubts whether they come within the description of the second clause of the second section of the fourth article of the

Constitution of the United States, which provides for the demand and surrender of fugitives from justice, I have thought it due to you that a full and clear statement of all the material facts should accompany the requisition."

I thought it but respectful to you to delay my action for a few hours that I might give to your note and the accompanying documents, the consideration to which they were justly entitled, but after weighing all the circumstances, which you were kind enough to present for my consideration, notwithstanding the doubts to which they have given rise, I saw no reason to change my previous opinion, and have accordingly issued a separate warrant for each person named in your requisition in the ordinary and proper form.

The doubts to which you allude, I am not allowed to suppose, are entertained by your Excellency, as upon the facts presented to me, you have an official demand for these persons as having "fled from the justice of Ohio," and taken "refuge within the State of Kentucky." I could not do you the injustice to suppose that you would issue a requisition in any case where you were not satisfied that it was embraced by the clause of the Constitution of the United States to which you refer. You alone are supposed to be fully cognizant of all the facts upon which your requisitions are based, and when made by you, they carry with them not merely the sanction of your name, but the authority of a sovereign State, that the persons demanded have fled from justice. If, however, the object of your Excellency in suggesting that doubts had arisen whether these persons were fugitives from justice within the meaning of the Constitution, was to give me the benefit of such doubts under color of which I might refuse to deliver them up, I beg leave to say that the people of Kentucky without regard to party, acknowledge the paramount obligation in letter and spirit of the Federal Constitution, and the supremacy of all laws made in pursuance thereof. They would be the last to justify their evasion by any mere quibble or technicality. A person, who has in any manner left the State within whose jurisdiction he is charged to have committed a crime, in the sense of the Constitution is a fugitive from justice. If he has departed from the place where the crime was committed, he has fled from justice, whether such was his intention or not. If a person should commit a crime in Kentucky and be immediately seized and transported across the river to Ohio, we in Kentucky should consider him a fugitive from justice and a proper subject for the requisition of the Governor of Kentucky. If while at large in Ohio he should commit a crime and stand charged with it, although he had been forcibly brought to this State upon the requisition of the Governor upon a similar requisition from your State, we should not hesitate at the proper time to send him back again to be tried for the crime of which he there stands charged. The Executive authority of this State has heretofore acted upon this construction and I entertain no doubt that it is in accordance with the true meaning and spirit of the Constitution of the United States. If you deemed it necessary to send here distinguished counsel to argue this question before me, I can but regret your appreciation of Kentucky character. While I take great pleasure in hearing testimony to his urbanity and high gentlemanly being, I may be allowed to add that no argument is even necessary with us to enforce a ready and willing obedience to the mandate of the supreme law of the land. Have the persons demanded been indicted for a crime committed while they were in Ohio and are they now here? If so they must be yielded to the violated law of your State. I make no question as to the object of finding an indictment against some of these persons, or as to the evidence upon which it was formed. I do not consider that this is a matter for my investigation. Nor have I any disposition to complain of other matters in connection with this transaction, which have produced some feelings in Kentucky. All that I have felt it my duty to do, was to construe correctly the clause in question of the supreme law of the land, and to act in obedience to it. While the people of Kentucky are justly sensitive in regard to the violation of their constitutional rights in the multiplied impediments thrown in the way of the execution of a kindred provision of the Constitution, they are unwilling to make it a ground for a similar violation by them of the rights of a sister State.

The persons demanded by you are slaves, persons held to labor under the Constitution and laws of Kentucky. They are to be carried to a State where slavery is prohibited, to be there tried for a high crime. In issuing my warrant for their apprehension, I acted in the same manner I would have done, had the requisition come from the State of Tennessee or any other slave-holding state. I would have been justly amenable to the censure of an enlightened constituency, if I had resorted to any subterfuge, however plausible, to evade the performance of a plain duty. Having performed my constitutional duty in the event that these slaves are not convicted of the crime for which they stand charged, it will be for the authorities of Ohio in turn to perform their duty. I cannot allow myself to doubt for a moment if any of these slaves should be acquitted of the charge against them, that the proper tribunals of Ohio in obedience to the dictates of honor and of justice will restore them to their owners with the same promptitude with which I have issued my warrants for their apprehension, and removal to your State for trial.

Hoping that the fraternal relations between our respective States may be thus preserved unimpaired, I have the honor to be very respectfully,

Your Obt. Servt.

C. S. Morehead

Liberator, March 21, 1856

Here the Liberator, *the abolitionist weekly edited by its founder, William Lloyd Garrison, brings to its readership excerpts from the* Cincinnati Daily Commercial's *report on the riverboat collision and Cilla Garner's drowning. Although Garrison's paper never had more than about three thousand subscribers, a majority of them black, its reach, and its notoriety, extended much farther: its stories were at times reprinted in newspapers all over the country, including some Southern papers deeply hostile to Garrison and his point of view.*

THE CINCINNATI SLAVES—ANOTHER THRILLING SCENE IN THE TRAGEDY.

Gov. Chase, of Ohio, made a requisition upon Gov. Morehead, of Kentucky, for the slave woman Peggy, charged with the murder of her child at Cincinnati. It was understood that Peggy was held subject to this demand; but on Friday, the 7th, she was sent to Louisville, and shipped on board the Henry Lewis, which left that port on the evening of that day for the South. The Cincinnati *Commercial* gives an account of the whole affair, which we abridge somewhat.

On Thursday, Joe Cooper, of Springfield, left for Frankfort, with the requisition. It is supposed that his errand leaked out, for when he reached Frankfort, Gaines with the negroes was on his way to Louisville. Gov. Morehead granted the necessary documents, and when Cooper returned from his fruitless search, he expressed himself warmly indignant at the conduct of Gaines, saying that that individual had trifled with him and deceived him, and had insulted the dignity of the Commonwealth of Kentucky.

'On the train of cars for Frankfort which conveyed Cooper, were four slaves of Gaines, being sent South. They had attempted to escape after the flight of Margaret and the others, but had been overtaken on the Kentucky side. One of them was a very likely and rather pretty mulatto girl, which our informant said Cooper had a great notion to buy, to save her from the Southern excursion to which she was destined. These negroes were in charge of Marshal Butts, of Covington, who did not permit them to tarry at Frankfort, but put them on the first train for Louisville, and with them Margaret. So that, it appears, Cooper arrived in Frankfort before Margaret was taken away. After Cooper's interview with the Governor, he took the first train for Louisville, and reached that town two hours after the Henry Lewis had started. He then returned to Cincinnati.'

Now comes the most interesting part of the story. The Henry Lewis, on her passage down the river, came in collision with another steamer and was much damaged, and several lives were lost. The *Commercial* gives the narrative of events as follows:—

'When the accident occurred to the Henry Lewis, the negroes were in the nursery, (as a place between the cabin and steerage in the stern of the boat is called,) ironed by couples. After the disaster, they were heard calling for help and to be relieved of their handcuffs. Some one happened to be on hand to save them. Margaret had her child—the infant that she hit on the head with the shovel when arrested here—in her arms; but by the shock of the boat that came to the assistance of the Lewis, (as one story goes,) she was thrown into the river with her child and a white woman, who was one of the steerage passengers, and who was standing by her at the moment. This woman and the child were drowned, but a black man, the cook on the Lewis, sprang into the river, and saved Margaret, who, it is said, displayed frantic joy when told that her child was drowned, and said she would never reach alive Gaines' Landing, in Arkansas, the point to which she was shipped—thus indicating her intention to drown herself.

Another report is, that, as soon as she had an opportunity, she threw her child into the river, and jumped after it. Still another story has it, that she tried to jump upon the boat alongside, but fell short. It is only certain that she was in the river with her child, and that it was drowned, while she was saved by the prompt energy of the cook. We are told by one of the officers of the boat, that Peggy was the only female among the slaves. It is probable, therefore, that the story about the good-looking mulatto girl, who was being sent South, and attracted attention and sympathy, is a romance. The last that was seen of Peggy, she was on the Hungarian, crouching like a wild animal near the stove, with a blanket wrapped around her. Our readers will, we presume, be struck with the dramatic features of the Fugitive Slave Case, and that it progresses like a plot wrought by some master of tragedy.

First, there were the flight and the crossing of the frozen river in the twilight of morning, the place of fancied security, the surprise by the officers, the fight with them, the murder of the child, the arrest, the scenes about the court-room and in the jail, the long suspense, the return to Kentucky, the removal to Frankfort, the separation there, the approach of the messenger with the requisition for Peggy, her removal to Louisville, the pursuit of the messenger, the boat on which she was to have been taken South leaving two hours ahead of Cooper, with the writ from Gov. Morehead—then the speedy catastrophe to the steamer, the drowning of the babe of the heroine, and her own rescue, as if yet saved for some more fearful and startling act of the tragedy; and, lastly, the curtain falls, leaving her wet and dismal, on a boat bound South, perfectly careless as to her own fate, only determined never to set her foot on the soil of Arkansas. There is something fearfully tragic about this, which must occur to every mind, and we shall look with much interest for information of the catastrophe which will complete the dramatic unity of the affair.

'And here an incident, related to us as occurring during the awful moments when the Henry Lewis was sinking and breaking, suggests itself to us. It is not wholly authentic, but is worth telling, any how. Marshal Butts, of Covington, who had charge of the negroes, is said to have been inflated somewhat with the importance of his position, and talked of his charge as his niggers, and displayed an immense amount of cutlery and fire-arms, with which he expressed himself resolved to slaughter whole armies of Abolitionists; and it happened that he exchanged some sharp words with a gentleman on the steamer about the Fugitive Slave case, &c. When the accident occurred, he was in his room, and one of the tables rolling against his door, he could not get out, and yelled tremendously for assistance. Some persons heard him, and went to work cutting a hole through the roof to let him out. The most active of those so engaged was the man with whom he had had the quarrel.

"When a hole was made large enough to let the rescuer and the prisoner communicate with each other, but not sufficient to crawl through, the man with the axe learned for the first time whom he was laboring to save, and called out, "Hallo, Butts, is that you" D——n you, if I'd known that, you might have drowned. And [after a moment's reflection] you shall any how, if you won't give your word to let those niggers go." There was no time to be lost and Butts, fearing that he might be left to perish, said—"To tell the truth now, I don't own the niggers; if I did, I'd let 'em go. I'm only the agent." "Well," said the man holding the axe of deliverance or death, "take the irons off them, any how." That Butts agreed to do, and the opening being enlarged, he crawled out, and began to inquire with some anxiety, "Where's them d——n niggers?" and was much gratified when he found that only the baby was lost.'

Cincinnati Daily Commercial, March 12, 1856

The story of the rescue of Butts on the Henry Lewis . . . is confirmed, and said to be even more interesting than we have related. The man would not let him out until he had promised to free the negroes.—Butts had previously pretended to be the owner of them, and when the alternative of emancipation or drowning was before him, he used the qualifying phrase, 'I'll free 'em as far's I'm concerned!' which, after he was safe, was explained to be meaningless as he did not own them.

We are now informed that Margaret did not throw her child into the river, but that she was hand-cuffed and could not hold it in her arms when she fell in. She was of course entirely helpless when in the water and was saved . . . by the cook. . . . What became of the four negroes that were sent from Covington on the morning that Cooper left for Frankfort, we cannot learn.—They were not on the Henry Lewis, and it seems that there was in their case a mysterious disappearance. There were no slaves on the Lewis, but Peggy and old Mary, young and old Simon, and the children. Col. Chambers received a dispatch yesterday, dated at Evansville, from Butts, which said that all the niggers in his charge were safe. Whether he forgot the drowning of Peggy's baby, or thought that so small a matter as not to be worth mentioning, or whether the baby was miraculously preserved, we have not the means of knowing. But the strong presumption is that Mr. Butts overlooked the death of the black baby.

Cincinnati Daily Enquirer, April 15, 1856

Assorted details in Archibald Gaines's chronology of events cannot be reconciled with the documentary evidence. For instance, it is not true that he had announced in the papers Margaret Garner's brief return to Covington. Nor, apparently, did he ever follow through on his concluding promise to publish her whereabouts once she was settled permanently.

Still, this letter tells us as much as any source how Gaines viewed the public spectacle in which he had become, surely against his wishes, a major character.

The Late Fugitive Slave Case

To the Editors of the Enquirer:

After my negro woman Peggy was delivered to me in Covington, under the laws of the United States, I retained her in Kentucky, in pursuance of an intention which I expressed before she was so given up, for the space of eight days and upward, holding her during all that time subject to a requisition from the Governor of Ohio, under the charge of murder which had been made against her by the Grand Jury of Hamilton County. When that period had elapsed, no requisition having come, I was constrained, by the accumulation of costs and a desire to get rid of such an incumbrance as the woman necessarily was, to send her, in company with her husband and children and her husband's parents, to the State of Arkansas. Before she reached my brother's plantation in that State the story of her crime had preceded her, and, consequently, he was unwilling to take so dangerous an inmate as she was into his family of slaves. It then became necessary to take them further South; and my agent accordingly took them all to New Orleans, where they were sold, all together, to my brother, A. Gaines. Soon after she was sent from Kentucky it suited the purposes of the Abolition newspapers of Cincinnati to clamor most vociferously against me for having, as they charged, been guilty of running off and concealing a fugitive from justice from the State of Ohio. After much hesitation and consultation with friends of intelligence and integrity, I concluded that, in order to satisfy even the clamors of fanaticism, I would have her brought back to Kentucky and there held a reasonable length of time, subject again to the demand of Governor Chase. This I accordingly did, and at heavy expense had the woman repurchased in New Orleans and brought back to Covington, Kentucky, by a special messenger. The fact that I had so sent for her was printed in several of the papers of Cincinnati some time before the arrival of the woman, and, as I am informed, when she did arrive in Covington, which was on Wednesday, the 2d day of April, the fact was generally announced in the daily papers of Cincinnati. Now, while I have no special interest in the administration of the criminal laws of Ohio, and no special motive for forwardness in bringing the murderess to justice, yet a desire to preserve my reputation as a law-abiding man, and to prevent and forever stop even the clamor of the Underground Railroad Abolitionists, induced me, after the woman had been in Covington for several days, to send a telegraphic dispatch, in my own name, to Governor Chase, at Columbus, announcing the fact that she was there, and subject to his requisition. Day after day, however, elapsed, and yet no requisition came. Not feeling bound to remain any longer in this attitude of expectation, and having, according to the opinions of many excellent and sensible men, done all that even a superfine regard for the susceptible feeling of the Abolition avengers of innocent blood could demand, I at last, on the ninth day after she had been brought to Covington, concluded to send her back to her husband and children in New Orleans, which I did at once.

Now, sirs, this is very briefly but truly the history of the case since the woman was surrendered to my ownership by the United States Commissioner; yet in the very teeth of these facts the Cincinnati *Gazette* and *Commercial* have seen fit again to commence a simultaneous attack upon me, without, however, asserting that I have done anything incompatible with the statement of facts which I have here given, but *insinuating* (notwithstanding the heavy expense incurred in sending an express messenger for her and bringing her back to Covington, and retaining her in jail there nearly nine days,) that I was only playing a part, and never meant in good faith to give her up.

How shall I characterize such bold-faced and atrocious yet shabby baseness?

Of course a negro-thief will steal negroes—it is their vocation; but when a cut-purse finds you have no money he will leave your throat uncut. Not so the Abolitionist; when foiled in his petty larceny enterprise he attempts to stab the character of the man from whom he attempts to steal.

Now, sirs, on my personal responsibility—and I trust the *responsible gentlemen* who edit the Cincinnati *Daily Gazette* and the Cincinnati *Daily Commercial* will understand what I mean—I must say that I am unable to perceive such difference between the slave-rescuer and the money-thief. Of this I am quite certain, if the conduct of those editors is to be regarded as a fair sample of *philanthropy,* then certainly an honest man may take a pickpocket to his bosom joyfully, rather than hold any communion with such cowardly stabbers, as I personally say they are.

How singular it is that, after the lapse of eight days before the woman was first sent to the South, and not until then, Governor Chase sent his requisition to Governor Morehead, and that it should arrive just in time to be too late! And how passing strange it is that, after a lapse of nine days, during which the woman was in Covington, subject to the requisition, no step was taken to enforce it until it was ascertained that she had again been taken to her home and family in the South!

I am morally sure that the Abolitionists care nothing for Peggy, either through regard for the offended majesty of the laws of Ohio or for any sympathy with her as an oppressed, down trodden persecuted, heart-broken, desperate woman; and I am equally sure that the atrocious scoundrels have a wider and meaner object in view—that they care nothing for negroes or their owners, and only wish to use both as material for the promotion of political ends, for the furtherance of their objects of treason to the Constitution and laws of the Union.

It may turn out that the publication of a letter from Governor Chase to Governor Morehead, which accompanied the requisition, will explain why the Abolitionists have managed to be *just in time to be too late* to get Peggy.

A.K. Gaines

N.B.—So soon as I hear of Peggy being permanently located in any State I will make publication of the fact in the Cincinnati papers that the State authorities may know where their requisition will reach her.

A.K.G.
April 14, 1856.

Chase to John T. Trowbridge

"WASHINGTON, *March 13, 1864.*

My Dear Sir: The Garner case comes next in order, and is invested with a peculiar interest by its tragic circumstances.

It is impossible to state the facts except in the merest outline; but even an outline will convey a pretty accurate idea of the whole transaction.

On the night of the 27th of January, 1856, a party of slaves escaped from Boone County, in Kentucky into Storrs Township, adjoining Cincinnati, on the Ohio River. Among the persons composing the party were an old man, named Simon Garner, and his wife—so far as a slave woman could be a wife—Mary; a son of the old man, also named Simon, and Margaret, his wife, and their four children.

They took refuge in a colored man's house, near the river bank, below Millcreek, a stream which divides Storrs from Cincinnati. They were tracked immediately, and a warrant for their apprehension was obtained the next morning, Monday, the 28th, from one Pendery, a commissioner appointed by Judge McLean, under the fugitive slave act of 1850. Provided with the warrant, the United States Marshal—named Robinson—with a gang of officers and the slave claimants, hastened to the house where the fugitives had taken refuge. Their entrance was resisted. Young Simon, who was armed with a six-shooter, fired four shots on the party of official and unofficial slave-hunters, before he and his companions were seized. While this was going on, his wife, Margaret, who was naturally of a violent disposition, and now frenzied by excitement, seized a butcher knife and, declaring she would kill all the children before they should be taken across the river, actually succeeded in killing one, a little girl of three years of age, named Mary. . . .

The slave act commissioner in this case was a weak, mercenary fellow; but his decision is written in judicial style, and bears the marks of a very different order of intellect from his. Who wrote it? . . .

On Thursday morning, however, Judge Leavitt announced his decision in the case which had been argued before him. He declared, to the surprise of every one, unless some had foreknowledge of his conclusions, that the custody of the sheriff as against the claims of the marshal under the fugitive slave act was unlawful, and ordered the former to deliver the indicted prisoners to the latter. . . .

I had observed the proceedings in these cases with great interest and with deep solicitude for the fate of the slaves. All that I could do in their behalf, under the circumstances then existing, was done. They were represented by able counsel, and the power of the State was pledged to maintain the process of the State. No one imagined that any judge could be found who would undertake to transfer by a proceeding in *habeas corpus,* prisoners indicted under a State law to Federal custody under the fugitive slave act. Nor did any one imagine that persons held under an order of a State Court during the pendency of a writ of *habeas corpus,* would be carried off beyond the jurisdiction and in violation of that order. But such a judge was found, and such an abduction was perpetrated.

I could not prevent this any more than I could prevent the commission of other outrages. I could not foresee such transactions and if I could have foreseen, I had no more power to prevent them than any private citizen possessed, except in the single contingency that the sheriff might need the power of the State to enforce the execution of process in his hands. Except in that contingency, I had no power other than that, the whole weight of which was given to the side of the fugitive, in every form of encouragement, counsel, and support to those engaged in their defense. I was not in Cincinnati during the proceedings. The legislature was in session. I had only a fortnight before the seizure of the fugitives entered an office, wholly without experience in its duties, and my constant presence was required at Columbus. Had I been at Cincinnati, I do not now see that I should have been likely to add any thing to the ability or the zeal with which the cause of the fugitives was defended, or to suggest any thing which did not occur to them. And certainly, if they on the spot could devise no way to prevent the surrender and carrying off of the fugitives under the unanticipated circumstances of that day, it is not wonderful that I could devise none, while a hundred and twenty miles off and wholly uninformed of the outrage which was being enacted.

Some abolitionists distant from the scene have blamed me since, because I did not in some way prevent the carrying back to slavery of Margaret Garner. They saw the tragic circumstances of her case and felt peculiar sympathy for her; but they did not see the extraordinary efforts made to save her. That these efforts were unsuccessful all humane persons must lament; but how more effort could have been made, or with what more likelihood of success, no one has yet pointed out. And no one conversant with the circumstances and concerned in the efforts made in her behalf, has found fault with what I did. All those approved my action and were grateful for my support. It must be remembered that Margaret Garner was but one of seven fugitives, each of whom was entitled, if not to equal sympathy, certainly to equal rights and equal efforts for their protection. None of them were forgotten or neglected.

After they were surrendered the prosecuting attorney sent me copies of the indictment and proceedings, and suggested that though the indicted prisoners could hardly be considered as having fled from justice in Ohio, yet it might be proper to regard them as having constructively done so, and to issue a requisition for their delivery to an agent of the State, to be brought back within its jurisdiction. I felt keenly the humiliation of being reduced to this mode of asserting the right of the State to the custody of persons indicted under the laws. It was obvious that when returned to the custody of the sheriff they would be in precisely the same relations as when they were taken from his custody by Judge Leavitt's order, and there would be no legal obstacles which did not exist to the original order to a repetition of it. A friend, however, volunteered, if I would issue a requisition, to go with the agent and purchase the freedom of the three children; and it seemed probable, if the others could be brought back, that an arrangement might be made also with their claimants for the relinquishment of their claims on them. So I overcame my reluctance to adopt the theory of constructive escape and issued the requisition.

My agent and the gentleman who had volunteered to accompany him, immediately departed on their mission and obtained a warrant of extradition from the Governor of Kentucky, who doubtless gladly embraced the opportunity of making a precedent of constructive escape, which he hoped would be useful to claimants of slaves found in Ohio, but not actual fugitives from a slave State.

With the warrant thus obtained the agent proceeded to Louisville, but the slave-masters continued to evade him, and the slaves were sent South notwithstanding all efforts to recover them.

Subsequently, hearing that Margaret had been brought back to Covington, I wrote to the prosecuting attorney to go over and demand her. He went, and was told she had been there, but was again sent South. It is doubted whether she was, in fact, ever brought there.

Nothing has been heard of the Garner family since. Perhaps the Rebellion has restored the liberty of which the cause of the Rebellion caused the loss; and we may yet hear of these slaves as among those rejoicing in the new-found freedom which God's Providence has given to so many.

CHAPTER 5

WHOSE SOVEREIGNTY?

Courts in Conflict

The most dramatic moments in the Garners' legal struggle for freedom unfolded in Commissioner Pendery's court, but the case was fought in four different legal venues; in competing ways, assorted officials and judges asserted the right to hold the fugitives in custody or rule on their fate. Antislavery activists regularly sought to use state laws and officials to thwart federal fugitive slave proceedings, and such conflicts were especially familiar in a border city such as Cincinnati, but Margaret Garner's killing of her daughter made the legal struggle all the more complex. With the encouragement of the family's lawyers, the local prosecutor pursued an indictment of Margaret for murder before Judge Samuel Carter of the Court of Common Pleas. Although various lawyers and officials argued in that court in several sessions during February, and though the pending murder charge was repeatedly invoked in the struggles in the other legal venues, the arguments in Judge Carter's court never got far enough for any of the Garners to be brought in or for a trial to begin.

Even before appearing in Judge Carter's court, however, the family's lawyers had sought a writ of habeas corpus from Hamilton County Probate Judge John Burgoyne, whom they chose not for the relevance of his court (by rights it had little to do with such cases) but because of the strength of his antislavery credentials and his power to put them to use. There was reason to hope that a writ from Judge Burgoyne would remove the Garners from the custody of federal marshals, place them in the custody of the city sheriffs, make them available for legal proceedings on the murder charge, and—the real objective—halt the proceedings before Judge Pendery, or at least prevent the commissioner

*from removing the family from Cincinnati. Judge Burgoyne proved
as cooperative as John Jolliffe had hoped. It was Burgoyne's orders to
Sheriff Gazoway Brashears that pushed the latter into his disputes with
Marshal Robinson during Pendery's hearings. Even though Brashears
ultimately lost those legal arguments, Burgoyne also ordered Robinson
not to take any of the Garners out of the city without first obtaining his
permission. When Robinson ignored the order and returned the family
to Kentucky and a life of slavery, an angry Burgoyne called him into
court and, eventually, found the marshal in contempt. In doing so, the
judge was clearly in violation of the Fugitive Slave Act. In defiance
of existing rulings by federal courts, however, he declared the relevant
provisions of the law unconstitutional, thus denying that Pendery had
the rightful authority to return the Garners to slavery. Robinson again
petitioned Judge Leavitt, who released him from jail and dismissed the
contempt charges. Leavitt thus ended Robinson's legal jeopardy, but the
decision hardly halted the larger American struggle over the validity
of the Fugitive Slave Act and the relative authority of state and federal
courts. Burgoyne's and Leavitt's opinions, artifacts of that struggle, are
reprinted here.*

Cincinnati Daily Gazette, March 19, 1856

Habeas Corpus for the Alleged Fugitive Slaves.
OPINION OF JUDGE BURGOYNE AS TO THE
MARSHAL'S RETURN

Judge Burgoyne yesterday delivered the opinion of the Court in this matter, as follows:

The return made by the Marshal to the writ of Habeas Corpus issued in this case, distinctly puts in issue the authority of this Court to compel the production of the bodies of those persons held in custody; and the main question to be decided is, therefore, how far the authority of the Court extends in such cases.

In a previous stage of the case the Court declared its deliberate judgment that the writ of Habeas Corpus could not be constitutionally suspended, and that so much of the Fugitive Slave Law as was designed to interfere with it was null and void. The authority to issue the writ in this case, as well as the duty of the Marshal to produce the bodies of the persons named in it, is, however, again denied, and the Court is asked to review its former opinion. The question is an important one, and has been carefully considered; but after full reflection and the consultation of numerous authorities, there has been found no reason to doubt the correctness of the decision pronounced on a former day, that the writ is properly issued in this, as in any other case of alleged unlawful detention. . . .

We would not be understood as carrying the idea that one Court can upon Habeas Corpus reverse the proceedings of another Court having proper jurisdiction, for irregularity. That is a totally different question, and one which it does not appear to be necessary to consider at the present time.

The right of an Ohio Court to cause to be brought before it a person alleged to be unlawfully restrained of his liberty within the State, that the cause of such restraint may be inquired into, is one thing; and the course to be pursued, as the result of such an inquiry, is quite another matter. —What is now decided, is, that the right to issue the writ is clear; and that, as a necessary consequence, it is the duty of the person to whom it is addressed, to obey its commands. . . .

The next question which is presented is, whether the proceedings before the Commissioner were such as would have induced this Court, if the bodies of the alleged fugitives had been duly produced and proper return made by the Marshal, to decline further interference in the premises, and the solution of this question, in the first instance, depends upon the validity of the law under which those proceedings were instituted.

It is well settled that Courts of Justice are not bound to obey the requirements of a legislative enactment when it has been passed in violation of the Constitution. . . .

It is of the first importance, then, to ascertain whether the propositions of the act of Congress, which authorized the proceedings before the Commissioner, are in conformity with the Constitution. . . .

. . . In considering the validity of the provisions of this act three questions arise, viz:

1st. Are the powers intended to be exercised by Commissioners judicial?

2d. Are Commissioners such inferior Courts as are within the meaning of the Constitution?

3d. Are the appointment, tenure of office and compensation of Commissioners such as the Constitution requires?

These questions will be briefly considered in the order in which they have been stated.

1st. Judicial power is the power to hear and determine cases at law or in equity, which is exercised by the Judge of a Court. It implies a controversy between adverse parties, which involves questions of law or of fact to be heard and determined in order that the proper remedy may be ascertained and enforced. Under the act of Congress a claim must be asserted and prosecuted, and it may be contested before the Commissioner, with the forms of process trial and adjudication that are usual in Courts.

The jurisdiction of the Commissioner is concurrent with that of the U.S. Judges in term or in vacation. . . .

And indeed it would be difficult to conceive of a definition of judicial power which would not embrace such powers as are conferred by this act upon Commissioners.

2d. To confer judicial power is not necessary to establish a Court. . . .

A Court is a place where justice is judicially administered; it requires the presence of a Judge, ministerial officers and parties. But the act in question erects no such tribunal. It constitutes no Court of which the Commissioner is the Judge. It simply confers judicial power upon an officer appointed to take affidavits, etc.; and the result is the same as if such power had been conferred upon the Clerk, the Marshal, or any other ministerial officer. The power is vested not in a Court, but in a person, and is adjourned, as it were, to his other duties. The Commissioner's Court is so called merely by courtesy, and has no legal existence. . . .

.3d. But if the other view of this subject should be taken, the result would not be more satisfactory. If, by the act of Congress referred to, a new class of Courts is established, then it is quite clear that the plain provisions of the Constitution have been disregarded. In providing for the appointment, term of office, and compensation of the Judges. If the Commissioners are Judges, they are required by the Constitution to be appointed by the President, to hold their offices during the good behavior and receive for their services a stated compensation, not to be diminished during their term of office. They are, *in fact,* appointed by the Circuit Courts removable at pleasure, and paid by fees dependent upon the result of their decisions.

The Court, after full examination and calm deliberation, is therefore clearly of the opinion, that so much of the Fugitive Slave Law, as authorizes Commissioners to examine and determine questions in reference to the surrender of persons claimed as fugitives from labor is an attempt to confer judicial power in a manner not authorized by the Constitution; and that the acts of Commissioners under its provisions are utterly null and void. If a due return had been made to the writ, therefore, and upon the production of the bodies of the persons named in it, it had been made to appear, that they were held in custody, under a certificate issued by Commissioner Pendery, according to the provisions of the Fugitive Slave Law, the Court would not have felt precluded by that certificate, but would have been compelled to deny the jurisdiction of the Commissioner in the premises. . . .

EX PARTE ROBINSON

Case No. 11,934 Circuit Court, S.D. Ohio From 20 Federal Cases *965, 1856 U.S.*

Opinion of District Judge Leavitt *[issued on April 23, 1856]*:

. . . The habeas corpus in this case, issued pursuant to the seventh section of the act of congress, passed March 2, 1833, which provides "that either of the justices of the supreme court or a judge or any district court of the United States, in addition to the authority already conferred by law, shall have power to grant writs of habeas corpus in all cases of a prisoner or prisoners in jail or confinement, when he or they shall be committed or confined on or by any authority of law, for any act done or omitted to be done in pursuance of a law of the United States, or any order, process, or decree of any judge or court thereof, anything in any act of congress to the contrary notwithstanding."

It is insisted by the counsel who oppose the discharge of the marshal that this provision of the act of congress applies only to the case of a federal officer who is confined or imprisoned by state authority under an unconstitutional state law; and reference is made to the historical fact that the act of 1833 was passed to meet the then existing exigency growing out of the threatened opposition of one of the states of the Union to the national legislation for the imposition and collection of duties on imports. To this it may be replied that whatever may have been the peculiar circumstances under which the act passed, the section above quoted is still in full force, and obligatory as a law of the United States. And it may be fairly inferred that while its purpose was, at the date of its passage, to provide against a great danger then pending, it has been deemed expedient that it should be continued as a remedy against nullification in any form in which it might be presented. But this point is not now for the first time presented for decision. It has been settled by eminent judges of the highest official position. In the case of Ex parte Jenkins, Judge Grier, of the supreme court of the United States, granted a writ of habeas corpus under the statute referred to, and released the person who applied for it, without the intimation of a doubt as to the authority it conferred. And in the well-known Rosetta Case which occurred about a year since, Judge McLean granted a writ of habeas corpus under the same provision of the statute, and released the marshal from custody under circumstances very similar to those involved in the case now before us.

The only inquiry, therefore, arising in the present case is, whether, from the facts proved, it sufficiently appears that the imprisonment of the marshal was "for any act done or omitted to be done in pursuance of a law of the United States." If this inquiry is answered affirmatively, it will follow that he is entitled to his discharge, as the precise case contemplated by the statute in that event is presented. . . . It has been before stated that the writ of habeas corpus from the probate judge issued the 21st of February, and that the decision of the commissioner, adjudging the fugitives to be the property of the claimant, was made on the 28th of that month. Between these dates the fugitives were in the custody of the marshal, under the process of the commissioner, and it was undeniably his duty to hold them, subject to the final action of the commissioner. Simultaneously with the decision on the claim of the owner, he made oath, pursuant to the provisions of the ninth section of the act of congress of September 16, 1850 [9 Stat. 465], that he had good reason to apprehend a rescue of the fugitives. This section provides that when such oath is made, "it shall be the duty of the officer making the arrest to retain such fugitive in his custody, and to remove him to the state whence he fled, and there to deliver him to said claimant by his agent or attorney." It is clear, from this provision, that the duty of keeping the fugitive in custody, after the decision of the commissioner, if in favor of the claimant, is as imperative as it is while he holds him under the warrant or order of that officer. With the obligation of this stringent and to him paramount law resting on him, was the marshal bound to obey the process of the probate judge? It would seem there was no intention on the part of the marshal to treat that judge with contemptuous disregard. He first appeared before him, and by his counsel exhibited all the facts as to the apprehension, custody, and disposition of the fugitives, submitting at the same time a motion for the dismissal of the writ of habeas corpus. This motion was overruled, and the marshal was required to make a return to the writ. He then presented an answer, couched in respectful terms, stating the reasons why he could not produce the bodies of the fugitives. Was this in contempt of the authority of the probate judge? The marshal states in his answer, duly sworn to, that in his conduct he was governed by what he regarded his duty under the constitution and laws of the United States. He was an officer appointed under the constitution, which he had sworn to support, and which declares "that this constitution and the laws of the United States, which shall be made in pursuance thereof, and all treaties made, or which shall be made under the authority of the United States, shall be the supreme law of the land, and the judges in every state shall be bound thereby, anything in the constitution and laws of any state to the contrary notwithstanding." [Const. art. 6.]

Now, if the marshal in good faith, and acting under what he regarded as an imperative obligation resting on him by virtue of a law of the United States, did or omitted to do the acts for which he is imprisoned by the sentence of the probate judge, is he not entitled to be discharged from imprisonment under the express provision of the act of congress before referred to? In the Rosetta Case, before noticed, this same marshal refused to obey a writ of habeas corpus issued by a state judge, commanding him to produce the alleged fugitive before him, on the ground that such fugitive was in his custody under process from a commissioner of the United States court; and for such refusal he was arrested by a warrant issued by the judge as for a contempt. On application to Judge McLean, that learned and distinguished judge issued a habeas corpus to bring the marshal before him, and, after argument and full consideration, discharged him from the custody of the state officer, under the act of congress already quoted. Judge McLean, in his published opinion, says: "The marshal omitted to do the act ordered to be done by the Honorable Judge Parker, because it would be in express violation of his duty under an act of congress. This is literally within the act." With the knowledge of this adjudication, in a case involving the same principle as in the habeas corpus issued by the probate judge, is it strange the marshal should have pursued the same course which had received the sanction of the eminent judge referred to? In the case decided by Judge McLean, the act omitted to be done was the bringing of the alleged fugitive before Judge Parker under a habeas corpus; and in the present case, it is the failure to produce the fugitives named in the habeas corpus before the probate judge. . . .

There is another high authority in support of the position that in cases arising under an act of congress the power of the federal officers is paramount to that of the states. I refer to the charge of Judge Nelson, of the supreme court of the United States, to the grand jury of the circuit court of the United States for the Southern district of New York. . . . That learned judge, admitting the right of a state judge to issue a habeas corpus for one in custody under federal authority, adds that "when it is shown that the commitment or detainer is under the constitution or a law of the United States, or a treaty, the power of the state authority is at an end, and any further proceeding under the writ is coram non judice and void. In such case, that is, when the prisoner is in fact held under process issued from a federal tribunal under the constitution or a law of the United States, or a treaty, it is the duty of the officer not to give him up, or to allow him to pass from his hands in any stage of the proceedings. He should stand upon his process and authority; and if resisted, maintain them with all the powers conferred upon him for that purpose." Authorities of the same import could be greatly multiplied, but it is unnecessary to adduce more. If judicial decisions are entitled to any consideration, it is clearly established that, though it may be competent for a state judge to issue the writ of habeas corpus in a case of imprisonment under the authority of a law of the United States, when the fact is made known to him, his jurisdiction ceases and all subsequent proceedings by him are void. Is it supposable the marshal was ignorant that the law had been thus settled by some of the ablest judges of the country, and was he guilty of a willful contempt in deferring to these high authorities? He might well conclude that when the probate judge became apprised of the fact that the fugitives were in custody under a law of the United States his jurisdiction ceased, and that the obligation was imperative on him, under no circumstances to permit them to be taken from his custody. . . .

The opinion of that judge, as published, on the question of the sufficiency of the marshal's return, shows clearly what his action would have been if the marshal had produced the fugitives. In that opinion he held that the proceedings before the commissioner, by which the fugitives were held in custody of the marshal, were unconstitutional and void. Although it was decided by Judge McLean, in the Rosetta Case, that it was competent for congress to vest in commissioners appointed by the circuit courts the powers conferred on them by the act of 1850, and that they could, therefore, legally and constitutionally exercise those powers, and although the same decision had been made by several other judges of the supreme court, the probate judge held otherwise, and that the acts of the commissioner were mere nullities; and it would necessarily result from this decision that the process by which the fugitives had been arrested was void, and that they were illegally in the custody of the marshal. I do not refer to this with any purpose of arraigning the conduct or impeaching the motives of the probate judge, but in proof of the fact that obedience to this writ by the marshal would have resulted in the discharge of the fugitives. . . .

In attempting to state briefly the conclusions to which I am brought in the consideration of this case, I have not deemed it necessary to notice all the views presented by the counsel resisting the motion for the discharge of the marshal. One of them has insisted, with much zeal and earnestness, that the fugitive slave law, on which proceedings in this case are based, is, in its most essential requirements, unconstitutional and void, and can not, therefore, form the basis of any valid action by any court or officer of the government. I can not take time to examine and refute this position, but will suggest, what will be most obvious to those who view the subject dispassionately, that a proper appreciation of my position and the obligations resting upon me will make its fallacy and unsoundness sufficiently apparent. The act referred to, whatever views may be entertained of its necessity and expediency, is a valid and constitutional law, and as such must be respected and enforced. No judge or other officer of the state or national government, or any citizen of either, so far as the rights of others are concerned, has a right to act on his private and individual views of the policy and validity of laws passed in conformity with the forms of the constitution. Until repealed or set aside by the adjudication of the proper judicial tribunal, they must have the force of laws and be obeyed as such. Any other principle must lead to anarchy in its worst form, and result inevitably in the speedy overthrow of our institutions. The petitioner is discharged.

CHAPTER 6

THE OHIO LEGISLATURE RESPONDS
Debate on the Floor

Just a few days after the Garners were captured, the events in Cincin-
nati provoked debate in Ohio's state legislature, as some representatives
and senators seized on the case as a vehicle for changing state law. The
arguments were intense and continued even after the family's forced
return South. Throughout Ohio's history, as the political climate and
partisan balance had shifted over the years, state laws on the claiming
of fugitives had changed back and forth, at times assisting claimants,
at other times posing barriers designed to protect those claimed as
slaves. Now, it appeared that it might be possible to alter the legal code
significantly in favor of fugitives. Ohio had entered a new era: like
other political institutions in the state, the legislature had undergone
dramatic changes in the 1850s, especially in the past year or so, when
Salmon Chase had helped forge a statewide Republican Party domi-
nated by those hostile to the extension of slavery and worried about
Southern imperialism. In the fall of 1855, the new party triumphed with
the election of Chase as governor.

 Led by James Monroe in the House and Oliver Brown in the
Senate, Republicans responded to the Garner case by pushing a series
of bills, including one that would punish individuals who aided in the
work of slave catching and another that prohibited the use of the state's
jails to hold captured fugitives. Many of these efforts failed, and others
would bear fruit only in the sessions of 1857. Despite the recent election
the balance of power in both houses was complex and precarious. Still,
two measures passed in April 1856. One was symbolic, a resolution with
no legal force: it asked the state's representatives in Washington to "use
their best exertions" to win the repeal of the Fugitive Slave Law "at the

*earliest possible time." Another, more practically important measure also
passed both houses and became law. Representative Monroe proposed
a habeas corpus bill designed to assist state judges who, like Judge
Burgoyne in the Garner case, sought to pry captured fugitives from the
hands of hostile federal marshals. The bill granted judges the power to
issue a writ of habeas corpus for the fugitives to whatever official seemed
most likely to execute it; those failing to comply with the writ were
subject to a fine of $1,000. On paper, at least, the bill also made it very
difficult to recapture fugitives who had been freed on such a writ: for
instance, anyone who reimprisoned or aided in reimprisoning a freed
fugitive was subject to a $5,000 fine. Monroe's bill passed the House on
March 13, by a vote of 62 to 40; the Senate approved it on April 1, and
the law was signed by both houses on April 5.*

    *The following documents give a glimpse of the content and tone of
the discussions on the bill, showing how the debate in the legislature
ranged well beyond the technical legal details. Here as in so many venues and media, those responding to the case moved from the details of
the Garners' circumstances to the broadest, most fundamental questions
dividing an increasingly polarized nation.*

Cincinnati Daily Gazette, February 1, 1856

*Senator Oliver Brown's bids to reform the state's laws pertaining to slavery
were among those efforts that would not succeed until 1857, when, on
April 17, the legislature passed one measure against slaveholding and
another against kidnapping. Although the latter law provided some
protections for the state's free black population, neither offered any real
assistance to fugitive slaves, as both laws exempted processes conducted
under the Fugitive Slave Act and explicitly deferred to all federal legal and
constitutional provisions concerning slavery. It was Brown, however, who
first brought the Garners' plight into the legislative debates, producing the
preamble and resolution contained in the following document.*

Ohio Legislature.

We copy from the Ohio *Statesman* the following proceedings in the Senate, with reference to the Fugitive Slave Case:

    Mr. Brown offered the following preamble and resolution:

WHEREAS We have authentic information that certain quiet, peaceable persons in the city of Cincinnati, county of Hamilton and State of Ohio, guilty of no offence known to our laws, were, on Monday last, attacked by one Ellis, and a large body of assistants, citizens of said county, under the lead of Archibald K. Gaines, and a Major Murphy, of Kentucky:

AND WHEREAS, one of the party thus assailed finding Ellis and his assistants about to gain a victory over a weak mother and her four infant children, and, in order to save those children from a life every moment of which was to be infinitely worse than death, with a mother's devotion to her offspring, took the life of her youngest child, and sought with her own hands to take the life, also of her three remaining children:

Resolved, That the Judiciary committee be requested to report a bill to prevent the recurrence of such scenes in our State, and further to prevent the wicked, depraved and abandoned from participating in them.

. . . The resolution was adopted. The preamble was adopted. Yeas, 24; nays, 7. The vote by which the preamble was adopted was reconsidered, and the preamble was referred to Mr. Brown for revision.

Ohio Statesman, February 19, 1856

———

Representative Monroe's more substantial and immediately successful bill, HR 71, was debated several times at length before passage. The next two documents are drawn from the reporting on those debates. Representatives Burns and Jewett would ultimately vote for the bill; Representatives Sawyer and Upham would oppose it.

Speech of Mr. *Sawyer* in the House of Representatives,
on the Habeas Corpus Bill, Friday, Feb. 15.

Mr. Sawyer addressed the Chair . . .

I doubt if this bill will add to the rights of the people of Ohio. I am not lawyer enough to determine, and have been, since its first reading, beset with constant apprehension, that it was not all right, and am not yet relieved; although I am assured it will be all that is claimed for it. I fear it has for its object negro stealing and aiding the underground operations to run off slaves from their masters, I would not take part against it, if I thought it was not intended to contribute to this end, and to throw additional difficulties in the way of recovering slave property that has been enticed away from their masters, or have made escape to this side of the river. It is a known fact that there are men in Cincinnati and elsewhere, actively engaged in inducing slaves to leave their owners, and run them off, in direct opposition to the Constitution and right. . . .

Now, I have fears that the object and intention of this bill is to assist the Abolitionists to rescue slaves from Kentucky labor, due to their masters. I am one of those who believe the master is entitled to the service of his slave, guarantied to him by the Constitution of the U.S., and even here in the State of Ohio, it is proper to assist him to take the slave back, escaping from his service, notwithstanding the abhorrence with which the institution of slavery may be viewed. If the slave makes his way to this side of the river, and secretes himself in Cincinnati, the master has a right to take him away by force, and it is not brotherly, it is not in accordance with the great charter, which we all should respect, bequeathed us by the wisdom of our fathers, to interfere to throw obstacles in his way, to prevent him from recovering his property.

In a conversation with a high functionary, very recently, a friend of Governor Chase, motives were shown that weigh no little upon the character and object of this bill. He said it had been determined those very slaves that have made so much excitement at Cincinnati and elicited so much false philanthropy, should be rescued from the hands of their masters and conducted safely to Canada. The only way was to make them amenable to the charge of the murder of the child, was to have them imprisoned, and set at large by the Governor, when the Underground Railroad was to complete the operation. I was assured it would be done! Is it dealing fairly? Still it has been the plan since the Underground Railroad was established, to decoy, steal, coax away the slave, and offer every inducement for him to leave his once happy home, to struggle and buffet for a hard living in a strange land. This is not just, nor honest according to my sense of right. I could never tolerate, much less be guilty of such acts. I approve of the Fugitive Slave Law, because it is founded upon right. The constitution of the United States fully authorizes such a law. . . .

I have never been guilty of that sin—no, I will not so express it— of the act of running after a negro. He might go without my helping or stopping. I should neither connive at the one, nor trouble myself about the other. . . .

Mr. Sawyer said he was clearly at the opinion from manifestations in this House that there was a party here whose object was to place the blacks on a level and equality with the whites. His friend first preceding him had said they were an inferior race. He thought so too. All the philanthropy and sympathy that could be manufactured could not make him think otherwise. Speak of making them equals!

It is my purpose, said Mr. Sawyer, to trace the history of the Republican party, as it is now called, from my earliest recollection to the present time. At first it was called the Amalgamation party. Yes, that's it, the Amalgamation party.

A voice. Who called it so?

Mr. Sawyer. The gentleman's party. That was its name then.

Mr. Upham. It was another, not the Republican party.

Mr. Sawyer. It was the party of the gentlemen who hold caucuses here, and shape their course by caucus.

Mr. Burns. There are none here.

Mr. Sawyer. I mean they are here.

Mr. Burns. Tell what and who were the Republican party then.

Mr. Sawyer. Arthur Tappan and Garrison, and others, of New York and Boston. They affected to hold the blacks in high estimation, and treated them as free and equal.

Mr. Burns interrupted.

Mr. Sawyer. If the gentleman will let me alone, I will explain.

Mr. Burns. Then the doctrines of the Democratic and Republican parties were the same.

Mr. Sawyer. It was the doctrine of these Amalgamationists to do away with all distinctions of color—to go to church on the Sabbath, the negro woman and white man, and the white man and negro woman, and there be seated promiscuously, affording a piebald spectacle indeed. At length it became so repugnant to every thing like a sense of decency that it was absolutely shocking as well as ridiculous.

Mr. Sawyer said he never came to make a set speech, that he was not prepared. He had taken the trouble to procure the documents. Gentlemen had seen proper to throw the gauntlet, and he was determined they should have quite as much as they bargained for. He had witnessed transactions in this House but yesterday that he had never seen tolerated on the floor of any House before. When it had been proclaimed that the black was equal, if not superior to the white, it broke out in cheering from men and negroes from the gallery, and even men here on the floor loudly cheered. It was disgusting to any one of even moderate sensibility. . . .

Mr. Burns. Is not the Declaration of Independence true? Were not the blacks here then?

Mr. Sawyer. Now the gentleman thinks he has got me; but he hasn't. I have a place to get out yet, and not a small hole either. . . .

. . . I did not believe that all men are created equal, although I believe the Declaration of Independence. If I believed as gentlemen do I would make the negro socially and politically equal with the white. Will gentlemen tell me why they have not been made so? I will tell you why. It is because such a sentiment as they avow does not pervade community, is repugnant to taste and abhorrent to appearance. . . .

But let gentlemen carry this thing out. Let them make this negro their equal—an impossibility I think, at least they cannot make him mine.—I say let them make him their equal, make him a member of their families, make him the companion of your wives and children, marry to your daughters, and your sons to their daughters. You say we are all of one blood, and should be equal—that we should go to vote together, send our children to the same schools, intermarry indiscriminately—we cannot carry out the doctrine of equality, unless it is observed in every thing, unless we practise amalgamation in its fullest extent. The liberty party, or Abolitionists of this House, yesterday, inculcated this very doctrine. Let us see how it will look, practically illustrated. Suppose I have six sons; three are married to white ladies and three wedded to the pouting lipped descendants of Ham. After a while, at some birthday or family anniversary, they are all gathered under the old rooftree, and around the cozy fireside, grandpapa seated in his old arm chair, a numerous progeny grouped around him, of various hues, "from snowy white to sooty," or half a dozen little fair skinned fellows on one knee and as many little darkies on the other, would we not have a fine time of it? It would be a rich family picture; and must excite the admiration of all lovers of equality!

Having shown the tendency—nay the absolute consequence to which the sentiments of one party here must lead, I turn to another, who inculcate the doctrine that foreign-born citizens should be here twenty-one years, before they shall be entitled to the right of suffrage. I must say something for their benefit. Many of them are not averse to the heresy of investing the negro with this right, between which and the foreigner they would place such a barrier—I am not one to think as they do. The most of them could fully appreciate the right of suffrage before they left their fatherland. They understood the principles of freedom. They had examined the basis of our government, and were satisfied with its advantages.

They were Americans in heart, before they came here. Gentlemen say "Americans shall rule America." So say I. . . .

I want them to mingle their blood with our people. Although I do not like the amalgamation of white blood with that of the negro, for in that case, ours is sure to deteriorate, although theirs may improve. I have no objection to the rosey-cheeked, bright-eyed Dutch or Irish girl, for they would improve the stock, and the gifts they bring would be a credit to any country. It would be the pure Anglo-Saxon blood, and elevate the new race not only in the attributes of intellect, but in the glorious physical development of strength and proportion.

I can show gentlemen, that I am a much better friend of the negro than they are, with all their boasted philanthropy. I would take the African from his degraded state here, and colonize him. He should be returned to his native clime. I would remove him to Liberia, where he might become President, Judge, or some high functionary, and indulge and cultivate all those aspirations which can never be successfully cultivated here. . . . Here such a thing cannot, and will not be permitted, as gentlemen have asserted upon this floor. This country agrees with and is peculiarly suited to the Anglo-Saxon race. Here is the place where Liberty loves to dwell. . . .

"The whole boundless continent was ours," and will be and shall be to the end, the abode of freedom,—not of the blacks, for the two races cannot live in juxtaposition harmoniously. Everything shows it. It is a physical as well as a moral impossibility—Nature itself points it out. The noble and spirited horse crossed with an inferior animal, is reduced one step, beyond which deterioration can never go, for nature has reserved to herself the power to prevent the multiplication of a still inferior grade. In no instance has the progeny been found to have been elevated in the scale of being. Then since they cannot be our equals—since they cannot mix with us to our advantage, the best thing for them and us is to colonize them. They have brought us into difficulties—caused us to think hard of each other; and have they not been the occasion of sedition being carried to the very foot of the Government? I am for colonizing them where they may benefit themselves and their race—where their intermixture with the people will be beneficial to the latter, and not hurtful to themselves. . . .

What is the African at home? He walks in the shadow of the most abject ignorance. He is scarcely the equal, much less the superior, of the dumb brute. Like the dog he is guided by his instincts or his master. He wallows like the hog, and has no idea of aught beyond the mere purposes of existence, and perpetuating the species. True, he was brought away from that delightful innocence—that Utopia of the dreams of some politicians, for a wicked purpose. Yes, say he was stolen away for wicked purposes; who knows but it may be converted into good, yet? The Savior of mankind was dragged to the cross, surrounded by a clamorous mob, hooting and upbraiding him with every ignominious epithet, and yet it was the harbinger of the salvation of multitudes. The brothers of Joseph stripped from him his coat of many colors, and sold him to bondage in Egypt. The act was wicked in itself but brought in its trains blessings incalculable. And so it may be with the negro. Although he was at first stolen from Africa, it had made him a better man, and might be the means of making his race respectable. . . .

Had the plans of colonization been carried out, and had not Abolition and Amalgamation entered the minds of white men, as means of obtaining political ends, there would not be a free black this day in the State of Ohio. . . .

Anti-Slavery Bugle (Salem, Ohio), March 29, 1856

REMARKS OF MR. JEWETT, ON MR. MONROE'S HABEAS CORPUS BILL

. . . Mr. Chairman, I have no fear lest I should characterize American Slavery by any too strong terms. . . . Neither have I any regret at being styled an Abolitionist, and if there be any other term in the English language that can express one's abhorrence of Slavery in stronger terms, then I wish to be designated by that term. Gentlemen here seem to have a great horror of that term, and every measure that has any squinting, or by possibility any bearing upon the subject of Slavery, before acting upon it they must feel of their scalps to ascertain whether wool is beginning to grow, or take a close look in a reflector to see whether they are changing in color. . . .

But Sir, the greatest and best men that ever graced our earth have been Abolitionists.

The leader of Israel was an Abolitionist, and through his agency under the Divine protection, some millions of as abject and degraded beings as now suffer in our disgraced country, were liberated. Every reformer in the Jewish polity from that time, were Abolitionists. They preached in favor of "breaking every yoke, and letting the oppressed go free." So the *Man* of sorrows, he who came to redeem us from sin and death, preached Abolitionism in every moral precept, and the inculcation and dissemination of his doctrine drove Slavery out of the Roman Empire.

So every true reformer from that time to the present, including Clarkson, Wilberforce, Granville, Sharp, John Wesley, George Washington, Thomas Jefferson, and a host too numerous to mention, were all Abolitionists. Sir, were a man in the Old Dominion to use such language as Thomas Jefferson used with regard to Slavery, he would be made acquainted with Judge Lynch, minus a jury. And here on this floor, in the so called free State of Ohio, were a man to use such language as he used to express his abhorrence of Slavery, he would be characterized as a woolly-head or fanatic, and thought by some of our good Union savers as a proper subject for one of our Asylums. . . .

This Bill makes provision for securing the citizens of the State of Ohio from the rapacity of men-stealers. It might be with all reason expected that those who had always stolen the earnings of a portion of their own population, would not be content without infringing upon the rights of their neighbors. So far as the Bill goes, it is well enough, and I shall support it on the same principle that I would make my supper on a cold corn dodger when I could not get anything better. I do assure gentlemen it is with me a meagre bill of fare. . . .

And, Sir, I can support such a law and not do violence to an agreement I entered into before that desk, to support the Constitution of the United States of America. . . . No, Sir, I do not believe that that time honored document is, as they affirm, "a covenant with death and a league with hell," but one of the best instruments for the purpose of securing the blessings of *Liberty* to all over whom the dominion of this nation extends, that ever emanated from fallible man, if its provisions were duly enforced. —But, Sir, I believe the *end,* the great object of that instrument, as is so clearly expressed in its preamble, has been sacrificed to a perverted meaning of some of its provisions. . . .

That [the framers] made a concession to Slavery, in permitting the African Slave trade to continue for twenty years, I freely admit; but that they also thought and expected that the extinguishment of the African Slave trade would do away with Slavery, no one conversant with the debates and history of the adoption of the Constitution, will deny. But the institution of Slavery had no legal existence before the adoption of that instrument, and no one will be, I think, so destitute of good sense as to expect to find a warrant for its legality in it. But when was Slavery legalized in this country? Can it be legalized? Was it ever legalized? I believe the best writers on common law say that Slavery is so abhorrent to justice, to nature, to morality, to the law of God, that it can never be legalized. . . .

Again, was Slavery legalized by the Declaration of American Independence, which was for years the only constitutional law of the land, and which has never been abrogated, and which starts with the declaration that "*all* men are created free and equal, and endowed by their Creator with certain unalienable rights, among which are life, liberty, and the pursuit of happiness?" On the contrary, had there been any Slavery in the colonies when the Declaration was made, it would have abolished it. And so the courts in Massachusetts decided, and to her eternal honor. She was the only one implicated in the evil that fully carried out the principles of that Declaration. . . .

The only remaining source of authority for slavery is the Constitution under which we live. What does that say of Slaves, Slavery or Masters? . . .

The only passages in it that is so often quoted here and every where as a compromise to Slavery. 4th article 2d section, and by which it is thought one may make a Slave of another, says nothing of Slaves or Slavery, and is an article needed to regulate the domestic intercourse of Massachusetts and Connecticut, and would be essential in the Constitution were there no Slavery in existence. —We can with all propriety talk of service or labor being due from one who has voluntarily entered into a contract, or has been bound by his parent or guardian to service. But it is all nonsense to talk of service or labor being "due" from one that can not make a contract. But suppose that the framers of that instrument had the recovery of a fugitive from Slavery in view when they framed that article, I find in the amendments to that compact a sweeping prohibition of Slavery.

Now an amendment to an instrument of writing has more force than any thing in the original body of the writing. It presupposes something defective in the previous part of it which is there remedied. An amendment to a constitution, like a codicil to a will, overrides every thing preceding. —It is something supposed to be adopted, upon more mature reflection, to remedy something wanting or defective. It is found in the fifth article of the amendment. Happily it is crouched substantially in these words: "No person shall be deprived of life, liberty or property without due process of law."

Can any language be clearer than this? . . . I ask then if every man illegally restrained of his liberty is not entitled to the benefit of Habeas Corpus; if he is not entitled to a hearing before the judge, and that his oppressors should be made to appear and show cause for his being restrained of his freedom?

Now, Sir, were it not for a disinclination to occupy the time of this House with motions which I know can not prevail, I should move that it be so amended as to give to every man that puts his foot on our soil his freedom, unless tainted by crime. —But as I know such a proposition cannot succeed, I shall vote for the present bill, which gives me greater security, as well as a large number of our community less fortunate than ourselves, who enjoy a certain amount of freedom, and whom it is our delight to oppress, and crush down every appearance of rising manhood.

But to the everlasting shame of Ohio, she is yet to continue the hunting ground for Slaves, and her citizens are yet to be permitted to engage in the damnable work of Slave catching and Slave hunting. And members can unblushingly acknowledge themselves in favor of the Fugitive Slave Law, and seek to deprive this poor bill of what little virtue it might by possibility possess, of permitting the judge to examine into the merits of the case. Sir, I would not wish to manifest any want of courtesy towards members here, but I have for a long time thought that I would not willingly trust my life or property in the hands of any man that acknowledged his willingness to comply with the requirement of the Fugitive slave Law. . . .

. . . I honor and revere Massachusetts for her noble stand on the subject of human liberty. I revere her as the only one of the original confederacy that practically acknowledges the truth of the declaration she had made. From the formation of her constitution, every man has been on an equality, and the experience of three-fourths of a century demonstrates that the mad dog, fanatical cry of amalgamation where equal rights are extended, has in her case been proved to have no foundation in fact. But what is the case in that quarter from whence this cry originated, and which is so readily taken up by apologists of Slavery here? Let the color of those held and fleeing from bondage answer. —Let the uncontradicted statement of Jefferson, that "the best blood of Virginia runs in Slaves," answer. Is it not a fact that the declaration of Henry Clay that Slavery "is destined to be obliterated by the inevitable laws of generation" has been practically carried out by every Southern man, (or at least not to have done so would be the exception,) the maker of that declaration not excepted. But, sir, this bill is very defective, in that it furnishes no protection to a man fleeing from Slavery towards the north star, if he happens to have any of the blood of the despised Ham in his veins. . . .

Should the fugitive belong to the same household of faith, should he plead for the sake of a common Saviour your aid and assistance, you must turn a deaf ear to all such silly entreaties, and brush them all away with the declaration that my *obedience to the Constitution of my country forbids* me to entertain any such *foolish notions of humanity.*

Mr. Chairman, should the time ever arrive when this nation shall become half civilized that generation will look back with horror to the time when their forefathers submitted to a law that compelled them to assist in hunting and catching men and women for the purpose of making them Slaves. And may we not hope that the historian of that era, as he records the lamentable fact, might be able to record the cheering intelligence that the same generation, in obedience to the dictates of their humanity, wiped the disgraceful fact from the page of history?

CHAPTER 7

THE BATTLE IN THE PRESS

Editorials on the Murder

Editorializing about Margaret Garner's attack on her children began as soon as she was captured in Cincinnati. A mother would kill her daughter before seeing her back in slavery—what did this suggest? The eight documents in this section are a small sampling drawn from the many editorial answers to that question. Although the commentary was most abundant in Cincinnati and Kentucky, the implications of the death of Mary Garner were elaborated and contested in the nation's capital and throughout the free states. Most of the editorials on this topic are dominated by hostility to slavery: those opposing the institution seemed far more willing to delve into the unsettling details of what happened at the moment when Gaines and the federal marshals recaptured the family.

New York Daily Tribune, February 8, 1856

At the time of the Garner trial, the Tribune *was, along with the* New York Herald, *the nation's most prominent and influential newspaper. Editor Horace Greeley, who had recently become active in the Republican Party, ensured that his paper treated the events in Cincinnati as a major national story, covering the case frequently and in detail both by reprinting accounts from the local press and through reports submitted to the* Tribune *by special correspondents. In this the paper differed markedly from the Democratic, militantly pro–Fugitive Slave Act* Herald, *which quickly abandoned the story.*

THE SLAVE MOTHER.

The case of the fugitives at Cincinnati is likely to incite more questions than those which have been argued so ably before the Court of the United States Commissioner. These are in themselves sufficient to arouse the attention of every man who is interested in an impartial administration of law; but beyond these is a moral question, addressing itself to the sympathies of all humane and noble hearts. The former we shall discuss in due time, and, therefore, confine our remarks for the present to the latter.

Our readers are aware that among the slaves arrested at Cincinnati was a mother, who preferred to put one of her children to death rather than it should be returned to the gripe of the slave-catchers. Her case is a remarkable one. We have heard a great deal of the beneficent influences of Slavery, and of the wonderful tenacity with which even the slaves themselves cling to its benefits. Every time that a poor negro, disappointed with the experience of free life, or longing for the flesh-pots of Virginia, returns to his original condition, the fact is trumpeted to the four winds of heaven. We are called upon to admire the beautiful effects of the institution which causes its very victims to fall in love with it, and to denounce that insane philanthropy which seeks to interfere with so happy a condition.

But what have such reasoners to say of the recent incident in Ohio? How do they account for the fact that a mother, fresh from the blessings of bondage, and with all a mother's sensibility and tenderness—will yet draw the knife across the throat of her innocent babe in preference to restoring him to the state from which she has just escaped? They will denounce the deed as a crime—they will ascribe it to a sudden and bewildering frenzy—they will say that the woman was demented—that she was overcome by a panic, of fear and that she knew not what she did.

Well, we will admit the crime, and granting the intense excitement under which she labored, ask how it was that she was thrown into such a madness of feeling? If Slavery is so agreeable a condition to the slaves; if they are so well nurtured and cared for under it, how comes it that this woman was crazed by the thought of being returned to it? How comes it that she could forget all the dictates of a mother's heart, and condemn her child to death by her own hands, rather than relinquish the possession of it to its pretended owner? How comes it that her companions, who are arrested as accomplices in this crime of murder, say that they would rather be tried for their lives, and afterward marched to the gallows, than be sent back to Kentucky? They know what Slavery is, and they know what death is, and, with many that have gone before them in this world, they cry, "Death before Slavery."

Our Southern friends who extol the delights of servitude will have to revise their theory, or leave events like these out of the account. These slaves, it seems to us, are, after all, men, with all the feelings, instincts and aspirations of men. There is something in them which tells of higher objects of life to a human being than "possum-fat and hominy," or the most delectable external relations. There is something which whispers to them that the body is more than raiment, and the freedom of the soul infinitely greater than the comforts of the body. Like the rest of us, they yearn for freedom, and having achieved freedom, though but for a few days, they welcome the grave as the alternative to bondage.

But, in doing this, they have in history some pertinent and illustrious examples. The annals of man are filled with similar incidents. There are names that have been rescued from that mortality which follows all human affairs, solely on the ground of such exhibitions as we have seen in Cincinnati. Not to mention the thousand occurrences in rude barbarian times—where fathers and brothers despairing of safety have destroyed those who were most dear to them—let us recall one or two from the pages of more civilized story. When Mithridates was defeated by Lucullus he ordered the sacrifice of his wife and sister to prevent their falling into the hands of the enemy; and the writers who narrate the tale are accustomed to dilate upon the act as a proof of the dignity and grandeur of his soul. When Virginius, summoned by Appius Claudius to surrender his daughter as a slave, plunges the dagger into her bosom rather than yield to the demand, the pen of the historian warms into eloquence as he describes the heroic spirit of the Roman father, and the imaginations of the poets are kindled into tragic sublimity.

The finest of the Lays of Rome, written by Macaulay, is decidedly that in which he tells the tale of the hapless Virginia; one of the most touching and effective of recent tragedies is founded upon the same pathetic subject. We have seen the latter, indeed, as enacted upon the stage, melt the eyes and stir the inmost depths of emotion in large audiences, in whose shuddering sympathy with the child was always mingled a lurking admiration for the stern heroism of the parent. Yet in what respect does the act of the Roman Virginius differ from that of the poor slave-mother on the banks of the Ohio? In the one case the daughter was claimed as a slave, under an infamous law of Rome, trumped up for the occasion, and the father, rather than submit to it, plunged his knife in the heart of that daughter. In the other case the child is claimed as a slave, under an infamous law of the Union, passed in a moment of political fanaticism, and the mother, rather than yield to it, draws the knife across the throat of that child. In the former, however, the crime becomes classic; history celebrates it; artists spread it upon their canvas; poets embalm the memory of it in undying lines; and the world does not cease to admire it, while it shudders, as a manifestation of the sternness and grandeur of Roman courage. But, in the latter case, where there is even more to excuse the criminal aspect of the transaction, and more to highten its pathetic interest, because the perpetrator is a woman and a mother, the poor creature is hurled to prison as a murderess, either to suffer the penalties of the law, in that character, or to be restored to a bondage which she regards as infinitely worse than death.

Whatever may become of her—and we trust that the issue will be left to a Jury of the free citizens of Ohio, who have hearts in their bodies, rather than to the tender mercies of those who drove the wretched one to so dreadful an alternative—let no one hereafter talk of the love of slaves for their servile condition. A great many of them, no doubt, who know no better, are contented with their lot, just as a great many white men here at the North are satisfied to live in ignorance; but the instinct of Freedom is in a majority of them an irrepressible one, which will assert itself when it has an opportunity. How strong and mighty it is in some, we behold in the incident before us, where the most powerful dictates of nature and affection were overcome by it, and a mother was made to imbrue her hands in the blood of her own offspring rather than consent to its return to the subjection from which she fondly thought she had delivered it forever. Ah no! "Disguise thyself as thou wilt, Slavery, still thou art a bitter draught," [end.]

Cincinnati Daily Enquirer, February 14, 1856

(COMMUNICATED)

FUGITIVE SLAVE CASE—*Messrs Editors* I have seen it stated in several papers that cruel treatment, by the owners of the slaves, whose protracted trial is still pending before the United States Commissioner in your city, was the cause of their attempted escape, and also the murder of the child. Standing in the relation of physician, neighbor and friend to these gentlemen, and knowing the absolute falsity of this charge, I feel unwilling that it should remain uncontradicted.

I have known A. E. Gaines and James Marshall, the owners of the Negroes, for more than twenty years. I have lived in a mile or two of James Marshall about that length of time, and as near or nearer to Mr. Gaines since his return from the South, some eight or ten years ago; I have attended the families of these gentlemen; both white and black, as physician; have been at their houses and negro-houses in the day and in the night, in every season of the year; have seen their Negroes at work indoors and out, and feel assured that cruelty or inhumanity to their slaves could not have been hid from my observation in all that time and under all these relations. I have never witnessed cruelty or inhumanity in either of them toward their slaves, but, on the contrary, have seen them well cared for in health and in sickness—well-housed and well-clothed and well-fed, and looking as contented and happy as Negroes generally do; and they are generally, when let alone by *false humanity,* the most contented and happy beings to be found anywhere. I have seen the children of the woman Peggy brought into Mr. Gaines' own house in sickness, and attended them there, and seen them tenderly cared for by the white family in their sufferings. And I have no doubt that it has required much and long persuasion to induce her to leave her comfortable house and home for the untried mercies and tender care of her Abolition friends, whose bowels of compassion seem just now to be so hungry and thirsty for her blood, that they cannot wait the regular delays of the law. She has offended against the laws of Ohio, by pouring out the blood of her child as an offering to her free soil. The majority of Ohio's laws must be maintained; and the yelping curs of Abolition raise a piteous howl for the blood of their deluded victim, even in defiance of the laws of the United States. Abominable hypocrisy! Do they not know that their senseless iniquity and utter disregard of the laws of the land has been the cause of this crime, and that they stand accused of this murder by every honest conscience? Do they not know that they stand guilty of sending hundreds of slaves to the extreme south against their wills, and against the wills and wishes of their owners. Do they not know that they are daily tightening the bonds of slavery, and diminishing the privileges and comforts of the slave? They would drive the owners to cruelty and inhumanity, if it were not true that a cruel master in this community would be held as only one remove above an Abolitionist.

And after all is said, what do they care for the poor fugitive who has been hurried to the inhospitable North, or lives in filth and penury in their midst, forever fleeing from, and, perhaps, never pursued by his owner? It is all false, deceitful, dishonest. I do not mean honest anti-slavery men and women. I do not mean law-abiding emancipationists. We have many such in Kentucky, and there would have been many more among us if there never had been a negro deceiving Abolitionist.

Respectfully, Yours, & etc.

B. SMITH CLARKSON

BOONE CITY, KY., February 11, 1856.

Cincinnati Daily Times, February 15, 1856

FREEDOM AND ITS ETHICAL CODE

We do wish people would distinguish between a name and a thing—and that names are not always things. The reports of parliamentary committees to the British Parliament prove a more degrading bondage, more moral depravity, and intellectual poverty and physical suffering among the laborers of England than is to be found anywhere on the globe, and yet England is a free country, there being no sufficient mutual obligation and responsibility between capital and labor, to prevent the inflictions of misery and want upon the honest, the good, and the industrious. There is ever, in all conditions, liberty to man to realize the goods and the truths that belong to him, and it is the duty of those of higher intelligence and purer affection to instruct and lead those below them as a condition precedent to all true freedom. How is it, then, when murder is counselled, with all its train of demoniac passions and reflections?—when laying aside christian precepts, pagan philosophy and pagan example is cited, as an encouragement to a violation of the decalogue? The sermon on the mount teaches no such phrenzied code of ethics.

All men are subjected to laws, which exist of necessity, for if all men "had the law written on their hearts" there would be no necessity. Freedom, it seems, in New York, according to Rev. Mr. Pease, has its dark side; yet there is no imperative obligation to guard the victims of neglect, of superior intelligence and enterprise, and virtue, *and* capital, against the extremes to which free competition reduces them, as there is elsewhere. We go against *all* slavery, that of the North, as well as that of the South, that of England, Scotland and Ireland, as of the West Indies and Brazil; —but in saying this, we are compelled to look at matters naturally not fanatically, not abstractly, but relatively, else in rectifying an evil, a worse one be committed. We do not believe the world was made and set agoing, and then left to man's guidance; but that there is over all a guiding Providence, so particular that even a sparrow cannot fall to the ground without notice; how much more then is the process of individual and national progress protected by mercy, love, and wisdom. Even devils and evils have their uses. There are many spokes in the wheel, but these parts are too apt to consider themselves the whole wheel, and that they only are sufficient.

Anti-Slavery Bugle, February 23, 1856

The Bugle *was the official organ of the Western Anti-Slavery Society, the main institution of abolition activism not only in Ohio but also in Indiana, western Pennsylvania, and southern Michigan. The paper at this time hewed close to the Garrisonian line, eschewing participation in electoral politics and challenging the morality of remaining in a union with slaveholders.*

From Frederick Douglass' Paper.
THE BEAUTIES OF SLAVERY—A SLAVE CHILD KILLED BY ITS MOTHER

We give elsewhere in our columns, a full report of the particulars of the dreadful tragedy in Cincinnati, which resulted in the death of a slave child by the hands of its mother. It seems that she was one of a party of eight slaves, who had escaped from Kentucky. The brave fugitives were pursued soon after their departure, and captured after the most desperate resistance. The frantic mother, finding that she and her little ones would be captured, determined they should never return to the house of bondage, and with a butcher knife commenced the work of death. She succeeded in killing but one of the children, though she states that it was her intention to kill them all, and then herself, preferring DEATH to Slavery. And now while in prison she constantly avows that she will never more be a slave, but will take her own life whenever an opportunity presents itself. Her husband and parents also declare that they would rather die than be replunged into the burning hell of Slavery.

What a commentary upon the "blessed" realities of American Slavery, Republican Despotism, Fourth-of-July Democracy! A slave mother, on the soil of the "Free" States, hunted like the wolf, and rescuing her little ones from the grasp of her pursuer, by delivering them into the jaws of Death, preferring to see them weltering in their hearts' blood, rather than to see them slaves! And this is the "land of the free, and the home of the brave!"

What a terrible protest have we here against the infernal enactment, which allows the hunting of a poor and defenceless mother with her little babes, whom she prefers seeing locked in the arms of Death, than in the clutches of the tyrants of Free and Democratic America! The act of this despairing slave mother, is vastly more expressive than tongue can tell of the wrongs, and cruelties, and miseries of Slavery. How perfectly happy and contented the slaves must be in their "normal," "Heaven-appointed" condition! Where is Rev. NEHEMIAH ADAMS, of "South Side" notoriety? Here is a fine opportunity for gazing upon a North Side picture of the "Patriarchal Institution. Let him gaze upon it, until his eyes are red with weeping, and heart o'erflows with penitence. And then let him gather every number of his "South Side view," and burn them at the base of Bunker Hill.

The name of this brave slave mother, the heroic act which she performed, and all the circumstances connected with it, will never be forgotten. History tells us of a Roman maiden who was sacrificed by her father in order to preserve her chastity. The deed has been immortalized in verse; music, painting, history, oratory, the drama, all, all, have kept the ashes of the Roman Father, glowing as it were, in eternal beauty. And so shall the name of this heroic slave mother never die. The "wide, wide world" will do her homage. The poet will gather inspiration from this offering of blood to the goddess of Freedom; History will hand down her name to the latest generation. Yes, MARGARET, THE SLAVE MOTHER, will furnish an inspiring theme for the painter's pencil, and the poet's song. She will not be viewed as a *murderess* but as a *heroine,* who loved her little babes too well, to behold them slaves, and therefore, fled for refuge to the grave; aye, to the grave—for *"there the servant is free from his master, and the voice of the oppressor is heard no more.*

Sleep on, child of the Slave Mother! No blood hound will e'er be upon *thy* track. Thou art free! Sleep on! The cruel task-master cannot reach thee in thy secure abode. There are no whips or chains, or slave-holders in the place where thy *spirit* dwelleth. The voice of thy blood cri-eth unto Heaven from the ground. Sleep on! Retribution is on the wing.

Liberator, February 29, 1856

Liberty or Death—Ohio and Kansas—Anthony Burns Excommunicated for running away, &c.

CLEVELAND, O., Feb. 15, 1856

Dear Garrison:

Events growing out of and deeply affecting antislavery in the West, and every where, crowd so rapidly one upon another, that one hardly knows what to speak of. Two events in this State have sent a thrill through every county and town and city, and the end is not yet.

. . . [S]econd . . . is *the Cincinnati Tragedy.* MARGARET GARNER, that loving, heroic mother, who cut her child's throat rather than see Christians (?) consign it to the horrors of slavery, bids fair to live on the record of time when the names of Patrick Henry, of Washington, Jefferson, and their compeers, shall have been forgotten. Patrick Henry spoke the words—'Give me liberty or give me death!' Margaret did the deed, and with her own hand took the life of her child, dearer to her heart than her own life, and would have done the same to her other three children, and then to herself, had there been time, to save herself and them from the cruelties and sufferings which Christians (?) and Republicans (?) would have inflicted on them. Who can blame that mother? Not one who thinks it right to take life at all. Will not Wendell Phillips, Theodore Parker, Henry Ward Beecher, Mrs. Stowe, and Dr. Lyman Beecher, deliver orations and sermons, and write eulogies on that slave mother, and make her name, her fame and heroism, known to the ends of the earth, as one who, like that Roman of old, could put the knife into the heart of her child, to save it from its Christian and Republican ravishers? Margaret acted not blindly nor inconsiderately, but she had deliberately made up her mind to kill all her children, and then herself, rather than again be subjected to the pollutions and cruelties of American slaveholders. Why do not all the ministers and churches, poets and orators, politicians and statesmen, who believe it right to kill to save themselves from slavery, combine to spread the name and heroism of MARGARET GARNER to the ends of the earth? She sought not to injure her cruel oppressors; she sought to destroy her own life and the lives of her children, to escape the doom of what the Reverend Doctors, Adams, Lord and Blagden call the God-ordained and Christ-sanctioned institution of slavery. That tragedy has appalled the whole State; it may well appal [*sic*] the world, that Christians (?) and Republicans (?) should inflict such cruelties on innocent, helpless women and children, rather than have them subjected to them. Where are Nehemiah Adams, Nathan Lord and George W. Blagden now? Why do they not come forth and arraign Margaret Garner before God and man as a murderer, because she killed her babe rather than have it fall into *their* pious, reverend, slave-catching hands?

But Margaret is in the hands of the coadjutors of these Rev. Doctors, and Ohio, with her two millions of people, has no way to rescue her, but to arrest her on the charge of MURDER! What will Salmon P. Chase, Governor of Ohio, now do? It is for him alone to say whether that mother and her still living children shall be given up to slavery. If they are sent back he and the Republican party of this State must be held accountable, for they now have an opportunity to array the State in a victorious conflict with the slave-hunting Union. Will the Republicans, who now control the State, protect that mother from the fans of the slaveholding Union? We shall see. If they do, the entire State, and the North too, I think, will sustain them. Be assured, nothing has ever occurred in Ohio which has so deeply and so painfully moved the hearts of the people as this.

What can I say of a religion and government which drive even loving mothers to such fearful deeds, to save their little ones from the outrages and cruelties which they would inflict? Can I but loathe a system of God-worship which can perpetuate and sanction pollutions and crimes in its adherents, that drive their victims to such fearful deeds to escape them? The slaveholding God of the American Church and Republic is a malignant, bloody fiend; for one, I scorn his worship and defy his power. Better no God at all than such an object of worship. With disgust I turn from such a polluted and bloody shrine, and lovingly and reverently bow to the loving, just and humane God of anti-slavery.

I am asked often—Did Margaret Garner do right? Perfectly right, just and noble, according to her own standard of right, and according to the standard of nearly universal Christendom; but perfectly wrong, according to my standard. Had she cut the throats of the master and of all who sought to enslave her, and should the slaves of the South cut the throats of all their oppressors, they would do right, as the church and clergy of this nation count right. But their bloody standard is not mine; their God of 'hot wrath, of revenge and war,' is not my God. The absolute sanctity of human life is the only principle that can save this world from slavery, war, anarchy and murder. This is the lesson taught every day by passing events.

I have been in Ohio about three weeks. Yesterday morning, the mercury, at sunrise, was twenty-four degrees below zero where I was, and the snow sixteen inches deep on a level. Many poor, thinly-clad fugitive slaves have suffered heroically to gain their freedom. Lake Erie spreads out before me, showing one solid mass of ice; a great chance for ice merchants, but a dreary sight to the fugitives from American stripes and chains.

HENRY C. WRIGHT.

Provincial Freeman (Chatham, Canada West), March 22, 1856

====

The Provincial Freeman, a militant abolitionist paper that generally touted the superiority of life in Canada and that paid particular attention to the status of women, was published in the midfifties by black men and women in what is now Ontario.

Loss of the Steamer H. Lewis.

We call attention to the account of the loss of the steamboat Henry Lewis, copied into our columns of to-day. Here is exhibited another reckless loss of life by the sheerest neglect and carelessness, on the part of those who should have attended to their business, on that despicable stream of human misery, woe and destruction, the Ohio river. A doomed stream it seems to be, as if the avenging angel of the Almighty, had cursed its portentious waters.

Though many other valuable lives were lost in this sad catastrophe, yet none attract our attention nor excite our reflections so much as that of the child of *Margaret Garner* (called in the notice "Peggy") the noble moral heroine and slave mother, who like her ancient prototype, the Carthagenian mother, put her own darling infant to death, rather than it should live to be a slave.

We have but one sentiment of reflection on this subject, and that is, the hope and wish, that the just retribution of Heaven's displeasure may sooner or later be dealt to their discomfiture, upon the head of each and every scoundrel, including Kentucky slaveholders, Ohio slave-catchers, Marshall, Commissioner, U.S. Attorney, constables, guards, steamboat, steamboats-men and all, who in any way or manner have any sympathy against, or anything whatever to do with the re-enslavement of that more than model of modern women.

The name of *Margaret Garner* shall live in the minds, and be cherished in the hearts of every true man and woman, when those of the contemptible wretches, who sought to enslave her shall have gone down to the earth from whence they came.

"Unwept, unhonored, and unsung." Margaret Garner *shall not be a slave—she must* and *will yet be free!*

Negroes and Negro "Slavery": The First an Inferior Race: The Latter its Normal Condition, J. H. Van Evrie, (1863)

New York doctor, publisher, and white-supremacist author, John Van Evrie published versions of this book under different titles before, during, and after the Civil War. The later editions resurrected the Garner case for his polemical purposes.

A few years since a "slave" woman escaping from Kentucky to Ohio was recognized and taken back to her home, but on the way down the river cut the throat of her child, whom she had carried off in her flight. The Abolitionists, of course, admired and praised this bloody deed, and declared that, rather than her child should live a slave, she, with Roman sternness and French exaltation, herself destroyed its life. If they had said that the mother had killed her child because it was not permitted to have a white skin, or straight hair, or to have any other *specialty* of white people, it would have been quite as rational and as near the truth as to say that she killed it because it was not to grow up with the freedom of the white man. The woman was doubtless a mulatto or mongrel, who in revenge possibly for the supposed wrong, inflicted this punishment on those whom she had been taught to believe had wronged her. But while this unnatural crime was quite possible, as indeed any unnatural vice or crime is always possible to the mixed element, it is scarcely possible to the negress, whose imperative maternal instinct, as has been observed, shields her from such atrocity. The negro mother has always control and direction of her offspring at the South so long as that is needed by the latter. The master, of course, is the supreme ruler—the guide, director, the common father, the very providence of these simple and subordinate people, but while his is the directing power that sees to all their wants, and protects them in all their rights, the relations of mother and child are rarely interfered with, for both the interests of the master and the happiness of the mother demand that she should have the care and enjoy the affection of her own offspring. This, however, is confined to a limited sphere when contrasted with the instinctive habitudes and enlarged intellectualism of our own race. The negro child, in some respects, at the same age, is more intelligent than the white child. This same fact is manifested by our domestic animals. The dog or calf of six months is vastly less dependent on the mother than the human creature. The negro child, with its vastly greater approximation to the animal, is also less dependent at a certain age than the white child.

CHAPTER 8

THE BATTLE IN THE PRESS

Editorials on the Trial, Return, and Requisition

Fugitive slave cases always harbored the potential to incite struggle over the appropriate relations among regions, races, and state and federal governments, but the conflict over these matters in response to the Garners' situation was especially fierce. Never before had a fugitive facing rendition under the Fugitive Slave Act been answerable to a charge of murder in a free state. Since it was not clear to all that the legal priority of federal fugitive slave processes applied in so extraordinary a situation, antislavery commentators had some hope that Ohio officials might have the authority to block the Garners' return. The uncertainties and diversity of legal venues and arguments helped prolong the case and give political activists and the press more opportunities to comment on the issues. The resulting editorials span a broad range of opinion, and the debate reached the deepest levels of disagreement on the legal, constitutional, political, moral, and religious questions to which American slavery gave rise.

Cincinnati Daily Gazette, February 1, 1856

The Fugitive Slave Case.

. . . A deep sympathy with the fugitives prevails throughout the city and State, but we observe a general willingness to submit to the law. It was noticed in our paper yesterday morning that a meeting would be held at SMITH & NIXON's Hall last night to sympathize with the fugitives.

This we regarded as untimely and uncalled for, and we were glad to find last night that the proprietors of the Hall had refused to allow it to be used for that purpose and the use of other halls was also refused so that no meeting was held. No good would result from such a meeting at this time. If the fugitives are legally entitled to their freedom, no one will dare to deny it to them; If this cannot be established, they will be returned to bondage. However much we may despise the law; and however deep our sympathies may be with the unfortunate negroes, we would not counsel or encourage resistance to the law, because such resistance would manufacture pro-slavery sentiments ten thousand times more rapidly than the work can be accomplished by the slavery propagandists of the South. We profess to be a law-abiding people, and we have always backed up our professions by our acts, notwithstanding the charges that have been and are still made to the contrary. Instead of the passage of resolutions and the utterance of patriotic speeches in their behalf, their friends should take steps to aid them *materially.* If they should be set at liberty, they will require assistance; and if returned to their master, their freedom may be purchased. Men and women, in whose hearts there beats such a strong desire for freedom as has been exhibited in this case, should have their freedom *purchased,* if it cannot be legally secured, and with a proper effort this may be done. If a subscription can be started for this purpose, contributions will come in from all parts of the State. Some of the papers suggest the erection of a monument to the woman, who spared not her own child, when she supposed it must be returned to bondage. Let her freedom be secured first, then it will be time enough to talk about the monument.

Cincinnati Daily Commercial, February 9, 1856

The Fugitive Slave Case—Conflict of Processes.

The conflict between the processes of two different jurisdictions, that is now going on in the city, wherein the subject matter is the custody of certain fugitives from labor in the State of Kentucky, is exciting some attention among our citizens, and there is, we doubt not, some difference of opinion as to what are the real legal rights of the parties, in the premises. The negroes are at present in the charge of the U.S. marshal for the

Southern District of Ohio, having been arrested under the act of Congress providing for the capture and re-delivery of fugitives from labor. Subsequent to the escape of these individuals from Kentucky, and while they were within the territory of Ohio, an act of homicide was committed by one of them upon the person of another. For this act, the guilty party stands charged under the laws of the State—the others being also accused as accessories. Upon complaint, process has been issued from a judicial officer of the State, having jurisdiction of the offense, and has been delivered up to the proper executive. That which is now sought to be settled is, Which party has the paramount right to the possession of the double defendants?

It is probable that were this case divested of all prejudice, of all party significance, and all feelings of private interest, it would present no especial difficulties. The laws of the United States do not declare one thing and the statutes of Ohio another and a different thing, neither is there any question as to which Court is empowered to try the issue upon the ownership of the slaves, or to which has been committed the duty to hear and decide under the criminal *prosecution.* Neither tribunal stands in the position of questioning the authority of the other in its legitimate sphere; neither, so far as we are aware, manifests the slightest disposition to arrogate powers not to its own, to stretch its authority, or to condemn or deny the constitutional authority of the other. The question is, which claim in this case is first in order of precedence—that of the Marshal, representing the property of the master in the slave, or that of the Sheriff representing the right of the State as a sovereign power, to punish offences committed within its territory?

Were the Ohio river removed, and the boundary between this and the neighbor State obliterated, there would be no question remaining. —Kentucky punishes the slave equally, at least, with the freeman for the offenses which he commits. Public justice does not ask of the master the privilege to hang or imprison his property. The good of *that* society demands that the wrong-doer shall be punished—why not the good of *this?* The peace of the State of Ohio is of as much importance as that of the State of Kentucky, and the right to use all proper measures to secure the same is as perfect in one case as in the other. Shall it be said that servitude gains under the fugitive law—enacted, as we have been taught to believe merely for purposes of recaption—qualities in the free States that it does not possess at home? Is slavery a stronger bond—a higher right in Ohio than in Kentucky? Not such, certainly, was the intention of the framers of the Constitution; not such were the professed designs of the makers of the law. By being, through the force of the Constitution, temporarily transferred to the free States, slavery requires no new prerogatives. It is merely continued as a tenure for one purpose and for one alone—that of the return to his master of the person held to labor.

When the United States assumes the duty to catch and return the negro to his owner, and enters the boundaries of a sovereign State for that purpose, it does it subject to all those restraints and limitations which necessarily belong to the nature of the service and which the sovereignty of the State may rightfully impose. Granted that the National is, within its own sphere, the paramount Government, so too is the State, within its sphere, also paramount. Except where especially invested by the Constitution, the Union has no power whatever. First and highest of all the rights and prerogatives of Government, is that by which society provides for the continuance of its own existence, by enacting laws for the punishment of crimes committed within its territory. Under our form of government, this right belongs to the States. In this respect, the authority of the State is paramount, and whatever office the Union assumes to execute, it does it subject this authority. The Union may take the negro and return him to his master; but if during his residence among us he has committed a crime against our laws, he has made himself the legal subject of those laws, and must remain under their penalty, within their power, until his crime is expiated. The laws of the sovereign State of Ohio, know none so high as to be beyond their reach, none so low as to be beneath their grasp, no party so privileged that they may be set aside in his favor.

It is to be hoped that this matter will be properly and peaceably adjusted. While it is proper that the Marshal of the Southern District of Ohio should conform strictly to the line of his duty, executing fully and accurately the provisions of the Fugitive Law, and all proper orders of the Court thereunder, it is neither necessary nor seemly, nor creditable, to go a step beyond the line of his legal duty, either to commit any injustice to the fugitive, or a wrong against the sovereignty of the State, by his return to slavery. —Let slavery in Ohio stand upon the law and the law alone. Let it have its legal flesh and blood and no more. And on the other hand, let the friends of the slave be careful. For their own sake—for the sake of the cause which they profess to hold so dear, let them abide by the law. He who does that which may inaugurate the reign of mob law in this city, is neither a good citizen nor a consistent philanthropist. No good cause can be benefitted by means entered upon in the face of the law, and dangerous to the peace of society; and we feel assured that if all magistrates and, officers and citizens confine themselves strictly to the conscientious performance of their respective duties, this cause of disagreement may be gotten over without a disturbance.

Liberator, February 29, 1856

From the Boston Evening Traveller.
A FEMALE ADVOCATE IN COURT.

We are not familiar with the method of procedure in the courts of law in Cincinnati, and we do not know therefore that it is not considered rather a matter of course than otherwise for strong-minded women, and others who have no connection with the case which is pending, to address the court and the audience during the progress of a trial, and give their sentiments upon the case itself, and upon matters of law and morals generally. Such a proceeding seems rather novel, to be sure, in this region, where a reverence for proper forms in the administration of the law has not yet been altogether swept away by a disregard for the law itself, and a disrespect for its ministers.

But it seems that in Cincinnati such things are allowed to happen and they appear to excite no special wonder. Miss Lucy Stone—under protest, Mrs. Lucy Blackwell—has thought it incumbent on herself to express her sympathy with the negro woman, claimed as a slave by Mr. Gaines, in a speech delivered in the court-room, just after the adjournment of the court. Before the adjournment, one of the counsel for the slave asked that Mrs. Blackwell have leave to speak; but objection being made, the speech was deferred until after the adjournment. Mrs. Blackwell then proceeded, in the presence of the bar and the spectators, to deliver herself of one of those rhapsodies about freedom, which long practice at the meetings of such patriotic associations as the New England Anti-Slavery Society has made familiar to her mouth; and in the course of her remarks, she expressed her regret that she had no knife to hand to the slave woman, that she might have the means of freeing herself.

All this passed in the court-room, while the court was but temporarily absent; and nothing seems to have been done by the officers to prevent this fanatical female from proceeding with her very foolish but very mischievous talk about a case then pending before that tribunal. There is certainly a strange apathy on the part of the officers of justice in

Cincinnati, in the maintaining of their dignity and their independence. They seem to yield to the prejudices and passions of the multitude in all cases where the popular feeling is aroused. This disposition on the part of the courts has emboldened the people to interfere in their proceedings to a greater or less extent, and not unfrequently to endeavor to influence their action. That such things should be allowed is discreditable enough to the judicial authorities; but if such trifling with the dignity of a court, and such a desecration of the halls of justice as Mrs. Blackwell has been guilty of, should be permitted to pass without rebuke, it will indicate that the tribunals of Cincinnati have become more degraded than we are yet willing to believe them.

Cincinnati Daily Enquirer, March 2, 1856

The Late Fugitive-slave Case—Reflections Upon it.

Now that the fugitive slave case, which for more than a month has caused some feeling and excitement in this community, has been disposed of by the rendition of the parties to their claimants in Kentucky, we feel at liberty to indulge in some reflections upon it. Connected with this case there are points and circumstances which it is eminently proper the people should understand. The most extraordinary efforts have been made by the Abolitionists here to repudiate our constitutional obligation to the matter, and to trample the jurisdiction and laws of the United States under foot. The officers of the United States, judicial and executive, have encountered at every step the most formidable obstacles in the performance of their duty. For a time it seemed as if it would be impossible for the law to take its course. All sorts of frivolous questions were raised, every legal artifice employed, by shrewd Abolition attorneys and wire-workers, to prevent a proper decision in the case. The Colored-Republican press, forgetful of their proper sphere, and careless and reckless of consequences, have teemed with inflammatory articles, designed to influence and coerce the public authorities into a path different from that which the statutes and decisions of the higher courts had marked out. The circumstances in the case were briefly these.

On the 28th day of January last a party of fugitive slaves, from Boone County, Kentucky, were arrested by the United States Marshal, in pursuance of the provision contained in the Constitution of the United

States, and the law of Congress of 1850, which enforces it. While the arrest was being made a slave woman barbarously murdered one of her little children, and attempted to take the life of two or three more. For the commission of this deed of blood the Abolitionists eulogized this woman, and compared her to some of the most sublime characters of antiquity. They indignantly scorned the idea that she had committed a crime deserving of any punishment; but, while taking this ground, they were eager to prosecute her for murder. They thought they saw in this circumstance a point which, if skillfully pressed, would not only defeat the operation of the Fugitive-slave Law in her case, but in that of all the other fugitives. It afforded a fine and plausible pretext for getting up a conflict of jurisdiction between the State and General Governments. Although the coroner's inquest which investigated the "murder case" found only the woman guilty, a Grand Jury was got, by skillful maneuvering, that indicted the rest of the slaves, with the exception of the children, as accessories to the murder. This was done without a particle of evidence to justify it. No one—not even the Abolitionists themselves—doubted that the mother alone was responsible for the death of the child; but, as the indictment subserved a useful purpose by detaining them upon a State offense, it was pressed against the "accessories."

Even before any proceedings had been taken upon the part of the State an effort was made by the Abolitionists to release the slaves from the custody of the Marshal by means of a writ of *habeas corpus,* sued out before Judge BURGOYNE, of the Probate Court. It was well known that they were legally in his possession, yet certain parties, holding that everything was fair that would defeat the execution of the United States law, were not ashamed to resort to such trifling. In this move, however, they were foiled. The Marshal still retained their custody. The trial proceeded before the Commissioner, and was allowed by that functionary to drag its slow length along for several weeks. The evidence was perfectly plain that they were fugitives from service, yet the ingenuity of the "higher-law" counsel raised a number of irrelevant questions, all of which were generally taken into long consideration by the Commissioner. Long before the case was concluded the indictment we have alluded to was found. It was now sought by the Abolitionists to take the fugitives out from the custody of the Marshal and the United States jurisdiction, which had attached, and try them in the State Court, without waiting for the former to finish its process. The Sheriff, acting under orders, accordingly seized upon them in jail, where they had been placed by the Marshal for safe-keeping, agreeably to the law of Congress, and refused to deliver them to that functionary when called upon. The pretext of this interference with the United States Courts was that a violation of the criminal law of Ohio by the fugitives *entirely overlayed proceedings* under the Fugitive-slave Act, which they termed but a civil process.

It is true, the law itself says that its operation shall not be stayed by any process whatever from a State Court, but it was construed not to apply to violation of criminal law. The Mayor took this ground, and gave instructions to the police, in case of collision between the Sheriff and Marshal on the question of jurisdiction, to place themselves upon the side of the former. Under this view of the matter the United States law would soon be a dead letter. All that fugitives from service would have to do would be simply to commit some petty larceny or an assault and battery in the State where they had escaped to, and they could be immediately taken from the United States Marshal's custody.

It was alleged that a proper regard for "State rights" and dignity demanded that we should pay no respect to the prior jurisdiction of the United States Courts, but trample it under foot. They scorned the idea that the State should wait until the proceedings before the Commissioner had terminated, and then, if necessary, the Governor of Ohio could make a requisition upon the Governor of Kentucky for the redelivery of the fugitives to answer to the charge of crime committed here. This manifestly proper course, which avoided all conflict of jurisdiction, and kept both the State and General Governments in their respective orbits without clashing, they did not desire to be pursued. It was generally believed that the Abolitionists intended to convict the slaves, if possible, of some penitentiary offense, have them pardoned out by Governor CHASE in a short time, and hurried off to Canada by the quickest possible route. However this may have been, it was disconcerted by the decision of Judge LEAVITT, of the United States District Court.

After a careful investigation of the law and facts in the case, and finding nothing that would justify an interference with the United States process, he issued a writ directing the Sheriff to deliver the fugitives to the Marshal. That officer, (the Sheriff,) whose conduct throughout the whole trial was eminently fair and honorable, complied. The slaves were then taken by the Marshal to Kentucky, agreeably to the order of the Commissioner, who found them to be fugitives from service. The sovereignty of the United States was vindicated; that of the State not infringed, for then the law shall be honorably and faithfully carried out. They know that the delivery of fugitives from service is an essential stipulation in our national compact, and that he is not a good citizen who will throw obstacles in the way of its execution. They desire to see no conflict of jurisdiction between the State and the Union, and, to prevent it, they see that there is no other way than to allow that sovereignty which commences proceedings to finish them before the other commences, for otherwise we should have continual wrangling and confusion.

New York Daily Tribune, March 3, 1856

RENDITION OF THE FUGITIVE
DECISION OF JUDGE LEAVITT.
OUTRAGE AT COVINGTON.

Correspondence of The N.Y. Tribune.

Cincinnati, Thursday, Feb. 28, 1856.

The case is ended!

This afternoon Judge Leavitt decided in a very brief manner that the custody of the parties belonged of right to the Marshal, and not to the Sheriff, that the arrest of the parties by the latter officer was illegal, and that the fugitives should be given over to the custody of the United States Marshal.

The Judge anticipated, according to Mr. Headley's view, the question whether an arrest made subsequent to the rendition was illegal, and so the Sheriff made none. At about 4 p.m. the United States Marshal and his posse moved to the jail, took thence the negroes and carried them across the river.

So they are in the Paradise to which Mr. Finnel, in his speech in behalf of the claim, made such touching mention.

It has been during the trial (and I have not been absent from the Court-room much) a source of great wonder where such another set of officials from the Commissioner down to the Assistant-Deputy United States Special Marshal could be found. The Sims Brigade was bad enough but this was more than a match for that in the various qualities necessary to "Union-saving officers." I noticed to-day at the jail one young man volunteering his services as a Marshal who in company with another youth (*par nobile*) attempted to free Kissane, the forger from his imprisonment, and was caught in the jail-yard with the tools, if I remember correctly, in his hand. He is an intimate friend of Mr. Commissioner Pendery, an inmate of his office, and if we judge a man by the company he keeps, we cannot form a high opinion of the moral or legal acquirements of Mr. P. The following will give you a better idea of the posse than anything I can say:

Some 20 or 30 of them offended by an article in one of the morning papers called at the office to-day and demanded the name of the writer of the offensive article. The proprietor refused to give it. The band after learning that two individuals whom they suspected were absent, threatened the proprietor with violence. After some parley the mob went out the front way and the proprietor the back, and the matter ended.

The case has a North-side view and a South-side.

Looking at it from the former point of view some very important effects are seen.

The community are thoroughly and deeply moved with a philanthropy that is not satisfied with words, but goes to the pocket. A prominent merchant of this city yesterday met Mr. Jolliffe and asked him whenever these people needed money to draw on him for $100, and if exigencies required it, to buy the children and the business-men of the city would make up the purse.

Ohio sees too, that no crime is too great to go unpunished when the Union demands the return of fugitives.

Seven slaves were carried back to-day, and it is some consolation to know that seven crossed the Ohio last night and are now safe on free soil. Peggy Garner and her three children were captured, but during her trial *fifteen of her relations escaped from Slavery.*

A South-side view, I am sorry to say, is not wholly favorable to the efforts of certain fanatics.

"Why, Sir," said a merchant to me to-day, "one of my best customers (a man from Crittendon, Ky.,) came to my store yesterday and paid his bill, and said he should henceforth deal in Louisville. He wouldn't come to a place that treated the South so."

I could only point the merchant to the glorious sacrifice of to-day upon the shrine of the Union as a source of consolation. He left me in sadness, yet in hope.

I do not know that I mentioned yesterday that Judge Burgoyne commanded the Marshal to keep the children in this State until he decided. Such was the fact, and Mr. Robinson has a prospect of imprisonment for contempt of Court. Sheriff Brashears, it is thought will be impeached for not rearresting the parties to the murder.

Of all these things I will try to keep you duly informed.

AJAX. . . .

Frederick Douglass' Paper, March 7, 1856

By the time of the Garner case, Frederick Douglass had already published
two autobiographies and was among the nation's most famous ex-slaves.
This renown is what enabled him to use his own name in the title of his
newspaper (which succeeded his first paper, the North Star, *in 1851).*
Earlier in the decade, he had broken with his mentor, William Lloyd
Garrison over, among other things, Douglass's conversion to the view that
the Constitution was not an intrinsically proslavery document. This makes
particularly interesting the following editorial's scathing analysis of the legal
opinions that authorized the Garners' return to slavery. Not surprisingly,
Frederick Douglass' Paper *featured the Garner case prominently in the first*
few months of 1856; the following document is only one of several editorials
on the return of the fugitives published in the March 7 issue.

Rendition of the Heroic Garner Family

The slave-catching Commissioner Pendery, not having the fear of God
before his eyes, has, for the sum of ten dollars, returned the noble and
heroic Garner family to their alleged owners, who will have an opportunity of glutting their vengeance upon them prior to their transportation to Vicksburg, Mississippi. The decision was not unexpected by those
acquainted with the antecedents of the man who had hitherto obeyed
with so much alacrity the behests of the Slave Power.

Pendery admits the fact of their having been brought voluntarily
into the "free state" of Ohio. He declares that had they then claimed their
Freedom, by no process of Law could they have been reconsigned into
the clutches of Slavery. But as they did not then claim their freedom, but
were taken back to Kentucky, they were again the property of their master. In this decision the laws of the state of Ohio, have been laid aside, and
the illegal enactments of Kentucky substituted.

Freedom, according to Commissioner Pendery, is something which
is to be worn by one portion of Humanity, as Christians are commanded
to wear the world, viz., as a loose garment. Slaves brought into a free
State, are free by the Laws of the State, whether they return into a slave
or not. The Law is "ONCE FREE, ALWAYS FREE." The fact of their return
into a slave State cannot nullify the Laws of the State of Ohio, by which
these slaves were declared free. They could not thereafter be re-enslaved,
except for crime. —But if the views of this ten dollar slave-catcher be

correct, they threw off Freedom as a mantle, upon their return to Kentucky. Thus can the garb of Freedom be worn and cast off ad libitum. We live in a strange country. The decision having been rendered in favor of the claimant, the Sheriff still maintained his right to hold them on the indictment for murder. This was an ugly case for the Marshal, but Judge Leavitt, another panderer to the pro-slavery interest, one who glories in the title of the United States District Judge, instantly loomed up in the horizon; and in order to wrest them out of his hands, they were brought before this "upright Judge." We have read the decision in the case, a decision which presents the State of Ohio, with its Free Soil Governor, before the world in a most humiliating aspect. The impressions of the Judge were in the outset strongly in the position that, as the claim of the alleged owner, in the proceeding under the Fugitive Act, was the mere assertion of a civil right, it must be subordinate, and yield to the right of the State to assert and enforce its criminal laws. But after "mature deliberation," (wishing to save the Union), he adopted a different conclusion, viz., that, notwithstanding the indictment for murder, they were in the custody of the Marshal, under lawful process of the Commissioner, and that it was not competent for the Sheriff to arrest them, under the process of the State, while they were so held under process issued by authority of the laws of the United States.

After the usual judicial nonsense concerning the sanctity of human enactments, in which any thing in form of an enactment is regarded as a LAW which must be respected and obeyed "while it is law," Judge Leavitt remarks: "In holding, as I must do in this case, that the right of the Marshal to the custody of the persons in question must be respected, I am not to be understood as asserting that a fugitive slave is not responsible for a violation of the criminal laws of the State to which he may have fled. It is the undoubted right of every State to punish crime committed within its limits. —A State destitute of this right, in its freest and fullest exercise could have no claim to sovereignty. And if an escaped slave could violate law with impunity, many States of this Union would be in a most defenseless condition. It is not asserted, therefore, that they are not liable to punishment, but merely that if they are in custody of an officer, under a law of the United States, before their arrest for crime against the State law, the latter arrest cannot be enforced till the disability existing by the prior arrest is removed. In other words, the slave being in the custody of an officer, acting under the authority of another, and, for the purposes of this question, a foreign jurisdiction, he cannot, by the mere force of a subsequent arrest, be delivered from such custody." But if Judge Leavitt be correct, any "escaped slave" may "violate the law with impunity." He may, indeed, be delegated by his master to murder some citizen in the Northern States with whom he (the master) has had a difficultly; and if he be demanded under the Fugitive Slave Act, as a fugitive slave, prior to his arrest as a criminal, the criminal code must be set aside, and the slave returned to his master. —But in such a case, says one, the Governor can demand him. Yes, he may demand him, and be welcome to him, if he can find him. Will the citizens of the Northern States quietly submit to be thus trampled on?

The unsuccessful heroes, under this decision, have been delivered to the Marshal, and carried to Kentucky, under a guard of 200 deputies, when a sort of jollification meeting was held in honor of the transaction.

Lexington Kentucky Statesman, March 7, 1856

Lexington was the center of the Kentucky slave trade, and the Statesman *followed the story with interest. Most of its reports were drawn from papers closer to the scene, but the paper also presented its own views. After praising both Commissioner Pendery and Marshal Robinson, this editorial focused on Judge Leavitt's decision and the lessons of the way the case was finally resolved. That portion of the editorial is reproduced here.*

FUGITIVE SLAVE CASE IN CINCINNATI.

. . . This decision was based upon principle and authorship, and we cannot but rejoice that in our sister State, amid the fanaticism of the times, a Judge should be found faithful and rule to vindicate it. He deserves and should receive the praise due to a just and upright Judge.

While we may denounce and defy the rancorous fanaticism of the abolitionists of Ohio, we cannot but congratulate ourselves upon this triumph of law, over violence and an unholy band of traitors. The surrender of a few slaves, as far as their value is concerned, is a matter of very little importance to the people of this Commonwealth. The determination of a great City upon our border to maintain her fealty to the Union, removes much of the asperity of feeling, and assures the South and the Union, that there are true friends over the border, whom it would be faithless to malign or desert.

Messrs. Gaines and Marshall, deserve the highest commendation for the vigorous and unshrinking prosecution of rights in which they could be little benefited as individuals, but in which the honor of the State, and Union, was seriously concerned.

We confess it is with profound regret and astonishment, that we see a paper of the standing of the Cincinnati Gazette, expressing the opinion than [*sic*] an execution of an acknowledged Constitutional act of Congress, should be regarded as an "attendance at the funeral of the Sovereignty of the State of Ohio."

New York Daily Times, March 11, 1856

═══════

Only five years old in 1856, the Times *had already become one of the country's most significant papers. Like the* Tribune, *the* Times *featured the Garner case regularly and prominently as national news, and weighed in on the fugitives' side in its editorial pages.*

The Cincinnati Slave Case.

The slave mother at Cincinnati, who killed her boy to save him from the patriarchal blessings of servitude, was claimed as a fugitive from Slavery, and delivered up. She was given up, notwithstanding a strong *prima facie* case existed to show that having been permitted at former times by her master to visit free soil, she had so become free; notwithstanding a higher claim over her person was urged by the laws of Ohio, on whose soil the homicide had been committed; notwithstanding the warmest sympathy of the whole population of Cincinnati, and indeed of the whole North, with the heroic confessor of liberty. There was no popular resistance to the execution of the Fugitive Law; and compliance with its requirements was carried so far, that the service of regular legal process from a State Court for her arrest upon the charge of felony was suspended in order that the Federal authority might be thoroughly vindicated in her rendition.

The same act of Congress—that of Feb. 12, 1793—which creates the right of reclamation for fugitives from service, creates the right of reclamation for fugitives from justice. The duty of surrendering slaves and criminals is enforced by one law. Accordingly, the Chief Magistrate of Ohio, Mr. CHASE, has addressed his requisition to the Governor of Kentucky, Mr. MOREHEAD, for the person of the murderer. She is required to stand trial for her life. Will she be surrendered? We do not for a moment believe so. By so much more elevated as are the exactions of Slavery over those of justice, are we to measure the probabilities of such compliance with the laws of the Union. By the fidelity with which every compromise touching Slavery has been complied with by the slaveholders are we to judge the future execution of this. By the Constitution, slaves were to be enumerated and represented, on condition of being taxed; they have always been represented and have never been taxed. By the Missouri act, Slavery was to be perpetually excluded from one side of a line, on condition of its admission upon the other. The whole energy of slaveholding is directed to its introduction upon both. So obvious and uniform is the disposition to submit only to so much Federal legislation as accrues to their benefit, and to nullify all the rest, that to indulge the hope of fairness in the present case is the part of extreme credulity. We have no idea that Gov. MOREHEAD will deliver up the infanticide. What he would do if Henry CLAY were alive, and the honor, and justice, and chivalry of Kentucky alive with him, we very well know; but such influences no longer rule in the State. We shall await the event with interest. Should the requisition be responded to, the general feeling will certainly be one of profound surprise. If it be denied, curiosity will be keenly excited to learn upon what tissue of special pleading and sophistry this specific form of nullification is grounded. The subject is as interesting as it is important.

Frederick Douglass' Paper, March 21, 1856

The Cincinnati Slave Case
by Cincinnati Correspondent J.W. Duffin, Geneva, March 3rd, 1856

My Dear Douglass: —The Fugitive Slave Case just decided in the "Queen City of the West," is so heart-rending in all its circumstances and details, that it seems to me, if we should not speak, the very stones in our streets would cry out. It is true that we have been called upon to witness some trying scenes of this nature in the cities of New York and Boston; and we wondered, then, why such things were permitted, and we thought that the first case would be the last, and when the second came, we said there would never be another—that the Fugitive Slave Bill was a dead letter, and so we have been drifting on from one tragical scene to another, until the case of that heroic woman, Margaret Garner, and her family, breaks upon our ears, in all its enormity and heart-rending horrors. It seems to have been reserved to Commissioner Pendery, to out-Herod Herod himself, and place himself at the head of the list of atrocious Judges; but I have more to do with others than the Hallets, Ingrahams, Curtises, Kanes, and Penderys of our land. God will take care of them as he has done of their kind that has gone before them. It is true that we expected much from the Free Soil State of Ohio; we were not prepared to believe that with her Free Soil Anti-Slavery Governor, a fugitive slave could be taken from her midst, but we had still stronger and more abiding faith in her vanguard, the free people of color. Who would have believed that the colored men and women of Cincinnati would have suffered that poor woman into whose soul the iron heel of slavery that entered so that she felt it to be worse than a thousand deaths, to be carried back again. O, shame where is thy blush! The Marshal, with his two hundred miserable Satellites, permitted to march through the streets of that city, containing thousands of free men and women of color, who ought, above all others, to have rescued her and her family, though they died in the struggle. I would ask to what purpose are the free people of color living in this country? We spend much time and money in holding conventions, passing resolves, and, as Horace Greeley says, "jawing about our rights." Would to God that we had the courage when occasion required to fight for our rights, and thus clear ourselves of the charge of delivering up to the master the bondman that is escaped unto us. We hear much now a days about Sharp's rifles. Minister and Laymen are extending their power in bringing Border Ruffians to recognize the rights of white men in Kansas, but where are the colored men that have signalized themselves, by their defense of the poor black man—nay, the poor black woman that flees from the prison house of Slavery and implores us for protection from what is—worse to her than a thousand deaths. I would have this Fugitives Slave Bill, (not Law), set at defiance in practice, as well as theory, throughout the land, and more especially by the Colored People; the fugitive should be rescued before a Commissioner sat in judgement upon them; their mandates should be no more obeyed than were the mandates of Herod when he commanded the Hebrew widows to murder their children. Let us make battle ground of every foot of free soil where an attempt is made to get a fugitive back. If Liberty is dear to white men, let us feel that it is equally dear to black men; and if Sharp's rifles are to be used to defend the rights of free white men in Kansas, let us use them to defend free black men upon free soil.

National Anti-Slavery Standard, March 22, 1856

In the 1850s, public discourse on slavery was more open and contested in Kentucky than in any other slave state. Still, the antislavery Newport News *exceeded the limits of acceptable speech. In the face of celebrations over the return of the Garners, the* News *used the case to advance its "free labor" critique of slavery as a system that benefited rich owners at the expense of ordinary white citizens. Although Editor William Shreve Bailey believed he spoke for the interests of the majority, his views drew violent opposition. The paper's offices were burned down by angry mobs at the beginning and the end of the decade, and Bailey ultimately had to flee to England. No copies of the* News *survived the flames, which is why the version of the editorial printed here is the one republished by the* Standard. *The official paper of the American Anti-Slavery Society, the* Standard, *like the rest of the abolitionist press, gave the Garners' story ample room in its pages.*

RIDICULOUS—VERY

. . . [T]he citizens of Boone and Kenton Counties have made application for an appropriation from the public treasury to defray the expenses of Archibald K. Gaines and James Marshall incurred in endeavouring to reclaim their fugitive slaves in Cincinnati, and also praying for the raising, by tax, of a State fund to be expended by the citizens of Kentucky in such cases.

Now, if this will not awaken the people of Kentucky to a sense of their duty to themselves, their fellow-men and to the State, we cannot imagine anything which would have that effect. Tax the people and the State, forsooth, for expenses incurred by individuals in reclaiming their fugitive slaves! If a negro oppressed and overburdened, flee from his master, for the purpose of gaining a liberty which is dearer than anything else to the human mind, he must be pursued, taken and brought back, not as the property of his owner, and at his own expense, but at the expense of a tax upon the people, and a drain of the public treasury. This is the last and greatest specimen of human effrontery of which we have ever heard. The citizens of Boone and Kenton Counties—magnanimous and generous as they would have us imagine them—will probably next petition the General Government for an appropriation from the treasury of the United States to pay the expenses incurred by them in having their boots blacked, or in purchasing the proper materials wherewith to tar and feather school teachers.

Of all the ridiculous things which have come to our knowledge, from the capture of a flock of geese by the immortal Don Quixote and his faithful Squire, Sancho, down to the action of Judge Leavitt, a few days ago, in Cincinnati, in declaring that although a fugitive slave murder her child in Ohio, she may not be delivered to the proper authorities, but must be remanded back to her master and to bondage, we have never heard of anything half so absurd. And yet, the people of Boone and Kenton Counties expect to have the people submit to an institution which will drive men and women to murder and self-destruction, and then, if their negroes, their private property, stray or run away from them, they expect to tax the State for the purpose of capturing and bringing them. Why not, at the same time, petition the Legislature to capture their hogs, horses and cattle, and bring them back and then say, "you may pay the expense incurred out of the State fund."

The people of these Counties certainly need Free Schools, if they need anything. They are in want of intelligence and enlightenment if they suppose this measure, even if passed, will be submitted to by the citizens of the State, and they are sadly mistaken if they suppose their "peculiar institution" will much longer need the support of State laws. A few more acts of this kind will secure the freedom of Kentucky from an evil, which all would acknowledge if they would but look at the matter in its right light, as much greater than any other which has ever cursed a State or a Nation.

Covington (Kentucky) Journal, March 22, 1856

Beginning on March 22, 1856, the Covington Journal *began a series of open letters to the people of Cincinnati, signed by "Justice." Of the surviving written sources, this series, which ran intermittently through August, offers the most intellectually ambitious proslavery response to the case. Justice opened by attempting to establish an authoritative account of the events and the constitutional and sectional issues at stake. In the ensuing months, he (and given the time, locale, and venue, it seems a near certainty that the author was male) broadened his discussion into an extended, at times rambling, argument for the biblical authorization for slavery. The two early letters reprinted here are notable for their continuing sense of outrage*

*over what had transpired and their picture of a nation on the verge of
dissolution. While contemporary readers have no reason to accept Justice's
venomous characterizations of the Garners and their allies, his commentary
on the abolitionist response to the case remains of interest for its awareness
of the images and stories that were mobilized by those who turned Margaret
into a heroine. He also offers a classic expression of the proslavery argument
for the constitutional obligation to return fugitive slaves. Perhaps because
it was so forceful, his version of this argument prompted a vigorous challenge. Beginning on April 12, "Truth" attacked Justice's legal and religious
analysis, and used the Garner case to launch a critique of slavery itself.
(Lacking either Justice's access to the paper or his relentlessness, however,
Truth confined himself to two letters in April.)*

*We cannot definitively establish the identity of either author, but
this much is certain: the exchange between Truth and Justice offers
an unusually good view of the intramural argument over slavery in a
slaveholding state as the political crisis of the 1850s intensified.*

For the Covington Journal.
To the People of Cincinnati

The fugitive slave case which has recently caused so much excitement
and interest, and is still exciting interest on both sides of the Ohio river, is
suggestive of much and grave reflection. It confirms an opinion, long held
by us, that the South, as a people, are more obedient to the laws, more
faithful to the constitution, and are possessed of higher moral qualities
than the North.

We have been taught, as the progress and result of this case, that the
constitution and laws of the United States may be nullified with impunity
in the State of Ohio; that the fugitive slave law is utterly valueless to the
slave holding States, whose wrongs it was made to remedy.

The slaves of Gaines and Marshall left their homes on the morning of the 28th of January last, and were captured before 12 o'clock on
that day, on the bank of the river, or very near to it. The river was firmly
covered with ice, and could have been crossed in ten minutes with all the
negroes, without the smallest difficulty or danger to any one. The proposition was made to Gaines to take them over immediately, without waiting any warrant or process of law; but this he positively refused to do,
or permit it to be done; determining not to violate any law of Ohio; fully
relying upon the power of the United States to vindicate her laws, and
render him justice. He did not, in the whole process of the case, violate

any law, or show the smallest disposition to do so. Even after the case had gone far enough to convince him, and every honest mind, that justice would be denied, the law nullified, and his property sacrificed, he refused to permit an effort, that I have scarcely a doubt would have been successful, to be made to bring them over, and thus put an end to this vexatious, dishonest and expensive delay. How favorably does his conduct and bearing in this whole controversy contrast with that of his and our adversaries? It must strike every honest and law loving citizen of Cincinnati; I still hope there are a few of them there. Every pretext, and artifice, and subterfuge, that dishonest ingenuity could conceive and suggest, was tried to prevent the execution of the law, deny justice and produce delay and consequent expense.

Vile incendiary speeches, and publications, and prayers, and sermons, were scattered broad-cast over the city, to excite the evil passions of deluded fanatics, runaway negroes, and thieving pretenders, to violence and blood. The constitution and the law was so denounced and derided that the Judge upon the bench was driven from his self-possession, and sacrificed his dignity in piteous moans, that it was his sad fate to be under the necessity to obey such a constitution and such vile laws; forgetting all the while that his agency in the matter was voluntary and for pay. The poor, deluded matricide was held up to the public gaze as a Roman heroine, whose glorious example of infantile murder, should be perpetuated in story, dramatised, and Uncle Tomatised as fit food for the unhallowed appetites of knaves and fools, and deluded fanatics—whose Websterian forehead and intellectual and soft and gentle countenance attracted and fascinated all beholders (especially the Gazette man, and Joliffe, and Fisher and Mrs. Lucy Stone.) The funeral of the poor murdered child was preached by some divine from I Peter chapter ii, verses 13 to 19, inclusive, or perhaps Titus ii, 9, and 10.

And the fate of poor Simon Garner, jr., was most feelingly lamented in the prayer meeting, by a Mr. Miller, because poor Simon had to stop on the way to buy shoes for the poor bare-footed children, and the delay, consequent upon this merciful and fatherly act, made him a *little too late for the underground care,* and the result was his master caught him. Now the truth is, Simon is a great liar and thief—and the respectable negroes of the neighborhood would not, generally, associate with him. One of my negroes was quite offended at being asked by Simon to come and see him the day before he run off. And Mr. Miller, if he had sense enough "to speak in meeting," ought to have known that this story of shoeing his children was simply ridiculous. Simon started to runaway about midnight, and crossed the river about daylight. Now what merchant in Kentucky, does Mr. Miller suppose, got out of his bed at that hour of the night, to shoe these children, without making some comments on the unseasonable call? The absurdity shows Mr. Miller's proclivity. And the truth is, Peggy is a very common cross tempered, flat nosed, thick-lipped negro woman, whose father was a very bad character. She was cruel to her children at home; she lied when she said "white man hit her" and made the scar on her face, if she did say so, as published by some of her abettors, or accomplices, or friends. The murder of the child was the result of vexation and disappointment, arousing to a pitch of phrenzy a revengeful and devilish temper, inherited from her father, and her new formed friends taught her the beautiful morality found in the *higher law,* that it was a noble act to cut the throat of her offspring. It is strange that they want to hang her for it, now that she is returned to the horror of slavery.

It is asserted that a very large majority of the citizens of Cincinnati are law abiding and Union loving people; opposed to *horse stealing and thieving in general,* and that the number of citizens in favor of stealing in particular, is quite small. Is this so? Kentuckians trading in Cincinnati come back and say so. —They tell us that the number of abolitionists is small—that the business men talk of them as we do. The vote cast in opposition to Chase last fall, strengthens the opposition. But I am not satisfied, nor will the reflecting be satisfied that such is the case, until there is a decided public demonstration made by the respectable, law abiding, Union and order loving citizens of Cincinnati, against the disorganizing, law-breaking, meddling fanatics. There never has been a day, or an hour, that such a majority of the respectable portion of the inhabitants of Cincinnati, as are said to be opposed to these babblers, who set at naught the laws of God and man, could not have frowned down and blasted them with an indignant and decidedly expressed public sentiment. Until this public demonstration, which Mr. Webster said was more terrible than the whirl-wind, is made, it is simply the dictate of common caution to distrust, if not to hold them all alike enemies. I shall lose no opportunity to impress this dictate of common sense and prudence, upon every man on whom I have the least influence, until it is made. If it is true they are all alike corrupt and evil disposed to us, we cannot know it too soon.

We have learned, from this and previous cases, that the *Union is no longer perfect*—that it is virtually dissolved already. The laws of intercommunication are violated; the rights of transit secured by constitutional provision denied; ordinary comity insultingly and barbarously withdrawn. The ties of kindred, of common origin and inheritance, are

rudely severed; we are unceremoniously given over to the tender mercies of the devil. Robbery and murder are justified and advocated from the pulpit to the sewer. Can there be perfect union, justice, domestic tranquility, &c., in this state of case. . . .
JUSTICE.

Covington (Kentucky) Journal, March 29, 1856

For the Covington Journal.
To the People of Cincinnati

The constitution of the United States was made "in order to form a more perfect Union, establish justice, insure domestic tranquility, provide for the common defense, promote the general welfare, and secure the blessings of Liberty to ourselves and our posterity."

Here we have succinctly stated the very desirable objects had in view by the wise framers of our federal Constitution. They represented the patriotic old thirteen States, who had previously been united by the spirit and blood of 76 to achieve a glorious liberty and independence, the blessings of which they now desire to secure to their posterity as an inheritance forever, by the formation of a more perfect Union, founded in justice, insuring domestic tranquility, providing for the defense of all, promoting the welfare of all. The wisdom of men never made an instrument better proportioned to the end in view. Shielded by it we have grown and prospered beyond all previous growth and prosperity known to human governments. So long as our Union continued perfect, and the constitution was reverenced as the supreme law of the land, paramount to all other law, justice was established—the welfare of the people every where promoted—domestic tranquility preserved—the eagle of America bidding defiance to foes from without or foes within—good will and brotherly kindness spreading over all our border.

It is not so now. We have fallen upon evil times. We cannot shut our eyes to the truth that the Union is no longer perfect. Justice is withheld and the rights of property disregarded—the general welfare is interrupted—domestic—tranquility is disturbed—the supreme law trampled upon and degraded—its plainest provisions unheeded and its solemn sanctions derided.

The flood gates of pollution and pest have been raised high by one section to deluge another with its loathsome miasmata; until they are bound in self-defense to dike and quarantine their border against the pestiferous breath of brothers turned adversaries. Whence this evil change? Is it not the same Constitution made for us by our fathers—having appended to it, the name of Geo. Washington, 'President of the Convention of Framers, and deputy from Virginia'—that same *Southern emancipationist,* who died a slaveholder, and who has left a name and a renown that is and will be unapproachable forever—and who Mr. Senator Sumner has the cool impudence to tell the American People, could not now be elected President if he were alive. And that same Virginia, too, who is the mother of States as well as Statesmen, for she freely offered up for the general welfare, that abundance of Territory, an empire in extent, out of which rich and populous States, have grown, ungrateful and degenerate children, and now belching forth a disgusting malaria upon their sister (Kentucky) as well as upon their mother? Is it not the same Constitution under which we have lived and flourished from infancy to manhood, from weakness to strength?—whose strong right arm, even now, encircles us all from the Atlantic to the Pacific—from the cold North, to the fiery South? It is the same. There is no change in the instrument. It has all the internal power for good that it ever possessed—all its provisions are intact; all its agreements and concessions stand as they did when Washington, with his own hand appended his name to it—and for eight consecutive years administered the government established by it. The cause for this change is not a change in the instrument itself; but grows out of a higher and more refined humanity—a higher degree of intellectual development—a spirit of improvement and progress in religion and morals reaching higher and higher, until, in its advance, it has discovered the *Higher Law Doctrine* in regions beyond the confines of the Bible, and planting itself upon this exalted eminence, even dares, impiously, to threaten the Throne of God with terms—demanding an Abolition God and an Abolition Bible. It grows out of an improved and progressive philanthropy, found only in this Higher Law Doctrine, which teaches, that their ways are higher than His ways, that their thoughts are better than His thoughts. It grows out of a restless itching for notoriety—a wretched longing for consequence and office—a pruriency for fame leading to base prostitution of talents, and corruption and degradation of virtue and morals. Inventive genius is racking her brain and sacrificing every principle of right and justice to find the byways, and alleys, and devious paths, leading to high position, that should ever be held as the reward of merit, and not of vice. The Chases, the Sewards, the Sumners, the Wilsons, and the Greelys, are striking out boldly in the dark wave now rolling over the North, each hoping as he bursts the stormy billows that some lucky surge may throw him on the top. And must this last hope of Freedom—this more perfect Union be dissolved to gratify the unhallowed passions, the inordinate ambition of wicked and selfish men? Is it true that the fraternal spirit and wisdom of our fathers is clean gone forever? Are the ties of blood—of common origin—of common inheritance, of interest and of glory so soon surrendered? Is it true, as said by your Senator Wade, that no two nations on earth are as hostile to each other as the North and South? Is it determined, as announced in New York by Rev. Theodore Parker, that a day is to be decreed, fixed and certain, when slavery shall cease in the States where it now exists, and that if it does not cease on that day, then they shall be taken possession of and made free? That a day is to be fixed when no Southerner shall hold office in the United States; that no fugitive shall ever be returned to his owner again; that the pursuing owner shall be branded and imprisoned as a Kidnapper—that the buying and selling of slaves in the slave States shall be made piracy? And all this is to be done, to promote the general welfare, and to insure domestic tranquility, without violating the constitution or impairing his more perfect Union? For Mr. Parker says "you have the right to interpret the constitution for yourselves and the Union need not be disturbed." None are to be put on guard in future, but men who are Higher Law men—men who love the Higher Law God, and the Higher Law men, in the meaning if not the language of Mr. Parker, who with Mr. Parker believe an oath has no sanction, and with Rev. Henry Ward Beecher, that Sharp's rifles are better than Bibles! Countrymen of Washington of Adams, Jefferson, of Hancock, of Madison, Webster, has it come to this? Can it be that these men of virtue and renown, did not understand this constitution, which they had made, and administered, and expounded? Shall the shining 'glory' which clustered in the mental vision of old John Adams, in that hour of peril, be realized in 'gloom' to his descendants? Oh, no! let us turn again to the times that tried men's souls, and invoke the spirit and wisdom of the great dead, to touch our souls 'as with a live coal,' that we may be imbued with the spirit and wisdom which animated them, to discern our true interests, and know our duty to posterity as they did theirs. Let us look at the difficulties surrounding them and follow their noble example. Let us remember that slavery is older than the constitution and government which they gave us, that it was a legacy entailed upon them by mother England, which they, as administrators without the will of the mother, were bound to distribute among the legatees. They had won for us a common inheritance of land and slaves, of rights and privileges. The rights of the heirs were equal—their dignity the same. The distribution must be just and equitable, of this possession, and the privilege of each to use his portion perfect—but the rights of his co-equal must be respected.

Hence the signature of all the legatees is required to this Federal agreement or Constitution—the 21 Section, 31 Clause with Article of which reads as follows. And is as binding to day as when it was signed by all the States: "No person held to service or labor in one State, under the laws thereof, escaping into another, shall in consequence of any law or regulation therein, be discharged from such service or labor, but shall be delivered upon claim of the party to whom such service or labor may be due."

This clause of the Constitution provides in plain and imperative terms, that the fugitives held up to service or labor in one State, escaping into another, shall be *delivered upon* claim of the party to whom service or labor may be due; and that no law or regulation in the State *shall* operate to discharge the runaways from the service or labor, due in another State. It makes it the duty of the State, and the citizens thereof, unto whose territory the fugitive shall escape, to *deliver* him up when claimed by the party to whom such service or labor may be due. The meaning of the clause cannot be mistaken by the commonest understanding the least tinctured with common honesty. This provision of the Constitution, in a 'perfect Union', with a very little honesty and a little comity, is sufficient without the enactment of any other law, to insure the return of every fugitive slave or apprentice from one State to another. It is very plain that this grave instrument, made to form 'a more perfect Union, &c.' when it says '*shall be delivered up*' means *delivered up*—not secreted to prevent delivery—not aided to escape his owner—not delivered up and stolen or taken by mob violence—but *captured and delivered up* in good faith. It is an instrument full of dignity, and gravity, and solemnity, that intends no fraud, or subterfuge, or perversion. It was made and signed, by sovereign States, coequals, and coparceners in its agreements, concessions and benefits. —These sovereign States agreed that no law or regulation, made by either of them, should operate to discharge a fugitive from the obligations to pay labor or service due in another State; but that such fugitive should be delivered up on claim.

But these wise framers forseeing that the obligation imposed by this provision upon themselves by the States "To deliver up on claim," might, in the distant fugitive, become an ungrateful and disagreeable duty, had to be discharged in good faith, provided in the 2d clause of the 6th Article that "this Constitution, and the laws of the United States which shall be made in pursuance thereof, shall be the Supreme law of the land; and the Judges in every State shall be bound thereby, any thing in the Constitution or laws of any State to the contrary not withstanding," and then, as if prophetic dread of coming evil warned them that no human work was perfect, they endeavored to close the last door to the ingress of civil discord, by the solemn sanctions of an oath remembering that God had said, thou shall not swear falsely, providing in the 3d clause of the same article (6) "that the members of the several States Legislatures, and all the executive and judicial officers both of the United States and of the several States, shall be bound by oath or affirmation to support this Constitution."

JUSTICE

Covington (Kentucky) Journal, April 12, 1856

For the Covington Journal.
To "JUSTICE"
"We stand firm upon the Bible and the Constitution and the Laws."
Justice.

If it is indeed true that you stand upon the Bible at all—that is to say, if the present and the future of American slavery stand upon the eternal right—then there is little necessity for many words upon the subject, and less cause for fear no matter what one set of men may say, or what another set may do. But little consolation can be drawn from the Constitution and laws, for if they are wrong they can be made right—the way to amend even the Constitution is clearly pointed out in the instrument itself.

It is true that slavery, in different forms has existed under different dispensations; but does this afford any argument for the *perpetuity* of American slavery? God permitted his own chosen to be enslaved four hundred years, but He fixed the time for their deliverance, and it was effected through the destruction of those who sought to make their bondage perpetual! You say that the fugitive slave law is ineffectual. It was expected that the repeal of the Compromise would restore again the equilibrium. It has had the contrary effect. Is it not a little singular that the *very* measures upon which our hopes for the perpetuity of slavery were based, have had in every instance an effect directly opposite from what was expected?

It is not utterly futile to suppose that the Union can be dissolved by force—by civil war? Have you ever made the calculation—not as to the amount of blood it would take to effect it—but how long the slave States could stand out against the general government and the free States combined and in alliance with the slave?

However bravely we might fight, or nobly die, in such a year would it not only seem to hasten the event that we sought to avert—while freemen, if any such survived, would themselves be subjugated! Is not this self evident? Is it not the Bible inference, not only, but the Bible teaching? Is slavery a natural and just element of American society and therefore to be perpetual? TRUTH

Kenton county, April 6th.

Covington (Kentucky) Journal, April 26, 1856

For the *Covington* Journal.
TO "JUSTICE"

After all you have written upon the subject of slavery, you have left us unenlightened as to the real question at issue. Is slavery a natural or just element in American Society or civilization, and therefore to be perpetual?

Now, slavery is not natural because it was forced upon us, against the will of our fathers, as also against the will of the enslaved. It is not just because it had its existence only in force, and is only perpetuated by force. Its perpetuity therefore, is simply a question of time—of power.

We have before intimated, that the servitude imposed upon Ham and his descendants was not a personal, unconditional service; and it is capable of demonstration, that the Bible nowhere recognizes the unconditional enslavement of a single human being against his will. . . .

You have, as if by accident, fallen upon the fact, that the servitude imposed upon Ham and his descendants, was to prepare the promised land from which they were to be exterminated. Now the African has done all he can do for American advancement. Indeed he has become a dead weight upon society. His presence among us disgraces free labor and sinks the poor white man below the slave. Less than a million slaveholders controle the destinies of more than twenty millions of free men. Three millions of slaves, reduced to a servitude, more abject than their own, more than three times the number of freemen, who, if the curse of slave labor were removed, would succeed to wealth and usefulness. Remove slavery from Kentucky and in ten years her increase in wealth, prosperity and happiness would be tenfold. She possesses natural advantages, equal, if not superior to Ohio; there is no reason, aside from the effect of slave labor, why she has not excelled or equaled her in wealth and influence. These are facts that cannot be controverted, and the day cannot be far distant when they will be realized.

At all events, it is the dictate of wisdom to ameliorate the condition of the slave rather than to make it more abject. Make the marriage relation inviolable—educate the slave and teach him to respect himself; and then the distinction between free and slave labor will cease to exist, and the greatest curse of slavery itself will be abated. . . .

TRUTH

Cincinnati Daily Commercial, Wednesday, April 16, 1856

The Slave Case Continued

The last scene of the Fugitive Slave Drama, which will forever be associated, in history and tradition, with the name of this city, giving its fame a dark and bloody tinge of tragedy, is the most peculiar and, in some respects, the most startling of all. Our readers remember well the several *acts* of this affair so strangely dramatic. The "Old Kentucky Home"—the flight over the snow—the capture—the passage of the frozen river—the place of shelter—the surprise, the flight, the murder, the capture—the scenes in the courtroom—the Marshal's office, the jail—the exciting incidents of the trial—the procession that crossed the river, bearing back the slaves— the revel in Covington, and the mob that followed—Peggy's adventures through Kentucky, then on the Ohio—the wreck of a steamer—Peggy's rescue; her shrieks of joy that her babe was drowned—the refusal of the Arkansas planter to the permit the fugitives to land—the sale of the family in New Orleans. These, in ordinary cases, would seem to complete the tragedy. It is time for the curtain to roll down and leave the audience (which is the civilized world,) to meditate in mournfulness on the solemn spectacle, with its many sad lessons. But no! Another surprise awaits us! A new installment of the play, quite unanticipated, is presented. It is a pantomime. Covington is the stage—the Ohio river the mystic line of foot lights. Peggy, the murderess, is exhibited to us, as it were, in the glare of blue fire burned to give a picturesqueness to the closing scene, and is suddenly withdrawn, as by magic, at the moment the arm of the State of Ohio, (to which there was some pretense of a purpose to surrender her) was extended, in vindication of its own sovereignty, to take her. The trick of the pantomimist is a touch ahead of the supernatural things indulged in by SHAKESPEARE. "Truth is stranger than fiction"—nature's dramas are more Shakespearian. No sooner does Peggy vanish—being spirited away into a dismal cloud over the South, which is impenetrable, save by glimpses—than, at the moment people are vexing themselves with wonder whether they have been victims of a hallucination, or have had a glance at reality—whether it was the veritable Peggy or a fictitious female that was made a dodging puppet amid the Covington scenery— we are told by the players that the identical Peggy had been within our grasp—that it was altogether our own fault that we did not come into possession of her—that she had been thrust under our very noses, and deliberately rejected by us; and at last we are abused for not taking her into Ohio when we had sent a requisition for her! All of this, when we were not quite certain that Peggy had been within a thousand miles of us, since she had been shipped to New Orleans and sold, or that the vague rumor of her presence was not founded entirely on an optical delusion, until we learned that she had been hurried away, whither we know not. We had no positive knowledge concerning her last appearance until it was ascertained that she was gone. . . .

The *Enquirer* of yesterday has a letter from Gaines himself (chapter 4), which . . . abound[s] in flimsy falsehoods. . . .

Mr. Gaines rests his defense chiefly on the fact that he states that Peggy was nine days in the Covington jail; but neglects to mention that the authorities of Ohio were not informed of her presence a sufficient length of time for them by the most strenuous exertions to issue a requisition before she was taken away. Within twenty-four hours of the time that Gov. Chase was informed that Peggy was in Covington, she was on her way to New Orleans. And when Mr. Gaines paraded around the declaration that he would keep Peggy until Thursday, he omits to mention that he had her removed on Wednesday. . . .

The duplicity of the man is palpable, and need not be further exhibited. His own lawyers do not attempt to justify him. His best friends maintain that his intentions are honest, but concede that he has had very bad advisors, and being a weak man has stumbled. No gentleman in Kentucky, or out of it, who is conversant with the circumstances, can endorse him. He endeavors to be quite personal and severe on us. In reply we have to say: There he stands—look at him. . . .

CHAPTER 9

SILENCE IN THE DEEP SOUTH

The Case of Charleston, South Carolina

While the Kentucky press covered the Garner case extensively, the South responded with censorship. Some papers that otherwise reported regularly on events in Cincinnati, fugitive slave cases, and the doings of white abolitionists evidently could not find suitable words for telling the story of a slave mother who would rather kill her children than see them taken back to slavery. For instance, such major news organs as the New Orleans Times Picayune *and the* Richmond Daily Enquirer *could be represented here only by a blank page, for they did not mention the case at all. If total silence leaves nothing to document, we can, however, record the partial and strategic silences that marked reporting on the case in Charleston, a capital of militant proslavery ideology. The elliptical and confusing stories reproduced below comprise the complete coverage of the case as it appeared in the city's two dailies in the winter of 1856. Readers who relied exclusively on one or even both of these papers for news would have had a hard time piecing together an accurate chronology, let alone gauging the breadth and intensity of the public contest over the case that raged in other regions of the country—though such details as the charge of murder, the habeas corpus issues, and the escort of two hundred special officers would have allowed an attentive reader to recognize that the fugitive slave case unfolding in the Queen City was something out of the ordinary.*

Charleston Mercury, February 16, 1856

━━━━━━━

THE SLAVE CASE AT CINCINNATI—The grand jury at Cincinnati have found a true bill for murder against Peggy, as principal, and the rest of the adult Kentucky fugitive slaves as accessories, to the murder of the child. The writ was placed in the hands of the sheriff, who, when the fugitives were brought to the jail by the marshal for safe-keeping, turned the key upon them, and they are now in his possession. The case grows more and more complicated. No decision has yet been made as to the ownership of the slaves.

Charleston Daily Courier, February 18, 1856

━━━━━━━

In consequence of the frequent occurrence of runaway slave troubles in Cincinnati, the Mayor of the city has seen proper to address written instructions to the chief of police and his subordinates on the subject of their course on such occasions. He considers that the action of the United States authorities, under the fugitive slave law, should not be interfered with, but, nevertheless, an indictment of any of the slaves or other parties, by a grand jury, is evidence that the case demands the attention of the State tribunals, and hence the police must render all possible aid in executing the state process.

Charleston Mercury, February 25, 1856

━━━━━━━

CINCINNATI FUGITIVES. Major J. J. Faran, o[f] Cincinnati, has discharged two of the city police for aiding in the capture of the fugitive slaves now on trial in that city. The Mayor holds that city police has nothing to do with fugitive slaves, unless called upon by the United States officers to aid them in arresting or retaining custody of such fugitives. He holds that any man who will neglect his regular business and assist in hunting up runaway slaves, without authority of law, and for the sole purpose of obtaining a reward, is unfit to be a city policeman. —*Plaindealer.*

Charleston Daily Courier, February 28, 1856

On Thursday last United States Commissioner PENDERY, at Cincinnati, ordered the fugitive slaves recently arrested there, to be brought before him that he might announce his decision. The Sheriff, in whose custody they were, refused to deliver up the adults, he holding them on a charge of murder. The Commissioner then adjourned the Court until Tuesday next. His decision is understood to be adverse to the claim of the slaves to their freedom. A habeas corpus has also been issued by the State Court to obtain possession of the slave children, held in custody by the United States Marshal. Writs also been issued against the Sheriff to show cause why the adult slaves should not be restored to the custody of the United States Marshal. These writs were made returnable on Saturday last.

Charleston Mercury, February 29, 1856

CINCINNATI, Feb. 27.—The fugitive slave case in this city has been decided in favor of the owners. The Sheriff holds the slaves under an indictment for murder. The Ohio river is open.

Charleston Mercury, March 1, and **Charleston Daily Courier,** March 3, 1856

The Fugitive Slave Case.

CINCINNATI, Feb. 28.—Judge Leavitt decided today that the fugitive slaves were in the custody of the United States Marshal. They were delivered to him and were escorted across the river by two hundred special officers.

CHAPTER 10

SPEECHES, SERMONS, AND "INTERVIEWS"

Many of the nation's most prominent opponents of slavery spoke out in public about the Garners during and after the case, at political meetings, and in the pulpit. The examples in this section show the varying uses to which both Margaret's conduct and the legal outcome were put. Included here, too, are accounts of direct encounters with the Garner family, though, as the scare quotes around "interview" in the chapter title are intended to suggest, the written versions of these encounters give reason for skepticism. Antebellum journalists had not developed the interview in the way we understand the term now: although public speeches were often reprinted as close to verbatim as the reporter could make them, journalists reporting on their conversations with those they had questioned did not as a rule aim for the kind of detailed transcription that today's readers tend to take for granted (and that marked much of the coverage of the Garner trial). Furthermore, it was considerably less likely that a reporter would feel bound to render the precise words spoken by a black interview subject (even when free, and even in the North). Even as produced by those whites most sympathetic to the antislavery cause, the written record that survives today reflects the era's prevailing assumptions about the political agency and intellectual authority of the nation's black population.

New York Daily Tribune, March 7, 1856

Profiling the Reverend Theodore Parker in its account of the same speech reprinted here, the New York Daily Times *referred to him as "one of the most remarkable men of the age." A member of Ralph Waldo Emerson's circle of Transcendentalists and a minister in the Unitarian Church, Parker was a leading figure in the national antislavery cause. His involvement was active and practical, as when, for instance, he hid the fugitive Ellen Craft in his house or played a central role in another of the most momentous fugitive slave cases of the era, the 1854 struggle in Boston over the fate of Anthony Burns. The federal government even filed charges against Parker for his role in that case. His reputation rested still more, however, on his passionate and militant sermons, speeches, and writings. (It was Parker, addressing slavery, who first made a remark that, in pithier form, was later made famous by Martin Luther King Jr.: the "moral universe" has an "arc" that, though long, "bends towards justice.") This speech on the Garner case was delivered at the Broadway Tabernacle, a New York church with intimate ties to both the abolitionist and the women's suffrage movements.*

THE DUTY OF THE NORTH.
LECTURE OF THE REV. THEODORE PARKER
AT THE TABERNACLE.

. . . MR. PARKER said: . . . The BATTLE between SLAVERY and FREE-DOM—WHAT SHALL THE NORTH DO? That is the theme, ladies and gentlemen, to which I ask your attention to-night. A few weeks ago we were startled by a strange tale, yet not a strange one, which came to us from Cincinnati. We were told that a mother, rather than suffer her child to go into bondage, overcame in a moment what is supposed to be the strongest instinct in a woman's heart—the love of her child—and slew with her own hand her first-born son. When she was asked whether she would go back to bondage or be tried for murder, with a chance of being hanged, she said: "Rather than go back to bondage I will go dancing to the gallows." Ladies and gentlemen, she did not have an opportunity to go dancing to the gallows. The United States Judge Livingston decided that if a fugitive slave commits a murder in the State of Ohio, the slave-master's claim takes precedence over Ohio law, and the murderer must be delivered up into bondage, and the laws of Ohio trodden under the hoof of the Slave Power. Just now, the great question before America—the greatest question she ever had—is, What shall we do with Slavery, or what shall Slavery do with us? It is very plain that either Freedom must go down or else Bondage must perish, and this generation is to decide which of the two shall prosper. Now, Slavery exists by the act of the American people. It is a Federal institution; it has been the favorite of the American Government for seventy years. I know it is common to suppose that Slavery belongs to the individual States, and they alone are responsible for it. No mistake can be greater. The Constitution, in the fourth section of the fourth article, has these remarkable words: "The United States shall guarantee to every State in the Union a Republican form of government." That clause puts Slavery completely in the power of the Federal Congress. Whensoever that Congress shall declare that Slavery is not a Republican institution, down Slavery goes. . . . Slavery exists, not by the act of Carolina and Mississippi and the other Slave States, but by the act or the acquiescence of the whole people of the United States. It is not the Slave States who extend Slavery: it is the United States. . . .

There are without doubt, two forces in the country; one is the power of Freedom and the other is the force of Bondage. These two have been recognized, but it is an old saying that if two will ride on the same horse one must ride behind. [Laughter]. Ladies and Gentlemen, these two parties have been on one horse ever since the adoption of the Federal Constitution, and all the time Slavery has sat in the saddle, and Freedom has been glad to sit on the crapper [Renewed laughter]. . . . Slavery is advancing. In 1776 it only reached on the Atlantic coast from Massachusetts to the Gulf of Mexico; but in no case did it go 250 miles into the interior. Now it has spread over all our territory; it has crossed the Alleghenies, and finds a home in the great basin of the Mississippi. It is to be found even in California; and, notwithstanding their Constitution prohibits bondage, yet I tell you slaves are to be found there, and their masters are protected by the authorities. It is the boast of Great Britain that a slave cannot breathe her free air for a moment—instantly on touching her soil his shackles drop from his limbs, and he is no longer a bondman. It is the boast of Yankee land that a slavehunter can kidnap his man wherever he will. . . .

The satanic Democracy is made up of the raw Irishman and the vulgar snob. Their aim at present is to completely destroy all Democracy in America. Some declare it; others know but declare it not. Their first treason is to restore Slavery to all territory that is now free. The fugitive Slave bill is one step to that. . . . The South, though few in numbers, but imperative, demands the North to surrender their slaves; and the North, which is populous and strong, says, "I will;" and further, if they commit murder on our soil we will send them back. The slave-hunter has his lair in the South, but is going North and then South. His dog lives in the North. The Fugitive Slave bill is the hunters call to their dogs. We have whole families of dogs in Boston. [Laughter.] . . .

If slavery progresses for the next eighty years as it has for the last eighty years, there will be thirty-two million slaves—three quarters white. If this be realized, the fate of America is the fate of the Republic of old. Free Church, free schools and free every thing will go down. Massachusetts will be like Georgia, and New York be like Arkansas. Ten years like the last and we are undone. . . . Three great battles have been fought. First, between the Anglo-Saxon people in the sixteenth century and the Pope. The Saxon conquered. In the seventeenth century the question was: Shall there be a limited monarchy, and in which the powers of the throne shall be limited by the representatives of the parliament? How did that turn out? Oliver Cromwell hewed off a neck of one king, and stout William the Dutchman banished another. Kings were taught that they had joints in their necks. Anglo Saxon blood prevailed. Next came the question of the right of a people to self-government, which was settled here. Three times has Anglo-Saxon blood fought for human rights and conquered. What if these questions had been answered differently? A different world would we have now. . . . Now, in the nineteenth century, comes the fourth great question for Anglo Saxon blood to decide; and shall it, who has three times striken down oppressions, now turn and strike down freedom? Shall 30,000,000 of men aid 300,000 wicked men to keep down 3,000,500 of poor bondsmen? I say the Anglo-Saxon is not going to "cave in" before 300,000 slaveholders. But the question must be soon solved. The North has a duty to perform—to put Slavery down, "peacably if it can, forcibly if it must." There are two ways to go to work to do this: One is to dissolve the Union, and leave the South to settle the matter for itself. Mr. Garrison, my friend, goes for the dissolution. He is a great man, and I love him [hisses and cheers]. The nation does not yet quite appreciate him, and it does not surprise me that there are some who hiss as well as applaud [Hisses and applause]. But when they who hiss are beneath the ground the world will be searched for marble white enough and gold pure enough to build his monument and inscribe his epitaph [Applause]. I do not agree with my friend Garrison, in the dissolution. To do it now would be attended with bloodshed. . . . But rather than one more fugitive slave should be sent back I would let the Union be

broken into fragments no larger than the space upon which this building
stands; and then I would place myself upon a little piece of free soil which
was not contaminated with my brother's blood. But it seems to me that
the dissolution of the Union is unnecessary. Let us see what we can do
without disturbing it. The Free States can choose for its officers men who
are men—men made by Nature and not by Nature's journeymen. Then
let New-York pass a Personal Liberty bill refusing to give up a fugitive
slave, and that every slave shall be free when he steps upon our soil. Then
pass a law to punish kidnappers by imprisonment in the State Prison.
Then punish those who are in the American slave trade the same way
you do those who are in the African slave trade. All this they could do in
Albany without violating the Constitution—for you are a sovereign State
and have a right to interpret the Constitution for yourselves. Then in
national point of view repeal all Fugitive Slave bills. Then abolish Slavery in the District of Columbia and all the Territories. Abolish the entire
State slave trade and make it piracy. Then make slaveholding incapaci-
tate a man from holding any office. Then reconstruct the United States
Judiciary—they need not remove the Judge from office, but remove the
office from the man. Then in their places I would take honest men who
love God and love men, and then the Constitution would no longer be a
Pro-Slavery document. There are things in that document that are bad
things, which I would tread under my foot. But there are other things
which are noble, and they preponderate. Then, at least, I would decree
a day, fixed and certain, when each State should abolish Slavery, and if
they did not do it, the Government should take possession of them and
form a Republican Government. In the next six months we can place a
Republican man in the Presidential chair, and if that is accomplished,
Freedom will triumph. . . .

Our masters one, we are many; they are poor, we rich; they are ignorant; we learned and intelligent. But yet we crouch down before them.
Will you wait and not resist them? Will you wait until necessity, through
the throat of the cannon, says: "Do or die?" I would not wait so long. To-
day we can check bondage with our votes; wait another Presidential term
and we can only efface bondage from the continent by wiping out with
the sacrifice of some of the best blood which runs in American hearts.
When we triumph, how rich will America become! America, the youngest of the nations, will be the mother of a continent, having a church
without a bishop, a State without a King, a community without a lord,
a family without a breeder of slaves; and we shall show the nations how
divine a thing a people can be [Loud applause].

National Anti-Slavery Standard, March 15, 1856

The author, Reverend Bassett, visited Margaret Garner in jail while the case was before Commissioner Pendery. However we judge the usefulness of Bassett's presentation of her state of mind, his is one of the few such reports based on a conversation with her. The resulting document is the source that, over a century later, brought the case to the attention of Toni Morrison, sparking the interest that culminated in her novel Beloved.

A VISIT TO THE SLAVE MOTHER WHO KILLED HER CHILD.
From The American Baptist.

LAST Sabbath, after preaching in the city prison, Cincinnati, through the kindness of the Deputy Sheriff, I was permitted to visit the apartment of that unfortunate woman, concerning whom there has been so much excitement during the last two weeks.

I found her with an infant in her arms only a few months old, and observed that it had a large *bunch* on its forehead. I inquired the cause of the injury. She then proceeded to give a detailed account of her attempt to kill her children.

She said that when the officers and slave-hunters came to the house in which they were concealed, she caught a shovel and struck two of her children on the head, and then took a knife and cut the throat of the third, and tried to kill the other—that if they had given her time, she would have killed them all—that with regard to herself she cared but little; but she was unwilling to have her children suffer as she had done.

I inquired if she were not excited almost to madness when she committed the act? No, she replied, I was as cool as I now am; and would much rather kill them at once, and thus end their sufferings, than have them taken back to slavery and be murdered by piece-meal. She then told the story of her wrongs. She spoke of her days of suffering, of her nights of unmitigated toil, while the bitter tears coursed their way down her cheeks, and fell in the face of the innocent child as it looked smiling up, little conscious of the danger and probable sufferings that awaited it.

As I listened to the facts, and witnessed the agony depicted in her countenance, I could not but exclaim, O how terrible is irresponsible power, when exercised over intelligent beings! She alludes to the child that she killed as being free from all trouble and sorrow, with a degree of satisfaction that almost chills the blood in one's veins. Yet she evidently possesses all the passionate tenderness of a mother's love. She is about twenty-five years of age, and apparently possesses an average amount of kindness, with a vigorous intellect, and much energy of character.

The two men and the two oldest children were in another apartment, but her mother-in-law was in the same room. She says she is the mother of eight children, most of whom have been separated from her; that her husband was once separated from her twenty-five years, during which time she did not see him; that could she have prevented it, she would never have permitted him to return, as she did not wish him to witness her sufferings, or be exposed to the brutal treatment that he would receive.

She states that she has been a faithful servant, and in her old age she would not have attempted to obtain her liberty; but as she became feeble, and less capable of performing labour, her master become more and more exacting and brutal in his treatment, until she could stand it no longer; that the effort could result only in death, at most—she therefore made the attempt.

She witnessed the killing of the child, but said that she neither encouraged nor discouraged her daughter-in-law—for under similar circumstances she should probably have done the same. The old woman is from sixty to seventy years of age; has been a professor of religion about twenty years, and speaks with much feeling of the time when she shall be delivered from the power of the oppressor, and dwell with the *Saviour,* "where the wicked shall cease from troubling; and the weary are at rest."

These slaves (as far as I am informed) have resided all their lives within sixteen miles of Cincinnati. We are frequently told that Kentucky slavery is very innocent. If those are its fruits where it exists in a mild form, will some one tell us what we may expect from the more objectionable features? But comments are unnecessary.

P. C. Bassett.
Fairmount Theological Seminary, Cincinnati, O, Feb. 12, 1856.

Liberator, May 16, 1856

The Reverend H. Bushnell's florid account of the case includes what appears to be an embellished version of the conversation recounted by Bassett. For his other likely borrowings, it is worth comparing this text with the excerpt from Uncle Tom's Cabin *reprinted in chapter 12.*

THE CASE OF THE SLAVE MOTHER, MARGARET,
AT CINCINNATI.

Extract from a sermon recently delivered in Cleveland, (Ohio), by Rev. H. BUSHNELL, from the following text: —"and it was so, that all who saw it said there was no such deed done nor even from the day that the children of Israel came up out of the land of Egypt unto this day: CON-SIDER IT, TAKE ADVICE, AND SPEAK YOUR MINDS."—*Judges* 19:20.

A few weeks ago, just at dawn of day might be seen a company of strangers crossing the winter bridge over the Ohio river, from the State of Kentucky, into the great city of our own State, whose hundred church spires point to Heaven—telling the travellers that in this place the God of Abraham was worshipped, and that here Jesus the Messiah was known, and his religion of love taught and believed. And yet, no one asked them in or offered them any hospitality or sympathy or assistance. After wandering from street to street, a poor laboring man gave them the shelter of his humble cabin, for they were strangers and in distress. Soon it was known abroad that this poor man had offered them the hospitalities of his home, and a rude and ferocious rubble soon gathered around his dwelling, demanding his guests. With loud clamor and horrid threatening they broke down his doors, and rushed upon the strangers. They were an old man and his wife, their daughter and her husband with four children; and they were of the tribe of slaves fleeing from a bondage which was worse than death. There was now no escape—the tribes of Israel had banded against them. On the side of the oppressor there is power. And the young wife and mother, into whose very soul the iron had entered, hearing the cry of the master: "Now we'll have you all," turning from the side of her husband and father, with whom she had stood to repel the foe, seized a knife, and with a single blow nearly severed the head from the body of her darling daughter, and throwing its bloody corpse at his feet, exclaimed—"Yes, you *shall* have us all! take that." and with another blow inflicted a ghastly wound upon the head of her beautiful son, repeating— "Yes, you *shall* have us all—take that!" meanwhile calling upon her old mother to help her in the quick work of emancipation—for there were two more. But the pious old grandmother could not do it, and it was now too late—the rescuers had subdued and bound them. They were on their way back to the house of their bondage—a life more bitter than death! On their way through that city of churches whose hundred spires told of Jesus and the good Father above; on their way amid the throng of

Christian men, whose noble sires had said and sung—"Give me *liberty,* or give me *death."*

But they all tarried in the great Queen City, of the West—in chains, and in a felon's cell. There our preacher visited them again and again. There he saw the old grandfather and his aged companion whose weary pilgrimage of unrequited toil and tears was near at its end. And there stood the young father and the heroic wife Margaret. Said the preacher— "Margaret, why did you kill your child?" "It was my own," she said, "given me of God to do the best a mother could in its behalf. *I have done the best I could!* I would have done more and better for the rest! I knew it was better for them to go home to God than back to slavery." "But why did you not trust in God—why not wait and hope?" "I did wait, and then we dared to do, and fled in fear, but in hope;—hope fled—God did not appear to save—*I did the best I could!"*

And who was this woman? A noble, womanly, amiable, *affectionate mother.* "But was she not deranged!" Not at all—calm, intelligent, but resolute and determined. "But was she not fiendish or beside herself with passion!" No, she was most tender and affectionate, and all her passion was that of a *mother's fondest love.* I reasoned with her, said the preacher; tried to awaken a sense of guilt, and lead her to repentance and to Christ. But there was no remorse, no desire of pardon, no reception of Christ or his religion. To her it was a religion of *slavery,* more cruel than death. And where had she lived? where thus taught? Not down among the rice swamps of Georgia, or on the banks of Red river. No, but within sixteen miles of the Queen City of the West! In a nominally Christian family— whose master was most liberal in support of the Gospel, and whose mistress was a communicant at the Lord's table, and a professed follower of Christ! Here, in this family, where slavery is found in its mildest form, she had been kept in ignorance of God's will and word, and learned to know that the mildest form of American slavery of this day of Christian civilization and Democratic liberty was worse than death itself! She had learned by an experience of thirty years, that it was so bad she had rather take the life of her own dearest child, without the hope of Heaven for herself, than that *it* should experience its unutterable agonies, which were to be found even in a Christian family! But here are her two little boys of eight and ten years of age. Taking the eldest by the hand the preacher said to him kindly and gently, "Come here, my boy; what is your name?" *"Tom,* sir." "Yes, *Thomas."* "No sir, *Tom."* "Well Tom, how old are you?" "Three *months."* "And how old is your little brother?" "Six *months,* sir." "And have you no other name but Tom?" "No." "What is your father's name?" "Hav'nt got any!" "Who made you, Tom?" "Nobody." "Did you ever hear of God or Jesus Christ?" "No, sir." And this was slavery in its best estate. By and by the aged couple, and the young man and his wife, the remaining children, with the master, and the dead body of the little one, were escorted through the streets of the Queen City of the West by a *national guard of armed men,* back to the great and chivalrous State of old Kentucky, and away to the shambles of the South—back to a life-long servitude of hopeless despair. It was a long, and, silent procession down to the banks of the Ohio, and as it passed, the death-knell of free-dom tolled heavily. The sovereignty of Ohio trailed in the dust beneath the oppressor's foot, and the great confederacy of the tribes of modern Israel attended the funeral obsequies, and made ample provision for the necessary expenses. And it was so, that all who saw it said, *there was no such deed done, nor seen from the day that the children of Israel came up, out of the land of Egypt unto this day,* "CONSIDER OF IT, TAKE ADVICE, AND SPEAK YOUR MINDS!'

Anti-Slavery Bugle, May 24, 1856

Speaking before sympathetic colleagues at the annual meeting of the American Anti-Slavery Society, and having had several months to reshape the remarks she made in Commissioner Pendery's court (see chapter 2), Lucy Stone again told of her encounter with Margaret Garner. It is interesting to compare the two accounts, as here her conversation with Margaret is made notably more elaborate. The poem Stone quotes is Mary Livermore's widely circulated rendition of the case (see chapter 12).

TWENTY-THIRD ANNIVERSARY
OF THE
AMERICAN ANTI SLAVERY SOCIETY
Reported for the Anti-Slavery Standard by William Henry Burr

SPEECH OF LUCY STONE BLACKWELL.

. . . For the last year I have been living directly on the slave-border, and almost every day I have been able to see over on to slave soil, where I know that neither I nor you, known as the slave's friend, can walk in safety—so much is this "glorious Union" worth—where also daily may be seen the selling of human beings. And even where I live I am surrounded by a class of people whose highest anti-slavery idea is, "Let there be no more slave territory." It is greatful, therefore, to come back here and look into the faces of those whose motto is, "Without concealment, without compromise"—whose sentiment is not "slavery sectional, and freedom national"—but who are seeking the destruction of slavery everywhere and altogether. I am glad to meet such friends on every recurring anniversary; I am glad to take them by the hand while we pledge ourselves, each to the other and to all, anew to this great work of the immediate and unconditional abolition of slavery.

Ladies and gentlemen, I have but a single thought that I wish to speak, and it is this: The anti-slavery cause has now passed through an era of indifference, when men said, "It is no business of ours; let it alone; it is only the negroes at the South that are concerned." I say it has passed through that stage, and men now see very well that slavery, with its Argus eyes and Briarian arms, is clutching everywhere at the rights of white humanity as well as black; and they are beginning to say now, "Hands off from us." But as yet they do not see, standing on the mount of vision, that the gain or loss of one of the least of God's creatures is the gain or loss of all; they are only asking that slavery may be limited. . . .

. . . Charles Sumner says, "freedom is national—slavery sectional." And Governor Chase's motto is, "No slavery outside of the Slave States." Now, who does not know that these men all hate slavery? And yet, when they stand up and utter their sentiments in regard to it, the most they can say is, "No slavery outside of the Slave States," which, as Wendell Phillips justly observes, means just this: "Let there be just as much slavery as there is." They do not propose to strike a single blow at it where it is now. . . . We, on the contrary, a little handful, strong only in the might of our right, feel that it is not enough to say that slavery shall be confined to this or that region and there let alone, but that now here in the wide universe of God shall a slave clank his chains. (applause.)

Only a few weeks ago, in Cincinnati, my present home, I stood by the side of that heroic slave mother, Margaret Garner, whose tale has made your ears tingle and your hearts ache. I said to myself again and again, what to her and to the millions of victims of slavery are the words "No slavery outside of the Slave States?" What to that mother, that father at her side, and those children clustered around them, are those words? God had bridged over the Ohio for more than seven hundred miles, and made a literal union between the North and South by connecting the two shores of that river by ice that could not be broken. Over that bridge of ice slaves by hundreds were making their way to the North. Margaret and Simon Garner, with their four little children, and their aged father and mother, bowed down by the sorrows and toils of a long life of slavery, saw there was a chance of making their way all together over the river. With the love of liberty which God had implanted in their souls, they started to make their way to Canada. When they had reached the Ohio side, there, in the Queen City of the West, they fondly hoped to find shelter and kindness for the little hour they needed for rest, and then to hurry from a country, the dissolution of whose Union people fear so much, where human beings charged with no crime, find no protection. That mother, that father and their family were overtaken. Was there any strong arm in Ohio to help them? Was there any one who, in trumpet tones, could call people to their rescue? The popular voice in Ohio had only said, "No slavery outside of the Slave States." So Margaret Garner was overtaken, and in the wild desperation of the hour, when she knew that there was nothing in the future for her and her's but the life of a slave, she drew out from her side a dagger she had concealed, and, taking up one little daughter, but three summers old, a child of surpassing beauty, knowing too well from her own experience the life that awaited that child, than which any death was preferable—that mother drew across its throat the sharpened dagger and the life blood of that little daughter lay in a pool at her feet. She did not stop to see it gasp, but hurried to take another child to send it back also to the angels. But her pursuers saw the work of ruin and wrenched the dagger from her hand. Then calling to her husband's mother, "Help, oh help me," she cried, "save this child from being made a slave." A billet of wood was the only weapon within her reach, and, maddened by the dreadful torture of slavery, she seized it and tried to take the life of that other child. I was present when the Court held its session. The living children were brought into the Court, and there I saw the fresh marks made by that mother on her little child. I went and stood beside that mother. I took her hand, hardened by unrequited toil, in mine, and said, "Margaret, we are glad that with the Constitution against you, the law against you and the Court against you, one of your children has found its freedom with the angels." For a moment her lip quivered and her cheek grew dark with the agony which no word could speak, and she raised her dark eyes so full of despair, and, "I didn't know what might happen to her here, but now I know where she is." And as I stood by the side of her so powerless, with one babe on her knee and two little ones on her side, I saw on one side the slave Commissioner, and the Marshal on the other; a half-a score of deputies guarding that woman, lest by some desperate effort she should force her way from that crew and escape. And to guard her the more securely, the stairway was thronged with the most ruffianly looking men I ever saw, all sworn as special marshals to help in the rendition of Margaret to slavery. I asked her if there was anything we could do for her. As she held my hand in hers all the response she made was to grasp my hand still tighter, expressing by that detaining grasp more than she could have done by words. I know well what she wanted. It was not that we should say, "no more Slave States," but that going up and down, and scattering far and wide on the nation's heart the living coals of truth, we should arouse such a public sentiment, that slavery, exposed to the withering scorn of the people, could not find room to breathe. (applause.) Then Margaret Garner will need no more of you or of me, for, her humanity recognised, standing up as a human being, she can make her way in the world as you and I make ours.

I stood again by the grated bars where she was confined, and taking her hand I bade her have courage if it were possible.

Again she went on her way down the river in chains, with her babe in her arms. The fearful tragedy seemed to be played on. The boat in which she was sailing ran into another boat and sank. Margaret and her babe, together with the whole crew, were plunged into the river. Oh that little baby, that sat on her knee in the Courtroom in innocent unconsciousness, patting its mother's cheek! Was it wrong, was it wicked for her to abandon that little babe to the waters? With one gurgling groan that babe went down, and Margaret clapped her hands with joy that that babe, too had gone to God.

Again, that mother goes on her way to New Orleans with such emotions as you and I can understand. She is brought back by a requisition from Gov. Chase; but it is unavailing; again she is carried away to the Southern prison-house.

I heard the law expounded in the Court upon that trial, and the only strong defence in her favor was made, based upon the Constitution and the atrocious Fugitive Slave law. And, as I heard it, oh, deeper than I can express it, I said, curses on that law.

Oh, thou mother, maddened, frenzied, when the hunter's toils ensnared
Thee and thy brood of nestlings, till thy anguished spirit dared.
Send to God, uncalled, one darling life that round thine own did twine;
what shall they say to thee when, stripped of all disguise, we stand
before our common Father?—Can they plead either Church, or Union,
or Constitution?

Now, the one word I have come here to say is this, and I want to say it emphatically to women. I know you are disfranchised, but do not think for that reason that there is nothing for you to do. I say, then, do you who are mothers, by all that Margaret Garner suffers to-day, by all she has suffered in the agony which impelled her to do the deed she has done, see to it that in spite of law and in spite of everything that weights down upon the slave, you make common cause with those who are at work to root out the system of slavery. I know there is no more tender cord than a mother's love. If sickness threatens your child, you summon physician and friends, and your own word is, "show me some way to save my child from the grave." —But so dreadful is slavery that all that Margaret Garner says is, "show me some way to hide my child in the grave that she may escape from the evils that impend over her." Go then, mothers, to the Anti-Slavery Office, there you will find Anti-Slavery Tracts by thousands. Take them, and wherever you find an empty hand put into it a tract. It is not, as was truly said by Mr. Remond it is not the logic of the head that people want; it is not the logic of the heart that is needed now; for there is not a man or woman living who does not know that the system of slaveholding is one stupendous wrong, and ought immediately to cease to be. Then carry to the heart that which makes the head right. These Anti-Slavery Tracts which shall go forth with thoughts that breathe and words that burn will help to create just that public sentiment which we need. . . .

Like the snow flakes gently falling, so will these tracts scattered abroad diffuse the pure principles of humanity over the land. They will reach a thousand homes where the voice of the anti-slavery speaker is never heard and where an anti-slavery newspaper never goes. The little tract is God's messenger. It is your duty to help create such a public sentiment that the merchant will find that he can no longer say, "We can't afford to let you succeed." That is not a truly anti-slavery feeling which says "Let not slavery go into Kansas." True anti-slavery feeling is that which undertakes to root out slavery where it is, and not merely to prevent it from going where it is not. So long as we find fugitive slaves held to trial and without judge or jury sent back to bondage we have a great work to do. Margaret Garner was tried by a Commissioner—a man who listens not to the voice of Him who sits in the circle of the Heavens bidding us to execute judgment in the morning and deliver him that is spoiled out of the hands of his oppressor but one who simply squares his conscience to the law of the Constitution. Such men have yet to learn that there is a law higher than the edicts of men—a law that claims our obedience and that calls upon us to trample under foot all laws made by men in contravention of God's law.

We are not many who are engaged in this crusade against slavery, but we do not require it to be many. Truth is mighty; what we need is to give it utterance. We need to have the truth uttered, that there is no safety or security in compromises with slavery. . . . .

I believe, too the religious sentiment of the country, now offered its worship to the unknown God, not the God of freedom or of justice, can be made to sympathize with the millions now suffering with Margaret Garner. When men find that they can keep their churches only when Margaret's heart is bleeding, like true Christians they will let the church go, and take up that suffering victim, and build up a new church, in which humanity, irrespective of color or condition, shall be recognized, and all shall be acknowledged as brethren and children of one God our Father. (applause).

Anti-Slavery Bugle, May 24, 1856

Theodore Parker took up the case again when addressing the same conven-tion as Stone. This excerpt reveals him at his most militant. In a letter to Parker written two months later, Governor Chase would object to how he was portrayed in this speech, particularly in regard to his racial commit-ments. Parker's own views on "blood" and racial identity are on display in this speech as well.

Speech of Theodore Parker

. . . The primitive thing is to arouse a sense of humanity in the whites which should lead us to abolish this wickedness. Another way would be to arouse a sense of indignation in the persons who suffered the wrong—in the slave and to urge himself to put a stop to bearing the wickedness.

Two things there were which hindered this thing being attempted. First, the anti-slavery leaders were non-resistants. . . .

The other reason was, the slaves themselves were Africans—men not very good at the sword. If the case had been other—if it had been three and a half millions of Anglo-Saxons—the appeal would not have been to the oppressor to leave off oppressing, but to the victim to leave off suffering the oppression. For, while the African is not very good with the sword, the Anglo-Saxon is something of a master with that ugly weapon; at any rate, he knows how to use it. If the Anglo-Saxon hadn't been a bet-ter fighter than the African, slave ships would fill this side of Sandy Hook and Boston bay; they would not take pains to go the Gulf of Guinea. If the three and a half millions of slaves had been white men, with this dreadful Anglo-Saxon blood in their bosoms, do you suppose the affair at Cincinnati would have turned out after that sort? Do you believe Gov. Chase would have said, "No slavery outside of the slave States, but inside the slave States just as much enslavement of Anglo-Saxon men as you please?" Why, his head would not have been on his shoulders twenty-four hours after he said it. In the State of Ohio, when Margaret Garner was surrendered up, there were 400,000 able-bodied men between the ages of 18 and 45; there were half a million of fire-locks in that State; and if that woman had been the representative of three and a half millions of white persons held as slaves every one of those muskets would have started into life, and 400,000 men would have come forth each man with a fire-lock on his shoulder, and then 100,000 women would have followed, bringing the rest of the muskets. That is what the state of things would have been if she had been a white woman and not a black one. We should not then have asked Quakers to lead in the greatest enterprise in the world; the leaders would have been soldiers—I mean such men as your fathers and my fathers, who didn't content themselves with asking Great Britain to leave off oppressing them. They asked that first; and when Great Britain said, "Please God, we never will," what did Jonathan say? "Please God, we will make you," and Jonathan did it (laughter.) "Gods," we would have said, "can a Saxon people long debate which of the two to choose, slavery or death? No, let us rise at once, gird on our swords, and, at the head of our remaining troops, attack the foe." That would have been opened with prayers of men who trusted in God and kept their powder dry likewise.

But in this case it was otherwise. The work has not been to arouse the indignation of the enslaved, but to stir the humanity of the oppressor, to touch his conscience, his affection, his religious sentiments. . . .

Frederick Douglass, Speech on West Indian emancipation, August 3, 1857

(Originally published in Two Speeches by Frederick Douglass, *1857)*

One of the period's greatest wordsmiths and orators, Frederick Douglass, spoke about the Garners in a variety of venues. This speech was delivered in Canandaigua, New York. Every year, on the first Monday in August, anti-slavery activists in many communities staged public events commemorating

Britain's 1834–38 abolition of slavery in the West Indies. These celebrations, offering an abolitionist counterpoint to mainstream July Fourth festivities, typically drew multiracial crowds numbering in the thousands. Douglass's Canandaigua speech, only a small portion of which is excerpted here, is probably the most noted ever given at such an event. The poet he quotes is Lord Byron.

The world in which we live is very accommodating to all sorts of people. It will co-operate with them in any measure which they propose; it will help those who earnestly help themselves, and will hinder those who hinder themselves. It is very polite, and never offers its services unasked. —Its favors to individuals are measured by an unerring principle in this: viz.—respect those who respect themselves, and despise those who despise themselves. It is not within the power of unaided human nature to persevere in pitying a people who are insensible to their own wrongs, and indifferent to the attainment of their own rights. The poet was as true to common sense as to poetry when he said,

"Who would be free, themselves must strike the blow."

When O'Connell, with all Ireland at his back, was supposed to be contending for the just rights and liberties of Ireland, the sympathies of mankind were with him, and even his enemies were compelled to respect his patriotism. Kossuth, fighting for Hungary with his pen long after she had fallen by the sword, commanded the sympathy and support of the liberal world till his own hopes died out. The Turks while they fought bravely for themselves and scourged and drove back the invading legions of Russia, shared the admiration of mankind. They were standing up for their own rights against an arrogant and powerful enemy; but as soon as they let out their fighting to the Allies, admiration gave way to contempt. These are not the maxims and teachings of a cold-hearted world. Christianity itself teaches that a man shall provide for his own house. This covers the whole ground of nations as well as individuals. Nations no more than individuals can innocently be improvident. They should provide for all wants, mental, moral, and religious, and against all evils to which they are liable as nations. In the great struggle now progressing for the freedom and elevation of our people, we should be found at work with all our might, resolved that no man or set of men shall be more abundant in labors, according to the measure of our ability, than ourselves.

I know, my friends, that in some quarters the efforts of colored people meet with very little encouragement. We may fight, but we must fight like the Seapoys of India, under white officers. This class of Abolitionists don't like colored celebrations, they don't like colored conventions, they don't like colored Anti-Slavery fairs for the support of colored newspapers. They don't like any demonstrations whatever in which colored men take a leading part. They talk of the proud Anglo-Saxon blood, as flippantly as those who profess to believe in the natural inferiority of races. Your humble speaker has been branded as an ingrate, because he has ventured to stand up on his own right, and to plead our common cause as a colored man, rather than as a Garrisonian. I hold it to be no part of gratitude to allow our white friends to do all the work, while we merely hold their coats. Opposition of the sort now referred to, is partizan opposition, and we need not mind it. The white people at large will not largely be influenced by it. They will see and appreciate all honest efforts on our part to improve our condition as a people.

Let me give you a word of the philosophy of reform. The whole history of the progress of human liberty shows that all concessions yet made to her august claims, have been born of earnest struggle. The conflict has been exciting, agitating, all-absorbing, and for the time being, putting all other tumults to silence. It must do this or it does nothing. If there is no struggle there is no progress. Those who profess to favor freedom and yet depreciate agitation, are men who want crops without plowing up the ground, they want rain without thunder and lightning. They want the ocean without the awful roar of its many waters.

This struggle may be a moral one, or it may be a physical one, and it may be both moral and physical, but it must be a struggle. Power concedes nothing without a demand. It never did and it never will. Find out just what any people will quietly submit to and you have found out the exact measure of injustice and wrong which will be imposed upon them, and these will continue till they are resisted with either words or blows, or with both. The limits of tyrants are prescribed by the endurance of those whom they oppress. In the light of these ideas, Negroes will be hunted at the North, and held and flogged at the South so long as they submit to those devilish outrages, and make no resistance, either moral or physical. Men may not get all they pay for in this world, but they must certainly pay for all they get. If we ever get free from the oppressions and wrongs heaped upon us, we must pay for their removal. We must do this by labor, by suffering, by sacrifice, and if needs be, by our lives and the lives of others.

Hence, my friends, every mother who, like Margaret Garner, plunges a knife into the bosom of her infant to save it from the hell of our Christian Slavery, should be held and honored as a benefactress.

Warrington (England) Times, January 29, 1859

Born in Salem, Massachusetts, in 1826 to a free black family that would play a prominent role in both the abolitionist movement and the struggle against Northern racism, Sarah Parker Remond went to work for the American Anti-Slavery Society in 1856, the year the Garners made their bid for freedom. In 1858, after two years of touring the United States on behalf of the Society, she accepted an invitation to speak against American slavery throughout Great Britain. Her speech in Warrington—which drew many more people than the room could hold—met with an enthusiastic response and helped fuel an antislavery campaign in the area. The speech was reported in the American abolitionist press and in multiple papers in England. None offers a putative transcript of the kind found in the newspaper coverage of the speeches of Parker and Stone, but the local Warrington Times *provided a detailed account of what Remond said and how her English audience received her. Remond stayed in England throughout the war, moving afterward to Florence, Italy, where, in her forties, she attended medical school and became a doctor. As far as is known, she never returned to the United States.*

Lecture on American Slavery by a Coloured Lady

Miss REMOND commenced by thanking the audience for their kind manifestations towards her, and said that though she was 3,000 miles from home, and from loved ones, yet she felt that a common sympathy should unite all, for was not God their father, and were they not all brethren? She was there that evening as the representative of a race that was stripped of every right and debarred from every privilege—a race which was deprived of the protection of the law, and the glorious influences of religion, and all the strong ties and influences of social life. She was there as the representation of a race, which, in the estimation of American law, had no rights which the white man was bound to respect, and for what? For no other reason than that they were of a different complexion from the majority of American citizens. And this infamous doctrine had the sanction of the established courts of law in that country. Nine judges of the supreme court of America had met together and given this decision. . . . She would remind her audience that in 16 of the 31 States slavery did not exist by law; but in those States there were half a million, perhaps more, honourable men and women—descendants of the African race, varying in complexion from black to white, and yet these men and women in either of the 16 states where slavery was prohibited, were deprived of every privilege as citizens. They were, in one respect, just as much deprived of these rights before this decision was given; but this had given the final blow to any faint hope that existed, and now, throughout the 31 states, the black people found that this law was irrevocable, and must be obeyed—not the slightest chance appeared of alteration. She would tell them in America politics were corrupt. (Hear, hear.) . . . But she would tell them that the American churches were infinitely more corrupt than American politics. (Hear, hear.) The American churches were responsible for many of the worst features that existed in regard to the slavery of the African population. When that infamous decision was given that was before mentioned, the church did not set their face against it, but tamely said with the pro-slavery party at the north, "we must obey the law. It is necessary for the public safety that we should obey the law." But if there was an attempt made to pass a law in favour of the negro, there was no movement on their parts, or sympathy shown towards it. Thus the laws of America stood condemned—for they were insincere and inconsistent. Miss Remond then alluded to the disabilities of the negro population in various States. There was not an hotel in Boston but one that would receive a coloured man or woman. In Massachusetts there had been an improvement within the last five years. Black men and women were allowed to ride in the omnibuses. This had been effected by a few who had determined to stand by the weak; but the majority stood aside. These few individuals had renovated the public sentiment to the extent mentioned. But in New York and Philadelphia, if a coloured individual were ready to sink in the street through exhaustion, not a single omnibus would take him in. When they took into consideration that the American people, beyond all others, were making greater professions of liberty than any other nation; and then besides, any 4th of July to hear their Declaration of Independence, and the speeches that were made, when they heard all this, and looked a little farther, they saw in that same America an iron despotism crushing out the intellect, aye, the very souls of men and women, made but little lower than the angels! . . . Who could give the faintest idea of what the slave mother suffered? She would not spend a moment of the precious time she had to occupy in endeavouring to prove that slavery was a sin—that would be an insult to their understanding— an insult to their hearts. . . . Miss Remond then touchingly related the case of Margaret Garner, who determined to be free or die in the attempt. She was born a slave, and had suffered in her own person the degradation that a woman could not mention. She got as far as Cincinnati with her children. Cincinnati—the queen of the west—that city excelled by no other except New York. There she stood amidst magnificent temples dedicated to God on either hand, but no sympathy or help was afforded her. The slaveholder found her; as he appeared at the door she snatched up a knife and slew her first-born child, but before the poor frenzied creature could proceed further in her dread object, the hand of the tyrant was on her, when she called to the grandmother of the children to kill the others, as she preferred to return them to the bosom of God rather than they should be taken back to American slavery. Above all sufferers in America, American women who were slaves lived in the most pitiable condition. They could not protect themselves from the licentiousness which met them on every hand—they could not protect their honour from the tyrant. There were slaveholders everywhere in that country. There were no morals there; no genuine regard for womanhood or manhood. The slaveholders south of Mason and Dixon's line were as low in the scale of morals as it was possible to conceive; and Margaret Garner would rather that her children should suffer death than to be left in the hands of such beings as she had been describing. The courts decided that Margaret Garner must be returned to slavery under the Fugitive Slave Law—a law which had disgraced America so much, and which could find no parallel in history, ancient or modern. But the counsel of Margaret Garner had told her (the lecturer) that he could have raised 10,000 dollars if he could have rescued her from the hands of the tyrant, but the slaveholder said there was not enough money in Cincinnati to purchase his chattel! She was a thing! (Deep sensation.) Yes, every slave below Mason and Dixon's line was a thing! "Ah!" continued Miss Remond, in deep and thrilling tones, "what is slavery? who can tell? In the open market place women are exposed for sale—their persons not always covered. Yes, I can tell you English men and women, that women are sold into slavery with cheeks like the lily and the rose, as well as those that might compare with the wing of the raven. They are exposed for sale, and subjected to the most shameful indignities. The more Anglo-Saxon blood that mingles with the blood of the slave, the more gold is poured out when the auctioneer has a woman for sale, because they are sold to be concubines for white Americans. They are not sold for plantation slaves.". . . Ah! the spirit of revenge was forming—it was coming upwards in the breast of the slave, and she related circumstances which had revealed this to her. There were insurrections taking place constantly on the plantations, and the masters had to go about armed. This spirit of revenge would increase, and unless something occurred to free them from the thraldom, it was impossible to see the end of it. But she believed in the efficacy of preaching. She believed in appealing to that high moral feeling which every man's heart could appreciate—viz., the idea of love to God and man which was implanted in the heart of every man—for who had not felt these emotions in their breast?—and until that man had got to the utmost depth of moral debasement she believed there was a chance of reaching his conscience. This was the opinion of the American anti-slavery party; they had faith in great principles—in the eternal law of right. . . . [T]he great American republic was destined to be sundered. She thanked God for it. It would be severed, and no power could save it unless a sentiment could be created in the northern mind which would overrule the antagonism of the south. The work would go on. God, love, and truth would prevail. She concluded by saying that in the City of Washington if a slave landed there that night, and could not prove his freedom through a stone wall a number of inches thick, he was cast into prison, and after a certain length of time placed on the auction block and sold to the highest bidder to pay his goal fees! They were misrepresented by the American press, and that was one reason why they were bound to represent themselves. They shut up every avenue—every means was denied them by which knowledge could be gained—and then they turned round and said "You are an inferior race, and have no rights which a white man is bound to respect." Admitting they were an inferior race—which she did not—granting all their oppressors said on the matter to be correct—it was still their duty if they laid claims to the name of Christians and the name of humanity to protect them because they were weak. If a mother had a daughter or son who was weaker than his fellows, did she neglect and oppress them on that account, or did she not rather by all the means which God had given her succour and support by increased solicitude and affection such a one? Therefore they were wished that evening to give her race their sympathy, and to express their moral indignation against American despotism. Miss Remond then sat down amidst the most enthusiastic cheering, after speaking an hour and a quarter.

CHAPTER 11

FINAL DEVELOPMENTS

Although the Garners were periodically invoked for political purposes through the Civil War years, those occasional references were made in a factual void, for reporting on the family's circumstances ceased soon after Ohio's requisition effort failed. The documents included here stand out from that general silence, giving us glimpses of the main protagonists in later years.

National Anti-Slavery Standard, June 13, 1857

Except when weather made the river impassable, traffic back and forth across the Ohio between Covington, Kentucky, and Cincinnati was common and, for white people, not especially fraught or difficult. John Jolliffe proved an exception to this rule one day in June, when his acceptance of a social invitation in Kentucky put him in grave danger. It is not surprising that his erstwhile courtroom nemesis, Archibald Gaines, remained unfriendly to him, but the ferocity of the assault suggests that, even after winning legal victory and outmaneuvering Governor Chase's requisition attempts, Gaines nursed a sense of injury. At Gaines's subsequent trial for assault, his lawyer made much of how severely and unfairly his client's reputation had been attacked during Jolliffe's advocacy for the Garners. After initially deadlocking, the jury found Gaines guilty and fined him. The two stories reprinted below show how the opposing banks of the Ohio River offered very different views of the assault.

MR. JOLIFFE MOBBED IN COVINGTON.
From The Cincinnati Gazette, June 1.

JOHN JOLIFFE, Esq., a lawyer of this city, extensively known as the friend and advocate of the slave in cases arising under the "Fugitive law," was on Saturday last mobbed in Covington, and driven out of that town. Mr. and Mrs. Joliffe had been invited by Rev. Mr. Sage, of Covington, to dine, and Mrs. J. went over in the morning; between 12 and 1 Mr. Jolliffe started over. On the ferry-boat he inquired the way to Mr. Sage's.

Proceeding up town, Mr. Jolliffe was accosted near the first cross street, above the landing, by name. He extended his hand to the man, saying at the same time, "I don't recollect you." The man replied, "My name is Gaines. I know you d——d well, you d——d rascal—you d——d nigger thief. You came over here to steal our niggers." Mr. Joliffe, thinking this was only the usual Kentucky way, said, good-naturedly, "Oh, no, I came over here to dine with my friend, the Rev. Mr. Sage." A crowd collected around them and Gaines thrust his fist against Mr. Joliffe's breast, and into his face, using violent and insulting language at the same time, evidently with the design of provoking Mr. Jolliffe to some show of violence. Mr. Jolliffe, however, walked on, surrounded by the hooting crowd, beyond the Madison House, and finally went into Timberlake's store for protection.

Timberlake made some show of dissuading Gaines, and even holding him, but seemed very glad when he got Mr. Jolliffe out into the street again. Gaines then went to the corner of the street and made a proclamation that "Joliffe was a d——d nigger thief, and that all those interested in niggers had better look out, for he had come over to steal their niggers." This brought a still larger crowd out. Mr. Joliffe finding it was impossible to proceed to Mr. Sage's, turned to the crowd and told them that if they were determined not to permit him to go on, that he would return, and appealed to them for protection to the ferry. This gathering of Kentucky gentlemen (for there was a number of merchants and respectable looking men in it, with some rowdies) replied with one voice, "G——d d——n you, you need not appeal to us," and laughed in derision at the idea.

Mr. Jolliffe was in great danger of being seriously injured by the crowd, when Mr. Warnock (an ex-marshal) came up, and, taking Mr. Jolliffe by one arm, guaranteed to see him safely to the boat. Marshal Lett took the other, and they walked toward the ferry, Gaines and the crowd following. A large man walking with Gaines cried out, "Get a cowhide and cowhide him," and Gaines inquired at every house they passed for a cowhide. He finally got a whip and struck Mr. Jolliffe with it over the shoulders, when Marshal Lett turned and arrested Gaines. A German then came forward to assist in protecting Mr. Jolliffe, and he arrived safely on the ferryboat.

On the way down the crowd seemed determined on violence, crying out "lynch him," "cowhide him," "hang him," and were only deterred by the determined conduct of Mr. Warnock and Marshal Lett.

Mr. Warnock deserves great credit for his conduct in this affair. Though differing entirely from Mr. Jolliffe in his views on slavery, yet he is too high-minded and honorable a gentleman to permit even a political enemy to suffer by mob violence.

There is no doubt, from the spirit manifested by the mob, that but for the interposition of these men, Mr. Jolliffe would have suffered serious personal injury.

Gaines will be tried tomorrow at 10 o'clock before Mayor Foley, who, we understand, has expressed a determination to put a stop to such scenes. This Gaines became notorious as the master of Margaret, the Negro woman who murdered her little girl rather than see her returned to slavery. We presume he will receive but little sympathy in Covington, for he is regarded with great contempt by all honorable Kentuckians for his conduct in taking Margaret away secretly from Frankfort and selling her down South, when he had promised the Governor of that State to keep her to await a requisition from Governor Chase; not only breaking his own word (which was nothing), but also causing the Governor of Kentucky to break his, and thus bringing disgrace upon the State.

Covington Journal, June 6, 1857

The Gaines and Joliffe Affair

On Saturday last, Mr. JOLIFFE, a lawyer of Cincinnati, was assaulted on a public street in this city, by Mr. A.K. GAINES, of Boone county, Ky. The amount of personal damage was slight. GAINES struck or punched JOLIFFE once or twice with his fist, and struck him a few times with a whip. JOLIFFE, though much the largest man of the two, made no resistance, and piteously begged to be conducted to the other side of the river. Some of our citizens took him in charge and conducted him to the river.

The lookers-on who understood the matter, sympathized with GAINES, and made use of such expressions as, "Give it to him," "Let him have it," &c. Mr. GAINES was promptly arrested, and gave bail for his appearance on Tuesday. On that day a trial was had before the Mayor, and Mr. GAINES was fined some twenty dollars.

In making up an opinion in this case it must be remembered that JOLIFFE is an officious and pestilent abolitionist and volunteer counsel for fugitive slaves. GAINES was one of the claimants in the celebrated Marshall and Gaines fugitive slave cases. JOLIFFE was one of the attorneys for the fugitives. The case was a plain one, yet every imaginable quibble and subterfuge was resorted to by the defense to defeat the claim. The claimants were put to great expense and trouble. They, as well as slaveholders generally, were shamelessly abused by JOLIFFE. On Saturday last, for the first time since the trial, Mr. GAINES happened to meet JOLIFFE on Kentucky soil, and remembering the abuse that had been heaped upon him and other slaveholders, and the expense and vexation to which he had been subjected, could not resist the temptation to retaliate.

We regret the occurrence simply because it places Mr. GAINES in the attitude of a law breaker. The interests of the South hang upon faithful observance of the law, and the people of the South ought on all proper occasions to set an example of obedience to its precepts. But while people on the other side of the river continue to entice away our slaves, and persist in violating the law of the land by resisting its execution, the recurrence of such scenes as that which we have been speaking of must be looked for. To forgo retaliating when opportunity presents, would require the exercise of more forbearance than we choose to claim for our people.

New York Daily Tribune, September 22, 1862

_____

Little is known about the Garners' circumstances in the midst of civil war, so this document is especially notable. It is here that Margaret's death was announced in what had become the nation's most important paper—though the information would not lodge firmly in national memory, and diverse speculations on her circumstances would be offered for many years afterward. How much information the journalist really had and how he got it are, however, open to question. Though he invokes details provided in a letter from Robert (without directly saying that he has read the letter himself), the Tribune's *reporter provides a date for Margaret's death that is probably off by about three years. But we do know, from other sources, that Robert indeed survived the war and claimed to have served the Union cause (see next document).*

THE CASE OF THE GARNER FUGITIVE SLAVE FAMILY

The public will remember vividly the case of Margaret Garner, her husband, Robert Garner, and their family, who were arrested a few years ago under the Fugitive Slave act in Cincinnati, and finally surrendered to the claimant. They will remember how Robert Garner stood bravely in the door of his cabin, keeping the Deputy Marshal and his assistants at bay with his revolver, and such other weapons as were within reach, while Margaret was slaying her children within, rather than have them dragged back into a life of slavery. A darling daughter was killed, and a younger son wounded almost mortally, before the brutal hirelings of Slavery burst in and caught them all. They were finally carried off, and sold South. Robert could have escaped, having frequent opportunities, but he would not leave his aged father and mother, whom he was resolved to free. A letter has just been received in this city from Robert Garner, inclosed in a "red, white, and blue" envelope. He writes "from the U.S. gunboat Benton," being under the Emancipation Law a *free man*. His first effort is to learn his mother's condition and state of health. She is, we are informed here, yet a slave in Kentucky; but Mr. Foley, Provost-Marshal of Covington, recently seized some of Mr. Gaines's horses on the charge that he was a "Rebel." Why the mother of the heroic Robert Garner should not be free for the same reason as that which justifies the seizure of her master's horses, perhaps the President knows. Robert writes that his wife Margaret died on the 14th of May, 1861. Her sons Tommy and Sammy are still living. Robert will come North soon.

Cincinnati Chronicle, March 11, 1870

This report, which was reprinted in papers at least as far away as Philadelphia, gives us a late glimpse of Robert Garner (who may have died in Cincinnati the following year) and, through him, a clearer sense of the fates of others in the family. This is the most helpful known source for determining where Margaret lived in her final years and when she died. Even as

it rehashes the long-familiar outline of the Garners' escape, capture, and
return, this chronicle adds important new information. Yet, especially after
examining the texts gathered in the previous chapter, we have reason to
approach this interview with caution, too. Robert's words are conveyed in
the voice of the reporter and not as directly quoted speech. What should we
make, then, of this document's dramatic account of Margaret's "last words"?

A REMINISCENCE OF SLAVERY.
The Slave Mother, Margaret Garner.
HER TRAGIC SACRIFICE OF A CHILD IN THIS CITY.
INTERVIEW WITH HER HUSBAND
Subsequent History of the Family.

It cannot have passed from the mind of any reader who lived in this city
fifteen years ago, that one morning early in February, 1856, a great sensation stirred the whole community as it had scarcely ever been stirred
before. The river was frozen over solid, and the old "Mason and Dixon
line" between freedom and slavery was for the time almost as much obliterated as it is now; so much so, at least, that there were frequent stam-
pedes of the "sleek and well-fed" slaves, so poetically described by one
of the great champions of the peculiar institution. In consequence of this
facility for escape, United States marshals and detective police were vigi-
lant, their "itching palms" stimulating to duty, as the scent of blood incites
the hound to the chase.

Among those who improved the opportunity, and, like too many
others, fell woefully short of realizing their fond expectations, were a
family of Garners, the old father and mother about fifty years of age
each, and a son, Robert Garner, his wife Margaret, and four children—
two boys and two girls. The old people and Margaret [*sic*] belonged to
James Marshall, of Boone county, Ky., while the wife and children of the
latter belonged to Archibald K. Gaines, of the same neighborhood, the
husband, of course, having no control over or duties in regard to them.
But his desire to exercise such rights and privileges led him to hitch up
two of his master's horses to a sleigh in the dead hour of night, and, putting his old father and mother and his own family therein, drive rapidly
to the river.

Leaving the team on shore, opposite the foot of Western Row, they
all crossed on the ice, and were met on this side by a colored man named
Elijah Kite, son of "old Joe Kite," of notorious reputation, who had been
notified to assist them to the "underground railroad." He conducted

them to a tenement, occupied by himself, a few squares below Mill-creek bridge. He left them until he went out to arrange for their departure to Canada. He was to be back before day, according to the injunction of Robert Garner, but did not come until between nine and ten o'clock, when he was soon followed by a *posse* of officers, accompanied by the masters of the slaves.

The scene that followed was described by the newspaper reporters of that day, as obtained from the white persons present, all of whom had interests in conflict with those of the unfortunate negroes, and was colored accordingly.

Interview with Robert Garner.

We yesterday learned that Robert Garner, the principal mover in this affair, and whose wife was the tragic heroine in its bloody termination, was now residing in our city. We met him at the law office of Col F.M. Moore, with whom he is instituting a suit for damages against the steamer Robert Burns, for damages sustained in having his ribs broken in while engaged in the performance of his duty on the boat, and by the carelessness of the boat's deck-hands. He is now a man of about forty-five years age, and much more intelligent than the average of his race. We improved the opportunity to converse with him about the shocking scene of his attempted escape, and the subsequent history of his family.

Mr. Garner says that Elijah Kite was an own cousin of his wife's, and was, therefore, advised of their coming, and requested to assist in their escape; but instead of assisting them, he now believes, and then suspected him of being guilty of treacherously selling his kinsfolk back into the hands of their masters. His long absence, while professing to be making arrangements for their continued flight, which should have been ready beforehand, and his neglect to return before day to secrete them, is strong justification of the suspicion.

When the officers and masters arrived at the door and demanded admission, Robert drew a pistol with which he had provided himself, and said the first man who attempted to enter he would shoot dead. At the same time his wife Margaret seized a butcher knife that was lying on the table and declared she would kill every child she had before she would see them carried back into slavery. While some of the outsiders were banging against the door, another, a Mr. Patterson, of the Fourth ward, raised a window and was about to enter, when Robert shot him in the mouth. He fell back, but was not killed. On turning around, Robert saw that his wife had cut the throat of her girl Mary, three years old, from ear to ear, who was weltering in her blood on the floor, and was making a dash at his boy Samuel. He sprang to his rescue, calling on her to desist, and received part of the blow himself, the remainder taking effect on the child. Then the door was broken open, and he fired two or three shots at the intruder, who, by the way, was Clinton Butts, the present well-known marshal of Covington. They were then overpowered, and, with an immense mob at their heels, carried off to prison.

Of the hearing of the case before U.S. Commissioner Pendery, which lasted about two weeks, and in which they were voluntarily defended by that ever-ready legal friend of the slave, Mr. John Joiliffe, assisted by Mr. Gitchell, we need not now write. It ended, as all such cases did in those days, in remanding the whole party back to their masters.

Subsequent History of the Garner Family.

Robert, his wife and children, were speedily sent off to the South—the fearful purgatory of Northern slaves. Clinton Butts conducted them as far as Louisville, where they were shipped to a brother of one of their old masters, LeGrand Gaines, a cotton broker of New Orleans. On their way down, their boat was run into by another, and sunk, and among the lives lost was the infant child of the unhappy slaves. It was reported that the mother drowned her child, in accordance with her frenzied declaration, under fearful excitement, that she would kill all her children rather than see them all go back into slavery. But the father protests that such was not the case, and that his wife never attempted to injure her children afterward, although she frequently repeated her conviction that it would be better for them to be put out of the world than live in slavery.

In New Orleans, Robert hired his own time, and that of his wife, and supported his family, by hard work and in great destitution, until all were sold to a Judge Bonham and taken to Tennessee Landing, Miss., where they were forced to labor on the plantation. Here Margaret Garner died in 1858 of typhoid fever. Her last words to her devoted husband were, never to marry again in slavery, but to live in hope of freedom, which she believed would come soon in some way.

Robert heeded her injunction, remained at Tennessee Landing till the war broke out, when he made his way to the Union lines, entered the gunboat service, was in the siege of Vicksburg, and was in active service until the close of the war, when he received an honorable discharge. He subsequently married, and is now living in this city. His two boys, Thomas and Samuel, are living on a farm opposite Vicksburg, in Mississippi.

We conclude this hasty sketch by hoping that Robt. Garner, suffering from premature age, as well as almost fatal injury, may succeed in obtaining proper damages from the steamer Robert Burns, and that his declining years may receive the kind charity of all who know his painfully-checkered history.

CHAPTER 12

LITERARY SOURCES, LITERARY ECHOES

The Garners' story took literary form long before the publication of Beloved. Poetry about "the slave mother" appeared in the press even as witnesses were testifying before Commissioner Pendery. Fictional accounts of the case followed within weeks of its legal conclusion. Whatever their aesthetic and commercial aspirations, such literary representations were part of the broader political struggle over the meaning and implications of both the murder and the legal dispute. Fiction and poetry offered ways to plumb the deepest emotions stirred by the events and to put these emotions to work in ambitious interpretations of the entire controversy. These forms of expression also provided opportunities for women to engage the case in print at a moment when news and editorial writing in the daily press were almost entirely male preserves.

The literary renderings followed familiar patterns. The slave narrative, which echoes in some of the following documents, was a significant form of antebellum cultural expression. It was intricately connected to what had recently become the most broadly influential genre of antislavery writing—sentimental fiction. The astounding popularity of Harriet Beecher Stowe's Uncle Tom's Cabin, *first published as a novel in 1852, was still gathering force in 1856. That influence can be seen in the works in this section, but not only here. It would be a mistake to draw too clear a distinction between these self-consciously "literary" documents and the sources gathered in the earlier chapters of this book, given the echoes of melodrama and sentimental fiction in news reports, courtroom speeches, sermons, and editorials.*

A compendium of all of the key sources shaping the scripting of the Garner story would be far too large to publish in one volume, but some antecedent sources stand out as especially direct in their effects. Below are two particularly important examples, as well as key poetic and fictional responses to the case. Together, these documents reveal some of the main patterns, and the complexities, that mark the literary construction of this story as *a story. In doing so, the texts found here help us understand how to read the entire Garner archive.*

Virginius: A Tragedy in Five Acts, James Sheridan Knowles (1820)

The Roman character Virginius was one of the crucial touchstones for commentary on the events in Cincinnati, especially for those who presented Margaret as a heroine (see, for example, the editorial by the New York Daily *Tribune in chapter 7). It is just this usage that the* Cincinnati Daily Enquirer *anticipated, and sought to thwart, in its first report on the case (see chapter 1). As presented by the Roman historian Livy, Virginius was a brave centurion who killed his daughter, Virginia, to save her from the designs of the tyrant Appius Claudius. Through a dishonest legal scheme, Appius arranges to have it "proven" that Virginia is not the freeborn daughter of Virginius but instead a slave. As Virginius well knows, Appius's ultimate aim is to gain sexual control over the girl. When Virginius foils the plan by killing his daughter, the Roman people are so inspired by his example that they rise up in rebellion against Appius and restore their lost republic. By using a story that made the defeat of pernicious sexual designs the pivotal moment in the restoration of political liberty, antislavery commentators on the Garner case at once construed Margaret as would-be liberator and implied that she, too, was concerned about matters of sexual honor and violation. But in doing so, her sympathizers were probably not borrowing directly from Livy. The story had been invoked or reimagined by such figures as Botticelli, Chaucer, Petrarch, and Shakespeare. It was retold yet again in the nineteenth century in MacAuley's widely read* Lays of Ancient Rome. *The version American editorialists most likely had in mind, however, was that of the English playwright James Sheridan Knowles, whose drama was among the most popular plays in the United States from the 1820s through the Civil War. In his presentation of Virginia's death, reprinted here, Knowles departs fundamentally from Livy in making the killing an expression of a kind of madness brought on by parental grief.*

App. . . . . Separate them, Lictors!

Vir. Let them forbear awhile, I pray you, Appius:
It is not very easy. Though her arms
Are tender, yet the hold is strong, by which
She grasps me. Appius—Forcing them will hurt them
They'll soon unclasp themselves. Wait but a little—
You know you're sure of her!

    App. I have not time
To idle with thee, give her to my Lictors.

    Vir. Appius. I pray you, wait! If she is not
My child, she hath been like a child to me
For fifteen years. If I am not her father,
I have been like a father to her, Appius,
For even such a time. "They that have lived
'So long a time together, in so near
'And dear society, may be allowed
'A little time for parting." Let me take
The maid aside, I pray you, and confer
A moment with her nurse; perhaps she'll give me
Some token, will unloose a tie so twined
And knotted round my heart, that if you break it,
My heart breaks with it.

    App. Have your wish. Be brief!
Lictors, look to them.

    Virg. Do you go from me!
Do you leave! Father! Father!

    Vir. No, my child;
No, my Virginia—come along with me.

    Virg. Will you not leave me? Will you take me with you?
Will you take me home again? Oh, bless you, bless you!
My father! my dear father! Art thou not
My father? [*Virginius, perfectly at a loss what to do
looks anxiously around the Forum; at length his eye
falls on a butcher's stall, L., with a knife upon it.*

    Vir. This way, my child—No, no! I am not going
To leave thee, my Virginia! I'll not leave thee.

    App. Keep back the people, soldiers! Let them not
Approach Virginius! Keep the people back!

    [*Virginius secures the knife in the folds of his toga.*
Well, have you done?

    Vir. Short time for converse, Appius;

But I have.

    App. I hope you are satisfied.

    Vir. I am—

I am—that she is my daughter!

    App. Take her, Lictors! *[Virginia shrieks, and falls*
    half dead upon her father's shoulder.

    Vir. Another moment, pray you. Bear with me

A little—'Tis my last embrace. 'Twont try

Your patience beyond bearing, if you're a man!

Lengthen it as I may, I cannot make it

Long! My dear child! My dear Virginia! [*Kissing her*

There is one only way to save thine honour—

"Tis this!—[*Stabs her and draws out the knife.—She falls*
    and dies, L.

Lo! Appius; with this innocent blood,

I do devote thee to th' infernal gods!

Make way there!

    App. Stop him! Seize him!

    Vir. If they dare

To tempt the desperate weapon that is maddened

With drinking my daughter's blood, why, let them: Thus

It rushes in amongst them. Way there! Way!

    [Exit through the Soldiers.

Uncle Tom's Cabin, Harriet Beecher Stowe (1852)

When first serialized in the National Era *(Washington, D.C.), Stowe's*
Uncle Tom's Cabin *caused a sensation. In book form it sold 300,000 copies
within a year and went on to become the most popular novel of the century.
A still larger audience saw one of the many competing stage productions
that began to appear even before the novel first arrived in bookstores. Blackface minstrelsy was America's reigning form of commercial entertainment at
the time of the Garner case, and dramatizations of* Uncle Tom's Cabin *had
become the form's most popular expression. Stowe's characters were ubiq-
uitous: available for purchase on cups and lamps, forks and spoons, as figu-
rines, in card games, and in many other incarnations, they were emblematic
commodities of the nation's incipient mass culture. They had also already
been appropriated and attacked in the "anti-Tom" literature that sprung up
immediately, mainly—but not entirely—in the American South.*

It is hardly surprising, then, that Uncle Tom's Cabin *provided one of the most important narrative frames into which the Garners' contemporaries placed the events of the case. After all, like Stowe's Eliza before her, Margaret was a slave mother who fled from Kentucky to Ohio across the frozen river. But Eliza's celebrated and much-replayed flight was only one of many scenes through which Stowe produced a template or script for the Garner case. One particularly significant component of Stowe's framing of the case can be examined in another famous scene from the novel, Ophelia's encounter with Topsy. Even on the page, Topsy offers readers a pocket-sized minstrel show, reminding us that Stowe often generated powerful antislavery sentiment through the use of degrading racial stereotypes. How such performances were echoed in white representations of the Garners can be seen by comparing this passage with the Reverend H. Bushnell's account of the "interview" with Tom and Sam Garner in the portion of his sermon reproduced in chapter 10.*

The "young un" alluded to heard all these comments with the subdued and doleful air which seemed habitual to her, only scanning, with a keen and furtive glance of her flickering eyes, the ornaments which Jane wore in her ears. When arrayed at last in a suit of decent and whole clothing, her hair cropped short to her head, Miss Ophelia, with some satisfaction, said she looked more Christian-like than she did, and in her own mind began to mature some plans for her instruction.

Sitting down before her, she began to question her.

"How old are you, Topsy?"

"Dun no, Missis," said the image, with a grin that showed all her teeth.

"Don't know how old you are? Did n't anybody ever tell you? Who was your mother?"

"Never had none!" said the child, with another grin.

"Never had any mother? What do you mean? Where were you born?"

"Never was born!" persisted Topsy, with another grin, that looked so goblin-like, that, if Miss Ophelia had been at all nervous, she might have fancied that she had got hold of some sooty gnome from the land of Diablerie; but Miss Ophelia was not nervous, but plain and business-like, and she said, with some sternness,

"You must n't answer me in that way, child; I'm not playing with you. Tell me where you were born, and who your father and mother *were*."

"Never was born," reiterated the creature, more emphatically; "never had no father nor mother, nor nothin'. I was raised by a speculator, with lots of others. Old Aunt Sue used to take car on us."

The child was evidently sincere; and Jane, breaking into a short laugh, said,

"Laws, Missis, there's heaps of 'em. Speculators buys 'em up cheap, when they's little, and gets 'em raised for market."

"How long have you lived with your master and mistress?"

"Dun no, Missis."

"Is it a year, or more, or less?"

"Dun no Missis."

"Laws, Missis, those low negroes, —they can't tell; they don't know anything about time," said Jane; "they don't know what a year is; they don't know their own ages."

"Have you ever heard anything about God, Topsy?"

The child looked bewildered, but grinned as usual.

"Do you know who made you?"

"Nobody, as I knows on," said the child, with a short laugh.

The idea appeared to amuse her considerably; for her eyes twinkled, and she added,

"I spect I grow'd. Don't think nobody never made me."

"Do you know how to sew?" said Miss Ophelia, who thought she would turn her inquiries to something more tangible.

"No, Missis."

"What can you do? —what did you do for your master and mistress?"

"Fetch water, and wash dishes, and rub knives, and wait on folks."

"Were they good to you?"

"Spect they was," said the child, scanning Miss Ophelia cunningly.

Miss Ophelia rose from this encouraging colloquy; St. Clare was leaning over the back of her chair.

"You find virgin soil there, Cousin; put in your own ideas, —you won't find many to pull up."

New York Daily Tribune, February 9, 1856
========

Antislavery verse about the Garners appeared in abolitionist periodicals, in the daily press, and in books of poetry. Invariably, the poets, most of them women, focused on the drama of a mother driven to kill her children rather than see them remain in slavery. In its employment of this theme, "The

Slave Tragedy at Cincinnati" by Mary Livermore seems to have touched a chord. After its initial appearance in the high-circulation Tribune, *it was reprinted in many other papers. In addition to aiding the antislavery cause through her work as writer, speaker, and editor, Livermore would go on after the Civil War to become active in Republican Party politics and to play a prominent role in the suffragist and temperance movements, at times working together with Lucy Stone.*

THE SLAVE TRAGEDY AT CINCINNATI.
By Mrs. Mary A. Livermore.

BRIGHT the Sabbath sun is shining through the clear and frosty air,
Solemnly the bells are calling to the house of praise and prayer;
And with hearts devout and holy, thither many wend their way,
To renew to God their pledges;—but I cannot go to-day.

For my soul is sick and saddened with that fearful tale of woe,
Which has blanched the cheeks of mothers to the whiteness of the
    snow;
And my thoughts are wandering ever where the prison walls surround
The parents and their children, in hopeless bondage bound.

Oh, thou mother, maddened, frenzied, when the hunter's toils ensnared
Thee and thy brood of nestlings, till thy anguished spirit dared
Send to God, uncalled, one darling life that round thine own did
    twine—
Worthy of a Spartan mother was that fearful deed of thine!

Worthy of the Roman father, who sheathed deep his flashing knife
In the bosom of Virginia, in the current of her life!
Who, rather than his beauteous child should live a tyrant's slave,
Opened the way to freedom through the portals of the grave!

Well I know no stronger yearning than a mother's love can be—
I could do and dare forever for the babe upon my knee!
And I feel no deeper sorrow could the light of life eclipse,
Than to see death's shadows settle on its brow and faded lips.

Yet (oh, God of Heaven, forgive me!), baby sitting on my knee,
I could close thy blue eyes calmly, smiling now so sweet on me!

Ay, *my* hand could ope the casket, and thy precious soul set free:
Better for thee death and Heaven than a life of slavery!

And before the Judge Eternal, this should be my anguished plea:
"They would rob my child of Manhood; so, uncalled, I sent it Thee!
"Hope, and Love, and Joy, and Knowledge, and her every right they
    crave;
"So I gave her what they left her—her inheritance—the grave!"

And the Lord would judge between us, oh ye men of stony heart!
Even 'gainst the strong and mighty, for the weak He taketh part;
Think ye, hunters of His children, bowed beneath your iron rod,
With your heel upon their heart-pulse, this ye do unto your God!

But the day of vengeance cometh—He will set his people free,
Though He lead them, like his Israel, through a red and bloody sea;
For the tears and gore of bondmen, staining deep the frighted sod,
And the wailing cry of millions riseth daily up to God!

—Auburn, N. Y., Sunday, Feb. 3, 1856.

"THE SLAVE MOTHER, a Tale of the Ohio,"
Frances Ellen Watkins (Harper)
=======

(Originally published in Poems on Miscellaneous Subjects, *1857)*

*It is worth comparing the respective points of view, cultural references,
and stylistic devices offered by Mary Livermore and Frances Watkins,
particularly given each author's social position and experiences. Born just
under five years apart, both had worked as educators, had joined the abolitionist movement, and, though still young, had published multiple works
in the decade before the Garner case. Unlike the white Livermore, however,
Watkins (1825–1911), a freeborn black woman, had already spent several
years on the antislavery lecture circuit by that time. Since her poem apparently did not appear until a year after the Garners were sent South, it had
a less immediate effect than Livermore's, but Watkins (who took the name
Harper when she married in 1860) probably cut the larger figure at the time
and certainly now looms more prominently than Livermore in accounts*

of American literature. Watkins published Forest Leaves, *her first book of poetry, in 1845 and her second,* Poems on Miscellaneous Subjects, *in 1854. The latter was reprinted in multiple editions over the next two decades. By the time of the 1857 edition, which included her poem about Margaret Garner, ten thousand copies of the volume were in print. Watkins went on to become one of the most important African American writers of the century. Much of her work, including her influential 1892 novel* Iola Leroy *(which alludes very briefly to Margaret Garner) and all of her published poetry after the now-lost* Forest Leaves, *is still in print today.*

I have but four, the treasures of my soul,
They lay like doves around my heart;
I tremble lest some cruel hand
Should tear my household wreaths apart.

My baby girl, with childish glance,
Looks curious in my anxious eye,
She little knows that for her sake
Deep shadows round my spirit lie.

My playful boys could I forget,
My home might seem a joyous spot,
But with their sunshine mirth I blend
The darkness of their future lot.

And thou my babe, my darling one,
My last, my loved, my precious child,
Oh! when I think upon thy doom
My heart grows faint and then throbs wild.

The Ohio's bridged and spanned with ice,
The northern star is shining bright,
I'll take the nestlings of my heart
And search for freedom by its light.

Winter and night were on the earth,
And feebly moaned the shivering trees,
A sigh of winter seemed to run
Through every murmur of the breeze.

She fled, and with her children all,
She reached the stream and crossed it o'er,
Bright visions of deliverance came
Like dreams of plenty to the poor.

Dreams! vain dreams, heroic mother,
Give all thy hopes and struggles o'er,
The pursuer is on thy track,
And the hunter at thy door.

Judea's refuge cities had power
To shelter, shield and save,
E'en Rome had altars, 'neath whose shade
Might crouch the wan and weary slave.

But Ohio had no sacred fane,
To human rights so consecrated,
Where thou may'st shield thy hapless ones
From their darkly gathering fate.

Then, said the mournful mother,
If Ohio cannot save,
I will do a deed for freedom,
Shalt find each child a grave.

I will save my precious children
From their darkly threatened doom,
I will hew their path to freedom
Through the portals of the tomb.

A moment in the sunlight,
She held a glimmering knife,
The next moment she had bathed it
In the crimson fount of life.

They snatched away the fatal knife,
Her boys shrieked wild with dread,
The baby girl was pale and cold,
They raised it up, the child was dead.

Sends this deed of fearful daring,
Through my country's heart no thrill,
    Do the icy hands of slavery
Every pure emotion chill?

Oh! if there is any honor,
Truth or justice in the land,
Will ye not, as men and Christians,
On the side of freedom stand?

Abolitionism Unveiled; or, its Origin, Progress, and Pernicious Tendency Fully Developed, Henry Field James (1856)

The Garner case received multiple fictional treatments in the 1850s. For instance, The Bondwoman's Narrative, *a manuscript published for the first time in our century and now believed by some scholars to be among the first African American novels, appears to borrow some details from the case in one brief vignette. Other antebellum authors succeeded in getting their fictional responses to the case into press at the time. John Jolliffe, the Garners' lawyer, presented a heavily altered version of the escape, capture, and killing as an episode in his 1858 novel,* Chattanooga. *He was beaten to his subject by Harriet Beecher Stowe, Henry Field James, and Hattia M'Keehan. Stowe's novel* Dred, *published in the fall of 1856, devotes a few pages to the story of Cora Gordon, a woman who is captured and kills her children rather than see them taken into slavery (though Stowe fundamentally alters both the details of Margaret's history and the manner of the childrens' death). James's* Abolitionism Unveiled *appeared still earlier, in April 1856, while the press continued to debate Ohio's efforts to retrieve the Garners. It follows 'Squire Henry Gray, of Boone County, and his young, more naive nephew, David, as they travel through the North. A compendium of antislavery clichés and fantasies, the book presents unruly free blacks, impoverished and repentant fugitive slaves, and fanatical abolitionist windbags. James even reveals to readers that abolitionism is the result of a secret plot against the United States hatched at the highest levels of the English government. The fictionalization of the Garner case reprinted here is the novel's dramatic culmination. For his rendition, James earned praise from the* Covington Journal *for "dispassionate" views that might yet restore "peace and goodwill between the North and South."*

"I can tell you, David, this Higher Law party here, is but a fraction of the population. They are artful and designing, and can make a terrific outcry."

"They must, uncle, contrive some way or other, to give themselves great prominence. They have exasperated the South by their 'outside interference,' to a dangerous degree."

"So they have, David, and their conduct is all the time producing border difficulties greatly to be deplored. Why should it be so? Kentucky has adopted Slavery, as she has a right to do, and has aimed to guard and protect her citizens in the possession of that species of property, by severe legislative enactments; because it would be perfectly ridiculous for a State to confer *legal rights,* without at the same time, enacting the necessary Laws to enforce their observance."

"Your penal statutes, uncle, ought to be a sufficient warning to *all persons* to abstain from *tampering* with Slaves."

"They ought to be, David, but they have proved insufficient to prevent this great evil. You know I am fond of walking alone of a night, indulging in the serious contemplation of the wondrous works of the Universe. Upon one of those occasions, while the moon diffused her mild rays upon this earth, and the stars shone with unusual brilliancy, I chanced to espy JIM CROW, wending his way to a negro cabin, which he entered, and closed the door. I was tempted to draw near, and place my ear within hearing distance. He thus commented:

"'Well, Sam, I thought I would just drop in to-night. You have a warm, comfortable room, good bedding, a wife, and four pretty children; but still you lack one thing to make you happy.'

"'Pray, mist'r,' replied Sam. 'What can that be?'

"'It is only, *freedom.*'

"'Shere, man, how can I get dat? You know, mast'r aint gwine to let dis nigger go.'

"'Oh, Sam, we care mighty little whether he wants you to go or not. We don't consult his feelings about it at all.'

"'Den how does you do, Mist'r Crow?'

"'That, I will tell you, Sam, at the proper time—all you have first to say, are you disposed to leave?"

"'I tells you, Mist'r Crow, dat be a mighty hard question. Dere is many t'ings to be t'ot on, when we talks about such t'ings. S'pose I start, and be ketch, den you know what follows—dis nigger has to be sent off.'

"'Don't fear that, Sam, we are your friends, and do not intend to worst your condition. If you will place yourselves in our care, we will go security, you will not be caught.'

"'Now, does you say dat, Mist'r Crow; you knows I am well sitiwated now. My mast'r is kine enuff—I works no harder dan he does. We gets along mi'ty well togeder. He gis us plenty to eat, an' you sees he gis us a good house to lib in. An' we has a kine missis too. What more den, does we want?'

"'There is one thing lacking, Sam, and that is, to be *free*. To get that, you have only to say, you are willing—that's all you have to do.'

"'Hush, Mist'r Crow, don't fool dis nigger—mast'r won't be slow hunting up dis Sam, his wife, an' leetle ones, if dey be gone. I knows him, an' he arn't a-gwine to let us get off so berry easy.'

"'I don't care, Sam, how quick he is, he can't catch you on our 'underground railroad.' That does business rather too rapidly to be overtaken.'

"'Dere it is, Mist'r Crow—what sort ob a darn t'ing is dat, as what runs under de ground.'

"'Never mind that at present, Sam, just say you will all come at a certain time, our Director will furnish you with through-tickets, and before you can say Jack Robinson, you'll all be snugly landed in Canada.'

"'Dere, aint dat curis, Mist'r Crow, but s'pose our ole hoss cums 'pon us 'fore we gets in dat dark 'ole, what den?'

"'Oh, we will hide you, Sam, too nicely for that; but we furnish another sort of a passport, that seldom fails—(draws a revolver) don't you see this lovely instrument? That is yours, if you consent to go.'

"'La! what a nice lookin' t'ing dis is, Mist'r Crow—how does you work him to make him talk loud—dere be six leetle holes in dis t'ing— how can you make each on 'em do his part?"

"'All you have to do, Sam, is to keep pulling the trigger, and it will keep working around, until the six loads are discharged.'

"'What a curis t'ing dis is, 'pon my word. Does you say, de white man will stand back, when he sees dis feeful instrument? Does you say it's mine, if we'll 'gree to go?'

"'Yes, Sam, it's yours, if you say you'll come.'

"'Dere, Mist'r Crow, you temp' dis nigger too much.'

"'Now, Peggy, my wife, what say you to gwine wid our children?"

"'Oh, Sam you're crazy, you know we're comfortably fixed now— has good homes where we may live our life-time; but if we try to get off and fail—t'ink of dat. What would become of us!'

"'But you know, Peggy, Mist'r Crow aint gwine to lie 'bout sich t'ings, and he says, dere aint no danger.'

"'Alas! I wish Mist'r Crow had staid at home, and mind his own business—not to come to dis cabin, to put sich bad noshens in dat head ob your'n.'

"'Fear not'in, Peggy, all well kum out rite.'

"'Why, Sam, does you inten' to hazar' all de blessin's we enjoys, for dis unsartin business?'

"'I mus' confess, Peggy, new t'ots has bin put in my poor head. I begins to sigh for dat strange land.'

"'Mis'ry, mis'ry, Sam; if we starts, I feels a kin' of bodin' well be brought back, an' den we'll be undone.'

"'Oh, Peggy, you conjer up so many bogobows—dey won't fin' us, and den how kin dey catch us?'

"'Don't believe eberyt'ing, Sam; you knows not what may happen. We may be obertaken, an' be bro't back. Oh, how awful de very t'ot. I'm so easily frightened, an' den I don't know what I might do. To be sent to de Souf, de berry noshen nearly kills me. All dese t'ings, dear husband, if we should be taken, will rush upon me at once; I shall become de'perate, and what I may be tem'ted to do, God only knows.'

"'Don't t'ink ob dem t'ings, Peggy—dey cotch us—all but dat; when we gets into dat dark 'ole, as what leads to Candy, dey'll no see us any more.'

"'If I goes, God knows, Sam, it will be with a tremblin' heart—I sees woe a-plenty a-head but I will foller you de world ober—if go you will.'

"'Den, Mist'r Crow, we'll be in de City next Sunday night.'

"'God bless you, Sam, be as early as possible; we will be prepared to give you dispatch.'

"The conversation having ended, I resumed my meditations."

"Well, uncle, let us have the sequel of the story!"

"On the very Sunday night mentioned, Sam, wife, and children, with the master's horses and sleigh, departed to this city; crossing the river upon the ice, they arrived at old Joe Kite's about the dawn of day, too late, as luck would have it, for underground railroad operations. Therefore, they had to remain in the safe-keeping of their good old friend, Joe, for the day."

"Did not the owner pursue, uncle?"

"Yes, he was on the trail bright and early in the morning—and soon tracked them to their den. He then got out a warrant from Commissioner Pendery, placed it in the hands of a United States' Marshal, who, accompanied by a *posse*, went to old Joe's, to arrest the fugitive slaves. The party entered, after bursting open the door—Sam, relying upon his revolver, discharged it two or three times, until it was wrested from his hands by one of the Deputy Marshals, who was slightly wounded. The mother in the meantime, in a fit of desperation, had cut the throat of one of her children, and wounded two others."

"What a horrible affair, uncle; ought not Abolitionism to be the more detested, for placing those poor, unsuspecting creatures in so dangerous a position? Had they let them alone, this would not have happened."

"If our Slaves, David, were voluntarily to elope, without any 'outside interference,' and then commit such tragedies, we would have no *right* to censure others for it. But it seems to me, where great persuasion is used to induce slaves to abscond, under the assurance of a perfect immunity from apprehension, the party bringing about this change, in all justice, ought to be answerable for the consequences that ensue."

"I do suppose, uncle, if Sam, Peggy, and children, had remained contentedly at home, this tragedy would not have happened. Upon whose hands shall the blood be fastened?—that is the grand inquiry."

"To decide that question fairly, David, let us consider the respective parties engaged: First, the owner. What did he do to bring about this fearful result? Did he, in any particular, transcend the law, either of his State, or the Union? It is not pretended he did. He pursued his absconding slaves, as he had a legal right to do, into the State of Ohio. There, out of a pure reverence for the law, he adopts legal steps for the recovery of his slaves. They go to arrest them by the highest and most sacred legal authority, bringing to their aid sufficient force to accomplish the object, and no more. If the mother, under those circumstances, thought proper to commit the unnatural deed of sacrificing the life of her child, surely he stands *guiltless* of the deed. It was not his will or wish."

"That, uncle, is evidently a legitimate conclusion. To arraign the owner for what may happen, is equivalent to cutting off his claim altogether. If the Slaves escape, he is legally empowered to pursue and recapture."

"That is true enough, David, but let us see how the account in the next place, stands with *Abolitionism*. If I might personify her, I would say, stand up thou at the bar of public opinion, and let us see if thy garments are pure and unspotted! As the serpent crept into the garden of Eden, and by his subtlety tempted Adam and Eve to depart from their holy estate, so hast thou sought to entwine thyself around the heart of the poor, ignorant, confiding Slave, and lead him through the labyrinth of ruin. Happy and contented at his home, thou didst find him and poured thy poisonous breath into his ear, and brought upon him irretrievable ruin. The blood of infants, like Moloch of old, has stained thy hands, because thou didst induce the mother to escape, who, if not tempted by thee, would have remained at her home, happy and contented. Thou didst draw her into that perilous condition, the most frightful to the Slave, in which, by the instigation of the Devil, if not by thyself, she felt herself constrained to pour out the blood of an innocent and harmless child. But here, let the curtain fall—I have done with Ohio."

Liberty or Death; or Heaven's Infraction of the Fugitive Slave Law, Hattia M'Keehan (1856)

M'Keehan's self-published novel appeared in July, a mere three months after Fields's book. Unlike the latter, or Stowe's and Jolliffe's subsequent novels, it is devoted entirely to a fictionalized retelling of the Garners' story, moving back and forth between the vantage point of Gazella, the Margaret character, and Mr. and Mrs. Nero, her owners. Like other antislavery commentators, M'Keehan makes a heroine of Margaret. But she essentially writes Robert out of the story and renders Gazella considerably lighter-skinned than Margaret was. Both moves facilitate one of her most distinctive narrative choices: in the first of the three scenes reproduced below, the novel presents a more explicit discussion of the sexual component of the case than can be found in any other antebellum source. In the second excerpt, the novel goes farther than most accounts of the day in presenting the deliberation that lay behind the slave mother's killing of her daughter. The third selection reveals that Toni Morrison was not the first to turn the Garner case into a ghost story. However heavy-handed in M'Keehan's execution, the ghostly visitation expresses an impulse that coursed powerfully through the antebellum antislavery imagination. Jolliffe's Chattanooga *presents a similar encounter, and the episode that may have inspired both Jolliffe and M'Keehan, Cassy's haunting of Simon Legree in* Uncle Tom's Cabin, *is one of Stowe's most vividly rendered scenes.*

"*Our* family! Do you say *our* family? O my Lord, I'll choke, I'll choke! Mr. Nero! Mr. Nero!" screamed the excited lady, as if she were being murdered.

"What! what! what's the matter? cried Nero in alarm; for his lady's scream had awakened him from a horrid dream of howling fiends and wandering goblins; nor did he look unlike a messenger from Tophet himself, standing in the door, wildly gazing, hair on end, and having nothing on but a linen nether garment, —none too liberal in length, and well calculated to remind one of the Scottish bard's "Cutasark."

"O, this miserable, audacious slave," said his wife, "presumes to claim relationship, and arrogantly asserts she's my sister-in-law! Only think of it—the vile nigger!"

"Ha! ha! ha!" roared Nero, "is that all? I verily thought you were about to be murdered. —And Gazella and you are sisters-in-law? Ha! ha! ha!"

"Laugh, do you? Heavens and earth! Is the man insane? Cooly laugh when a base born slave claims to be a blood relation!"

"There's no use getting excited, my darling; such relationships are fashionable, only they're considered matters of some delicacy, and not to be too freely talked about."

"Mercy! mercy! I can—hardly—get—my breath!"

"Gazella you should avoid alluding to these little matters," said Nero, addressing the servant in a chiding tone.

"Great God of vengeance!" exclaimed the lady, more excited than ever, "shall she a moment be spared?"

Nero now turned about, feeling pretty well aired, and again sought his bed chamber; soliloquising as he went, in the following style:

"There's no use denying it, Gazella's my father's daughter, and it was his dying request she should be freed; but 'tis clear, I've now got to sell her, or there'll be a fuss in the family. As to little Rosetta, I'll see to it that hereafter she's less imposed upon for I strongly incline to think she's still nearer related to me than is her mother—yet I'm not exactly sure of it; —her mouth and eyes are very much like mine, or else I imagine it. Talk about not knowing who's who in the slaveholding States, —by thunder, we don't know our own children! Then the idea of a man making slaves of his own offspring—Great God! it makes me feel like cutting my infernal throat!"

With these unhappy reflections preying on his mind the slaveholder reclined his head upon his downy pillow; but long, restless hours passed, ere he was able to compose himself to sleep. . . .

. . . Little Rosetta stood leaning on her knee. Looking up into its mother's face, the child said:

"Ma, is this 'Hio State?"

"Yes, my child," replied Gazella softly, still looking towards the river, "we're in the State of Ohio."

"Is we now free?" inquired the innocent prattler.

"Yes, this is a free country," answered the mother, affectionately turning to caress, for a moment, the endeared one, and plant upon its tender cheek a mother's kiss.

"Then can I go to school, Ma?"

"Some of these days, when we get a home at the north."

"Will we learn to read?"

"Yes, and write, too; for Ma intends giving all her children a good education."

"Then we'll have nice books won't we?"

"Ma will buy you pretty books."

"Like them in Master's library that he wont let us look at?"

"Dont say Master; call him Mr. Nero."

"Isn't he our master any more?"

"No, not now; colored people have no masters on this side the river."

"Can't Master—there, I said Master again, —can't Mr. Nero come here and whip us, Ma?"

"They don't allow whipping in Ohio,"

"Tom couldn't make me kiss his big toe in State of 'Hio, could he, Ma?"

"No."

At this moment the woman who was preparing breakfast came in, looking much alarmed, and said:

"Gazella, I just now saw two suspicious looking men peeping in at the side window at you."

Springing to her feet and feeling for the knife fastened in her waist-ribbon, and concealed by a broad cape which hung from her shoulders, she proceeded to the side window, saying in a resolute tone, as she went— "If there are but two I'll be sufficient for them." Seeing no one, she said to her hostess:

"Seemed they to be Irishmen, Mary?"

"Very ruffian-like they looked and may have been Irish."

"I dare say 'twas Sputtles and Dobbins. This knife for their throats was whetted, or else for mine and my children's."

"O Gazella! Would you kill yourself and children?"

"Rather than go back into slavery."

"Should the wretches bring a large pack of ruffians to assist, they'd overpower you at once."

"In case of a formidable attack, I'd slay my children first, and then sell my own life dear as possible."

"I'll send over to the other house, sha'nt I, and have all the fugitives to come here so as to make a stronger defence, all being together?" Without waiting for Gazella's reply she immediately dispatched a little boy with a message to the other fugitives, who were but a short distance off.

At this juncture Mark Martin entered, almost breathless, saying:

"Gazella, Nero's coming and a great gang of ragged, desperate looking men, following at his heels!"

"My God! my God!" exclaimed the unhappy woman, clasping and wringing her hands, "what shall I do?"

"Do nothing rashly, Gazella?" said Mary Martin, "perhaps you'd better quietly give yourself up, —for what else can you do?"

"Death is better than slavery!" she answered with emphasis, at the same time clutching the hilt of her knife.

"But O do not, I beseech you, think of destroying yourself and children."

"Can I, O can I slay my innocent ones? Heaven be not angry with me—my children I love, and must place them beyond the tyrant's power," and drawing the deadly weapon from its concealment, she said—"Now, my soul, be strong—to die is but the pang of a moment, slavery's the pang of a lifetime!"

The intense and heart-crushing emotions of her mind rendered difficult her respiration, and caused her brain to grow dizzy; she reeled and was near falling to the floor, but recovering, and hearing a noise without, she exclaimed:

"They're coming upon us! —my children!"

"Ma, you wont kill me?" said little Rosetta, in a sweet, gentle tone, while with mingled fear and confidence she looked up into the livid face of her distracted mother.

"Heaven support me!" cried the despairing woman in tones of agony.

"Here they are!" was the ruffian shout, accompanied with profane oaths and vulgar epithets. And now crash went a window; and then, in an instant, the door was forced from its hinges.

"Rush upon them!" vociferated the chief of the police.

Gazella, with burning brain and boiling blood, wildly gazes upon her dear child—and while she gazes thinks of the horrid life to which slavery dooms the female held in its iron clutches. That thought determines the deed—the glittering steel is raised—a moment 'tis tremblingly suspended in air, while the frenzied eye of the mother marks the blue vein upon the tender neck of the lovely Rosetta, where the fatal stroke she aims, —like the lightning's flash the murderous knife descends—weltering in blood, the innocent victim falls to the floor.

"Liberty, heaven and immortality are thine!" exclaimed the frantic mother; but, pausing not, she drew again the cruel blade, all dripping with gore, and strikes her noble boy; he falls, but is not slain, —the gash is deep, but the wound not mortal.

Now, seized by ruffian hands, the knife was wrested from her grasp, and her arms pinioned. . . .

As Gazella was dragged from the house she exclaimed:

Let me but finish my work of death—my children send to freedom in heaven, then drag me away, ye inhuman monsters!"

"Murderer," said one of the officers, "you'll hang for the killing of your child."

"Would to God!" she responded, "I'd slain the remaining three, — then could I have gone to the gallows laughing!"

. . . Mrs. Nero sat some hours, wincing and fuming over the loss they had sustained in the death of Rosetta. At length her husband, rousing from his slumbers, enquired the time of night.

"Near twelve," the lady replied in quite an ill-humored tone.

"Do my eyes deceive me?" said Nero, rising upon his couch and resting on his elbow, "what's that looks like murdered ghost?"

"A murdered ghost?" iterated she in great astonishment.

"I swear 'tis Rosetta, with her throat cut!"

"Where? where?" demanded the terrified woman, glancing round the room with wild, glaring eyes, and mouth open to its utmost capacity.

"Standing at the threshold," replied he, "now turning," he continued, "a withering look on you."

"O horror! horror!" she shrieked, on beholding the apparition, and hastily flew to her husband for protection,

"Fear nothing," said he, "I'll speak to it."

"Do not, I pray, for fear 'twill answer. Murder! murder! its eyes, like daggers, pierce me through!"

"Pale ghost," said Nero, "why come ye here? Go haunt thy wicked mother, 'twas she that shed thy blood."

"Ungodly man," replied the apparition, "thou didst slay me. And heartless woman, thou art my murderer."

"How canst thou say so?" returned Nero, "'twas thine own mother's hand that struck the fatal blow."

"But 'twas the hand of oppression that compelled her to it. The maternal blow was in kindness given, and hath delivered me from the power of cruel oppressors, and many long years of miserable, heart-crushing, mind-destroying bondage! Accuse not my mother, ye are the murderers." And it vanished. . . .

Harper's Weekly, "The Modern Medea—The Story of Margaret Garner," May 18, 1867

Thomas Satterwhite Noble (1835–1907) was born in Kentucky, studied painting in France, and served in the Confederate army. In 1865, just after the war's end, he began what would become a series of eight large canvases featuring scenes from slavery. Perhaps the most well known dates from 1867, when Harlan Roys, a New York leather broker and sometime art dealer, commissioned Margaret Garner. *Noble presented the most dramatic moment in the Garner story in a visual style indebted to French history painters such as J.-L. David. The picture helped make Noble's career. Displayed at the National Academy of Design,* Margaret Garner *received enthusiastic reviews in both art journals and the daily press. Matthew Brady's photograph of the painting was turned into an engraving, which was in turn published in* Harper's Weekly *and reprinted in a variety of papers. Noble's original painting was ultimately lost (though a much smaller version, painted in 1868, survives), but the engraved image reproduced here may have had greater social importance, as it reached a far broader audience.*

It was Harper's *that added the title "The Modern Medea." In Greek mythology, Medea kills her children in order to take revenge on a husband who has just abandoned her for another, more prominent woman. In a brief text accompanying the illustration,* Harper's *opines that Margaret Garner, seeking to save her children from slavery, acted from "a far nobler jealousy." Still, in invoking the myth, the text and title departed significantly from the terms of the 1856 controversy: during her time in Ohio, Garner had not been cast as any kind of Medea. At the time Noble painted his picture, however, a European stage production of a modern version of* Medea *was touring the United States, to great acclaim. It is not possible to determine the extent to which this influenced Noble or the editors at* Harper's. *Nor is it clear why a New York businessman would want a large painting that spectacularly represented a confrontational scene of child murder, or what led to the Garner story's sudden reemergence into public discourse. What is clear is that the political and cultural context for Noble's rendering was fundamentally different from that surrounding Margaret Garner's actions in Cincinnati. In a nation partway through ratifying the Fourteenth Amendment, the conflict over slavery and abolition had given way to an equally fierce debate over equality, black autonomy, and the terms of Reconstruction. It is worth pondering how that struggle, and its attendant anxieties, shaped the painter's and the magazine's reconstructions of the facts of the Garner case. One might, for instance, compare Noble's version of Garner's demeanor and appearance with that found in the earlier reporting, or ask why Margaret's light-skinned daughter, Mary, was transmuted into two dead sons.* Harper's *did not ask. Indeed, its text presented Noble's work as "really historical," the "true story" of how Garner had killed two of her children. Unlike some other sources, the magazine did not purvey fantasies that Garner was still alive, but this was not because it had more accurate information to convey: the* Harper's *report concluded by telling readers that "while being returned to slavery [Margaret] eluded the watchfulness of her guard and plunged into the Ohio River and found freedom there."*

The Modern Medea—The Story of Margaret Garner. Print collection of the New York Public Library. Print by Brady, after a painting by Thomas Satterwhite Noble. Courtesy of Photographs and Prints Division, Schomburg Center for Research in Black Culture, The New York Public Library, Astor, Lenox, and Tilden Foundations.

Letter of E. A. Burke (1901)

Nested in another letter in the archives of the Kentucky Historical Society is a typed transcription of a portion of a letter reportedly written in December of 1901 by E. A. Burke, niece of Archibald K. Gaines. That puts this document at a questionable remove from its source, but then as a guide to the facts of the Garner case the letter is thoroughly unreliable, anyway. As unwitting evidence of how understandings of the case have always been entwined with powerful fictions, however, the document registers an important cultural truth. In the putative recollections of Mrs. Burke's "mammy," we find an inverted recognition of the relationship between the Garners' story and the famous novel that had been published several years before they made their short-lived bid for freedom. Burke is not alone in this: various literary critics, over the years, passed on the rumor that Margaret Garner claimed to have been the inspiration for Stowe's Eliza. Also contrary to Burke's report, antebellum responses to the Garner case did not discuss scars on Margaret's back—but over a century after Margaret's death, and nearly nine decades after the writing of this letter, Morrison would make the "chokecherry tree" on Sethe's back one of the most compelling images in Beloved.

The following is an extract of a letter written 22 Dec, 1901, by Mrs. E.A. Burke. Mrs. Burke was the niece of Archibald K Gaines, referred to in the extract, and was born 1842. . . .

"His (Archibald K Gaines) mother's negroes were run off to Ohio by the Abolitionists, followed and recaptured by Archibald K forming basis of the "Peggy" case in Mrs. Stowe's Uncle Toms Cabin. My old mammy now here, 96 years old, remembers "Peggy" well and has given me the history of the scars on her back. They were not made by a Gaines, Peggy was Grandma Gaines' housegirl. Nellie was the Cook, they were always fighting when Archibald K. Gaines was away, his father being dead. (Abner Legrand Gaines died 1839).

Archibald had some bundles of beech switches cut and whenever Peggy and Nellie were reported as fighting, he would tell them to have it out, giving each a bundle of switches and they would go at each other until they got enough. This is the history of the scars found on "Peggy's" back. She was run away by her husband and two underground Railroad emissaries to Cinc, they stealing three fine horses for the purpose. When found by the sheriff in Cincinatti Peggy killed two of her children and later killed the third. Her husband remained in Ohio. I knew Nellie, Grandma's cook, and was always afraid of her, she looked so ferocious and was so fond of fighting, also knew Peggy the house girl and her children. She was a fine looking woman, and we children liked her, in fact she was Grandma's pet servant. This kind old lady never laid a hand on 'Peggy' whose fault seemed to be a violent temper."

ACKNOWLEDGMENTS

Over the years since I first began thinking about the Garner case and how it might best be understood and presented to a nonspecialist audience, many people helped me locate sources, make sense of them, and think about the unsettling events recorded in those documents as well as the broader context of antebellum American culture and politics.

The initial research for the project was supported by a fellowship from the National Endowment for the Humanities. Williams College students Sabrina Fève and Elise London were invaluable in the early stages of discovering and sifting through primary material; students Elissa Shevinsky, Kylie Anderson, and Lexie Hunt all assisted ably with specific research tasks in later stages. The collections and staffs of many libraries and archives were important to investigating this case. I particularly thank Alison O'Grady and the Interlibrary Loan staff at Williams College's Sawyer Library for obtaining so many antebellum newspapers on microfilm, and Lisa Long of the Ohio Historical Society, who researched the legislative history of the bills prompted by the Garner case and provided copies of all relevant records of the Ohio House and Senate. Ruth Brunings generously shared much information about local history in Boone County as well as several documents from her own research into the case. Donna Chenail and Peggy Weyer transcribed the vast majority of the sources republished here, cheerily unraveling the mysteries of nineteenth-century typography and penmanship.

The final form of this book profited from the insights and suggestions of anonymous reviewers for the University of Minnesota Press. The Introduction incorporates revised versions of portions of my essay "Who Speaks for Margaret Garner? Slavery, Silence, and the Politics of

Ventriloquism," published in *Critical Inquiry* in 2002; early drafts of that article were presented to audiences at Northwestern University, State University of New York at Albany, the Law and Society Association, and the American Political Science Association. Over the years, I received helpful commentary from Samuel Delany, Tom Dumm, Abigail Jackson, the late Michael Rogin, Karen Sanchez-Eppler, and, several times, George Shulman, for whose encouragement I am especially grateful. For their invitations, responses, and suggestions I thank Mieke Bal; the late Paige Baty; Lauren Berlant; Stuart Clarke; Charles Dew; David Edwards; Peter Euben; Sophia Mihic; Sara Monoson; Shawn Rosenheim; Geoff Sanborn; Mort Schoolman; David L. Smith; Williams College colleagues in the political science department, the American studies program, and the Oakley Center for the Humanities and Social Sciences; and the students in my "Fugitive Identities" and "Representing Slavery" seminars.

Finally, I thank my children, Simon, Max, and Dulce Reinhardt, to whom this book is dedicated, and my wife, Molly Magavern, for her support and patience as I worked on this project. The Garner case is a painful reminder that being able to offer thanks of this kind is a matter of privilege and good fortune.

Privilege and fortune were among the matters explored in my seminars on slavery. One focus was how slavery and its legacies have continued to haunt American political, cultural, and social life, and one wager of those courses—a wager shared by this book—was that it can be productive to grapple honestly with the formative role of racial subordination in the making and remaking of national identity. But the contemporary status of slavery, especially when placed in a global context, is unfortunately more than a matter of the echoes of the past. Slavery is still with us in the most literal sense: millions of men, women, and children around the world are subject to some form of involuntary servitude. Nothing, and certainly no telling of her story, can reverse what was done to Margaret Garner and to so many of her contemporaries. Today's slavery, however, can perhaps be undone and is being contested. One group in the forefront of the effort to bring slavery to an end is Free the Slaves, and all author's royalties from the sale of this book will go to that organization.

TEXT OF THE FUGITIVE SLAVE ACT OF 1850

SECTION 1

Be it enacted by the Senate and House of Representatives of the United States of America in Congress assembled, That the persons who have been, or may hereafter be, appointed commissioners, in virtue of any act of Congress, by the Circuit Courts of the United States, and Who, in consequence of such appointment, are authorized to exercise the powers that any justice of the peace, or other magistrate of any of the United States, may exercise in respect to offenders for any crime or offense against the United States, by arresting, imprisoning, or bailing the same under and by the virtue of the thirty-third section of the act of the twenty-fourth of September seventeen hundred and eighty-nine, entitled "An Act to establish the judicial courts of the United States" shall be, and are hereby, authorized and required to exercise and discharge all the powers and duties conferred by this act.

SECTION 2

And be it further enacted, That the Superior Court of each organized Territory of the United States shall have the same power to appoint commissioners to take acknowledgments of bail and affidavits, and to take depositions of witnesses in civil causes, which is now possessed by the Circuit Court of the United States; and all commissioners who shall hereafter be appointed for such purposes by the Superior Court of any organized Territory of the United States, shall possess all the powers, and exercise all the duties, conferred by law upon the commissioners appointed by the Circuit Courts of the United States for similar purposes, and shall moreover exercise and discharge all the powers and duties conferred by this act.

SECTION 3

And be it further enacted, That the Circuit Courts of the United States shall from time to time enlarge the number of the commissioners, with a view to afford reasonable facilities to reclaim fugitives from labor, and to the prompt discharge of the duties imposed by this act.

SECTION 4

And be it further enacted, That the commissioners above named shall have concurrent jurisdiction with the judges of the Circuit and District Courts of the United States, in their respective circuits and districts within the several States, and the judges of the Superior Courts of the Territories, severally and collectively, in term-time and vacation; shall grant certificates to such claimants, upon satisfactory proof being made, with authority to take and remove such fugitives from service or labor, under the restrictions herein contained, to the State or Territory from which such persons may have escaped or fled.

SECTION 5

And be it further enacted, That it shall be the duty of all marshals and deputy marshals to obey and execute all warrants and precepts issued under the provisions of this act, when to them directed; and should any marshal or deputy marshal refuse to receive such warrant, or other process, when tendered, or to use all proper means diligently to execute the same, he shall, on conviction thereof, be fined in the sum of one thousand dollars, to the use of such claimant, on the motion of such claimant, by the Circuit or District Court for the district of such marshal; and after arrest of such fugitive, by such marshal or his deputy, or whilst at any time in his custody under the provisions of this act, should such fugitive escape, whether with or without the assent of such marshal or his deputy, such marshal shall be liable, on his official bond, to be prosecuted for the benefit of such claimant, for the full value of the service or labor of said fugitive in the State, Territory, or District whence he escaped: and the better to enable the said commissioners, when thus appointed, to execute their duties faithfully and efficiently, in conformity with the requirements of the Constitution of the United States and of this act, they are hereby authorized and empowered, within their counties respectively, to appoint, in writing under their hands, any one or more suitable persons, from time to time, to execute all such warrants and other process as may be issued by them in the lawful performance of their respective duties; with authority to such commissioners, or the persons to be appointed by them, to execute process as aforesaid, to summon and call to their aid the bystanders, or posse comitatus of the proper county, when necessary to ensure a faithful observance of the clause of the Constitution referred to, in conformity with the provisions of this act; and all good citizens are hereby commanded to aid and assist in the prompt and efficient execution of this law, whenever their services may be required, as aforesaid, for that purpose; and said warrants shall run, and be executed by said officers, any where in the State within which they are issued.

SECTION 6

And be it further enacted, That when a person held to service or labor in any State or Territory of the United States, has heretofore or shall hereafter escape into another State or Territory of the United States, the person or persons to whom such service or labor may be due, or his, her, or their agent or attorney, duly authorized, by power of attorney, in writing, acknowledged and certified under the seal of some legal officer or court of the State or Territory in which the same may be executed, may pursue and reclaim such fugitive person, either by procuring a warrant from some one of the courts, judges, or commissioners aforesaid, of the proper circuit, district, or county, for the apprehension of such fugitive from service or labor, or by seizing and arresting such fugitive, where the same can be done without process, and by taking, or causing such person to be taken, forthwith before such court, judge, or commissioner, whose duty it shall be to hear and determine the case of such claimant in a summary manner; and upon satisfactory proof being made, by deposition or affidavit, in writing, to be taken and certified by such court, judge, or commissioner, or by other satisfactory testimony, duly taken and certified by some court, magistrate, justice of the peace, or other legal officer authorized to administer an oath and take depositions under the laws of the State or Territory from which such person owing service or labor may have escaped, with a certificate of such magistracy or other authority, as aforesaid, with the seal of the proper court or officer thereto attached, which seal shall be sufficient to establish the competency of the proof, and with proof, also by affidavit, of the identity of the person whose service or labor is claimed to be due as aforesaid, that the person so arrested does in fact owe service or labor to the person or persons claiming him or her, in the State or Territory from which such fugitive may have escaped as aforesaid, and that said person escaped, to make out and deliver to such claimant, his or her agent or attorney, a certificate setting forth the substantial facts as to the service or labor due from such fugitive to the claimant, and of his or her escape from the State or Territory in which he or she was arrested, with authority to such claimant, or his or her agent or attorney, to use such reasonable force and restraint as may be necessary, under the circumstances of the case, to take and remove such fugitive person back to the State or Territory whence he or she may have escaped as aforesaid. In no trial or hearing under this act shall the testimony of such alleged fugitive be admitted in evidence; and the certificates in this and the first [fourth] section mentioned, shall be conclusive of the right of the person or persons in whose favor granted, to remove such fugitive to the State or Territory from which he escaped, and shall prevent all molestation of such person or persons by any process issued by any court, judge, magistrate, or other person whomsoever.

SECTION 7

And be it further enacted, That any person who shall knowingly and willingly obstruct, hinder, or prevent such claimant, his agent or attorney, or any person or persons lawfully assisting him, her, or them, from arresting such a fugitive from service or labor, either with or without process as aforesaid, or shall rescue, or attempt to rescue, such fugitive from service or labor, from the custody of such claimant, his or her agent or attorney, or other person or persons lawfully assisting as aforesaid, when so arrested, pursuant to the authority herein given and declared; or shall aid, abet, or assist such person so owing service or labor as aforesaid, directly or indirectly, to escape from such claimant, his agent or attorney, or other person or persons legally authorized as aforesaid; or shall harbor or conceal such fugitive, so as to prevent the discovery and arrest of such person, after notice or knowledge of the fact that such person was a fugitive from service or labor as aforesaid, shall, for either of said offences, be subject to a fine not exceeding one thousand dollars, and imprisonment not exceeding six months, by indictment and conviction before the District Court of the United States for the district in which such offence may have been committed, or before the proper court of criminal jurisdiction, if committed within any one of the organized Territories of the United States; and shall moreover forfeit and pay, by way of civil damages to the party injured by such illegal conduct, the sum of one thousand dollars for each fugitive so lost as aforesaid, to be recovered by action of debt, in any of the District or Territorial Courts aforesaid, within whose jurisdiction the said offence may have been committed.

Section 8

And be it further enacted, That the marshals, their deputies, and the clerks of the said District and Territorial Courts, shall be paid, for their services, the like fees as may be allowed for similar services in other cases; and where such services are rendered exclusively in the arrest, custody, and delivery of the fugitive to the claimant, his or her agent or attorney, or where such supposed fugitive may be discharged out of custody for the want of sufficient proof as aforesaid, then such fees are to be paid in whole by such claimant, his or her agent or attorney; and in all cases where the proceedings are before a commissioner, he shall be entitled to a fee of ten dollars in full for his services in each case, upon the delivery of the said certificate to the claimant, his agent or attorney; or a fee of five dollars in cases where the proof shall not, in the opinion of such commissioner, warrant such certificate and delivery, inclusive of all services incident to such arrest and examination, to be paid, in either case, by the claimant, his or her agent or attorney. The person or persons authorized to execute the process to be issued by such commissioner for the arrest and detention of fugitives from service or labor as aforesaid, shall also be entitled to a fee of five dollars each for each person he or they may arrest, and take before any commissioner as aforesaid, at the instance and request of such claimant, with such other fees as may be deemed reasonable by such commissioner for such other additional services as may be necessarily performed by him or them; such as attending at the examination, keeping the fugitive in custody, and providing him with food and lodging during his detention, and until the final determination of such commissioners; and, in general, for performing such other duties as may be required by such claimant, his or her attorney or agent, or commissioner in the premises, such fees to be made up in conformity with the fees usually charged by the officers of the courts of justice within the proper district or county, as near as may be practicable, and paid by such claimants, their agents or attorneys, whether such supposed fugitives from service or labor be ordered to be delivered to such claimant by the final determination of such commissioner or not.

Section 9

And be it further enacted, That, upon affidavit made by the claimant of such fugitive, his agent or attorney, after such certificate has been issued, that he has reason to apprehend that such fugitive will be rescued by force from his or their possession before he can be taken beyond the limits of the State in which the arrest is made, it shall be the duty of the officer making the arrest to retain such fugitive in his custody, and to remove him to the State whence he fled, and there to deliver him to said claimant, his agent, or attorney. And to this end, the officer aforesaid is hereby authorized and required to employ so many persons as he may deem necessary to overcome such force, and to retain them in his service so long as circumstances may require. The said officer and his assistants, while so employed, to receive the same compensation, and to be allowed the same expenses, as are now allowed by law for transportation of criminals, to be certified by the judge of the district within which the arrest is made, and paid out of the treasury of the United States.

Section 10

And be it further enacted, That when any person held to service or labor in any State or Territory, or in the District of Columbia, shall escape therefrom, the party to whom such service or labor shall be due, his, her, or their agent or attorney, may apply to any court of record therein, or judge thereof in vacation, and make satisfactory proof to such court, or judge in vacation, of the escape aforesaid, and that the person escaping owed service or labor to such party. Whereupon the court shall cause a record to be made of the matters so proved, and also a general description of the person so escaping, with such convenient certainty as may be; and a transcript of such record, authenticated by the attestation of the clerk and of the seal of the said court, being produced in any other State, Territory, or district in which the person so escaping may be found, and being exhibited to any judge, commissioner, or other office, authorized by the law of the United States to cause persons escaping from service or labor to be delivered up, shall be held and taken to be full and conclusive evidence of the fact of escape, and that the service or labor of the person escaping is due to the party in such record mentioned. And upon the production by the said party of other and further evidence if necessary, either oral or by affidavit, in addition to what is contained in the said record of the identity of the person escaping, he or she shall be delivered up to the claimant, And the said court, commissioner, judge, or other person authorized by this act to grant certificates to claimants or fugitives, shall, upon the production of the record and other evidences aforesaid, grant to such claimant a certificate of his right to take any such person identified and proved to be owing service or labor as aforesaid, which certificate shall authorize such claimant to seize or arrest and transport such person to the State or Territory from which he escaped: Provided, That nothing herein contained shall be construed as requiring the production of a transcript of such record as evidence as aforesaid. But in its absence the claim shall be heard and determined upon other satisfactory proofs, competent in law.

CHRONOLOGY OF KEY EVENTS, 1856–71

1856 JANUARY 27

Late in the evening, the eight members of the Garner family flee Richwood, Kentucky, on a horse-drawn sled, heading toward the Ohio River.

JANUARY 28

Around 10:00 a.m., federal marshals, Archibald K. Gaines, and others capture the Garners in Cincinnati at the home of the Kites, relatives on Margaret Garner's side. Margaret's daughter Mary dies almost immediately after capture. The family is taken first to the U.S. Court House, where Gaines and Thomas Marshall ask Commissioner John L. Pendery to order the Garners' return to Kentucky. Citing the need for more documentation, Pendery postpones the hearing and orders the Garners to be kept overnight in the Hammond Street station house, in the custody of federal marshals. Contentious crowds surround the station house.

Hamilton County sheriffs arrive with a writ from Probate Court Judge John Burgoyne, claiming custody of the Garners. Sheriffs and marshals dispute custody for much of the evening, which ends with the matter still ambiguous but the fugitives lodged in the county jail.

Coroner's inquest on Mary Garner's death begins.

In the evening, Burgoyne heads to Columbus to confer on the case with Governor Salmon Chase. Chase assures Burgoyne that the state will stand behind the judge if he intervenes.

JANUARY 29

The inquest concludes with verdict that Margaret killed her daughter; two jurors vote that Simon and Robert were accessories.

Custody struggle between sheriffs and marshals continues.

1856
(cont'd)

JANUARY 30

Hearings begin before Commissioner Pendery on James Marshall's claim to Simon, Mary Garner, and Robert Garner, and Archibald Gaines's claim to Margaret and the surviving children. Pendery decides to split the case in two, first considering Marshall's claim, then Gaines's. The court is packed with spectators, but only whites have been admitted.

A large, racially mixed crowd of men and women agitates outside the courtroom all day, making it difficult for the marshals—who control movements outside the county jail—to bring the Garners into or out of the courthouse. Two black men, Minstin Hayes and Jerry Fassett, are arrested for disturbance.

In the Ohio legislature, the first of many debates over resolutions and bills responding to the case.

Warrant issued to all four adult Garners on the charge of murder, but it is not served, as the federal case is continuing before Pendery.

JANUARY 31

Case of Simon, Mary, and Robert begins with witnesses for claimant James Marshall. All witnesses are white men.

Two or three hundred persons, mostly of color, again throng outside courtroom. One "colored man" is arrested, reportedly for throwing a stone at officers on the omnibus used to transport the Garners. That night, citizens of color hold a public meeting to condemn their exclusion from the proceedings.

Marshal Robinson departs for Washington, D.C., seeking to consult on case with high-ranking members of the Pierce administration. (There is no solid evidence that he succeeds.)

Four more of Archibald Gaines's slaves escape, probably heading for Canada. There is no record of their ever being captured, and sources conflict on their identities.

FEBRUARY 1

Case before Commissioner Pendery continues with witnesses for the Garners, mostly free Cincinnatians of color.

FEBRUARY 2

More witnesses for Garners testify.

Cincinnati police now excluded from court, with order inside enforced by police from Covington and deputy marshals hired specially for this case. Most accounts indicate that the number of deputies hired by Marshal Robinson in the coming days will reach about 400.

FEBRUARY 4

Final testimony for both sides; beginning of final arguments.

FEBRUARY 5

James Gitchell, John Jolliffe's assistant counsel, makes closing arguments for fugitives.

FEBRUARY 6

Jolliffe makes his final argument for fugitives. Audience in court is now racially mixed.

A Hamilton County grand jury indicts Robert and Margaret for murder and Simon and Mary as accessories. On receiving the indictments, Sheriff Gazoway Brashears evicts the marshal and deputies from the county jail, asserting custody over the fugitives.

FEBRUARY 7

At the opening of the day's session before Commissioner Pendery, the Garners do not arrive in court as scheduled. Sherriff Brashears reports that he has custody and has not brought them, because of the murder charge. Eventually, Brashears agrees that he will continue to bring the family to Pendery's courtroom, and Pendery agrees that he will not interfere with the sheriff's de facto exercise of custody. After the fugitives arrive, Francis Chambers presents a five-hour concluding argument for claimant. End of proceedings on the first case. Pendery announces that he will decide outcome after hearing the case of Gaines, Margaret, and the children.

FEBRUARY 8

Most of the central parties are absent from Pendery's court, as the custody battle between the sheriff and the marshal resumes and consumes the day. The sheriff seeks a formal grant of custody from Pendery, making possible the pursuit of the murder case; Marshal Robinson contests this request. Press accounts are contradictory, but it appears that Pendery takes the issue "under advisement" while insisting that marshal at present retains *legal* custody, though not immediate physical control.

FEBRUARY 9

Beginning of the case of Margaret and her children. Women are majority of the audience. Opening witnesses for claimant, Archibald Gaines.

FEBRUARY 10

One Reverend Bassett, of Cincinnati's Fairmont Theological Seminary, visits Garners in jail; his account of the encounter will circulate in the antislavery press and, over a century later, help inspire the novelist Toni Morrison to begin her novel *Beloved*.

1856
(cont'd)

FEBRUARY 11

Conclusion of testimony for Gaines, beginning of testimony for Garners. Over fierce objections, Pendery grants Jolliffe's motion to allow Margaret to testify for her children. She becomes perhaps the only fugitive slave to testify in a proceeding held under the Fugitive Slave Law.

FEBRUARY 12

Concluding arguments for fugitives, beginning of concluding arguments for claimant.

FEBRUARY 13

Claimants' final arguments. Pendery adjourns, announcing that he will give his decision on March 12. A crowd remains in court, and a public meeting is declared so that the well-known abolitionist and women's rights advocate, Lucy Stone, can speak about the case. Her speech celebrating Margaret's heroism is widely reproduced in the Northern press.

FEBRUARY 20

Brashears appears in the Court of Common Pleas before Judge Samuel Carter in response to Carter's order that the sheriff take possession of the fugitives, for pursuit of the murder case. Under pressure from Carter, Brashears agrees to say he has custody—despite Pendery's prior declarations on the matter.

FEBRUARY 21

Pendery is expected to announce his decision on the Garner cases, but the sheriff will not release the Garners to the marshals or allow them to be taken to the commissioner's court. After consulting with Marshal Robinson, Pendery adjourns for the day.

In probate court, Judge Burgoyne issues a habeas corpus writ for the Garner children, served on Robinson. Robinson gives his word that he will not turn any of them over to the claimants without first appearing before Burgoyne.

In district court shortly thereafter, Robinson seeks to thwart Burgoyne's efforts, pressing federal Judge Humphrey Leavitt for two habeas writs, one for the Garner adults and another for the children. Leavitt grants the writs, making them returnable on February 26.

FEBRUARY 23

In Florence, Kentucky, citizens of Boone County hold a public meeting to address the current "crisis" in the rights of slaveholders. Gaines and other participants in the Garner case appear before the assembly.

FEBRUARY 26

Habeas hearing begins in Judge Leavitt's court.

In the early afternoon, while the Garners remain in jail, Pendery delivers his decision in the courtroom, finding for the claimant in each case: the Garners are fugitives who "owe labor and service . . . for life" and must be returned to Kentucky. Afterward, Gaines submits an affidavit to Pendery, expressing fear that the Garners will be "rescued by force." Pendery orders the marshal to deliver the Garners to Kentucky. Pendery's rulings cannot be enforced, however, until Judge Leavitt rules on the custody issue. Judge Burgoyne and Judge Carter's writs also remain pending.

FEBRUARY 27

Hearings before Judge Burgoyne on the marshal's detention of the fugitives continue. Marshal Robinson requests a dismissal of Burgoyne's writ, arguing that Burgoyne has no authority to intervene in processes being conducted under the Fugitive Slave Act. Jolliffe asks Burgoyne to rule the Fugitive Slave Act unconstitutional. Saying he will decide the issue soon, Burgoyne issues an order barring the fugitives' forcible removal from Ohio in the meantime.

FEBRUARY 28

Judge Leavitt finds for the marshal in the custody dispute.

Marshal Robinson and hundreds of deputies remove the Garners from the county jail, taking them across the river to Covington, Kentucky. There, Kentuckians and supporters of slavery hold public celebrations, with speeches. The Cincinnati *Daily Gazette* journalist Edmond Babb, reporting on the scene in Covington, is assaulted by a mob; only the intervention of several federal marshals from Ohio, with guns drawn, saves him.

FEBRUARY 29

In the Court of Common Pleas, prosecuting attorney Joseph Cox presents Sheriff Brashears's response to Judge Carter's writ: Brashears cannot return the fugitives as he cannot find them; they were discharged from his custody by Judge Leavitt. Carter tells Cox that, though the sheriff should have tried to rearrest the fugitives after their discharge, the only recourse now is for the prosecutor to ask Governor Chase to requisition the Garners from Kentucky. Cox replies that he has made that request.

MARCH 1

Marshal's counsel again asks Judge Burgoyne to quash his habeas writ. Judge Burgoyne rejects the motion, ordering Robinson to make a return on the writ—to produce the fugitives or explain why he has not done so—in court by March 7.

Citizens of Covington, Kentucky, hold public meeting to condemn the assault on Edmund Babb.

1856
(cont'd)

Beginning today and continuing for much of coming week, Archibald Gaines will send various Garners, in different combinations, to different parts of Kentucky, in an apparent effort to make them difficult to locate. Surviving accounts of these movements are sketchy and contradictory.

MARCH 4

After several days of deliberation and delay, Governor Chase completes his requisition for return of the adult Garners.

MARCH 5

Joseph Cooper and Edward Hamlin agree to deliver the requisition to Kentucky governor Charles Morehead. They leave for Cincinnati. Hamlin is also seeking to meet with Gaines and arrange the purchase of the children's freedom.

MARCH 6

With the prosecuting attorney Joseph Cox, Cooper and Hamlin travel from Cincinnati to Frankfort. For the latter part of the route, they share a train car with the Covington sheriff, Clinton Butts, who is escorting four of Gaines's slaves south. It appears that, unbeknownst to the Cincinnati delegation, the four include Robert, Margaret, and infant daughter, Cilla. Butts and his captives continue on to Louisville, while Cooper and the others get off at Frankfort, delivering the requisition to Morehead in the evening. On receipt, Governor Morehead sends a telegram to Louisville, asking Gaines to hold Margaret ready for turning over in Louisville or to return with her to Frankfort. Gaines has reportedly promised to comply with any such request.

MARCH 7

In the morning, Butts brings the Garner family aboard the steamer *Henry Lewis* and sets off with them down the Ohio River, heading toward the Mississippi River, and ultimately Arkansas.

Governor Morehead issues warrants for adult Garners. He again telegraphs Gaines, asking the latter to hold Margaret ready for delivery to Ohio. Cooper's party takes the next train to Louisville. On arrival at the jail where the Garners had been kept, they are informed that Gaines had shipped the whole family south that morning. Given what Morehead has assured them, the Ohio contingent does not believe this; they search for Margaret.

In Cincinnati, in Judge Burgoyne's court, Marshal Robinson makes his return on the habeas writ. Robinson explains that he cannot bring the fugitives, as he does not have them in his control. Robinson claims he was obliged under federal law to return them to Kentucky. Arguments from lawyers for Robinson and the Garners consume a full day of hearings.

MARCH 8

Before dawn, on the Ohio River, just past Troy, Indiana, the *Henry Lewis* collides with the *Edward Howard*. Margaret's daughter Cilla drowns.

Cooper's party searches Louisville for the Garners, eventually realizing that they have indeed left.

In Cincinnati, concluding arguments begin before Judge Burgoyne.

MARCH 10

Gaines arrives in Cincinnati, publicly defending his conduct throughout the case, and proclaiming his willingness to have Margaret returned should legal processes so require.

The Garners arrive at Gaines Landing, Arkansas, delivered to cotton-grower Benjamin Gaines, Archibald's brother. Sources conflict, but the preponderance of evidence suggests that Benjamin refuses to keep them and that the Garners are soon shipped to New Orleans and sold to brother Abner LeGrand Gaines. (Although the timeline is not certain, it is clear that by *some* point in the spring, the Garners arrive in New Orleans and are hired out.)

MARCH 13

Ohio House passes HR 71, Representative Monroe's *Habeas Corpus* bill, which furthers the power of state judges to control the custody of fugitive slaves.

MARCH 17

Ohio Senate passes and sends to Governor Chase a resolution asking him to provide copies of all correspondence pertaining to the requisition of Margaret Garner.

MARCH 18

Judge Burgoyne rules that Marshal Robinson's return on the habeas ruling is inadequate, therefore finding Robinson in contempt of court. Robinson defied an order not to bring the Garners out of Cincinnati, and his defense, that he was following the Fugitive Slave Act, is not sufficient. Burgoyne further rules that the provisions in the Fugitive Slave Act authorizing commissioners to decide claims about fugitive slaves are unconstitutional. Burgoyne orders proceedings against Robinson on the contempt charge.

MARCH 21

Archibald Gaines, who for the past week has been attacked in the Cincinnati and national press for his conduct in the requisition, defends his actions in a letter published in the Cincinnati press. He promises to make all possible efforts to help recover Margaret for trial.

1856
(*cont'd*)

APRIL 1

Ohio Senate passes Monroe's *Habeas Corpus* bill.

APRIL 2 OR 3

Summoned by Archibald Gaines, Margaret arrives back in Covington and is placed in the Kenton County jail, ostensibly so that she is available for requisition. (Reports are contradictory as to which date.) The available evidence indicates that, contrary to his later public claims, Gaines does not publicize this return.

APRIL 5

Habeas Corpus bill HR 71 signed by both houses and becomes Ohio law.

APRIL 8

By telegram Gaines finally informs Governor Chase, who had not previously known, that Margaret is in Covington jail and will be removed on April 10, if not requisitioned by that time.

APRIL 9

The prosecuting attorney Joseph Cox receives papers from Chase, authorizing his retrieval of Margaret. Sheriff Brashears provides Cox with two deputies to assist him.

At night Margaret is removed from jail by a man bearing written orders from Archibald Gaines.

APRIL 10

Cox and deputies arrive at Kenton County jail in the morning and are informed that Margaret is gone, with destination unknown.

APRIL 11

Sheriff Brashears, hearing that Margaret is being sent to New Orleans via Louisville, cables Louisville sheriff asking for arrest of Garner for the requisition. Receives no reply.

Margaret is again sent south from Louisville.

Ohio legislature passes Senate Joint Resolution 20, calling on the state's federal representatives in Washington, D.C., to do all they can to ensure the repeal of the Fugitive Slave Act "at the earliest practicable time."

APRIL 15

After new stories in the press again accusing him of duplicity in sending Margaret back south, Gaines publishes a second defense of his conduct in the Cincinnati *Daily Enquirer.*

Judge Burgoyne issues order giving Marshal Robinson two days to explain why he should not be jailed on contempt charges.

APRIL 17

Marshal Robinson appears before Judge Burgoyne. Robinson's position is that he had been performing his official duties under U.S. law, and he denies the probate court's jurisdiction in such matters. Burgoyne fines the marshal $300 and orders him jailed "until he obeys the order of the Court." Robinson taken to county jail by deputy sheriff.

Robinson requests a habeas writ from Judge Leavitt. Leavitt orders sheriff to bring the marshal before him immediately. Hearings begin on whether to void Burgoyne's contempt ruling. Matter unresolved at day's end. Marshal returns to jail.

APRIL 18

Judge Leavitt continues hearing on marshal's request that he void Judge Burgoyne's contempt proceedings.

APRIL 23

In *Ex Parte Robinson,* Judge Leavitt releases Robinson from jail, ruling that Robinson was acting as directed by valid federal law and could not be subject to conflicting orders from a state court.

MAY 15

Cox sends Chase a copy of the murder indictment, asking him to requisition Magaret and the other adult Garners from New Orleans. Nothing comes of Cox's request.

1856–58 At some point, Abner LeGrand Gaines sells the Garners to Judge Bonham of Tennessee Landing, Mississippi; Garners labor as slaves on Bonham's plantation there.

1857 MAY 30

Archibald Gaines, encountering John Jolliffe on the streets of Covington, assaults him as a large crowd watches.

JUNE 2

Gaines is tried and convicted for the assault, and assessed a modest fine.

1858 In all likelihood, Margaret dies of typhoid in Tennessee Landing. (See next two entries.)

1862 SEPTEMBER 2

A *New York Daily Tribune* journalist describes in detail a recent letter from Robert Garner. According to the report, Robert says he escaped and is aboard the Union gunboat Benton, and that Margaret died on May 14, 1861.

1870   MARCH 11

The *Cincinnati Chronicle* publishes an interview with Robert Garner, who is living in the city, severely injured from a workplace accident the previous year. It is here that Robert reports Margaret's death of typhoid in 1858. He says that Sam and Tom are living near Vicksburg, Mississippi.

1871   APRIL 20

A Robert Garner, identified as a black man originally from Kentucky, with an age estimated at forty-three years, dies in Cincinnati.

NOVEMBER 11

Archibald Gaines dies of lockjaw at home in Richwood, Kentucky, after stepping on a rusty nail. His obituary in the *Covington Journal,* referring to him as "universally respected for those traits of character which mark the kind husband and father—the good citizen—the upright man," makes no mention of the Garner case.

NOTES

Preface

1. Pittsburgh Visitor, as reprinted in the (Ohio) Anti-Slavery Bugle, February 16, 1856. Among those making such predictions was the National Anti-Slavery Standard, which speculated that perhaps Margaret Garner's "heroism . . . will be remembered . . . two thousand years hence" (February 8, 1856).

2. When *Beloved* was published, Morrison remarked that after coming across the interview (see chapter 10), "I did a lot of research about everything else in the book—Cincinnati, and abolitionists, and the underground railroad—but I refused to find out anything else about Margaret Garner. I really wanted to invent her life" (Mervyn Rothstein, "Toni Morrison, in Her New Novel, Defends Women," *New York Times*, August 26, 1987). For the most thorough scholarly account of the case written before *Beloved*, see Julius Yanuck, "The Garner Fugitive Slave Case," *Mississippi Valley Historical Review* 40, no. 1 (1953): 47–66.

3. Steven Weisenburger, *Modern Medea: A Family Story of Slavery and Child-Murder in the Old South* (New York: Hill and Want, 1998). Drawing on years of archival research and a vast body of material, Weisenburger's study was far more ambitious and wide ranging than any previous work on the case, and it remains the most comprehensive and significant scholarly source available. Although I have substantial disagreements with Weisenburger on assorted points of fact and interpretation, and have questions about his handling of evidence (some of which are noted at various places in the next chapter), I remain fundamentally indebted to his work. Other accounts of the case include Ruth Wade Cox Brunings, "Slavery and the Tragic Story of Two Families—Gaines and Garner," *Northern Kentucky Heritage* 12, no. 1 (2004): 37–45; Paul Gilroy, *The Black Atlantic: Modernity and Double Consciousness* (Cambridge, Mass.: Harvard University Press, 1993), 63–71; Avery Gordon, *Ghostly Matters: Haunting and the Sociological Imagination* (Minneapolis: University of Minnesota Press, 1997), 137–90; Stephen Middleton, "The Fugitive Slave Crisis in Cincinnati, 1850–1860: Resistance, Enforcement, and Black Refugees," *Journal of Negro History* 72 (1987): 20–32; Mark Reinhardt, "Who Speaks for Margaret Garner? Slavery, Silence, and the

Politics of Ventriloquism," *Critical Inquiry* 29, no. 1 (2002): 81–119; Angelita Reyes, *Mothering across Cultures: Postcolonial Representations* (Minneapolis: University of Minnesota Press, 2001), 33–78; Cynthia Griffin Wolff, "'Margaret Garner': A Cincinnati Story," *Massachusetts Review* 32 (1991): 417–40. The opera *Margaret Garner* was first performed in 2005. Morrison wrote the libretto, with music by Richard Danielpour. For a critical discussion of how the opera's approach to the Garner case differs radically from that of *Beloved,* see Catherine Gunther Kodat, "*Margaret Garner* and the Second Tear," *American Quarterly* 60, no. 1 (2008): 159–71.

Introduction

1. On Minkins, Sims, and Burns, see, respectively, Gary Collison, *Shadrach Minkins: From Fugitive Slave to Citizen* (Cambridge, Mass.: Harvard University Press); Stanley W. Campbell, *The Slave Catchers: Enforcement of the Fugitive Slave Law, 1850–1860* (Chapel Hill: University of North Carolina Press, 1970), 117–21, 124–30; Albert J. Von Frank, *The Trials of Anthony Burns: Freedom and Slavery in Emerson's Boston* (Cambridge, Mass.: Harvard University Press, 1998). A good, brief overview of many of the prominent clashes over captured fugitive slaves is provided by Lois E. Horton, "Kidnapping and Resistance," in David W. Blight, ed., *Passages to Freedom: The Underground Railroad in History and Memory* (Washington, D.C.: Smithsonian Books, 2004), 149–93.

2. The Rosetta Armstead case involved the same federal marshal, Hiram Robinson, and federal slave commissioner, John L. Pendery, as the Garner case; Salmon Chase, who at the time of the Garners' capture had just taken office as governor, was the lawyer who obtained the initial habeas corpus for Armstead. For an example of the journalistic response, see the coverage in the *New York Daily Times* (*NYDT*), April 3, 4, and 26, 1855. For scholarly accounts, see Robert Cover, *Justice Accused: Anti-Slavery and the Judicial Process* (New Haven, Conn.: Yale University Press, 1975), 183–84; and Paul Finkelman, *An Imperfect Union: Slavery, Federalism, and Comity* (Chapel Hill: University of North Carolina Press, 1981), 175–77.

3. I discuss the broader patterns of the fugitive slave experience later in this chapter.

4. The mid-1850s saw the collapse of what historians and political scientists have sometimes called the "Second Party System," in which the key parties were the Whigs and the more dominant Democrats. Whether this is the most useful terminology, a point on which contemporary scholars disagree, it is clear that the old regime broke down in the early years of the decade, and, after a brief period of multiparty turmoil, the Republican Party emerged by 1856 as the most important party in the free states. One key point of contention in accounts of this transition is whether the intensification of the conflict over slavery is better viewed as cause or consequence of the breakdown of the old party system. For classic, contending accounts, see Eric Foner, *Free Soil, Free Labor, Free Men: The Ideology of the Republican Party before the Civil War* (New York: Oxford University Press, 1970); and Michael Holt, *The Political Crisis of the 1850's* (New York: Norton, 1983). On the intertwining of electoral politics and

mass spectacle, see Eric Foner, *Politics and Ideology in the Age of the Civil War* (New York: Oxford University Press, 1980), esp. 15–56. For particularly illuminating (and again competing) accounts of the role of slavery on the popular stage in national racial politics, see Eric Lott, *Love and Theft: Blackface Minstrelsy and the American Working Class* (New York: Oxford University Press, 1993); and Michael Rogin, *Blackface, White Noise: Jewish Immigrants in the Hollywood Melting Pot* (Berkeley: University of California Press, 1996).

5. Steven Weisenburger calls the Garner case "the longest [and] most expensive" of American fugitive slave trials, a claim that is echoed in other sources (*Modern Medea*, 5, 192, 314n24). This assessment seems persuasive. Pendery ruled twenty-nine days after the Garners' owners first appealed to him, and twenty-seven days after full proceedings, with the Garners and their lawyers present, began in his court. None of the other famous cases was nearly as long. Although many fugitive slave cases are lost to the documentary record, making it possible that some other, now obscure case was even longer, it seems highly improbable: any case so protracted would, presumably, have become a matter of significant commentary in the press and in later scholarly discussion.

6. American Anti-Slavery Society, *Annual Report, Presented to the American Anti-Slavery Society, May 7, 1856* (New York: Kraus Reprint, 1972), 44.

7. Most early documents, including the reporting on courtroom exchanges, list the boys as Tom and Sam. Postwar documents refer to Thomas and Samuel. Details from my retelling are drawn from "A Terrible Affair," *Cincinnati Daily Times* (*CDT*), January 28, 1856; *Cincinnati Daily Commercial* (*CDC*), January 29, 1856; "A Tale of Horror!" *Cincinnati Daily Enquirer* (*CDE*), January 29, 1856 (chapter 1); "Arrest of Fugitive Slaves," *Cincinnati Daily Gazette* (*CDG*), January 29, 1856. Here and in the following paragraphs, I rely primarily on the local Cincinnati and (to a lesser extent) Kentucky papers whose reporting on the initial events of the case was most detailed. Whenever possible, citations include article title. My narrative of the events is highly compressed, omitting many complexities and points of contention. The documents in chapters 1–4 of this book and the chronology that makes up the appendix offer additional details—although even when read in conjunction with my discussion here, they cannot spare the reader the uncertainties, ambiguities, and contradictions that mark the entire archive of the Garner case.

8. *Reminiscences of Levi Coffin* (New York: Arno, 1968), 559.

9. Robert's suspicions are reported in the *Cincinnati Chronicle,* March 11, 1870 (chapter 11). The *Cincinnati Daily Enquirer* reported that the marshal's office had been informed of the location. Since the paper was edited and published by the chief marshal for the area, the paper seems a reliable source on this particular point, but the story gives no clue as to whether Kite betrayed his relatives, or Gaines simply had a good guess as to where the Garners would go, or the source was someone wholly unknown to the Garners. See "A Tale of Horror!" (chapter 1). For other details in this paragraph, see "A Tale of Horror!"; "A Terrible Affair"; "Arrest of Fugitive Slaves"; "The Dreadful Affair Yesterday!" *CDT* January 29, 1856; *CDC,* January 29, 1856; "Horrible Affair!" Louisville *Daily Courier* (*LDC*) January 30, 1856 (chapter 1); *CDE*, January 30, 1856.

10. "Horrible Affair!"

11. The story of the threat appeared, in notably different versions, in "Horrible

Affair!" and in *CDC,* January 29, 1856, though the latter paper's coverage on the next day included comments from the sheriff claiming that the initial account exaggerated the ferocity of the conflict. For other details in this paragraph, see "Arrest of Fugitive Slaves"; "The Dreadful Affair Yesterday!"; "Dreadful Tragedy in Cincinnati," *National Anti-Slavery Standard (NASS),* February 9, 1856; "The Slave Case in Cincinnati," *NASS,* February 16, 1856.

12. For many more details on the trial, see the thorough reporting in the documents gathered in chapter 1 of this book.

13. "The Fugitive Slave Case," *CDG,* February 27, 1856 (emphasis added) (chapter 2).

14. Leavitt's decision was reprinted in the *New York Daily Tribune (NYTRB),* March 3, 1856, as well as in the Cincinnati dailies. The official version is published as *Ex parte* Robinson, 20 Federal Cases (1856) (chapter 5). For other details in this paragraph, see "The Fugitive Slave Case"; "The Fugitive Slaves Safe in Kentucky—Their Arrival and Reception," *CDT,* February 29, 1856; "The Mob in Covington," *CDC,* March 1, 1856; "Rendition of the Heroic Garner Family," *Frederick Douglass' Paper (FDP),* March 7, 1856.

15. *LDC,* March 10, 1856; *CDC,* March 11, 1856; "Peggy Southward Bound," *CDC,* April 14; *CDC,* April 15; "The Gaines Case—The Woman Peggy," *CDE,* April 15, 1856; *CDC,* April 16, 1856; Chase, letter to Trowbridge, in Robert B. Warden, *An Account of the Private Life and Public Services of Salmon Portland Chase* (Cincinnati: Wilstach, Baldwin, 1874), 346–50 (chapter 4).

16. Commentary from the Civil War and Reconstruction eras frequently said as much, as did such secondary scholarship as Yanuck, "The Garner Fugitive Slave Case"; and Angelita Reyes, "Rereading a Nineteenth-Century Fugitive Slave Incident: From Toni Morrison's *Beloved* to Margaret Garner's Dearly Beloved" *Annals of Scholarship* 7, no. 3 (1990): 465–86.

17. On the bloody knife, compare "A Terrible Affair" with "Horrible Affair!" On Mary's role, compare the conflicting testimony given at the coroner's inquest, as reported in "The Late Tragedy," *CDE,* January 30, 1856; "The Fugitive Slaves," *CDG,* January 30, 1856 (see chapter 1); and "A Visit to the Slave Mother Who Killed Her Child," *NASS,* March 15, 1856 (see chapter 10). On Robert's behavior, compare "The Late Tragedy" with "The Fugitive Slave Case in Cincinnati," *NYDT,* February 11, 1856. On the claim that Margaret was not the killer, see "The Gaines Case," *CDG,* April 14, 1856. This reprints or excerpts an article from the (now unavailable) *Louisville Democrat.* While the reporting on the day of the Garners' capture gives us a record that is contradictory and inconclusive on many matters, the evidence for the conclusion that Margaret killed Mary is overwhelming, and the claim that one of the Kites was responsible is wholly without either evidence or plausible speculative grounds.

18. William Lee Miller, *Arguing about Slavery: The Great Battle in the United States Congress* (New York: Knopf, 1996), 256. Miller is here quoting South Carolina Congressman Francis Wilkinson Pickens, who was objecting to a motion that the House receive a petition allegedly written by twenty-two slaves. I discuss the problem of slave speech later in this introduction and at considerably more length in "Who Speaks for Margaret Garner? Slavery, Silence, and the Politics of Ventriloquism," *Critical Inquiry* 29, no. 1 (2002): 81–119.

19. For general information about slave life in Kentucky, see Marion B. Lucas, *From Slavery to Segregation, 1760-1891,* vol. 1 of *A History of Blacks in Kentucky* (Frankfort: Kentucky Historical Society, 1992). Drawing on archived correspondence and other relevant documents, Weisenburger develops by far the most detailed account of the pre-escape lives of the Garners and the families of Marshall and Gaines (*Modern Medea,* 16–49 and *passim*). As my primary focus in this book is on the public controversy after the Garners escaped, my treatment of their situation in Kentucky is brief and relies at many points on Weisenburger's research. Those looking for a more extended focus on this aspect of the case should consult his book. It is, however, a source to approach with more than ordinary caution. Weisenburger's treatment of Richmond life is at times imprecise or misleading in its handling of sources, and some of his speculations rest on shakier foundations than he allows. I discuss some examples below.

20. Combining census records and maps from 1850, Weisenburger puts the population in the immediate vicinity of the Garners at sixty-three whites and sixty-one slaves (*Modern Medea,* 19, 289n4). At this time, only 22 percent of Kentucky residents were slaves, a figure that would decline to 20 percent by 1860 (Lucas, *A History of Blacks in Kentucky,* xvi). According to Paul P. Tanner, the 1850 figure for Boone County as a whole was 18.8 percent ("Slavery and Its Aftermath in Boone County," *Northern Kentucky Heritage Magazine* 12, no. 1 [2004]: 48). The 1850 census listed Marshall as having eleven slaves and Gaines, twelve. Weisenburger points out that, had none of Gaines's slaves died or been sold, Margaret's three younger children would have brought the total to fifteen (*Modern Medea,* 295n67). On the role of hogs in the farming operations, see ibid., 19, 25, 51 and chapter 2 of this book.

21. In her court testimony, Margaret said she was born on June 4, 1833 (see chapter 2), which is consistent with the August 1850 census listing of a seventeen-year-old mulatta slave on Gaines's farm. On life with John Gaines and the sale to Archibald, see both the court testimony in this book and *Modern Medea,* 20–35. Weisenburger notes that by the time of sale Gaines and Marshall "had consented to an 'abroad marriage'" between Margaret and Robert (34). Weisenburger provides no source, but Margaret had obviously taken Robert's name, and neither owner disputed the marriage during the arguments in court. Tom's age can be dated by the 1850 census, in which he was listed as five months old (*Seventh Census of the United States (Slave Schedule), 1850, Boone County,* p. 354, National Archives microfilm, roll 223), as well as by the discussion in the court testimony. The latter also provide ages for the other children. See chapter 2 of this book and also *Modern Medea,* 39, 44.

22. In a report sent by a local correspondent, Margaret is referred to as "the pregnant woman." See "The Kentucky Slaves," *NYDT,* February 16, 1856. Although the report's dubious handling of some other details suggests it is not an entirely reliable source, it appears to be accurate on this point, for at one moment during the court proceedings, the fugitives' lawyer, John Jolliffe, referred to Margaret as "in a delicate situation," a nineteenth-century euphemism for pregnancy (*CDG,* February 7, 1856 [chapter 2]). Information about the pregnancy is, however, strangely elusive. As Weisenburger points out, Robert Garner's postwar interview makes no reference to Margaret's having had a fifth child (*Modern Medea,* 275). As Weisenburger does not acknowledge, this silence is in keeping with most of the Garner archive: if I have not overlooked a relevant report (and Weisenburger's vagueness about sources makes it

impossible to know which evidence he has considered on this point), there are no other confirmations of Margaret's pregnancy, and no primary source offers an estimation of how advanced the pregnancy was (though Weisenburger speculates that Margaret was three to four months along). To be sure, social conventions at the time favored ambiguity or indirection on the subject of pregnancy, when it was even allowed into public discourse, but the scarcity of allusions in the Garner case remains striking and perplexing. In general, abolitionists made much of the sexual exploitation of female slaves, and in Margaret's particular case many documents reveal a fascination with the parentage of her children; as discussed below, a few women such as Lucy Stone were much more direct in suggesting that Margaret's children were evidence of a degrading sexual submission to her master or other white men. Yet neither Stone nor any other commentator pressing this issue gives even the most indirect indication that Garner was pregnant at the time of her escape, an indication that would have served their purposes.

23. For the work conditions of the Garners on the respective farms, see testimony in chapter 2 of this book, and Weisenburger, *Modern Medea*, 17–49. In addition to Mary's complaint about her eight children, she is also reported as citing cruel treatment as a reason for escaping in "The Fugitive Slave Case at Cincinnati"; and "Surrender of the Fugitive Slaves," *FDP*, March 7, 1856. Margaret's commentary on who owned her makes it particularly difficult to interpret her comment on cruel treatment, as the report gives no detail. See *CDG* January 30, 1856; and February 11, 1856 (chapter 2).

24. Quoted text from "The Fugitive Slave Case at Cincinnati." The differences over Robert and Margaret's names arise throughout the documents gathered in this book. Weisenburger offers perceptive comments on the struggle over "Robert," though he is in error in claiming that all stories in the press used "young Simon," prior to Jolliffe's courtroom insistence on "Robert" (*Modern Medea*, 121). See the use of "Robert" in, for instance, the *Cincinnati Daily Commercial* of February 29, 1856 (chapter 2) and "The Fugitive Case," *CDG*, January 31, 1856. For relevant scholarly discussions of the practices and politics of naming under American slavery, see Kenneth S. Greenberg, *Honor and Slavery* (Princeton, N.J.: Princeton University Press, 1996), 41–42; Herbert Gutman, *The Black Family in Slavery and Freedom, 1750–1925* (Oxford: Blackwell, 1976), 230–37; Eugene B. Genovese, *Roll Jordan Roll: The World the Slaves Made* (New York: Vintage, 1976), 443–47; Orlando Patterson, *Slavery and Social Death* (Cambridge, Mass.: Harvard University Press, 1982), 55–56. Toni Morrison also brilliantly engages the politics of naming and knowing in her elaboration of the relationship between *Beloved*'s fictional master, Paul Garner, and the slave (Baby Suggs) he calls "Jenny Whitlow," a name she does not recognize as hers, and in his calling most of his male slaves "Paul," after himself. If Morrison indeed avoided researching the particular details of the historical Garners' lives, her novel here captures Margaret, Robert, and Mary's struggles with an exactness that is nearly uncanny.

25. Mary Garner's religious vocation (another aspect of her life echoed by *Beloved*'s Baby Suggs) is described in "A Visit to the Slave Mother Who Killed Her Child." Quoted text on Margaret's joining the church is from *Richwood Session Book II,* page 14, entry for March 1855. Given the small population of both Richwood and the church (which had, with this addition, seven slave members at this point), the latter's close proximity to Maplewood, and the small number of other farms nearby, it

seems highly unlikely that the Margaret in question was a slave other than Margaret Garner. For the role of religion in slave life, see Albert Raboteau, *Slave Religion: The "Invisible Institution" in the Antebellum South* (New York: Oxford University Press, 2004).

26. As Weisenburger discusses, a few letters in the Gaines family correspondence indicate that there were moments when relatives sought to purchase slaves from Archibald and when he appeared inclined to sell them; on at least one instance, when the slaves were still owned by Archibald's brother John, it appears that a slave (probably Margaret's mother, Cilla) was aware of the possibility of a sale (*Modern Medea*, 31–32, 41–43). The letters, from the John Pollard Gaines Papers, can be read on microfilm at the New York State Library in Albany. See Abner L. Gaines to JPG, October 1, 1846, Reel 1, p. 00147; JW Menzies to JPG, August 8, 1851, Reel 2, p. 00635; Archibald K. Gaines, Jr. to JPG, September 14, 1852, Reel 3, p. 00120. On Hannah, see ibid., 52, and *Richwood Session Book,* although note that we cannot be *certain* that this Hannah was the Gaines slave. Weisenburger argues that her defiance was part of a broader pattern of difficult and resistant behavior by Maplewood slaves, difficulty that he claims (while providing only minimal support) is mentioned in the correspondence. He includes, for instance, histories of defiance by Margaret's father, Duke, in his account, but the specific evidence he cites is dubious—for it is a histrionic, proslavery editorial that, in the wake of the Garner trial, vehemently attacked the character of Margaret, blaming her alleged flaws in part on her father (see ibid., 33 and chapter 8 of this book). Weisenburger assumes that Margaret's mother's name Cilla is short for Priscilla, as it may be; at least one newspaper story refers to the baby in court as "Cilly (Priscilla)," but many newspaper articles also use "Silla," and it is clear from the archive as a whole that the names of slave children were not approached with great care or precision. Furthermore, while no Priscilla was among the handful of slaves belonging to the Presbyterian Church, there was a Drusylla, and it is also plausible that *she* was the woman known as Cilla (*Session Book II,* March 1856; I thank Ruth Brunings for calling this to my attention). Was Cilla, whatever her fuller name, among the slaves who successfully escaped Maplewood after Margaret's capture? Weisenburger suggests as much (*Modern Medea*, 127, 306n9), but once again the sources are not sufficiently consistent or detailed to justify a firm conclusion. News accounts are ambiguous and contradictory, though, as Weisenburger notes, no slaves fitting the descriptions of Hanna, Cilla (or Duke) are listed at Maplewood in the 1860 census. See "Another Escape of Slaves," *CDT,* February 1, 1856; *Covington Journal (CJ)*, February 2, 1856; *Eighth Census of the United States (Slave Schedule) 1860: Kentucky, Boone County,* A316, National Archives microfilm, roll 401.

27. On Chambers's attempts to keep the issue out of court, see "The Fugitive Slave Case," *CDG,* February 5, 1856; and The Fugitive Slave Case," *CDG,* February 11, 1856 (chapter 2xx). For primary evidence on Gaines and honor, see his April 15 letter to the *Cincinnati Enquirer* and, especially, in reports on his 1857 assault on John Jolliffe (chapter 11). Weisenburger offers a particularly insightful discussion of Chambers's maneuvering and Gaines's honor (*Modern Medea,* 160, 242–43).

28. *Modern Medea,* 44–48. In interpreting postcapture conduct, Weisenburger engages not only Margaret's killing of Mary but Gaines's immediate response. A distraught Gaines was observed carrying the dead body, with the aim, in the *Daily Gazette*'s words, of "taking it to Covington for interment in ground consecrated to

slavery" ("Arrest of the Fugitive Slaves," *CDG,* January 29, 1856). For Weisenburger's discussion of this response, see *Modern Medea,* 75–78.

29. Weisenburger reports that James Marshall sold Robert Garner in his childhood to one George Anderson (*Modern Medea,* 35–36, 293n39), who then resold Robert to Marshall less than a year before the Garners escape. But the very sources Weisenburger cites establish that it was Simon Garner ("old Simon"), not Robert ("young Simon"), whom Anderson purchased. In addition to the reports on court testimony in *CDG,* February 1, 1856 (chapter 2), see also "The Fugitive Slave Case," *CDE,* February 1, 1856; and "The Fugitive Slave Case at Cincinnati," *NYDT,* February 11, 1856. Simon's long stint enslaved to Anderson had an important effect on the legal arguments before Commissioner Pendery: even while insisting that all the other Garners had been allowed onto free soil in Cincinnati prior to the family's escape, Jolliffe ultimately had to concede that there was no evidence that Simon had left Kentucky (*CDG,* February 7, 1856 [chapter 2]). Even once father's and son's histories are disentangled, it remains true that Robert had also been hired out at various points during Margaret's child-bearing years, but it becomes too difficult to discern whether these shorter-term hirings would have prevented his fathering the children. Nor is there evidence sufficient to establish that no other white men in the area could have had sexual access to Margaret.

30. Weisenburger bases his analysis on Gaines birth dates of November 1852, November 1854, and March 1856. Margaret's son Sam was born some time in 1852, while Mary was born in May 1853, Cilla was born in April 1855, and the child Margaret was apparently carrying would have been some months after the trial in 1856. Relying on records kept in a Gaines family Bible, however, Gaines descendants contest these dates for the Gaines children, instead giving dates of April 21, 1851, March 29, 1854, and September 1856. If the latter dates are correct, then none of Margaret Garner's children was conceived during the final months of an Elizabeth Gaines pregnancy. Unfortunately, it is impossible to adjudicate this dispute while abiding by scholarly norms regarding publicly available evidence. The descendant in possession of the Bible neither wishes to make it generally available nor to be named in discussions of the case, and while I obtained a purported transcription with these dates along with photocopies of some other pages of this Bible, I have been unable to obtain a photocopy of the page with the children's birth dates. Thus, I invoke these counterclaims not as sound evidence that invalidates Weisenburger's dates but as one more example of how, at key points, the archive frustrates those who wish to move beyond the political battle over the case to the lives the Garners led before becoming public figures.

31. The most well-known and extraordinary firsthand account of a female slave's negotiation of the sexual demands of her master is Harriet A. Jacobs's *Incidents in the Life of a Slave Girl, Written by Herself,* ed. Jean Fagan Yellin (Cambridge, Mass.: Harvard University Press, 1987). Illuminating scholarly accounts of sexual relations between masters and slaves can be found in Saidiya Hartman, *Scenes of Subjection: Terror, Slavery, and Self-Making in Nineteenth Century America* (New York: Oxford University Press, 1997); Meltin A. McLaurin, *Celia, A Slave* (New York: Avon, 1993); and Deborah Gray White, *Ar'n't I a Woman? Female Slaves in the Plantation South* (New York: Norton, 1985).

32. John Hope Franklin and Loren Schweninger, *Runaway Slaves: Rebels on the Plantation, 1790–1860* (New York: Oxford University Press, 1999), 367n49. The

authors borrow this characterization from another, unnamed historian. Most slaves who did run off, they report, tended to make shorter journeys within the slave South—brief visits to friends or loved ones, "lying out" for weeks or a few months in a nearby swamp or forest, attempts to disappear amidst the free black population of a Southern city, etc. (ibid., 97–115). On this aspect of slave escapes, see also John Michael Vlach, "Above Ground on the Underground Railroad," in Blight, *Passages to Freedom,* 99–102.

33. Franklin and Schweninger, *Runaway Slaves,* 25, 116–17.

34. On the preponderance of young men, see Franklin and Schweninger, *Runaway Slaves,* 210–12, and also Herbert G. Gutman, *The Black Family in Slavery and Freedom, 1750–1925* (Oxford: Blackwell, 1976), 265. The tendency toward young single men traveling alone or with at most one or two others grew more pronounced over time; by the 1850s the share topped 95 percent (Franklin and Schweninger, *Runaway Slaves,* 229). On the tendencies of family groups to be small, see ibid., 63–65.

35. Combing through reported escape attempts in area papers after the passage of the Fugitive Slave Act, Weisenburger found "six parties totaling twenty-eight slaves ranging in age from sixty down to one year," and with only eleven of these fugitives adult males. One of these escapes (a dismal failure) took place just four weeks before the Garners' attempt (*Modern Medea,* 56, 297n75). Another multigenerational group of Gaines' slaves escaped even as the Garner hearings were beginning. See, for instance, "Another Escape of Slaves."

36. Franklin and Schweninger, *Runaway Slaves,* 66. On the role played by relatives, see ibid., 69; and Nikki M. Taylor, *Frontiers of Freedom: Cincinnati's Black Community, 1802–1868,* 141–43.

37. Population figures from ibid., p. 20, *The Seventh Census of the United States 1850* (accessed online at http://www2.census.gov/prod2/decennial/documents/1850a-27.pdf) and *The Eighth Census of the United States 1860* (accessed online at http://www2.census.gov/prod2/decennial/documents/1860a-01.pdf). For discussion of the scattering of races and classes across the city, see Taylor, *Frontiers of Freedom,* 24; and Henry Louis Taylor Jr. and Vicky Dula, "The Black Residential Experience and Community Formation in Antebellum Cincinnati," in Henry Louis Taylor, ed., *Race and the City: Work, Community, and Protest in Cincinnati, 1820–1870* (Urbana: University of Illinois Press, 1993), 96–125. The census at this time distinguished between blacks and mulattoes, as does Taylor and Dula's residential analysis. The distinction mattered not only in white perceptions but also in the self-organized social life led by Cincinnatians of color. Mulattoes were, for instance, especially prominent in the community's leadership. But the evidence also suggests that it *was* a community, and for my purposes, when writing in this section about the community of color in Cincinnati I have found it most useful to employ "black" or "black community" as an inclusive term encompassing black and mulatto members. On the roles and places of people classified as "mulatto" and as "black" in the community, see William Cheek and Aimee Lee Cheek, "John Mercer Langston and the Cincinnati Riot of 1841," in Taylor, *Race and the City,* 29–69; and James Oliver Horton and Stacey Flaherty, "Black Leadership in Antebellum Cincinnati," in Taylor, *Race and the City,* 70–95.

38. "Attorney-general" characterization reported in J. W. Schuckers, *The Life and Public Services of Salmon Portland Chase* (New York: D. Appleton, 1874), 52. Chase's role in the creation of the Republican Party, and the partisan dynamics of midcentury

Ohio, are best sketched in Stephen E. Maizlish, *The Triumph of Sectionalism: The Transformation of Ohio Politics, 1844–1856* (Kent, Ohio: Kent State University Press, 1983). For statistics on his election as governor, see ibid., 223; and Yanuck, "The Garner Fugitive Slave Case," 50. Republican Frémont won Ohio's presidential vote by 4 points, while Democrat Buchanan won Hamilton County by 13 points. Ohio's voting in this election is discussed in Joe Hallett, "Ohio and the Presidency," *Columbus Dispatch,* October 18, 2007, updated June 6, 2009. Detailed breakdowns of the results, including county by county figures, are provided in the online version at http://www.dispatchpolitics.com/dawson_maps/dawsons_maps_index.html#1856 (accessed July 2009).

39. This account draws on Taylor, *Frontiers of Freedom,* 32–35 and *passim*; and Cheek and Cheek, "John Mercer Langston," 31–32.

40. On the riots, see Taylor, *Frontiers of Freedom,* 50–79, 109–12, and 118–26; Cheek and Cheek, "John Mercer Langston"; and John Nerone, *Violence against the Press: Policing the Public Sphere in U.S. History* (New York: Oxford University Press, 1994), 97–106.

41. On the history of escapes managed entirely by the community of color, see the white abolitionist James Birney, quoted in Benjamin Quarles, *Black Abolitionists* (New York: Da Capo, 1991), 144–45. On the national primacy of black people in protecting fugitives, see James Brewer Stewart, *Holy Warriors: The Abolitionists and American Slavery,* rev. ed. (New York: Hill and Wang, 1996), 139. My description of the character of Cincinnati's black institutions and leadership draws especially on Horton and Flaherty, "Black Leadership in Antebellum Cincinnati," and Taylor, *Frontiers of Freedom,* 117–60. The convention of colored citizens is described in "Ohio Convention of Colored Men," *NASS,* February 16, 1856. The men the paper identified as the leaders of the convention are the very people that Oliver and Flaherty single out for their broader leadership role in the city.

42. Blacks statewide had won the legal right to public education in 1849, but were effectively prevented from exercising it by the city government. It took seven years of activism and a series of legal battles for Cincinnati's black community to overcome the impediments. See Taylor, *Frontiers of Freedom,* 138–60. Some of the activism leading to that result is sketched, if very briefly, in "Movement of Colored People" (Ontario, Canada West) *Provincial Freeman (PF),* February 23, 1856.

43. For Smith and the Beckley's roles in the Garner case, see chapter 2. Smith is identified as a member of the Daughters of Samaria in Taylor, *Frontiers of Freedom,* 264n45. The Beckleys are discussed in Taylor and Flaherty, "Black Leadership," and in Weisenburger, *Modern Medea.* The latter work identifies Jesse Beckley as a member of the Life Guards. In examining the sources Weisenburger cites in his assorted discussions of the family, however, I have not been able to find any evidence confirming that claim. Nor, using his cited sources, have I been able to confirm the specific involvement in the Garner case that Weisenburger attributes to the Life Guards (*Modern Medea,* 3–5, 71, 121, 182–83, 193, 195, 299n13, 305n2). On public transcripts, see James Scott, *Domination and the Arts of Resistance: Hidden Transcripts* (New Haven, Conn.: Yale University Press, 1992).

44. "Impudence of the Negroes," *CDE,* February 2, 1856. Compare this to the *Covington Journal*'s coverage on the meeting held in Florence, Kentucky, on February 23, to address the "crisis" in the affairs and rights of slaveholders. Unlike the meeting of

Cincinnati's blacks, this one was announced in the press beforehand, and the reporting afterward, though brief, gives the names of some of those who addressed the meeting, including Archibald K. Gaines. "Meeting at Florence Today," *CJ,* February 23, and *CJ,* March 1, 1856.

45. Coffin's narrative combines relatively brief and superficial moments of first-person recounting with long passages borrowed, without attribution, from many of the same newspaper sources used in part 2 of this book (*The Reminiscences of Levi Coffin,* 557–74).

46. "The Fugitive Slaves!" *CDT,* January 31, 1856. This story also reported that black men in the crowd had assaulted Cincinnati's mayor, James Farran, with a knife, but the next day the paper recanted, saying that Farran had in fact prevented a group of whites from attacking a black man (chapter 2). If this raises questions about the general reliability of the original report, the quoted account of the conduct of the crowds is generally similar to reports of the agitation by black spectators that appeared in the city's other dailies on the same day.

47. "The Fugitive Slaves!" *Cincinnati Daily Times,* February 1, 1856. For the arrest, though not the passage quoted here, see chapter 2.

48. "The Fugitive Slave Case," *CDE,* January 31, 1856 (see chapter 2).

49. "The Fugitive Slave Case at Cincinnati," *NYDT,* February 4, 1856, reprinting a report from the otherwise unavailable *Cincinnati Columbian* of January 31, 1856.

50. Coffin, who witnessed the courtroom escape and helped organize the flight to Canada provides a detailed account (*The Reminiscences of Levi Coffin,* 548–54). Unfortunately, Coffin again leaves black actors unnamed in his account and allows us no sense of black organizational networks.

51. See, for instance, Theodore Parker's two speeches in this book (chapter 10), which treat the Garners' return to slavery as evidence not only of white racism but black docility. Black commentators leveled criticisms, too. In his report to *Frederick Douglass' Paper,* the correspondent J. W. Duffin proclaimed the black failure to risk their lives to liberate the Garners shameful (chapter 8). Quarles reports that, stung by Parker's comments, John S. Rock later urged blacks to respond with actions demonstrating their courage (Quarles, *Black Abolitionists,* 228).

52. Weisenburger, *Modern Medea,* 146.

53. Under the terms of the Fugitive Slave Act, marshals were subject to fines of up to $1,000 for various forms of dereliction of duty in the handling of fugitive slaves. See appendix, "Text of the Fugitive Slave Act of 1850." Robinson may have had other reasons. Later reports in some papers alleged that he was involved in financial schemes to claim a disproportionate share of federal payments to the deputies. The scale of the federal bill for the deputies drew extended critical commentary in the Cincinnati and New York press, which estimated the cost of the deputy force at over $23,000, though the *Enquirer* disputed such reports. Accounts in the *New York Daily Tribune* suggest that the Pierce administration even investigated the marshal for his financial dealings. See the following sources: *CDG,* March 3, April 19, 1856; *CDE,* March 7, 1856; *NASS,* March 29, 1856; *NYTRB,* April 23, 28, 1856.

54. Although still potentially bloody, the conflict might have been very different had Governor Chase ordered state forces to protect the fugitives. With some justification, abolitionists would for many years question whether he did all he could to keep the Garners out of slavery. See chapter 12 and *Modern Medea,* 214–16.

55. Quotation is from Campbell, *The Slave Catchers,* 169. My account of the act skips some significant details. The appendix of the present volume contains the complete text.

56. The Fugitive Slave Clause of the Constitution (the third clause, Article 4, Section 2) read, "No Person held to Service or Labour in one State, under the Laws thereof, escaping into another, shall, in Consequence of any Law or Regulation therein, be discharged from such Service or Labour, but shall be delivered up on Claim of the Party to whom such Service or Labour may be due." For an account of the reluctance of some Founders to see the word "slave" in the document, see Paul Finkelman, *Slavery and the Founders,* 2nd ed. (Armonk, N.Y.: Sharpe, 2001), 3–37. On the fugitive as debtor, see Stephen M. Best, *The Fugitive's Properties: Law and the Poetics of Dispossession* (Chicago: University of Chicago Press, 2004), 80–82. In this paragraph, I borrow from Best's analysis and the related arguments of Hartman, *Scenes of Subjection,* 79–112.

57. Headington's arguments are reported in "The Habeas Corpus for the Fugitive Slaves," *CDG,* February 27, 1856; emphasis added. Just as Headington found advantages in momentarily recognizing the Garners' personhood, for similar reasons counsel for the sheriffs consistently sought to stress that the federal claim was a matter of property, for they argued that this made that claim of lesser importance than the Ohio murder charge. See "The Habeas Corpus for the Fugitive Slaves" and "The Fugitive Slave Case," *CDG,* February 9, 1856. Praise for Headington appeared in "The 'Habeas Corpus' before Judge Leavitt—Speech of Mr. Headington," *CDE* February 27, 1856.

58. *CJ,* April 5, 1856. In this paragraph, I rely heavily on Campbell, *The Slave Catchers.* On the percentage of cases won by the claimants, and the heavy use of federal marshals in returning slaves, see page 168; on the midfifties as peak years, see page 106. On Southern underestimation of claimants' successes in court and of the use of federal money in paying for returns, see pages 110–15 and 147. That the Fugitive Slave Act was successfully enforced does not mean that it succeeded in halting escapes. Although thousands escaped, only 191 slaves were claimed under the act prior to the Civil War, and, after the much-publicized 1854 trial of Anthony Burns in Boston, no further cases were brought in New England. But while the political climate of New England may have influenced slave owners' calculations, the primary obstacle was the logistical challenge of pursuing a reclamation so far from slavery (Campbell, *The Slave Catchers,* 168, 185).

59. Campbell notes that the Supreme Court never settled the question of fees (*The Slave Catchers,* 42). In 1859, in *Ableman v. Booth,* the Court did rule—briefly and virtually without argument—to reaffirm the Fugitive Slave Act, one part of a broader decision that the legal scholar Robert Cover called "the last and greatest blow of the Taney court against antislavery" (*Justice Accused,* 186–87). The law was repealed on June 28, 1864.

60. See Weisenburger's astute discussion, which points out that Jolliffe originated this argument in 1852 and would use it up through the onset of the war (*Modern Medea,* 100–101). See also *The Reminiscences of Levi Coffin,* 542–48.

61. On *State v. Farr,* Chase's role in laying the groundwork, and the aftermath in Ohio, see Finkelman, *An Imperfect Union,* 164–75. On Pendery's role in the Armstead case, see page 176. The history of the free soil doctrine is far more complex than

acknowledged in my main text, for it included distinctions among different kinds of encounters (e.g., "transit" across free territory vs. a more extended "sojourn" vs. "residence in it), and the willingness of courts to recognize the laws of other states shifted in various ways during the nineteenth century. This history is analyzed subtly and at length in both Finkelman's book and Cover's *Justice Accused*.

62. On Chase and Van Zant (5 Howard (U.S.) 215 (1847)), see Cover, *Justice Accused*, 171–72 and Finkleman, *An Imperfect Union*, 246–48. In *Strader v. Graham* (10 Howard (U.S.) 82 (1851)), the Supreme Court ruled that the meaning of free soil was a matter for the relevant state courts to resolve. They thus let stand a Kentucky Supreme Court decision that found for the owner. But in his opinion Justice Taney had simply declared that slaves who returned to a slave state became slaves again. The status of his declaration was still a contested matter at the time of the Garner case. See Finkelman, *An Imperfect Union*, 271–74; and Weisenburger, *Modern Medea*, 140–45. A far more detailed account was published, too late for my consideration, just as this volume was in press. See Robert G. Schwemm, "*Strader v. Graham*: Kentucky's Contribution to National Slavery Litigation and the *Dred Scott* Decision," *Kentucky Law Joural* 97, no. 3 (2008–9): 353–438.

63. Cover, *Justice Accused*, 183.

64. Michael Schudson, *The Power of News* (Cambridge, Mass.: Harvard University Press, 1995), 65. On the relationship between changes in the news and changes in the party system in the 1850s, I follow Thomas C. Leonard, *The Power of the Press: The Birth of American Political Reporting* (New York: Oxford University Press, 1986), 84–92.

65. Michael Schudson, *Discovering the News: A Social History of American Newspapers* (New York: Basic, 1978), 4–5; Hazel Dicken-Garcia, *Journalistic Standards in Nineteenth-Century America* (Madison: University of Wisconsin Press, 1989), 32, 89.

66. See, for instance, the attacks on the *Commercial* in the *Enquirer* of January 30 and February 1 and the rebuttal in the *Commercial* of February 2, 1856, or the similar exchanges between the *Enquirer* of March 7 and the *Commercial* of March 8, 1856. For the critical assaults on Robinson's expenses and conduct in organizing his force of deputies, see note 53 and the *Enquirer*'s counterattack of March 7, 1856.

67. "Cincinnati Correspondence," *New York Daily Herald*, February 9, 1856.

68. The *National Era* presented stories or editorials on the Garners throughout February and March 1856. Generally in the South at this time, legitimate public discourse on slavery was confined to robust defenses of the institution's intrinsic merits, but Kentucky had more ideological conflict and open newspaper discussions of slavery than did other slave states. See Nerone, *Violence against the Press*, 91, 110.

69. See the examples from Charleston, South Carolina, in chapter 9, and Weisenburger's discussion in *Modern Medea*, 134–45, 307n17.

70. "A Tale of Horror!"; "The Late Fugitive Slave Case in this City," *CDE*, January 30, 1856; editorial, *New York Express*, reprinted in "The Fugitive Slave Case," *CDG*, February 13, 1856; letter from "Justice" in *CJ*, March 22, 1856 (chapter 8).

71. Douglass, "The Significance of Emancipation in the West Indies," in *The Frederick Douglass Papers. Series One: Speeches Debates and Interviews. Vol. 3: 1855–63*, ed. John W. Blassingame (New Haven: 1985), 204. See chapter 10. *Anti-Slavery Bugle* (Ohio), February 2, 1856.

72. Webster, *An Address Delivered at the Laying of the Corner Stone of the Bunker*

Hill Monument (Boston: Cummings, Hilliard, 1825). For examples of uses of Bunker Hill in the Garner case, see letter from C. Wright, *The Liberator* (*LIB*), April 28, 1856, as well as the courtroom speech of Lucy Stone in chapter 2 of the present volume. For uses of Patrick Henry, see, for example, "A Virginius," *Anti-Slavery Bugle* (Ohio), February 16, 1856 (reprinting *Pittsburgh Visitor*); "The Wicked—the Disgraceful End," *Anti-Slavery Bugle* (Ohio), March 8, 1856; letter from H. C. Wright, *LIB*, February 29, 1856.

73. Jane Tompkins, "Sentimental Power: *Uncle Tom's Cabin* and Literary History," in Harriet Beecher Stowe, *Uncle Tom's Cabin*, ed. Elizabeth Ammons (New York: Norton, 1994), 504, 507.

74. Writing to her sister, Martha Coffin Wright, in February 1856, the abolitionist and women's rights activist Lucretia Coffin Mott recounted a dinner table conversation during which (responding to Lucy Stone's courtroom speech) at least one male guest criticized Garner's "selfish" taking of life, objecting strenuously to any celebration of it (*Selected Letters of Lucretia Coffin Mott* [Urbana: University of Illinois Press, 2002], 247). Surely others shared this view. It is hard to know how many, though, especially since this kind of criticism of Garner is not a notable part of antislavery public discourse about the case. Margaret Washington, who cites Mott's letter in arguing that there was a broader conflict among abolitionists over Garner's conduct, presents Mott and the other guests at dinner as accepting the critique of Stone and Garner. I do not, however, think the letter is clear enough to sustain any conclusion on this point. And while Washington may be correct in asserting that, as a "slave mother and pacifist" Sojourner Truth was "certainly" opposed to Garner's violence, too, this must be the biographer's inference, based on Truth's general principles, about a matter that Truth appears to have avoided taking up in public—for Washington cites no specific statement in support of her characterization. See Margaret Washington, *Sojourner Truth's America* (Chicago: University of Chicago Press, 2009), 273–74, 439n4.

75. On slave infanticide generally, see Mary Jenkins Schwartz, *Birthing a Slave: Motherhood and Medicine in the Antebellum South* (Cambridge, Mass.: Harvard University Press, 2006), 114, 207–11, 220, 223–24, and 314, and White, *Ar'n't I a Woman?* 87–88. Calling the Garner case "notable in its singularity," Schwartz adds, "Enslaved mothers did not typically murder their children, Margaret Garner notwithstanding" (210). Although White does briefly cite a few cases in which mothers who had killed their children claimed to have done so out of concern for their well being, she argues that child-killing was rare. Less than eight years before the Garner case, however, a dramatic case of child-murder had occurred just across the river from Cincinnati. One Mr. Rust, seeking to sell a slave family down the river, placed them temporarily in a jail cell in Covington "for safe keeping." The father of the family used a knife to kill his wife and children, and then attempted to kill himself. The aim, reportedly, was to avoid enslavement in the Deep South, and the wife allegedly collaborated with the plan. Like Margaret Garner, the father was compared to the Roman character, Virginius (see discussion below). Unlike Garner, this man—the report does not name him— did not become a significant figure in public discussion. The story remained obscure ("A Murder and attempted Suicide," *ASB*, June 2, 1848). The lack of a prolonged legal dispute providing daily occasions for new stories must account for part of the difference, as does the location in slave territory and the difference between the clashes of

the 1840s and the more intense post–Fugitive Slave Act battles of the midfifties. But the difference in gender is presumably relevant, too.

76. See Stowe, *Uncle Tom's Cabin,* 318, 373. In a wide-ranging discussion of literary treatments of infanticidal slave mothers, Weisenburger argues that "it was almost as if the icon had always awaited or demanded a Margaret Garner" (*Modern Medea,* 247). His lengthy analysis is illuminating in many ways, but I think on this point he underestimates the extent to which the Garner case disrupted the existing stories and images, the way the discourse around it was fueled not only by the familiar or expected elements but by everything that made it hard to assimilate to available genres. For his broader discussion, see pages 246–75.

77. *NYDT,* February 2, 1856; Elizabeth Spelman, *Fruits of Sorrow: Framing Our Attention to Suffering* (Boston: Beacon, 1997), 47–55. As Spelman and Patterson discuss in different ways, ancient Greek tragedians produced no works in which the protagonists were slaves, for slaves were not regarded as possessing the honor or importance necessary to the hero. See Spelman, *Fruits of Sorrow,* 6, and Patterson, *Slavery and Social Death,* 87.

78. Carolyn Karcher, "Lydia Maria Child's *A Romance of the Republic:* An Abolitionist Vision of America's Racial Destiny," in *Slavery and the Literary Imagination,* ed. Deborah E. McDowell and Arnold Rampersad (Baltimore, 1989), 83.

79. *Livy, With an English Translation,* by B. O. Foster. 13 vols. (New York, 1922), bk. 3.

80. "The Fugitive Slave Case," *CDT,* February 12, 1856 (chapter 2); *NYTRB,* February 8, 1856; *NASS,* February 9, 1856.

81. *Annual Report Presented to the American Anti-Slavery Society,* 45, 46. For two examples of uses from across the ideological spectrum of newspapers covering the case, see "The Slave Mother," *NYTRB,* February 8, 1856 (chapter 1); and Justice's letter in *CJ* March 22, 1856 (chapter 8).

82. *Oxford English Dictionary* (Oxford, 1971); *Black's Law Dictionary,* Sixth Edition (St. Paul, 1990).

83. See, for instance, "A Visit to the Slave Mother, *NASS,* March 15, 1856.

84. At least one major shaper of antislavery discourse noted the emphasis placed on Margaret's frenzy and, up to a point, resisted it: Harriet Beecher Stowe. Her novel *Dred,* published months after the Garners were sent South, refracted their case in the story of Cora Gordon. After killing her children to keep them out of slavery, Cora testifies in court: "I have heard some persons say I was in a frenzy. . . . They are mistaken. I was not in a frenzy; I was not excited; and I did know what I was doing! and I bless God that it is done!" Cora is calm and deliberate, yet she still acts from Christian maternalism. While acknowledging that what she did may seem, may even be, sinful, she adds, "I am willing to lose my soul to have *theirs* saved. . . . And now, if any of you mothers, in my place, wouldn't have done the same, you either don't know what love is, or you don't love your children as I have loved mine." It is telling that in order to give voice to such a perspective, Stowe fundamentally altered both the circumstances and the consequences of the Garner case. At the time she takes her children's lives, Cora is a widow who had married and been emancipated by her former master, living with him in freedom in Ohio. The children, born in Ohio, had never been slaves until the novel's scheming villain succeeded in claiming them. And Stowe renders the

children's deaths in the gentlest possible terms: "while they were asleep and didn't know it," Cora tells the court, "I sent them to lie down with the Lord." This act does not turn Cora Gordon into any kind of icon or fuel further rebellion; her case provokes no political struggle. While she is not frenzied, she is no Virginius either (though in what one could perhaps take as Stowe's sly allusion, Cora does tell those listening in court, "Your old proud Virginia blood is in my veins"). For all quoted passages, see Harriet Beecher Stowe, *Dred: A Tale of the Great Dismal Swamp* (New York: Penguin Books, 2000), 439–40.

85. Patterson, *Slavery and Social Death,* 5–10, 187, and *passim.*

86. Paul Gilroy is the commentator on the Garner case who has seen this most clearly. See his account of the "inclination towards death" in *The Black Atlantic,* 68. On the distinctive relationship of American slave mothers to kinship systems and the gender order, see Lauren Berlant's discussion of slavery's "maternal line of entailment without entitlement," in *The Queen of America Goes to Washington City: Essays on Sex and Citizenship* (Durham, N.C.: Duke University Press, 1997), 85; and Hortense J. Spillers, "Mama's Baby, Papa's Maybe: An American Grammar Book," *Diacritics* 17, no. 2 (1987): 65–81.

87. "The Fugitive Slave Case," *CDG,* February 11, 1856 (chapter 2), and "The Fugitive Slave Case," *CDG,* February 10, 1856. Very similar characterizations can also be found in many other papers.

88. *CDE,* January 29, 1856.

89. The "Editorial Introduction" to this edition (New York, 184–?) claims, "Few plays have been represented on the American boards as repeatedly as this," and calls it "the most popular tragedy of the day." Records of theatrical performances in New York City show frequent performances in multiple theaters for many years, starting with its American premiere in 1821 and including a number in the early 1850s. See T. Allston Brown, *A History of the New York Stage: From the First Performance in 1732 to 1901* (New York: Dodd, Mead, 1903).

90. "The Fugitive Slave Case," *CDG,* February 12, 1856 (chapter 2). Many major dailies reprinted the testimony. Though minor details vary, the tone and substance are the same across versions.

91. I base my account on the speeches or texts by Bassett, Bushnell, Stone, among others. See chapter 10. You may disagree. To justify my characterization, the argument made here and in the following two paragraphs would of course have to undertake a detailed reading of the texts in the manner of the discussion of Virginius above. Given the nature and purposes of this volume, though, I would rather have readers test my general claim against their own reading of the primary sources. Those interested in my own extended interpretation should consult Reinhardt, "Who Speaks for Margaret Garner?" *Critical Inquiry.*

92. See Douglass, *My Bondage and My Freedom,* ed. William L. Andrews (Urbana: University of Illinois Press, 1987); and Jacobs, *Incidents in the Life of a Slave Girl.* For the best and most thorough analysis of how slave narrators challenged the discursive constraints with which they worked, see William L. Andrews, *To Tell a Free Story: The First Century of Afro-American Autobiography* (Urbana: University of Illinois Press, 1986).

93. The phrase is from Stewart, *Holy Warriors,* 122.

94. "The Fugitive Slave Case," *CDG,* February 14, 1856 (chapter 2). The black abolitionist Sarah Remond offered much the same interpretation as Stone, in similar language, in addressing an English audience several years later (chapter 10).

95. March 22, 1856.

96. Correspondence from J. W. Duffin, *FDP,* March 7, 1856 (chapter 8).

97. The definition from *Webster's* is quoted in Albert J. Von Frank, *The Trials of Anthony Burns: Freedom and Slavery in Emerson's Boston* (Cambridge, Mass.: Harvard University Press, 1998), 15. My broader analysis of slavery, honor, and the Garner case is indebted both to Orlando Patterson's conception of social death and to Kenneth S. Greenberg's argument that the Southern press feared a symbolic emancipation of Nat Turner. See Patterson, *Slavery and Social Death*; and Greenberg, *Honor and Slavery,* 107.

98. For a fuller account of the legislative debates, and representative primary sources, see chapter 6. Secondary treatments of this legislative history are consistently inaccurate, but it can be followed not only in the news stories gathered here but in the *Ohio House Journal* for 1856 and 1857, and the *Ohio Senate Journal* for the same years. The volumes can be consulted at the Ohio Historical Society, Columbus, Ohio. For examples of hostile responses to the legislators' efforts, see "Nullification in the Ohio Legislature—The Fugitive-Slave Law to be Trampled Under Foot," *CDE,* March 16, 1856; and the letter from "Justice" in *CJ,* April 5, 1856. Campbell reports that the personal liberty laws that so enraged Southerners "did not prevent even one slave from being returned South where the claim was legitimate" (*The Slave Catchers,* vii–viii.

99. Later, Margaret's story was also invoked in detail by Senator Charles Sumner as part of the argument leading to the repeal of the Fugitive Slave Act in 1864. See U.S. Senate, Select Committee on Slavery and the Treatment of Freedmen, *Report (to accompany bill S. No. 141)* (Washington, D.C.: Government Printing Office, 1864), 20–21. Samuel J. May Anti-Slavery Collection, Cornell University Library Division of Rare and Manuscript Collections (http://dlxs2.library.cornell.edu/cgi/t/text/page viewer-idx?c=mayantislavery;cc=mayantislavery;q1=Garner;rgn=full%20text;idno =16855320;didno=16855320;view=image;seq=1;node=16855320%3A1;page=root;size =s;frm=frameset;).

100. The record places Robert in Cincinnati in 1870 (see discussion below, and chapter 11). Just over a year later, on April 20, 1871, a black, Kentucky-born man named Robert Garner, died of consumption in Cincinnati. I am aware of no later records that enable us to identify the Robert Garner of this book. Is the man on the death certificate, then, the same man? The certificate lists the deceased as forty-three, at least eight years too old. But the journalist who interviewed Robert in 1870 put his age similarly, at forty-five, suggesting he had aged considerably beyond his years. If appearance is all that the coroner had to go on, then the estimate of forty-three would not argue against the hypothesis that this is the same Robert Garner. The deceased is also listed as a widower, however, whereas the journalist says that the Robert who had been Margaret Garner's husband had remarried in freedom (see chapter 11)—though it is not completely clear from the newspaper account that Robert's second wife was still alive. The death certificate, then, gives reason for suspicion, but offers no certainty. My discussion here is based on a transcription of the death certificate, sent to

me by Ruth Brunings, as I was completing this book. The transcription identifies the certificate as from the Ohio Death Records, Hamilton County, Volume 3, Page 141, Record Number 237.

101. See chapter 11.

102. Rev. George Hawkins, *Lunsford Lane; or, Another Helper from North Carolina* (1863; rpt. New York: Negro Universities Press, 1969), 132; Chase, letter to Trowbridge (chapter 4). The critic imagining a free Garner in Cincinnati is Cynthia Griffin Wolff, who, after noting parallels between the Garner story and *Uncle Tom's Cabin* (published several years before the Garners escaped), writes, "Little wonder, then, that Margaret Garner had claimed some part in the genesis of that singular work." Though noting, skeptically, that there is no record of a black Margaret Garner in postwar Cincinnati, Wolff leaves open the question of the story's veracity, proving, apparently despite herself, unable to dismiss it altogether ("'Margaret Garner': A Cincinnati Story," *Massachusetts Review* 32 [1991]: 427, 434).

103. For the *Chronicle* story, see chapter 11. On the typhoid epidemic, I rely on Weisenburger, whose book was one of the first secondary sources to trace the Garners to Tennessee Landing and whose account of their time there remains by far the most substantial (*Modern Medea*, 275–78). The 1860 census does not list the names of slaves. It does list their ages and classifies them as black or mulatto. The census listing for those enslaved to Bonham was recorded June 1, when Margaret would have been twenty-six. No twenty-six-year-old mulatta is listed. One woman of twenty-six is, however, listed as black. Could Margaret's race have been registered differently in Mississippi? If we say "no," relying on antebellum racial taxonomies to remain stable across state boundaries and from observer to observer, a new puzzle arises: where is young Samuel Garner? There is every reason to believe that both Samuel, age ten, and his brother Thomas, eight, were there. In Thomas's case, the census records pose no obstacle to this assumption, as they list several ten-year-old black boys. But the only eight-year-old boys in the census are listed as black, and Samuel was described in the Cincinnati court documents and press accounts as a mulatto (*Eighth Census of the United States (Slave Schedule), 1860: Mississippi. Issaquena County*, p. 418, June 1, National Archives microfilm, roll 401). Weisenburger reports that the census lists "a mulatto boy whose age in 1860 corresponds to that of Samuel Garner," but this misrepresents the record. The only mulatto boy is ten years old (an especially odd match for Samuel, since in the same paragraph Weisenburger, inexplicably, identifies him as being only six years old [*Modern Medea*, 275–76]). The only way to place Samuel on the plantation is to assume that he, at least, *was* categorized differently in Mississippi. This assumption is particularly plausible because, when he appears by name in the next census, ten years later, in Madison Parish, Louisiana, he is listed as black, not mulatto (*Ninth Census of the United States, 1870: Louisiana. Madison Parish*, 6 [entry 13]). Once we allow that Samuel's classification could change as he moved, and realize that the ostensibly hard facts of the census turn out to be ambiguous, unreliable, resting as they do on the interpretive decisions of the census taker, can we be sure, after all, that Margaret is *not* the twenty-six-year-old black woman listed on Judge Bonham's rolls in 1860? The problematical quality of the era's practices of racial classification does not suffice to establish that she was still alive: even if one were to decide that the twenty-six year old listed on the census rolls *could* be Margaret, that hardly means that it *was* she. My aim is merely to note here, as elsewhere, how

uncertain matters become once we subject the unreliable and contradictory documentary record to critical scrutiny.

104. On other points, however, the two texts align more easily. For instance, Robert Garner claims in the 1870 interview to have served on Union gunboats and to have fought in the siege of Vicksburg. The 1862 report places Robert on the gunboat Benton, which participated in that siege. That accounts of Robert's remarks cohere does not, however, mean that they can be substantiated. Weisenburger, who here too has done the most ambitious research into the later lives of the Garners, reports that he could find no official record confirming Robert Garner's enrollment in the Union lists. He also speculates, however, that Robert is probably the "Robert Gardner," who appears in a note from the paymaster for the 71st Regiment of the United States Colored Infantry: "Gardner" complained to the paymaster that he had cooked for the regiment for six months without pay (*Modern Medea*, 284–85). (Weisenburger's book, though, makes no mention of the *Tribune* story.)

SELECTED BIBLIOGRAPHY

This bibliography is a selection from the scholarly literature useful for understanding the political, legal, and cultural context of the Garner case and the issues that arose in the struggle over the fate of this family. I compiled these recommendations from diverse disciplines, genres, and perspectives, but in the interests of brevity I included neither general histories of slavery in the United States nor relevant antebellum sources such as slave narratives and the writings of abolitionists, black and white. Readers seeking information about these often illuminating works will easily find it in other sources, including many listed here.

Andrews, William. *To Tell a Free Story: The First Century of Afro-American Autobiography*. Urbana: University of Illinois Press, 1986.

Berlant, Lauren. *The Female Complaint: The Unfinished Business of Sentimentality in American Culture*. Durham, N.C.: Duke University Press, 2008.

Best, Stephen M. *The Fugitive's Properties: Law and the Poetics of Transgression.* Chicago: University of Chicago Press, 2004.

Blight, David W., ed. *Passages to Freedom: The Underground Railroad in History and Memory*. Washington, D.C.: Smithsonian Books, 2004.

Campbell, Stanley W. *The Slave Catchers: Enforcement of the Fugitive Slave Law, 1850–1860*. Chapel Hill: University of North Carolina Press, 1970.

Cover, Robert. *Justice Accused: Anti-Slavery and the Judicial Process*. New Haven, Conn.: Yale University Press, 1975.

Fields, Barbara. "Slavery, Race, and Ideology in the United States of America." *New Left Review* 181 (1990): 95–119.

Finkelman, Paul. *An Imperfect Union: Slavery, Federalism, and Comity*. Chapel Hill: University of North Carolina Press, 1981.

Foner, Eric. *Free Soil, Free Labor, Free Men: The Ideology of the Republican Party Before the Civil War.* New York: Oxford University Press, 1970.

Franklin, John Hope and Schweninger, Loren. *Runaway Slaves: Rebels on the Plantation, 1790–1860.* New York: Oxford University Press, 1999.

Fredrickson, George M. *The Black Image in the White Mind: The Debate on Afro-American Character and Destiny, 1817–1914* (Middletown, Conn.: Wesleyan University Press, 1987.

Gara, Larry. *The Liberty Line: The Legend of the Underground Railroad.* Lexington: University Press of Kentucky, 1961.

Gilroy, Paul. *The Black Atlantic: Modernity and Double Consciousness.* Cambridge, Mass.: Harvard University Press, 1993.

Gordon, Avery. *Ghostly Matters: Haunting and the Sociological Imagination.* Minneapolis: University of Minnesota Press, 1997.

Greenberg, Kenneth S. *Honor and Slavery.* Princeton, N.J.: Princeton University Press, 1996.

Hartman, Saidiya. *Scenes of Subjection: Terror, Slavery, and Self-Making in Nineteenth Century America.* New York: Oxford University Press, 1997.

Holt, Michael F. *The Political Crisis of the 1850's.* New York: Norton, 1983.

Leonard, Thomas C. *The Power of the Press: The Birth of American Political Reporting.* New York: Oxford University Press, 1986.

Lott, Eric. *Love and Theft: Blackface Minstrelsy and the American Working Class.* New York: Oxford University Press, 1993.

Lucas, Marion B. *A History of Blacks in Kentucky, Volume I: From Slavery to Segregation, 1760–1891.* Frankfort: Kentucky Historical Society, 1992.

Maizlish, Stephen E. *The Triumph of Sectionalism: The Transformation of Ohio Politics.* Kent, Ohio: Kent State University Press, 1983.

Painter, Nell Irvin. *Sojourner Truth: A Life, a Symbol.* New York: Norton, 1996.

Patterson, Orlando. *Slavery and Social Death: A Comparative Study.* Cambridge, Mass.: Harvard University Press, 1982.

Peterson, Carla L. *"Doers of the Word": African-American Woman Speakers and Writers in the North (1830–1880).* New York: Oxford University Press, 1995.

Quarles, Benjamin. *Black Abolitionists.* New York: Da Capo, 1991.

Raimon, Eve Allegra. *The "Tragic Mulatta" Revisited: Race and Nationalism in Nineteenth Century Antislavery Fiction.* New Brunswick, N.J.: Rutgers University Press, 2004.

Reinhardt, Mark. "Who Speaks for Margaret Garner? Slavery, Silence, and the Politics of Ventriloquism." *Critical Inquiry* 29, no. 1 (2002): 81–119.

Reyes, Angelita. *Mothering across Cultures: Postcolonial Representations.* Minneapolis: University of Minnesota Press, 2001.

Rogin, Michael. *Blackface, White Noise: Jewish Immigrants in the Hollywood Melting Pot.* Berkeley: University of California Press, 1996.

Sanchez-Eppler, Karen. *Touching Liberty: Abolition, Feminism, and the Politics of the Body.* Berkeley: University of California Press, 1993.

Schudson, Michael. *The Power of News.* Cambridge, Mass.: Harvard University Press, 1995.

Spillers, Hortense J. "Mama's Baby, Papa's Maybe: An American Grammar Book." *Diacritics* 17, no. 2 (1987): 65–81.

Stewart, James Brewer. *Holy Warriors: The Abolitionists and American Slavery,* revised edition. New York: Hill and Wang, 1996.

Taylor, Henry Louis Jr., ed. *Race and the City: Work, Community, and Protest in Cincinnati, 1820–1870.* Urbana: University of Illinois Press, 1993.

Taylor, Nikki M. *Frontiers of Freedom: Cincinnati's Black Community, 1802–1868.* Athens: Ohio University Press, 2005.

Von Frank, Albert J. *The Trials of Anthony Burns: Freedom and Slavery in Emerson's Boston.* Cambridge, Mass.: Harvard University Press, 1998.

Weisenburger, Steven. *Modern Medea: A Family Story of Slavery and Child-Murder in the Old South.* New York: Hill and Wang, 1998.

White, Deborah Gray. *Ar'n't I a Woman? Female Slaves in the Plantation South.* New York: Norton, 1985.

Williams, Linda. *Playing the Race Card: Melodramas of Black and White from Uncle Tom to O.J. Simpson.* Princeton, N.J.: Princeton University Press, 2001.

Yanuck, Julius. "The Garner Fugitive Slave Case." *Mississippi Valley Historical Review* 40, no. 1 (1953): 47–66.

INDEX

The abbreviation "MG" stands for Margaret Garner. The abbreviation "FSA" stands for the Fugitive Slave Act of 1850.

abolitionists, 211; clashes between FSA enforcers and, 1–2; newspapers of, 30, 174; responses to Garner case, 170–72, 174–75, 195, 202–4, 289n22; views on MG's conduct, 32–33, 41, 298n74. *See also* antislavery movement
Act of 1833, 147–48
Alexander, Wm.: testimony of, 77
Amalgamation party, 156
American Anti-Slavery Society: newspaper of, 193; Stone's speech to, 219–24; views on MG's conduct, 3
American Party: newspaper of, 73
American Revolution: symbolism of, 33
Anderson, George: ownership of Robert and Simon Garner, 70, 292n29
Anti-Slavery Bugle: editorials in, 170–72; Mary's murder reported by, 32; Ohio Legislature coverage by, 159–63; speeches reprinted in, 219–25
antislavery movement: in Cincinnati, 1, 6, 17; infanticide examples used by, 31–33, 34, 37; legal fight by, 25; literature of, 244–48; MG as heroine

for, 285n1; newspapers of, 57, 58–59; sermons and speeches, 211–31; state laws used by, 143–51; West Indian emancipation celebrated by, 225–26. *See also* abolitionists
Anti-Slavery Sewing Society, 19
Armstead, Rosetta: fugitive slave case of, 2, 27, 148, 149, 150, 286n2
Armstrong, Charlotte: testimony of, 74–75
Armstrong, John: testimony of, 105
arrest of Garners, 1, 5, 6; newspaper accounts of, 51–52, 54–55, 57–58
Articles of Confederation & Perpetual Union (U.S.), 128–29. *See also* U.S. Constitution
Ashbrook, John: testimony of, 101–2

Bailey, William Shreve, 193
Baker, Dianah: testimony of, 103
Bassett, P. C.: interview with Margaret Garner, 215–16
Beckley, Jesse, 19–20, 294n43
Beckley, William, 20, 69
Bennett, George S., 66, 73–74; returns Garners to owners, 122, 125
Best, Stephen M., 24
blackface minstrel shows, 2, 34, 244, 245
Black Laws (Ohio), 18, 19, 153
blacks: in Canada, 1, 18, 22, 174; in Cincinnati, 1, 4, 16, 17, 18–22,

Mark Reinhardt is Class of 1956 Professor of American civilization in the Department of Political Science at Williams College. He is the editor of *Beautiful Suffering: Photography and the Traffic in Pain* and *Kara Walker: Narratives of a Negress,* and the author of *The Art of Being Free: Taking Liberties with Tocqueville, Marx, and Arendt.*